D1560070

PASQUALE PAOLI

General Pasquale Paoli by Richard Cosway

PASQUALE PAOLI

An Enlightened Hero
1725-1807

Peter Adam Thrasher

ARCHON BOOKS 1970

This edition first published
in the U.S.A. by Archon Books 1970
Copyright © 1970 P. A. Thrasher
Library of Congress catalog card number
70–107866
SBN 208 01031 9

945.5034092
P 21 H
1970

Printed in Great Britain

For Edith and Thomas George Thrasher

ACKNOWLEDGEMENTS

My sincere thanks for their help are due to the staff of the British Museum, both in the Print and Reading Rooms; and equally to the staff of the Public Records Office

In Paris I had much courtesy and assistance from officials at the Archives Nationales, the Archives du Ministère des Affaires Etrangères and the Bibliothèque Nationale. In Corsica the kindness and knowledge of the curator of the lovingly-kept Paoli museum at Morosaglia opened up many new paths to investigate.

The London Library and its staff have been on this, as on so many other occasions invaluable.

I am indebted to Mr T. O. Haunch, the Assistant Librarian of the United Grand Lodge of England, for his help in tracing the course of Paoli's life, particularly his masonic life, during his years of exile.

Mr M. S. Bowcher put much care and thought into the maps, for which I am duly grateful. I must thank Messrs William Heinemann Ltd for permission to quote from the Yale Editions of the Private Papers of James Boswell.

I must also thank Lord Pembroke for his permission to reproduce the Wilton portrait of Paoli by an unknown artist.

My deepest gratitude is due to Dr Eric Hobsbawm, but for whom I should not have had the courage to begin to write the life of Paoli, and to Professor Douglas Dakin who provided me with the opportunity, both of Birkbeck College in the University of London. They have, of course, no responsibility for any errors in the text.

Finally, the work would never have been written without the abiding patience and constant help of my wife.

London 1970   P.A.T.

CONTENTS

ILLUSTRATIONS

MAPS

THE INVASION OF
EMANUELE MATRA

In January 1756, Emanuele Matra landed on the east coast of
Corsica at Aleria. He was enthusiastically welcomed, both in the
town and its tiny fort, for Aleria had long been part of the
territory of the Matra Clan and the return of the chief of a clan
was an event for great celebration. He was not unexpected, since
it was common knowledge that, after having rebelled and been
driven out of the island by Paoli, the newly-elected General of
the Corsicans, in the preceding October, he had been busy in
Genoa obtaining men and arms so that he could return and
renew the struggle. He obtained both without difficulty, for the
Republic of Genoa was eager for an ally; its rule of Corsica which
had lasted for more than four centuries, had, in the past 25 years,
been threatened by repeated Corsican insurrections; Paoli was
the latest of the insurrectionary leaders and looked to be one of the
most formidable, for in less than a year he had not only driven the
Genoese troops from almost every town, village and hamlet in
the interior, but he had set up a dangerously efficient government in his mountain capital of Corte. The Republic was old in
the tactic of using the quarrels of clan chieftains to perpetuate
its rule; it was a measure of its respect for Paoli that the
500 Genoese who came with Matra were hardened regulars; a
powerful addition to Matra's main strength which lay in his
family glens to the north west of the port.

Matra did not continue long in the malaria ridden plains of
the east coast. After a few days, he marched across them to the
region where the long fingers of his clan's glens thrust into the
mountains; there he knew the support of his kinsmen and
followers awaited him. In his family glens he was received everywhere with the wild enthusiasm that was his due. He spent some
weeks in the duties proper to his station and his cause: visiting
his kinsmen, feasting with his retainers, entertaining the relatives
and followers of those chiefs who might prove allies, assuring all

that the newly-established power of Paoli would be of short duration. But when the first enthusiam aroused by his return had abated, he became increasingly aware that events on the island were occurring in a most disquieting way. His attempt to find allies was largely unsuccessful. Even where he was most confident he was disappointed. All his overtures to Tomaso Cervione, on whom he had counted most and who ruled the powerful clans to the north of the Matra territory, were rebuffed. Tomaso indeed, as Matra knew, had no enthusiasm for the new General; he considered himself slighted by some judgments which had been made in Paoli's courts; but his opposition to Paoli was shown only by a sulky retirement into his own glen and a refusal to have anything to do with the General's administration. The reason for the passivity of his resistance lay to a great extent in divisions within the Cervione family, but what had caused those divisions was of more general significance. In contrast to Tomaso, the women of the family, especially the chieftain's mother, were enthusiastic adherents of the General, for they had been greatly influenced by the clergy of their glen who, to Matra's alarm and irritation, appeared, like most of the clergy on the island, to be wholly in sympathy with Paoli. This was surprising, for the General himself, though a religious man, was certainly no devotee and had on more than one occasion spoken scathingly of what he considered to be the Corsicans' unnecessary superstition and dogma. But the Corsican clergy, to whom the Pope was remote and the Bishops Genoese, and who were, above all, patriots, made no bones about a little unorthodoxy when the General was the son of a leader whose devotion was famous; when the General himself was such a passionate patriot and when he had on his right hand a brother whose devoutness had become a legend. The way in which in almost all the glens of which he had knowledge, except his own, the Corsican clergy enthusiastically espoused Paoli's cause depressed the spirits of Matra and his followers.

As the weeks passed they were depressed still more. News reached them that clerical enthusiasm for Paoli was growing throughout the island, and indeed that in some places a Holy War was being preached against the invader. Everywhere, from the churches of clustered hamlets to remote convents perched high on their isolated spurs of rock above the valleys, prayers ascended to Heaven for Paoli, while curses rained down upon the head of Matra. In some of the more enthusiastic convents a solemn ceremony was performed, which was still remembered with a shudder many generations later by those Corsicans who had witnessed it. Before the altar, in a darkened church, a solemn procession of cowled monks circled round a set of tall candles arranged in the form of a coffin. As they went they recited the 68th psalm:

> Let God arise and let his enemies be scattered:
> let them also that hate him flee before him.
> As smoke is driven away, so drive them away;
> as wax melteth before the fire,
> so let the wicked perish at the presence of God.

At the end of each verse a monk would approach the coffin with a measured tread and suddenly extinguish a candle. As he did so, the rest thundered out curses on the Matra. The church grew darker and darker, until at last it was plunged into complete darkness as a symbol of that darkness which awaited the unholy invader; and in the darkness the words of doom echoed from walls and roof: 'Pour the vessel of Thy wrath upon them, O Lord. Blot them from the book of the living.'

The attitude of the Corsican church helped to isolate Matra, but the attitude of the clergy was only one element in his isolation. More credit was due to Paoli's evident selflessness and sincerity, already widely known and admired qualitities that played a great part in winning him a breathing space, for amongst those who were not Paolists, Tomaso Cervione's attitude was widely imitated. Even those powerful leaders in what the Corsicans called the 'other side of the mountains', the *Oltremonti,* that is in those glens which lay on the western side of the island, and which were very proud of their independence long preserved by the central mountain chain, stood aloof. They would not aid Paoli, the centralising tendency of whose government was regarded with some suspicion, but neither would they oppose him. They waited on events.

While Matra was engaged in the search for allies Paoli mustered his forces in the two most prosperous and most violently nationalistic parts of the island, the Castagniccia and in Balagna, and moved his headquarters to his mountain capital of Corte. Here, in the centre of the island, he marshalled and drilled his troops and prepared for the coming struggle with Matra. He was, as was his nature, unhurried and deliberate in his preparations. Matra had hoped that the Genoese, in their stronghold at Bastia, might concert their forces with his to attack Paoli, but in this he was disappointed. Aid to Corsican leaders was always a cold calculation on the part of the Serene Republic; the Genoese did not want to replace one leader with another; what they aimed at was an internecine war which would weaken the Corsicans and enable their own forces to assert once again the Republic's authority as the legitimate ruler of the island, an authority which the recent emergence of Paoli as a national leader had threatened.

In the middle of March, Paoli advanced his headquarters to the monastery of the Bozio, a remote mountain region whose ring of villages lay just over the crest of the mountain range from the heads of Matra's glens. Once the news was brought to Matra he determined to strike at once. His attack was a daring stroke by a bold and energetic man to end the conflict with one blow, for he hoped to overrun Paoli and the small garrison in the convent before the main body of Paoli's forces arrived to begin the attack on the Matra strongholds. Matra did not take long to organize his forces but, even so, the news that he was on the march reached Tomaso Cervione very quickly. Even while Matra was marching through the night for a dawn attack on the monastery, a great debate was going on in the Cervione household. There, Tomaso was furiously upbraided by his mother for refusing to go to the aid of Paoli. In the high Corsican fashion she denounced his inertia by appeals to his honour; throughout the night the same phrase was flung at Tomaso, again and again: 'Your honour and the honour of your clan will be stained forever by your refusal to go to the aid of the Saviour of your country.' But Tomaso remained obdurate. He had been slighted by Paoli and he would not go. He endured the reproaches of his mother sullenly, aware that the tirades could not be long prolonged, since in a few hours the question of Paoli or Matra would be irrevocably settled.

While this went on at Cervione, Matra passed the head of his glen, and out of the dawn mist he launched a furious attack on the convent of Bozio. Its speed, its fury and its unexpectedness almost ended the struggle at once. Paoli's sentinels were silenced, his outposts were carried and the vanguard of Matra's forces was in the courtyard of the monastery before the impetus of the attack was spent; but in the courtyard they were halted, then driven

16

back to the mountainside by Paoli's garrison. Reinforced, they attacked again and a furious struggle went on in the doorway of the monastery, the great doors themselves being set on fire in the fighting. Paoli, awakened by the rattle of musketry and the barking of the dogs which lay before his door, was a tower of strength for his hard-pressed garrison with his courage and his calmness. Giving orders with all the phlegm and self-possession of a professional soldier, he restored their confidence and raised their spirits. Somehow, and before the main body of Matra's forces arrived, the Paolists cleared the courtyard, barricaded the doors and prepared for renewed attacks – they were not long in coming.

The Paolists had some advantages; the monastery was in a good strategic position and Paoli, well-experienced in military engineering, had fortified it well. Like all Corsicans, his men were adept sharp-shooters and, thanks to the advantage of their position and the accuracy of their fire, they kept the Matrans pinned down on the hillside between the attacks that Matra repeatedly ordered, costly though they were to his side in men. But the garrison was heavily outnumbered and every attack that Matra launched and had driven back cost them precious lives. Their initial elation at having beaten off the first attacks slowly began to ebb away. Paoli said later that there was indeed a great danger from Matra and his men at that time, but there was a greater danger in the lowness of the garrison's spirits when they realised how large and experienced was the force opposed to them. All he could do was to encourage and upbraid them: 'If we cannot hold a fortified position like this,' he is reported as having said to them, we have a scant chance of ever governing the whole island'. Of his own feelings during that critical day there is no real record. When later he told the story of the attack on the monastery, he used an ironical depreciating tone when speaking of his part in the defence; a tone that he adopted very frequently when he was called on to speak of his own exploits. Yet, in spite of the offhand manner of its telling, the account is very revealing of his cast of mind. As there was nothing much for him to do between attacks, he said, he had time to think of the story of the Crusaders at Acre who, when they were on the point of surrendering the city to the besieging infidel, had come across a piece of the True Cross and who, reinforced by this Holy Relic, had sallied out to destroy their besiegers. Thinking there might be some equally useful relic around the monastery he had poked around, during the morning and the afternoon, to see what he could find. Since he was not successful in this search for an inspiring relic he fell back on the skills which he learnt as an officer in the army of the Two Sicilies and employed his time in making sure that no part of the defence had been overlooked.

Heaven, though not forthcoming in the way of relics, seemed, nevertheless, to be, at least vocally, on his side when, after some hours of fighting, a thunderous voice was heard booming through the mountains: '*Corággio patrioti! Corággio patrioti!*' above the rattle of muskets and the cries of the soldiers. Matra's incredulity, however, matched Paoli's in matters of this sort and the cries ceased abruptly when the soldiers he had sent to discover their origin, discovered a local priest, employing a famous local echo.

The day of fierce attacks wore away. As the sun descended, Paoli's followers were running short of ammunition. It was at this critical moment that one of his sentinels, stationed in the highest part of the tower of the convent, saw light flashing on the arms of his brother Clemente's forces as they marched up the glen from Corte to join Paoli. But Matra, too, had learnt that the forces were coming and launched a last attack on the monastery with all the troops he possessed, giving the order that it was to be taken, whatever the cost. Hardly had the attack begun, when he was enfiladed by a body of men who had crossed the mountain in his rear. They were the followers of Tomaso Cervione; the upbraidings of his mother and his other relatives, added to the doubts that existed in his own mind, had at last driven the leader of the Cervione clan to action. Caught between two fires, threatened by the whole of Paoli's army, which was now only a short march away, Matra's position was dangerous, but he was as brave as he was bold and in the Genoese regulars he still had a powerful force under his command that was used to the changing fortunes of war and was not likely to panic. But in the first exhanges of fire between his troops and the followers of Cervione, Matra was killed outright by a bullet in the forehead, and at this disaster the rest of his army broke and ran, making their way back as best they could over the mountains into the glens of their clan. As for Tomaso Cervione, he did not await the arrival of Clemente's troops or the thanks of Paoli. He did not intend Paoli to think that his help had been a gesture of reconciliation or that his pride was still not affronted. As soon as he saw that Matra's followers were in full flight, he ordered his own men to retire and before Clemente arrived they had returned as quickly and as silently as they had come.

After the brothers had met, and some sort of order had been restored to the monastery, Paoli went to where the body of Matra had been discovered on the hillside. He immediately ordered his followers to bury Matra with all military honours. Then, as the body of the insurgent chief was lowered into the grave, Paoli burst into tears. The followers of Paoli were surprised and disconcerted, for not only was Paoli accustomed to cloak his grief but Matra had always been his most determined and bitter enemy. When he was asked why he so lamented the death of a foe, he replied in words that went straight into Corsican legend: 'He was a brave man. In the fullness of time he might, if he had lived, have done Corsica great service.'

The battle had left Paoli with a debt that he was determined to settle. The next day, with a few followers, he set off for Cervione's home, and that same evening he presented himself at the door of the mother of the leader of the clan. 'Your son will not give me the opportunity to thank him for what he has done for me,' he said to her, 'well, I have already incurred one great obligation to the Cervione clan, now I make no scruple of incurring another. I come to ask you if you will give me a bed for the night.' The gesture was successful. On the morning of the next day Tomaso came to meet Paoli and in some hours of talking all their differences were reconciled and the two leaders began a friendship that was to be one of the most fruitful in Corsican history.

PART I

The Hero of an Enlightened Republic

— I —

THE ISLAND

Matra's expedition was, in itself, an epitome of the island's political history during the four and a half centuries of Genoese rule. It showed how that the Genoese had maintained their control over Corsica: cheaply, simply and brutally by means of a politic exploitation of the vendetta. While the vendetta existed in Corsica the Genoese could always raise a party to oppose any would-be liberator; a party which would demand no reward, only arms, ammunition and perhaps, in the last resort, a few troops of regular soldiers. While the vendetta existed in Corsica, and clan could be set against clan with the minimum of trouble, the Genoese knew that their rule was secure.

The origins of that ferocious custom are still unknown; they were usually vaguely attributed to the Moors but, whatever the origin, as Forester the mid-nineteenth-century traveller observed, hot blood, hot weather and the peculiar conditions of Corsican life went a long way to explain its persistence. Hunting and telling stories of their prowess were, Boswell noted, the two main occupations of a Corsican's life, and when the islanders were not hunting or boasting, time hung heavily on their hands in the villages of the glens during the long hot Corsican summers. Quarrels came easily. A blow once given and returned and the vendetta was in full swing. Such was its nature that even the most timid could pursue it. There was no code of conduct; a shot from behind a rock was as highly esteemed as a knife-thrust in a street of Bastia and considering the standard of Corsican marksmanship, liable to be more effective. Once it was launched, once an injury had been inflicted, a revenge achieved and the vendetta firmly established, revenge followed revenge, until over the passage of years the original quarrel was often quite forgotten, while its extension was bloodily pursued. Once begun, it did not merely involve an individual but spread to his whole family. Indeed, its nourishment was one of the occupations of the females of the family. Corsican annals are full of the part played by the women in the pursuance of the vendetta. Merrimé's *Colomba* springs at once to mind, but long before Merrimé visited the island there was almost a formalised ritual for the tardy. If any man had reservations about pursuing a quarrel with people whom he did not know, or revenging an injury of which he was ignorant, he was taken to the family chest to see the simple treasures of the newly-slain drawn forth. There would be usually a little money; sometimes lucky stones from Capo Corso or carefully-preserved hollow eggshells, lovingly painted and threaded on a string to be hung in the window at Easter; ribbons and gee-gaws of a visit to the markets of the seaboard; sometimes even a treasured book or pamphlet or printed prayer; some fine clothes for feast-days and always lastly, below a crucifix, the blood-stained shirt drawn out with wails and lamentations and curses upon the murderer. If all this failed to move the beholder the insulting word '*Rimbeco*' was hissed in his face. Few men cared to outface this and if any did he became an object of derision in his glen. With such persuasions was the vendetta sped on its bloody course over the generations.

The vendetta could divide families; it could divide glens and it could set glen against glen and clan against clan. It was when the clans were set one against the other that the Genoese found their allies. By means of such an alliance most of the would-be liberators of the country had been eventually destroyed. From Vincentello d'Istria in 1434 to Gaffori, Paoli's predecessor in 1753, there is a long record of Corsican leaders betrayed by their fellow countrymen. Even the greatest of them all, Sampiero da Bastelica, who achieved a European reputation in the first half of the sixteenth century and made Corsica, for a brief moment, a European concern, met his death at the hands of his fellow-countrymen, shot down by the Vittoli in an ambush.

Always in an emergency the pride and ambition of a clan chieftain were the targets of the Genoese. For, once the support of a clan chieftain had been obtained, all his clan came with him. The second step was inevitable; it was the natural result of the Corsican social system in which glens, or groups of glens (called *piaves* and used as an administrative or ecclesiastical unit) belonged to one clan. In Corsica there were often great differences between the customs of one glen and another, even the glens belonging to one clan. But whatever the differences between glens the clan which possessed them looked to their chief and his kinsmen for their leadership. Essentially, of course, it was the Celtic type of clan organization familiar in Ireland or in Scotland.

Some visitors to the island, Boswell included, tended to foist a European past on the island and made free with the term 'feudalism', which was supposed to be especially strong on the west coast, the *Oltremonti*, but even here, where the descendants of the half-mythical nobleman Hugo Colonna lived, the clan system only varied in the degree of the chief's despotism, rather than in the nature of his rule.

By contrast, in the north and east of the island, some of the chieftains could draw additional strength, paradoxically enough, from the tradition of a democratic past and the Caporali, who had been the elected leaders of their glen in the eleventh century, could be quoted as their forebears by the chiefs who ruled there.

But a past of feudalism or elective office alike was mere shadow play. The bond which united men was everywhere, except in the ports, loyalty to the head of a family, and the chiefs ruled without question in the glens, their power limited only by the ever-present Corsican sense of honour and *amour propre* and the duties due to blood and kindred. The demands of the vendetta were capable of confusing even this fundamental bond but, vendetta apart, loyalty to a chief was the real tie of Corsican society.

In the towns of the coast, however, the pattern was different. These were fortified, their existence was protected by the military power of the Genoese Republic and their inhabitants were, or a great many of them were, outside the clan system of the interior. It was in these ports, in Bastia the capital in particular, that the merchants, the doctors and the lawyers, who apart from the clan chieftains were the most prosperous of the Corsicans, flourished. Like all sea-ports, the towns on the coast were far more cosmopolitan than any of the other towns in the island. The most important of them, Bastia and Ajaccio, were also much bigger. In a population of about 200,000 Bastia accounted for something over 9,000 and Ajaccio something under 7,500. In the interior, only Corte with a little over 3,000 and Sartene with a little over 2,000 could compare with them. Bastia and Ajaccio, together with the seaports of Calvi, Algajola, San Fiorenzo and Aleria and some powerful fortresses in Capo Corso, close to the coast, such as Rogliano and Tomino, were the strong points of Genoese rule in the island, the last bulwarks in the event of a national rising, the spring-board for the eventual reconquest of the island. All provided with strong fortresses and large Genoese garrisons, they were easy to provision and to reinforce by sea.

But most of the inhabitants of the island lived in the interior, in those Corsican villages which were strung along the side of the mountain or ran along their rocky spines. There were few villages in the well-watered valleys or on the levels of the eastern plain, for there disease was widespread. Malaria was endemic in the island; it was not for nothing that statues to the plague saint, San Rocco, were prominent in every church.

The Corsican towns and villages of the interior were usually made up of hamlets bunched in close groups. Life in them differed greatly from the life in the seaports. For the Corsicans of the interior were, in spite of the normal presence of Genoese garrisons in the main towns, largely an unconquered people. Those who had nominally ruled Corsica over the centuries – the Moors, the Romans, the Pisans and the Genoese – merely ruled the sea coast. In the mountains of the interior the native Corsicans, heavily taxed and sometimes brutally oppressed, nevertheless preserved a life of their own.

Many travellers, especially those from Great Britian, compared the Corsicans to the Scots. This was partly because of the similarity of the clan structure, but even more because of the alleged similarities of character: the dourness and endurance of both. Dour the Corsicans certainly appeared; it was felt by the traveller from the first reserved greeting; the reserve of Paoli, as typical of his fellow-countrymen in this, as in so many other things, was one of the first things that those who met him remarked upon. This dourness showed itself in many ways. A French observer, seeking a symbol for the Corsican character, was quick to cite the grim, silent and joyless card-players of Bastia; the story was told of the Corsican father who found that his son had betrayed a patriot to the Genoese for money. Without a word, he took the boy to the wall of Bastia, shot him dead and left the body there with the tainted money scattered over it.

Yet this harsh exterior was deceptive and those who laid most emphasis on it were usually those whose acquaintance with the Corsicans was confined mainly to the sea-ports, where the islanders lived in the presence of their Genoese oppressors.

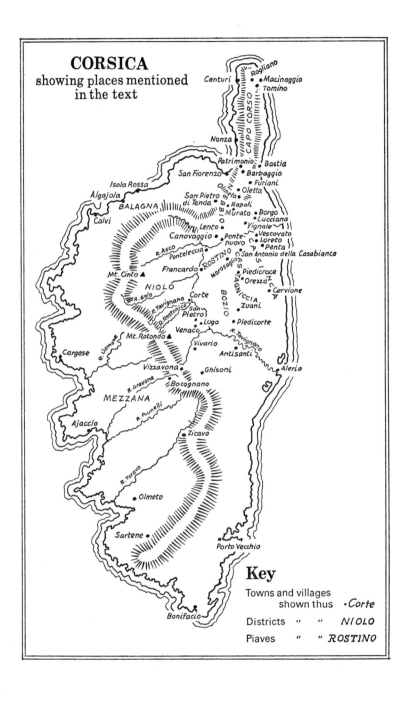

CORSICA
showing places mentioned in the text

Centuri • Rogliano
• Macinaggio
• Tomino

CAPO CORSO

Nonza •

Patrimonio •
San Fiorenzo • • Bastia
• Barbaggio
Isola Rossa • • Furiani
Algajola • • Oletta
BALAGNA San Pietro di Tenda • • Rapali
Calvi • • Murato • Borgo
• Lucciana
Lento • Yignale
Canavaggio • • Ponte-nuovo • Vescovato
R. Asco • Loreto
Ponteleccia • Penta
Francardo • ROSTINO • San Antonio della Casabianca
Mt. Cinto ▲ Morosaglia • Piedicroce
NIOLO • Orezza
R. Golo BOZIO • Cervione
R. Tavignano Corte
R. Rostonico • San Pietro • Zuani
Venaco • • Lugo
Mt. Rotondo ▲ • Piedicorte
R. Vecchiano Vivario • R. Tavignano
Cargese • Antisanti
R. Liamone Vizzavona • • Aleria
R. Gravona • Ghisoni
MEZZANA • Bocognano
R. Prunelli
Ajaccio • • Zicavo
R. Taravo
• Olmeto
Sartene • • Porto Vecchio
Bonifacio •

Key

Towns and villages
shown thus • Corte

Districts " " NIOLO

Piaves " " ROSTINO

Closer acquaintance revealed an underlying charm and gift of phrase, which, as in Ireland, was to be found widespread in the countryside, even often among the poorest peasants. As in Ireland, too, it could result in fine comforting distinctions, and even at times dissimulation. But it could also rise to a blazing eloquence which, in the Italian of Paoli or the French of Pozzo di Borgo, might exploit all the resources of language. And, out of sight of the Genoese, the honeyed words would be accompanied by a ready hospitality and an unfailing courtesy.

There was, however, no qualification to be made about the Corsicans' endurance which was indeed well attested by their enemies, both French and Genoese.

'There is not a Corsican who does not deserve to be broken on the wheel,' said the Genoese proverb, 'nor one who could not endure it.'

'You fight without hospitals, without ambulances and without surgeons,' said a French soldier to a Corsican prisoner. 'What happens to you when you are wounded?' 'We die,' said the Corsican.

This picture of the harsh and unyielding side of the Corsican nature was, of course, emphasised by the islanders themselves, for they had a hoard of anecodotes, many of which, heroic or horrible, stressed the darker side of their nature and ended fatally. One reason for their willingness to retail these stories to the enquiring traveller was not always fully appreciated. For telling them was one way in which the Corsicans could obliquely point out their separateness; one way in which they could emphasise how different they were from their other Italian, and particularly their Genoese, neighbours. For all Corsicans were very proud of their separateness and very conscious of their nationality. Sometimes, this led them to protest overmuch about their uniqueness, for their culture, although different in many particulars, was essentially Italian. Indeed, their most notorious trait, the vendetta, and their constant fratricidal strife could be seen as reflections of Italian manners, even as could their language and the eloquent use they made of it. Even their Church, in many of its aspects, was Italian, being Roman Catholic, forming the sole ideology of the island and being firmly threaded through their life, their customs and their culture. It had, too, many of the faults of the Italian Church, for along with frequent devoutness and sincerity often went superstition and ignorance. The priests were all too often as narrow and as unlearned as the most insular of their fellow countrymen.

But there were differences, too: differences in emphasis and perhaps, in the case of the Church, a difference in its very nature. With Genoese bishops whom they regarded more as enemies than as ecclesiastical superiors, the Corsican clergy formed, to a very large degree, a national Church. The priests were more concerned with their own villages than with any idea of a great and universal order. Their greater unit was Corsica, not Rome. Indeed, many of them closely approximated to that Savoyard Vicar of Rousseau, which was the ideal of so many men of the Enlightenment around the middle of the eighteenth century.

The island was to be full of echoes for the Enlightened; foremost for Rousseau himself, who saw the islanders as the modern inheritors of antique virtue, uncorrupted by Arts and Sciences, unshackled by laws and customs, 'the only people in Europe fit for legislation'. The Corsicans could be fitted into the cult of the Primitive reasonably easily; the first thing that struck the visitor to the interior of the island was the truly humble dwellings of most men.

In the interior, the houses of the population were, indeed, very humble. In the glens, only the houses of the clan chieftains, often of stone and having two or more stories with large, outside stone staircases, impressed the visitor. Most of the population lived in simple cottages of wood or local stone; cottages which consisted of a rude roof, set on four walls, in one of which was an opening which served as door, chimney and window alike. Inside this house there would be only a few, rough, wooden stools, benches and tables for furnishings. In the winter, a wood fire would burn in the centre of the room and the smoke would ascend to cure the hams and sausages which hung from the roof and which were staple parts of Corsican fare. These, together with the chestnuts, which were usually heaped in one corner, were the chief support of the Corsicans. The chestnut was, indeed, the potato of the island; ground down the chestnuts were made into flour for *balenta, fritelle, bricolli* and so forth, the dishes which diversified Corsican cooking.

The dress of the Corsicans was simple as their habitations. Rich and poor alike dressed in short jackets, breeches and long gaiters, all made of a coarse chocolate-coloured cloth. The same cloth would furnish them with a cap or *pelone,* a sort of cowl, which they threw over their heads in winter and which hung at the back of their necks in summer. Everywhere the men went armed with loaded muskets, slung over their shoulders. The shot and powder were carried in a *cachera,* or leather pouch, which was fastened to the waist. Often, too, they wore a cummerbund with a dagger or a pistol thrust through it. Women were universally dressed in dark-coloured garments, sometimes enlivened by a gayer kerchief or sash of brighter material brought from the mainland.

The economy of the island, too, was very primitive. There were only four regions that produced a surplus and so were comparatively flourishing: the Balagna, a fertile bowl of olive, vine and fruit trees which opened on to the coast, just to the east of the Genoese-held port of Algajola; Capo Corso, a long narrow mountainous peninsula thrust into the sea at the north of the island; the Nebbio, a fertile valley which channelled its produce through San Fiorenzo, and Paoli's own inland region of the Castagniccia, a region of abundant chestnut and oak groves, where a thriving wood-carving industry flourished and where chestnuts were gathered in enormous numbers. For the rest, the men were content to eke out their frugal existence with the chestnut as their potato and the abounding game as their meat.

The Genoese, for their part, did nothing to develop the economy of the island and, as a result, the Corsicans won, in the course of time, a dubious fame as a race of sharp-shooters and hunters who were congenitally lazy. But the more observant traveller suspected that it was despair of ever profiting from their labour, and not any inborn trait, which produced their indifference and torpor.

The rule of the Genoese was corrupt and oppressive. Corsica was regarded by Genoa as a country to be exploited, not as a possession to be guarded and developed. Although succeeding Doges of the Ligurian Republic added to, or lessened, some of the burdens imposed upon the Corsicans, there was hardly any serious or permanent attempt at improvement or reform. The greater and the lesser officers in the administration and the judiciary of the island were, almost without exception, occupied by Genoese, and their administrative record was an almost uniform one of corruption and exploitation. So much so, that in the Ligurian Republic itself a Genoese official or landowner who lived or worked in Corsica was regarded with some mistrust, since possession of office or land in the island implied a certain dubiety of character. Corsica was known as the field for adventurers and those with few scruples.

The rule of law was almost absent from the island. Corsican complainants in the first days of Genoese rule had their complaints treated extremely cavalierly and, with the passage of time, many of them ceased to have any recourse to Genoese institutions at all and trusted rather in the network of clan and vendetta. However, some of the more powerful of the Corsican clan chieftains and some of the Corsican merchants in the towns had sufficient connections and money to have their cases taken past the island's administration to Genoa. Few chose to do so, however. For their complaints were always referred to the Inquisitors of the State, who judged their cases in closed court and *ex informata conscientia* – which enabled them to neglect inconvenient parts of the evidence.

All commerce was channelled through the city of Genoa itself and, in trying to market their products, the islanders of the most fertile parts of the island were systematically exploited, not only by the Genoese factors, but by their own merchants. The little return they had for their labours increased their fury and diminished their industry. There was not even consistency in the machinery of oppression, for the Genoese were quick to vary their customs duties to suit the needs of a particular governor or his collaborators.

The governors themselves were very rarely men of principle. In common with the rest of the Genoese administrators in the island the Governor was often a senator of small fortune but some influence, who had been given his post in Corsica in order make, or redeem, his fortunes. He knew that during his stay in Corsica it was expected of him that he would keep the country quiet and, as a reward, he would be allowed to exploit it without question. The governor had a salary and the provisions for his table from the island, and he also received twenty-five per cent on the proceeds of all confiscations and fines. In the circumstances it was a common policy for the Governor to use every trick and quirk of the law to bleed the islanders white before he returned to his happy retirement on the mainland.

The Corsicans endured this over the centuries, sullenly and bitterly, but in 1724 the Genoese laid a new burden on them by appointing a second Governor who was to be resident at Ajaccio and who came, in the Genoese fashion, with an attendant Court and a new swarm of hopeful and hungry followers at his heels. Almost at the same time a new hearth-tax of *Due Seini* was brought into being, supposedly to replace the abolition of the sale of gun licences (which, however, continued). The new government, together with the new tax, caused great disquiet and general discontent.

To increase unrest, news was received in the island in 1729 of an insult offered by the government to Corsican soldiers on the mainland. The Corsicans who served in the Genoese regiments were one of the few sources of national pride Corsicans could claim. Hot-blooded and healthy young men in the glens, tiring of a life in which all their ways to wealth, fame and renown were blocked by the Genoese, often volunteered, at least in the first instance, for the regiments of the Genoese army and sought their fortune on the mainland in the ranks of Corsican regiments serving under the Genoese standard. Many of them seized the first opportunity to leave the Genoese service and join the French or the other Italian powers. Indeed, independently of the path through Genoa, some of them made their way to the mainland and began their military career in the regiments of the Neopolitans or the Tuscans. But for those who served with the Genoese there was a shattering insult in 1729. Just outside the great sea-port some Ligurian peasants, seeing a Corsican undergoing military punishment, jeered at him and were then fired on by Corsican soldiers; the soldiers were subsequently executed by the Genoese government after a mockery of a court-martial. This, when it became known, was taken in the island as an affront to the national pride and the country simmered on the edge of a revolt.

The refusal of an old man, in a remote village of the Bozio, to pay the new tax was the occasion for an outbreak. Pent-up anger and the unpreparedness of the Genoese, who had relied too long on the vendetta to manage the island for them, led to a complete and rapid overthrow of Genoese power in the interior and the Genoese were driven within weeks into the fortified sea-ports. Their attempts to reduce the Corsicans proved unavailing, and only the employment of German mercenaries, which were supplied by Charles VI in 1731, turned the scale and suppressed the revolt. On the departure of the Germans in June 1733 it

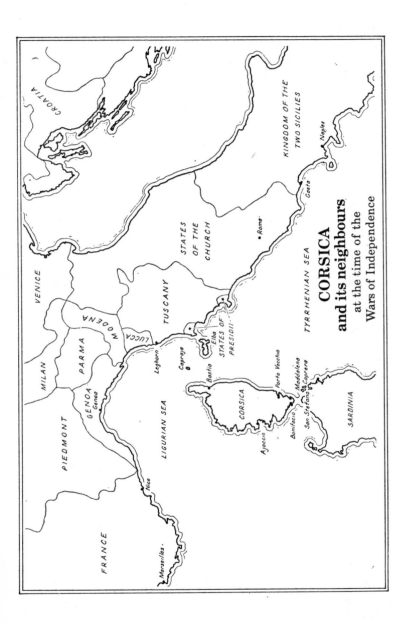

CORSICA
and its neighbours
at the time of the
Wars of Independence

CROATIA

KINGDOM OF THE
TWO SICILIES

Naples

Gaeta

Rome

STATES
OF THE
CHURCH

TYRRHENIAN SEA

VENICE

TUSCANY

MILAN

MODENA

PARMA

LUCCA

GENOA

Leghorn

Capraja

Elba

STATES OF
PRESIDII

Bastia

Porto Vecchio

Maddalena

Caprera

San Stefano

PIEDMONT

Genoa

LIGURIAN SEA

CORSICA

SARDINIA

Ajaccio

Bonifacio

Nice

FRANCE

Marseilles

B

flared up again and in 1734 Giancinto Paoli, the father of Pasquale, gathered together an assembly in the glens of Rostino, an assembly which swore to unite all Corsicans against the Genoese. The assembly at Rostino marked the resumption of the struggle which was to continue until it ended over 30 years later in the destruction of Genoese power.

Giancinto Paoli and Giafferi who were, together with Ceccaldi, invested with the rank of general in 1735, were, for the next four years until their exile, the soul of Corsican resistance, but the limelight was stolen from them by the arrival of King Theodore of Corsica, who so captured the imagination of his own and succeeding generations that of all the Corsicans before Napoleon he has had the most written about him.

King Theodore von Neuhoff, whose biography has been entertainingly written in English by Aylmer Vallance in *A Summer King,* was a Westphalian baron whose Corsican kingdom was merely an episode in a chequered career which ended with his death in an English poor-house. His bizarre arrival on the island, dressed in a scarlet silk caftan with Moorish trousers and yellow shoes, accompanied by ammunition, cannon and a great deal of *braggadocio* and the widely disseminated and greatly embellished stories of his exploits, made him, for a time, a European celebrity although the insubstantiality of his power and his later career reduced the Corsican struggle to the level of a comic side-show and provided Voltaire with a figure of fun in *Candide.* Yet in spite of all the King's failings, he gave the Corsicans heart at a critical moment in their history and he brought Corsica to the attention of all Europe; Paoli dealt graciously with him when he assessed the extent of the King's influence in his conversations with Boswell.

The aftermath of the King's descent on the island was the intervention of the French at the invitation of Genoa, and the overwhelming power the French commanded effectively brought this phase of the long rebellion to an end; in July 1739, Giafferi and Giacinto Paoli were compelled to leave the island and seek refuge in Naples, where they were given honorary colonelcies in the King's army.

European wars caused the French to return home and with their departure the Corsicans rose once more, with Count Domenico Rivarola and Gaffori replacing Giafferi and Paoli as the leaders of the islanders. In 1748, Rivarola died and the

French again invaded the island at the invitation of the Genoese, but this time Gaffori kept the Corsican forces intact and by able diplomacy he secured a truce with the Marquis de Cursay, who led the French, and obtained a *de facto* recognition for the Corsican government. De Cursay was disgraced in 1752 through Court intrigue and the French retired from the island. With the French gone, and Gaffori in possession of the whole of the interior and with a united nation behind him, it seemed, for a moment, as though the Genoese power in the island might be at an end. But the Genoese called the power of the vendetta once more to their aid. In one of the typically complicated situations created by the vendetta Gaffori's own brother was persuaded to betray the Corsican leader to the Genoese. In October 1753 Gaffori was suprised and murdered by the soldiers of the Serene Republic.

With the subsequent fame of Paoli, Gaffori and his influence were often overlooked by historians. Many of the events of Gaffori's rule foreshadowed that of Paoli. He had demonstrated by his sole command and by his diplomacy how much advantage was to be gained from having one leader of the island cause as opposed to the normal practice of a Junta of two, three or four chieftains. His diplomacy had shown that those who invaded the island on behalf of the Genoese, in this case the French, could be neutralised and divided from their Genoese sponsors. He also created in his time the national legend of a leader. His oval, sensitive, withdrawn face became known all over the island and symbolised Corsica itself. Legends concerning him passed into Corsican history: One tells of his wife, alone and besieged in Corte, faced with a cowardly conspiracy of her husband's followers to betray the town, seizing a lighted match and threatening to blow the Citadel and all its inhabitants into the sky, rather than surrender to the Genoese. Another tells of his refusal to suspend a cannonade of Bastia, even when the Genoese dangled his captive son from the battlements in direct line of his cannon. With his death, the Corsicans lost a national leader and were deeply conscious of it; they began to seek a new one to continue the struggle. The man they found was Filippo Antonio Pasquale Paoli.

2

PASQUALE PAOLI
AT NAPLES

The younger son of Giacinto Paoli and Dionisia Valentina, Pasquale Paoli was born on 5th April 1724 at Morosaglia in the *piave* of Rostino. His father was descended from the Caporali and was the chief of a clan which had for 700 years been in the forefront of the struggle for Corsican liberty. His mother, likewise descended from the Caporali, came from a prosperous, respectable family which lived close to Pontenuovo.

His father's house in which he was born, a large one by Corsican standards, stood at the head of the village, looking down over the sparkling, schist-covered roofs of the prosperous little glen. From the room where he was born one could look away across the mountains to the summits of Monte Cinto and Monte Rotondo, the two highest mountains in Corsica.

A few days after his birth, he was carried up a rough-hewn rock staircase to be christened in the tiny church of Santa Reparata, which stood on the hillside overlooking the village. He was to say later that he drank in liberty with his mother's milk, and, indeed, Morosaglia was at the very centre of the resistance to the Genoese. It lay deep in the wedge of the Castagniccia, some 20 miles from Bastia in the north-east of the island, among the huge chestnut groves which gave their name to the region. The region was prosperous and its strategic position important. Its northern edge looked down upon the valley of the Golo, along which ran the main west to east route through the mountains; the friendly groves of the Casinca connected it with the eastern plain; and to the south west it was protected by the mountains of the central range.

The Corsican revolt broke out some five years after Paoli's birth and his earliest boyhood memories of hunting and fishing were forever mixed with the excitement of arrivals in the village of the fierce Corsican chiefs who were joined with his father to overthrow Genoese rule. Sometimes, there were more exciting happenings. Years later, he remembered being taken to see the splendid figure of King Theodore on his arrival in the island.

But when he was thirteen years old all this came to an end. His father was compelled to go into exile at Naples and Pasquale went with him. He left behind his mother, his elder brother Clemente and a sister, Chiara.

Early biographers, French, Italian and German, all treat the years of his life in Naples until his return to Corsica in the manner of a saga. The hero first studies at the university under Genovesi until he becomes the incarnation of the devout Enlightened liberal. He then joins the Neopolitan army and makes himself conversant with the arts of war. While he thus learns the liberator's trade, he perfects his knowledge of men and manners by becoming a member of the brilliant, sophisticated society of Naples and, at the same time, he acquires the political arts by conversations with the politicians of the capital. The period of preparation past, he is recalled to his native country to lead the struggles of his countrymen for liberty. He sails from Naples with the blessings of his father ringing in his ears.

The reality which, thanks to the comparatively recent researches of M. Ersilio Michel, is now as clear as it probably ever will be, is very different and at first glance rather disconcerting. For Paoli appears during the years of his exile in Naples more as a figure from Stendhal, than from Snorri Sturlson; a Julien Sorel in spite of his uniform, rather than a Skarphedin. First, he was unnervingly poor. The only source of the family income was the pension disguised as a colonelcy which Charles III of Naples paid to his father. Paoli had no time for a leisured life of attendance at lectures at the University of Naples while he perfected his social graces. From the age of sixteen he was forced to earn his living in the Neopolitan army, first as a cadet and later as a junior officer.

Given the laxer standards of military service and university life in the eighteenth century, this does not mean for certain that he had no time to attend lectures at the university. But if he had, the attendance was hard won and his position very humble. Whether he attended lectures or not is now impossible to determine for the progress of his formal education is one of the tantalising gaps in the record of his early years. His military career, however, is recorded in far greater detail.

At sixteen, on 1st February 1741, he enlisted as a cadet in the

Corsican Regiment at Naples. The Corsican Regiment was composed, as its name implied, mainly of Corsican exiles. It was a workaday, unfashionable regiment whose task was mainly to garrison the towns of the Neopolitan peninsula. Paoli's first captain was Carlo Lusinghi, whom he regarded with affection and respect. For the next six years he was engaged in a round of garrison duties. From 1742-3 he was at Gaeta. From February 1743 to February 1745 he was at Pizza Falcone near Naples. From March until the October of 1745 he was at Gallipoli, a demure, white-walled town on the shores of the Adriatic. Later still, he was at Brindisi and in February 1746 he was sent on an artillery course to Naples and subsequently promoted to the temporary rank of *Alfieri* or second lieutenant. It was during this course that he might have visited the university and heard the lectures of Genovesi. But there is no record of it.

But whether he attended Genovesi's lectures or not, he could hardly have been unaware of the intellectual ferment in the capital which the reign of Charles III had provoked. Indeed, from Naples of that time one can draw fascinating parallels with Paoli's own subsequent rule in Corsica. He must have learnt a great deal from his residence in the Neopolitan kingdom, even if his role there was only that of an unusually observant spectator.

. From 1734, when Don Carlos of Spain began his reign as Charles III of the Two Sicilies and the Tuscan seaports of the Presidi, Naples had renewed her political and intellectual life. The first cause of this was the liberation of Italian energies at the end of Austrian rule. Charles' arrival meant a clean sweep of the Austrian supporters and their administration and under his rule Italians soon directed their own state. And with the end of Austrian rule went the Austrian baronial courts, which were soon replaced by the jurisdiction of the King's own advisers. From this beginning there soon arose a new breed of Italian administrators and these went to work busily reforming and improving the administration, carrying out extensive public works and supervising for the King and themselves the construction of a great number of new buildings, designed and furnished by some of the most talented architects, artists and decorators of the time. From the ranks of this new class of administrators, the dour Tuscan, Tanucci, emerged as Charles' chief adviser. He was the hoped-for darling of any Enlightened monarch, the loyal and

able administrator, whose only political passion was for the
status of the ruler. His management of political affairs, and
particularly his management of the Church, must have taught
the young Paoli a great deal.

For although, like Charles, Tanucci was personally devout
(he had the works of Voltaire burned at Naples) he was, in the
way of Enlightened administrators, very impatient of the pretensions and influence of the clergy. His conflict with them, and
his task in bringing them to order, was made much easier by the
love and affection in which Charles himself was held by the
populace.

The conduct of Charles, too, had lessons to teach. Charles
was simple, but shrewd. He was a good judge of men and loyal
to those who obtained his trust and to whom he, with great
success, left the management of politics. His great passion was for
his family and his domestic life was a blameless model for his
subjects. But alongside these more retiring virtues he had a great
passion for enriching his State with new buildings and for ex-
cavations to uncover the past (Pompeii began to be excavated
in his reign). He was also, for the comfort of his parish clergy,
impeccably devout; his devotion displaying itself visibly, indeed
ostentatiously, on feast days and holy days in elaborate proces-
sions and ceremonies. This pleased the Neopolitans who were
always avid for spectacle, but even more to their taste was the
laudable form his devotion often took of care for the poor,
exercised through the medium of the Dominican preacher and
evangelist, Father Rocco. For him, Charles founded in 1751 the
enormous *Reale Albergo dei Poveri* which had the task of
housing the homeless, the orphans and the destitute, and of
caring for, and educating, all those who might benefit from
education. Because of this and his works of charity, Father
Rocco aroused great enthusiasm in the *Lazzaroni,* that rabble
of half-naked idlers and beggars, which astonished all the
visitors to Naples and which in its numbers and in its propensity
to sudden rage constituted a threat to any government which
aroused its disapproval, as the Republican French were to find
to their cost. The feelings of great gratitude which Father Rocco
aroused in the *Lazzaroni* enabled him to exercise a remarkable
degree of control over them and they became, in the course of
time, a strong support to the government of Tanucci. Charles'
government then was liberalising, both administratively and

socially, with evident political returns for the strength of the régime.

Side by side with Tanucci's liberal measures went one of the most powerful liberal intellectual influences of the age in Genovesi. The pupil of Giambattista Vico, the famous Neopolitan savant and philosopher, Genovesi believed passionately in the free play of the intellect. Croce called him the 'evangelist of reason'. He abhorred dogmas and systems; he shared with all the men of the Enlightenment a robust belief in the virtues of commonsense and of the superior force of a rational and scientific approach to any problem. He was unreservedly opposed to the usual unquestioned acceptance of tradition and precedent. He was eager to investigate new scientific discoveries, and during his tenure at the university of Naples he introduced, among other innovations, lectures in the completely new subject of Political Economy.

That Paoli learnt from his Neopolitan experience, and that his subsequent reforms were framed in the light of Neopolitan practice, must have been the case. But there is little proof in what remains in his letters at this time, and, indeed, little proof, then or subsequently, that he treasured much affection for Naples. The balance lies the other way.

The fact that he was one of the founders of a Masonic Lodge at Gallipoli in 1745 is of far greater significance, for into the Masonic Lodges of that period were flocking the Enlightened of all Europe. The Lodges enshrined two basic principles of the Enlightenment – the Supremacy of Reason and the worth of natural man who exercised it. The membership of a Lodge was a sort of spiritual subscription to the ideas of Voltaire and Montesquieu. Essentially, the Enlightenment was an intellectual reaction against the stagnation of official and approved thought in the late seventeenth century and especially, since it originated in France, a reaction against the rigid orthodoxy of Louis XIV's twilight. But basically, the Enlightenment was an anti-clerical, though, at least in its early stages, not an anti-religious movement. To the dogmas and the finality of the Church it opposed the common-sense of rational man and the provisional certainties of Science (about which it could be argued it had, at least until Burke and the excesses of the French Revolution, far too few reservations). But since the Church and the Established Order frequently supported one another, it was quite prepared to kick the feet from under tradition in its attempt to bring down the towering pretensions of the Church to a human level. Voltaire, who was its epitome, provides a typical illustration of this in his essay on 'War' in the *Dictionnaire Philosophique*. The essay culminates with a violent attack on the hypocrisies of the Church. In speaking of the clergy's attitude to war Voltaire says:

The marvel of that infernal undertaking is that each chief of the murderers has his flags blessed and solemnly invoked God before setting out to exterminate his neighbour. If a leader has the ill fortune to kill only 2 or 3 thousand men he gives God no thanks, but when he has killed somewhere near 10,000 by fire and sword and when for a crowning grace some town has been completely destroyed, then they sing in four parts a long, tedious barbaric song in a language unknown to the warriors. The same song is used for marriages and for births as well as for murders: and this is unpardonable, especially in a country which is renowned for new songs.

Natural religion has a thousand times prevented citizens from committing crimes. A decent soul has no desire to commit crimes; a nervous soul would be frightened to commit them; it would be afraid of a just and vengeful God. But artificial religion encourages all the cruelties which are carried out by an army; conspiracies, seditions, brigandage, ambushes, the sacking of towns, murders. Everybody marches gaily to crime under the banner of his saint. A certain number of orators are everywhere paid to celebrate these murderous days. Some wear a short coat, over a long black close-fitting coat; some wear a shirt over a gown; over the shirts of others hang two pieces of multicoloured rope. They all speak for a long time and *à propos* of a battle in Vétéravie they cite what was once done in Palestine.

The rest of the year these people declaim against vices. They prove on three counts and, by antithesis, that those ladies who lightly add a little colour to their cheeks will be the object of eternal vengeance: that *'Polyeucte'* and *'Athalie'* are the works of a devil; that a man who has fresh sea fish that cost 200 *écus* a day served up at his table during Lent is sure of his salvation and that a poor man who easts $2\frac{1}{2}$ *sous* of mutton on Friday will go inevitably to the Devil.

Miserable doctors of souls, you cry out for well over an hour about a few inessentials and you say nothing of the malady which tears us in a thousand pieces! Moral philosophers you ought to burn your books.

But this sweeping attack on the clergy is led up to by a satirical explanation of how wars begin, which is bitterly critical of the Princes who prosecute them:

A geneologist proves to a Prince that he is descended in a direct line from a Count, whose parents had made a family pact three or four hundred years previously with a House of which not even the memory now remains. That House had distinct pretensions to a neighbouring province of which the last possessor has just died of an apoplexy: the Prince and his council conclude, without much difficulty, that that province belongs to him by Divine Right. That province which is some hundreds of miles away protests strongly that it does not know him and that it really does not desire to be governed by him; that in order to rule men it is necessary to have their consent; these objections only reach the ears of the Prince whose right is incontestable. He finds, without much trouble, a great number of men who have nothing to lose; he dresses them up in a cheap blue cloth, decorates their hats with a white band gets them to turn to the left and then to the right and marches off to glory.

The other Princes, when they hear of that enterprise, take part in it, each one according to his resources, and cover a little piece of earth with more murderers than Genghis Khan, Tamburlaine and Bajazet put together.

To comment on Europe and its rulers, the Enlightened philosophers evolved a series of lay figures, Chinese and Persian, Abyssinian and English, who rationally appraised what they saw and judged it by the standards of common sense. Naturally, their criticism was devastating. The English visitors, such as Lord Boldmind, were highly significant. For England represented, at least until the American War, a country which had advanced much further along the road to happy rationality. There, the Church was in its proper place, having learnt long since to abandon absurd pretensions. There, benevolent landlords concerned themselves with cultivating their own estates, and not with dancing attendance at Court. There, the peasantry was sturdy and independent and well-cared for and they were, as a result, loyal and patriotic. There, too, the King was not an all-powerful despot claiming Divine Authority for all his whims, but merely first among his fellows.

However, in spite of their dislike for despots, Voltaire himself went off happily to advise Frederick of Prussia, Diderot was content to become the librarian of the great Catherine and La Harpe, Voltaire's pupil, was honoured to be chosen as a tutor for Alexander I, the heir of all the Russias. For the *Philosophes* were no democrats. Or rather, they were would-be democrats if they could have found a people. The peasantry of Europe they did not regard as a people. Sometime, far in the future, they believed, the spread of education would enable all men to contribute to the establishment of a rational community, but at the moment in time with which they were concerned they held that the spread of their ideas amongst those in the most favoured position to put them into practice was the most rational step, and would indeed bring most benefit to the poor and humble. If Catherine in Russia or Frederick in Prussia or Joseph in Austria or Louis XIV in France might be won for the Enlightenment, then they believed to win them was the wisest course to pursue. That the Enlightened despots might have mixed motives and that unconsciously, and sometimes not so unconsciously, they might have more concern for their despotism than for their Enlightenment, they preferred to ignore – at least, until the divergence between principles and practice became too great in the 1780s. It would be a mistake to call the Enlightened Despots, hypocritical. They, too, believed in Rational Man. They, too, believed that the improvements in techniques, which were being made everywhere in agriculture and industry, and the new discoveries and researches that men were undertaking would enable mankind to advance into a happier and well-ordered future. And, naturally enough, they saw the pretensions of an obscurantist clergy and the conservatism of an inconvenient nobility as obstacles to mankind's progress. The fact that the clergy and the nobility limited their own power did not lessen, in any way, their desire to remove them from the path.

But if the inhabitants of the kingdom were not bowed down by the burden of centuries of superstition and out-worn tradition, both the *Philosophes* and the Enlightened despots believed that, with the knowledge that mankind had gained, and was every day gaining, at their disposal it might be possible, even in the space of a lifetime, to create a happy, democratic realm.

In Corsica, from a distance, these conditions seemed to exist. The Genoese obviously represented all that was bad in the unhappy world the Enlightenment thought to change. By the very conditions of their oppression the Corsicans had escaped the temptations and taints of Society. With only a slight adjustment of the mental vision the rude Corsican could be seen magnified into that huge wraith of the Enlightenment, '*The Noble Savage*'. The island's priests, remote from their bishops, looked from a distance very much like so many Savoyard Vicars. Indeed, all the island needed was a legislator, an Enlightened ruler who would apply the benefits of science and the reason of Enlightened men to the islanders and so lead them rapidly to a glorious future. All this was potential, of course. It was Pasquale Paoli who was cast to realise the potentiality, for Paoli, who all his life deeply believed in the ideas and the ideals of the Enlightenment and attempted to put its principles into practice, became its *beau idéal*.

There was an element of make-believe in all this. Few of the Enlightened knew anything of Corsica at first hand; fewer still had any idea of the nature of its society and it people. But when the doings of the islanders were put into the formal diction of the eighteenth century its laws and customs acquired a misleading solidity and familiarity.

Still the choice was not all that mistaken. Paoli shared the beliefs and assumptions of the European Enlightened, and indeed rooted his spiritual and intellectual being in its principles. He never deviated from them. The Paoli of 64 who wrote in 1787 that: 'The miracles of liberty are grander, more frequent and more useful than those of Saint Anthony of Padua' is the same Paoli as the young man of 30 who read Montesquieu as a preparation for his return to lead the Corsicans. The young man who had no desire to become a 'bobbing priest' is one with the old man who, on his death-bed, thought only of the education of his fellow-countrymen. The mature man whose democratic constitution was the amazement and envy of Europe's Enlightened idealists is one with the old man who wrote that the execution of Louis XVI was only an incident in the history of a people.

These Enlightened principles of Paoli dwelt, of course, side by side with a burning Corsican nationalism, intensified by his

years of exile. Chance and the hand of the assassin was to give him
an opportunity of serving both. But for most of his teens and
twenties any such opportunity seemed very remote and he had a
more immediate concern. The Corsican revolt occupied his mind
greatly, but so did the question of the slowness of his promotion.
Perhaps the two were not unnconnected. A report on Paoli,
which was sent to Paris by a French spy resident in Naples,
quotes him as having declared that peace with Genoa would be
worse for Corsica than death. Such extreme opinions could
easily have made him a marked man. And even in an intellect-
ually fermenting Naples, his Enlightened principles might have
hindered his advancement, for Tanucci was a bitter enemy of the
Masonic Lodges, which had been condemned by the Pope in
1738. Certainly something has to be explained, for by 30 he
was still only a lieutenant, and apart from the military talents,
which were to make him the admiration of Europe, all the
reports which his supervisors made on him during these years tell
of his application to study, his punctilious performance of his
military duties and his fine character; all remark that he would
be worthy of promotion in due time. There is of course, the
possibility always sobering to a biographer, that his own
deficiencies may have prevented him from rising. For although Paoli was to out-general the best commanders of the
Genoese Republic and defeat one of the finest armies in Europe
with an army composed mainly of peasants, his talents were
those of a strategist rather than those of a cavalry leader. And,
in the Neopolitan provinces where the duties of the troops were
to pursue bandits in the hills, and when he was still a very
junior officer, the talents of a strategist were not in great demand.

Nor did he shine in the Society of provincial Naples. Years
later, he said to Boswell that he could not endure the makers
of fine sayings and that he was thought to be a very singular man
in Naples, leaving the company when he had had enough of it.
Boswell repeated this with admiration, but really it is conduct
which accords rather better with the founder of a country than
with an aspiring young officer in an unfashionable regiment in a
foreign country. He appears, too, to have devoted a great deal
of his time to reading not only the literature of the Enlightenment
but also the classics. Many people throughout his life were to
remark on the extent of his reading and on his vast knowledge of
the Roman authors: one of the companions of his last days,

Cambiagi, remarked after his death that a reading of the classical authors was one of his greatest pleasures during the last years of his life. It is admirable, of course, but again it was not the relaxation designed to endear him to his military superiors in the provinces.

The picture that is built up of him in these days, from various fragments, is that of a rather solitary, embittered man, nagged at by his own slow promotion. There is no record of any tender passion and this is probably due to the lack of evidence, rather than the lack of emotion. The record of the more intimate details of his youth is tantalisingly deficient: all we have is the sententious remark to Boswell that he 'very seldom deviated from the paths of virtue' during his years at Naples; which may mean a great deal or nothing at all.

Certainly, he had enough outward graces to attract attention. He grew, in his twenties, into a very attractive figure – tall, fair and well made with a square, powerful face and large, bright eyes. A little later, when he became more prominent in Corsican affairs, his reserve was remarked on, but his frank, calm and modest manner was thought to be very winning and his deep voice made his eloquence, when his emotions were engaged, very persuasive. Moreover, beneath his attitude of reserve there is an enormous weight of evidence to show that he was a deeply emotional man; in his later life he proved capable of winning and retaining the friendship of men and women of the most diverse kind. But of love in Naples there is no record. Certainly, there were obstacles to a serious attachment. His relatively humble place in Neopolitan society, his poverty, his lack of prospects or connections and his foreignness when combined with his pride, provided reason enough, without recourse to psychological surmise or romantic speculation, for which in any case no evidence exists, to account for a lack of emotional involvement during his years from fourteen to thirty.

On 21st July 1749, he was successful in having himself transferred to a rather more highly esteemed regiment – that of the *Real Farnese,* where he found himself again under the command of Carlo Lusinghi. He was now transferred to Sicily and began a new round of garrison duty, passing from town to town of the island, from Trampani to Messina. His fortunes improved somewhat: he was promoted to the rank of first-lieutenant, although this rank was, once again, only acting and he was attached with

Lusinghi to the General Staff; he was also singled out for comment as being particularly well-versed in the theory of gunnery and military engineering; percipient judgment since his engineering skill was to become one of the keystones of his Corsican campaigns.

But the recognition was no compensation for the boredom and frustration he felt at being locked away in Sicily, and in spite of his promotion he was still very junior in rank. He was now 24 and very eager to make a name for himself in the world.

By a nice twist of historical irony, considering his future as a hammer of the French, he wrote on 20th November 1749 to Andrea Buttafuoco, a Corsican in the *Royal Corse* (a crack French regiment consisting of Corsican exiles, and founded during the War of Austrian Succession), to offer his services in the capacity of a captain. The offer was not accepted.

His increasing bitterness and disillusion, expressed in his letters home during these years, began to distress his father. The old Paoli had become saddened and resigned with the passage of the years. He had given up believing that Corsica, weak as she was and the prey of major powers, could ever hope for independence. Hs younger son's ideas were strange and foreign to him. From them he had a dim sense of disaster impending. He gave the best advice he could to his son. It was sensible advice, in its way, but addressed to young Pasquale, with his opinions, it was bizarre enough. Pasquale, he wrote, should seek a refuge from the disappointments of this world by entering the clergy. Many of Paoli's Corsican contemporaries in Naples, who had left Corsica with their fathers at the same time as the elder Paoli, had found a refuge in the religious orders – the Jesuits were especially favoured. There are records of a Roberti, a Molazio, a Francia, among others who entered the Society of Jesus. But addressed to Pasquale, the young idealist of the Enlightenment, this advice could only cause an explosion. Pasquale took his answer from a satirical rhyme. He had no desire he wrote to his father, to be a *'bobbing priest'*: 'Holiness does not seem to me to be found within the walls of a monastery,' he wrote angrily, 'I believe a man should praise his God by pursuing the way of life most proper to him.' His father did not try again to change his opinions.

During these years of frustrated ambition Clemente kept his younger brother closely informed of the progress of the struggle in Corsica. In that struggle Pasquale saw no place for himself. Gaffori steadily rose to be the undisputed leader of the Corsicans and although he was a true patriot whose exploits Pasquale respected, and indeed boasted of, he was a man of the old order in Corsica, who had one aim only and that was to drive out the Genoese. The ideals which meant so much to Pasquale did not touch Gaffori at all. Moreover, Paoli's elder brother ruled the clan in Corsica and Pasquale had no desire to dispute his precedence with him. Pasquale was the traditional younger son, who had to seek his fortune in other fields.

On 17th February 1752, he was given a regular commission as second-lieutenant and transferred to Longone for garrison duty in the Tuscan States of the Presidi.

Although he did not realise it, it was the turning point of his career. Longone was within easy reach of Leghorn and Leghorn had always been the landfall of independent Corsica. It was the clearing-house for Corsican news, its streets were full of Corsicans who had defied the Genoese ban and run cargoes to the Tuscan shore, or who brought news to Corsican exiles or requests for aid or information to Corsican leaders in the town. Its harbour was thronged with English shipping and the popularity that the Corsican cause had obtained in England brought to the Corsican exiles in the port the illusion of a common struggle with a great power behind them.

The young Pasquale was brought into closer contact with Corsican affairs than he had ever been before. He heard, embellished with a wealth of detail, of the immense reputation his brother Clemente had obtained as a guerilla leader. He heard of the rising power and influence of Gaffori and of the great affection he inspired in the islanders. He heard with excitement of Gaffori's brilliant diplomacy and campaigns. Then, like a thunderclap, in 1753, came the news of Gaffori's assassination.

Gaffori's assassination, and the confusion into which it threw the islanders, produced a sense of defeat in the permanent exiles in Leghorn. Their leader was Luigi Zerbi, an islander who, unofficially looked after all the interests of his countrymen in Tuscany. He was a deeply respected and very sincere man; a Corsican of the older generation, who, like many of the older Corsican exiles, had long had doubts of the ability of the Corsicans to obtain their independence and who, with the death of Gaffori, became convinced of the impossibility of Corsican freedom. Accordingly, with a group of Corsican clerics, he set afoot a proposal to place Corsica under the protection of the Grand Master of the Order of the Knights of Malta and this proposal obtained some powerful support from a group of Corsican clergy at Rome.

It was in opposition to this that Paoli first decisively entered Corsican politics. He threw all his weight against Zerbi's proposal. He wrote letters, he wrote broadsheets, he spoke against it whenever and wherever an opportunity afforded. The Maltese, he argued, were not regarded with respect in Europe; they were thought of as servile, and the proposal, even if it were successful, would only result in Corsica being turned into a nation more servile even than the Maltese.

His eloquence and his energy, joined to his famous name, made him a new and powerful ally to all the war party in Corsica and on the mainland. Acquaintance with him produced the heady realisation that, in spite of his comparatively junior rank, he was a well-trained and experienced soldier. Acquaintance did more; it conveyed the impression that he was highly intelligent and brimful of ideas. Strong links grew up between Pasquale and the Corsican adherents and supporters in Tuscany. Mariani, Colonel Fabrini and Ortioni, all powerful adherents to the Corsican war party, soon became his friends, and indeed began to encourage him to think of himself as a possible leader of his country. They and his brother spread his fame rapidly in the island. By the middle of October he was in direct contact with many Corsican chiefs.

Now the steady reading and thinking during the years of his garrison duty bore fruit. He bombarded the Corsicans with proposals. Over and over again he insisted that the war must be prosecuted. He would not tolerate any thought of peace. Corsica must be free and she could be free only by military victory. But, he argued, that victory must be built on a reformed administration and an economic plan. The first necessity was to stamp out the vendetta and establish the rule of law in the island. Then the judiciary should be completely reformed with new courts set up. Since the Genoese held the sea-ports, new outlets must be found for Corsican commerce and, if necessary, a new port should be established for its exports. The new port might need a navy to protect it and the Corsicans, too, should plan to create a fleet.

Paoli's excitement and enthusiasm, his profusion of ideas and the vigour with which they were expressed were infectious. In the island and on the mainland more and more men began to consider him as the General the island needed. Moreover, Paoli had a very powerful ally in Corsica itself: his brother Clemente. Clemente had a great reputation, which future years were to consolidate, as a brillant and intrepid guerilla leader. He seemed, in many ways, the mirror image of his brother. He was unaffectedly devout; the doctrines of the Church were sufficient for him and satisfied his every need. Of middle stature, dark, retiring and thoughtful he had brooded, during his early years, on a monastic life and even now, so the rumour ran, when he trained his gun on an enemy he offered up a prayer for his soul, should the bullet find him. He had no desire at all for a political life, however. But he had a great admiration of his younger brother's talents and education. Throughout the island he encouraged the islanders to support his brother.

There was only one possible contestant for the title of General in the island – the chieftain Emanuele Matra, whose powerful clan not only held the key port of Aleria, but also dominated the glens immediately south of the Castagniccia. Matra was courageous and he had dealt the Genoese some heavy blows in his encounters with them, but he lacked judgment and had little political ability. It was true, however, that not all the clan chieftains were eager to have a leader of great political ability. What was even more damning of his chances was that Alerio Francesco Matra, his cousin, had seven years previously, after leading Corsican troops brilliantly and successfully in many actions, suddenly deserted Gaffori for the price of a regimental command in the army of Charles Emmanuel of Savoy and by this action brought all his clan into disrepute.

Paoli's financial position in Tuscany seems about this time to have become easier. His father, up till now, had been extremely reluctant to supplement Paoli's rather meagre pay and, indeed, it could hardly be expected of him, since his own pay from the colonelcy was all that he could count upon. But now, hearing his son spoken of everywhere with respect and affection, he suddenly acceded to a long-standing request of Pasquale and provided him with the money to undertake a tour through Italy, in order that he could study the way in which states were governed and their resources managed. Pasquale set off enthusiastically, but his trip was curtailed by the news that an invitation was to be sent to him to return to Corsica and lead the Corsicans. Knowing his time was short he seized every opportunity during his return to study whatever industry fell in his way; he ended by visiting the iron mines of Elba. At the same time, he was steadily reading and preparing himself for the task of the Enlightened leader. Significantly enough, he took with him into Elba Montesquieu's *Spirit of the Laws*.

Everything was now prepared for his return. His brother wrote to him, urging him to hurry, for if he let slip this opportunity it might never return again. But before he went, there was a tragi-comedy to be played out. For his father had doubts of the whole venture once he knew its extent. He had seen too many good patriots perish in what he had come to believe was a hopeless and futile struggle. He had no desire to see his younger and favourite son swallowed up in the pursuit of a chimera. Angry exchanges took place between the father and son. To Paoli, the chance to escape the boredom of life in Naples and the opportunity to begin a useful, perhaps a great, career was within his grasp; to his father a dubious career leading to a shameful death seemed more likely.

'I think of my return to Corsica as I did once about the beginning of a feast-day, but you regard it as a passage to misfortune and death,' Pasquale wrote on 17th October 1745. 'At home I may be able to do some good, both to myself and to others; here, I am only an idler.' Some of the bitterness he felt against Naples and the scanty opportunities it had given him is visible in his letter: 'The air of Naples is ennervating for you; it is better that I fly in time for its subtle poison is evidently able to weaken even the most austere characters.' He rebuked his father gently for counselling him to take the path of safety: 'You would not have done much good with these sentiments you now press upon me. Tell me, would you have been able to take the bold resolutions you took so frequently in Corsica if you had such a disposition then? How are you able then to counsel and even to command me to show timidity?'

He grew increasingly annoyed at his father's determined opposition to his desire to return and lead the islanders. But it was not only the verbal approval of his father that he sought. A return to Corsica would involve him in additional expenses, for he had no money of his own and to return to Corsica penniless would, he realised, involve him in dependence on some faction; a dependence which he was determined to avoid. He looked to his father to provide him with enough money to make a brave show, both just before and just after his arrival in the island. As he grew to realise that his father was determined to keep him in Naples, if he possibly could, his tone became more bitter: 'Make an effort to overcome the fears of old age. Tell me, would you wish to see me at your death-bed knowing in your last moments that your son was a coward and a coward through your advice? Look back over your life. Was not the day of your departure from Corsica the last day of your glory? . . . Before you press on me religious sentiments, read and reread the Roman histories and recall to your mind those models you once sought to emulate. With these in your mind you will give me much better counsel.'

But Giacinto was obdurate; the struggle to free Corsica was, he held hopeless; his son would merely return to wage fruitless campaigns and die a useless death. Pasquale kept up the attack remorselessly, using every argument that suggested itself to his mind. He recalled his brother's solitary struggle, alone against the Genoese oppressor; the enduring sorrows of the Corsicans, the hope that patriots had in the name of Paoli; the poverty of a military career under the Bourbons; his desire not to remain a dependent on his father's slender resources. He hinted, too, that with Genoese cut-throats lurking in every alley, waiting to cut him down, he was no safer in Naples than he would be in Corsica. Pleading with the old man once more to put aside unworthy fears, he emphasised how valuable his father's advice would be to him once he had returned to the island. 'Why cry "wolf",' he wrote, 'before the wolf is even in sight?'

Paoli's persistence and his continual appeals to the memory of his father's past gradually wore the old man's opposition down. The burden of his letter now was the desolation he would feel when his son had left Italy. At the same time, realising that nothing could deter Pasquale from going, he sent him some money for the journey; but Pasquale considered the amount to be derisory and only another device to keep him from returning to Corsica. He was unjust; his father had only the pay from his colonelcy and he had to meet, too, claims on this slender income from other exiled members of the clan. There was really no justification for Paoli's bitter remark to his father: 'I know you are not rich; but the fashion of your giving is almost that of a miser.' However, he was of too generous and charitable a disposition not to realise once his return to the island had finally been determined upon, that his father had not been ungenerous.

Soon the correspondence between father and son became milder in tone. Paoli increasingly asked his father for advice and was eager to allay some of the old man's fears: 'Do not doubt,' he wrote in answer to Giacinto's warnings, 'that I will take great care not to become merely the head of a party.'

Pasquale planned to return to the island by the early days of May 1755. As the time for his return drew nearer, his letters to his father become crowded with his enthusiastic plans for the island: 'When I have arrived the first thing I will do is to arrange for the manufacture of salt near Aleria'; 'I will confiscate all the Genoese revenues and the tenth that the Bishops receive'; 'I will march with a thousand men from one end of the island to the other, putting everything in order and establishing peace'; 'I am determined that the "other side of the mountains" must form part of the Corsican State, all Corsica must be free' – an aim that must have cost Giacinto some uneasy moments, aware as he was of the proud independence of the 'other side of the mountains'; 'Once I have taken San Fiorenzo then all the Nebbio will fall into my hands'. Again Giacinto must have reflected sadly that his son had not yet assessed the magnitude of the task he was so enthusiastically undertaking.

His arrangements made, Pasquale sailed from Leghorn. There is no record of that touching scene of farewell where the old man blessed the hero before he undertook his labours; no record of Paoli making any journey to Naples. Perhaps tradition is right and the scene did take place; or perhaps, as is more likely from the tenor of the letters, he did not dare to risk confronting his father face to face and beginning again all the fruitless arguments about the wisdom of the task he had undertaken.

The journey to the island was uneventful. On 29th April 1755, Pasquale Paoli landed in the Bay of Golo.

3

BIRTH AND YOUTH OF AN
ENLIGHTENED REPUBLIC

From the Bay of Golo, Pasquale Paoli made his way to
Morosaglia and his old home. He received an enthusiastic welcome from those of his clan who were in the village, but his
brother and many others, whom he had looked forward so
eagerly to meeting, were not there to receive him: Clemente and
his followers had been called away at the last moment to deal
with bodies of Genoese soldiers who were attempting to break
into the mountain strongholds from Bastia.

When his numerous well-wishers had departed that evening,
Paoli wrote: 'the house seemed sad and empty'. It had changed
very little from the house he remembered as a boy. Clemente
had carried out some alterations; the most noticeable was that
there was now glass in the windows; but, Pasquale reflected, if
he had any illusions of the grandeur of his new post his
arrival would soon have dispelled them. Characteristically, he
had come provided for emergencies. He had brought with him a
camp bed, some cooking utensils, some knives and forks and, as
a concession to his new glory, some fine shirts. His household,
he considered as he settled in, provided a good lesson in the
virtues of frugality.

Clemente soon returned from his fight and, for the next few
weeks, he lectured Pasquale on the affairs of the island and on
the military dispositions of the Genoese. The house was soon full
of Corsican leaders who came from every part to assess the
qualities of their proposed new General.

In the first days of July, the Grand Council of the island met
together in the famous convent of San Antonio della Casabianca,
standing high among the chestnut woods between two great
valleys of the Casinca. Paoli waited outside, while the Council
deliberated on the choice of the island's leader, until he received
a formal request that he should come before them. Then, before
the representatives of the people and the clergy, he was solemnly

requested to undertake the Supreme Command of the Corsican forces. In his speech of reply, he said that he willingly accepted the honour, but, evidently with Matra in mind, he expressed a desire to share the responsibility with a colleague. This disconcerted the Council, in spite of the fact that Clemente had already warned them that Paoli had something of the sort in mind. Some attributed it to unnecessary Machiavellianism, a device to have it declared loudly that Paoli, and not Matra, was the unequivocal choice of the Council. Others thought it showed considerable political naivety in a leader they had selected partly because, from all the reports they had heard, he had considerable political maturity. Clemente argued that it was neither Machiavellianism nor simplicity, but part of Paoli's character. This seems the fairest judgment, for, although Paoli certainly did not lack ambition, his ambition was for the furtherance of his ideas for the nation, rather than for his own personal glory. He was probably quite willing to have Matra as a colleague if, in doing so, he could unite the nation in its struggle against the Genoese. But the Council soon decided that twin command was dangerous and that, in any case, Matra was more than a little suspect because of the relations of his family with the House of Savoy. They, accordingly, announced that they desired only one General for the nation and Paoli, thereupon, accepted nomination as the candidate. But he was not done yet with surprise. He proposed that the powers of the General in matters of great importance to the State be limited and that, if the Council so desired, all such matters should be referred to a plebiscite of the elected representatives. The Council, not without some uneasiness at all this new-fangled squeamishness, agreed.

On 15th July 1755, in the church of the convent, therefore, Paoli was solemnly adopted as the General of the Corsicans. It was a simple ceremony for the Genoese pressed the islanders hard at many points. Apart from the Council, most of the spectators came from the neighbouring glens. As Pasquale entered the church there was a *feu de joie*, wild cheering and the ringing of bells throughout the valley. That evening, there was a joyful celebration in all the surrounding glens. The Corsicans had found a new national leader; few of those celebrating realised that the spirit of the eighteenth century had also alighted in their valleys.

The first task of the new General was a quasi-military one.

The Council answered, or claimed to answer, for the whole island, but in some of the more remote glens their writ did not run strongly and Paoli had to demonstrate in the first few months, as he had planned at Longone, by a show of military force in the glens, that he was determined to prove his rule was no nominal one, but one which extended to all his countrymen without exception. But that this was only partly a military task is well-instanced by a letter which he wrote to his father at this time, calling upon the old man's knowledge of his fellow-countrymen to help him. Giving a list of the glens of which he had little knowledge, he wrote: 'Father, write and tell me what is the best way to govern these glens? What are their customs? What are the things they particularly cherish? How can I avoid antagonising their deeper feelings?'

He relied greatly in this instance, and in many others where political action impinged upon custom and tradition, on the knowledge and experience of his brother Clemente. But his father was far off and in some ways out of date, while Clemente was no politician. To increase his knowledge of the Corsicans at first hand, Pasquale began to make long journeys on horseback up and down the island and these journeys were to become a feature of his rule. In the glens of his followers he rode with only a few friends. Into some of the others he rode accompanied by an armed band. Always, he brought a camp bed with him to serve as a sort of symbol of his independence of particular clans. Everywhere, he mixed adjurations to the patriotic struggle with demands that the Corsicans take their affairs into their own hands, study the mechanism of government, obey the laws and respect the magistrates. Whenever possible, he stayed the night in monasteries rather than seem to commit himself by the place of his lodging to any particular faction.

There were, indeed, a great many monasteries to stay at: Basti estimated that there were forty convents of the Capucins, thirty-four of the minor observants of the Franciscans, fourteen of the Reformed or Conventual Franciscans, five of the Servites, two of the Jesuits and one of the Carthusians. There is a certain piquancy in seeing the man of the Enlightenment, the opponent of clerical obscurantism, collaborating, from his first arrival in Corsica so closely with the clergy, many of whom in the island might be numbered among the most superstitious and backward of ecclesiastics. But the feature of Paoli's rule was the caution and care with which he dealt with Corsican society. In his eyes the Corsican clergy, both regular and secular, had one redeeming virtue – they were completely and utterly patriotic and devoted to expelling the Genoese. Nor, of course, was he anti-religious himself; like most of the men of the first generation of the Enlightenment he was at heart a Deist. And the Church in Corsica was, for all practical purposes, the kind of Church the Enlightened were fond of – an Erastian Church. The clergy had little contact with their Genoese bishops and no desire at all to obey them. On the other hand, they were willing and eager to obey the edicts of the General. Where Paoli found clerical pretensions he acted ruthlessly and quickly. The Corsican clergy were left in no doubt that they, too, along with the laity, were subject to all the laws of the State. From the first, he abolished the right of sanctuary, which had been long-established and abused; and, whenever he found that his opponents and adversaries had been sustained by the clergy, he punished the clergy equally, along with the lay, as guilty of rebellion. Those priests who imagined that the power of the Church enabled them to outface the state were rapidly disabused of the idea by imprisonment and the confiscation of their property. But the occasions were not numerous. On the whole, the clergy were proud of the trust their General had in them, and if the more acute and intelligent sometimes had reservations about his ideas they were tactful, while he, for his part, made allowances too, convinced that, in the fullness of time, he could create an educated and responsible clergy throughout the island. One thing worried him somewhat, as it was to worry the French later. And that was the enormous number of monks there were in Corsica. The value of the institution of monasticism was as suspect to the Enlightened as it was to Luther. At the beginning of his rule, and at intervals thereafter, Paoli considered plans to restrict and reduce the number of both monks and monasteries. Boswell recounts that when he visited the island in 1765, Paoli was concerned with plans to make the embracing of a novitiate more difficult. But the monastic institution in Corsica was popular and unpretentious. Most monasteries were small and poor, most monks humble and no worse, if no better, agriculturists than their fellow-countrymen. They might have little place in the ideal Enlightened State, but, as a fact, they were among the most

loyal friends of the General and a sure support in every emergency. Paoli was never free enough from a foreign threat to
cause them to question these virtues too closely. Besides, he knew
the advantages both his causes, patriotic and philosophic, might
draw from the support of the clergy. On the one hand, his
summing-up of the role of religion sounds very Napoleonic:
'Religion is an essential part of public order,' he said, 'Without
a belief in God we would soon loose our confidence in victory';
and on the other, in more persuasive vein: 'You are the elected
instrument of the Holy Spirit to enlighten men. . . . I doubt
neither the Divine Protection nor your ability. Know that you
have in your keeping my honour, your honour: indeed the
honour of Christ.' The clergy had to be, indeed, the instruments
of the Enlightenment, for, with a few exceptions, they alone
could provide the body of educated men he needed to begin his
reforms. There was, for instance, the Abbé Geufucci, who had
formerly taught in the famous university of Florence. There was
Suzzione, who had lived many years in Germany and was well-
qualified to teach the German language. There was Gian Quilico
Casabianca, very learned in the history of the island and there
was Paoli's bosom friend and most able collaborator, the Abbé
Rostini, who seemed to Paoli the ideal cleric : a man, not only
extremely well-educated, but of a noble and generous temperament.

The support of the clergy was of the utmost importance to
Paoli from the very first and one of the first tasks in which its
support was absolutely essential was the preaching of the end of
the vendetta.

The suspension of the vendetta was not new. In the first
enthusiasm of a national rising, when hopes ran high and men,
for a time, thought of their nationality with a heightened aware-
ness, the vendetta had sometimes been tacitly suspended. Such
for instance was the case at the beginning of Gaffori's rule. But
the suspension was usually short-lived: Genoese money and
Genoese intrigues and the natural declension of high resolution
with time and mischance inevitably saw the resumption of bloody
quarrels.

Paoli had made its abolition the first great aim of his policy.
The part that it played in perpetuating the Genoese domination
of the island was recognised throughout Europe and Paoli himself had advised the Corsican chiefs, during his correspondence

with them from Longone, that only its replacement by the rule
of law could bring about the liberation of the Corsicans.

Usually, whenever he introduced a policy he proceeded
extremely cautiously, but his action against the vendetta was,
from the first, swift and harsh: 'the island will only know
efficient government,' he declared as soon as he had been proclaimed General, 'if the vendetta can be stamped out.'

First, he declared an amnesty. Then, on 3rd August 1755, he
decreed the penalty of death for all murders. He struck at that
family pride which was one of the great stimulants of the
vendetta by decreeing that, outside the house of any found
guilty of murder, a pillar should be erected with the name of the
murderer inscribed upon it, so that all men could see the shame
which had fallen upon the family. This was not entirely new;
it had been practised before in the island as a weapon against the
vendetta, but it had never been pursued as systematically as
under Paoli's government. Neither rank nor connection could
save the family of the murderer from the mark of public shame.
More than one observer thought that, considering the Corsican
temperament, the pillar of infamy had far more influence in
stamping out the vendetta than all the rigour of the law. One of
the first to be arraigned under the new statute was a relative of
Paoli's mother. The usual Corsican petitioning for mercy on
behalf of the condemned man was begun immediately the judgement was announced. It was commonly expected that Paoli
would intervene, for, in spite of his professions, few men expected
him to alienate those clans on which his own power ultimately
rested. They were soon undeceived. Paoli ignored all the pleas that
were made to him and replied to all the petitioners that, irres-
pective of family connections, it was essential that justice be
done. The execution duly took place. The shock was salutary.
Certainly, it must have done something to hold the island steady
when the Matra rebellion broke out in the autumn of 1755.

The occasion of the Matra rebellion was very much in the
line of Corsican history. A certain Ferdinando Agostini had been
condemned to banishment for his part in the plotting of a murder
in the pursuance of a vendetta. Tomaso Santucci, a member of
the General Council and a relative of Agostini, pleaded with
Paoli to rescind the judgement. Paoli refused. Santucci, angry at
what he considered an affront to his status and to his family,
accordingly entered into a plot with Matra to overthrow Paoli

and put the great clan leader in his place. In October 1755, a revolt broke out. It was soon suppressed by Paoli marching his troops rapidly into the Matra glens and defeating the insurgents. Matra, in the classical Corsican manner, fled to the mainland and enlisted Genoese aid in order to return for his ill-fated expedition in January 1756.

With the defeat and death of Matra, Paoli had demonstrated the reality of his power for all to see and the lesson was learned. As a result, he found himself free to put his principles into practice, undeterred for some time by the demands of war and survival. The next five years were probably the happiest in his life. Throughout the island there was no body of Corsicans who now opposed his rule. It is true that on the 'other side of the mountains', on the west coast, the edicts of his government were received more grudgingly and more critically than they were in the east; but they were obeyed and, if some of the more powerful chiefs murmured, there was no doubt that among the clansmen as a whole there was a great affection and respect for the General. It is true, too, that in Capo Corso, the Genoese held the three key fortresses of Rogliano, Tomino and Macinaggio and the strategically-planned ports of Bastia and San Fiorenzo and thus militarily controlled that fertile peninsula, causing the chiefs there, always fearful of brutal retaliation by the Genoese, to adopt an attitude of professed neutrality towards the General. But Genoese control really ceased at the gates of their fortresses and, as a proof of this, a steady stream of contributions to Paoli's exchequer, some of it indeed in the form of church-plate, came to swell his finances. Apart from Capo Corso, only Calvi and Algajola and the Matra fort of Aleria were secure from Paoli's forces.

The arrival of the French in 1756, who by agreement with the Genoese possessed themselves of the fortresses of Calvi, Ajaccio and San Fiorenzo on the outbreak of the Seven Years' War, was, although of course Paoli did not see it this way, a blessing in disguise. To Paoli, it was a new evidence of an old threat to Corsican independence. But the very presence of the French in the island was to give him time to consolidate his hold over the affections of his countrymen. The French were commanded initially by the tactful and diplomatic Marquis de Castries, and from the first, the Marquis was at pains to emphasise that they were neutral in the struggle between the

Genoese and the Corsicans. The Marquis lost no time once he had arrived in the island in getting in touch with Paoli and informing him that the French expedition had for an object only the guarding of the coastal fortresses against the English: once peace had been made they would immediately retire. Paoli, for his part, resolved to take no action against them. He issued orders that the French soldiery were to be treated with courtesy and kindness and announced that the interior of the island was open for their diversion. It gave him, too, an opportunity of demonstrating what Corsican government meant to another great European Power. Already, his letters to correspondents in Leghorn ensured that his version of events in the island was rapidly carried back to England by the masters and the crews of the English shipping which frequented the port. For Paoli, like the *Philosophes* whose spiritual pupil he was, had a very acute appreciation of publicity. Almost from the beginning of his rule he had pamphlets outlining the Corsican case against the Genoese printed in Leghorn and in Luca. In 1755, he had a printing press established at Oletta in the Nebbio; this was afterwards transferred to Cervione and then to Corte. Symbolically enough, the first work produced by his press was: *A justification of the Revolution in Corsica.* He pursued this policy of ensuring that the Corsican cause was known to the outside world throughout the period of Corsican independence. In 1764, the Corsicans began the publication of an official Gazette: *News of the Island of Corsica;* it appeared at infrequent intervals and was of course flagrantly propagandist.

The occupation by the French of Calvi, San Fiorenzo, Ajaccio and Algajola allowed the Genoese to concentrate all their forces at Bastia, and it was around Bastia that most of the fighting was done between Corsicans and Genoese up to 1760. To contain the Genoese in Bastia Paoli began, almost from the moment of his installation as General of the Corsicans, to construct fortifications at the hill-village of Furiani, from the fortress of which the Genoese capital was plainly visible and whose tower commanded the road to the south and thus provided the strongpoint from which attacks could easily be launched at the vital Genoese life-line between San Fiorenzo and Bastia. On the fortifications of Furiani he lavished all his engineering skill and experience. The hours of study that he had devoted to military engineering in

Sicily under Lusinghi now paid their reward. Furiani, in a short while, was turned into an almost impregnable citadel.

The Genoese could not reconcile themselves for some time to the new state of affairs in the island. They had recourse to all their old devices of bribery and of intrigue, to raise up a party against Paoli, but their efforts were ineffectual and they became increasingly aware of the General's growing power in the island. Forced at last to contemplate military operations of their own, they chose Furiani at which to strike the first blows, for its presence inhibited any campaign directed south against the seat of Paoli's power in the Castagniccia; they spent some months recruiting three or four divisions of soldiers in Switzerland and Germany before they began operations. They joined their new recruits to units of their own forces and placed the whole army under the command of one of the most experienced commanders, the Marchése Grimaldi. Grimaldi with his whole army then marched out to take Furiani. The effect of Paoli's work now became evident as attack after attack was repulsed by the defenders of the village with heavy losses to the besiegers. It was reported back to the General at Corte that, at the height of the attack, the village and its citadel had become a column of flame. But although the village was shattered the Genoese could not take it. Its capture became an obsession with them, and over the months they wasted a good deal of time and troops in vainly trying to storm the fortress.

In the meantime, Paoli's reforms were being steadily pursued. The rule of law was his standard text as, like a secular John Wesley, he rode up and down the island, steadily preaching and preaching again law and order.

On every possible occasion he emphasised the respect which must be paid to the magistrates and the meaning of the sovereignty of the elected representatives. Yet in spite of his insistence that the Corsicans trusted their fortunes to no one man, but always referred them to the State itself he could not, in those early days, in the absence of a large number of trained and reliable administrators, escape the role of judge and arbiter himself. He acted, indeed, at times as a one-man court of equity, a living assurance that justice was above the ties of loyalty and kindred. He trod, indeed, the razor's edge, for his insistence on the sovereignty of the people was, in the last resort, erosive of the traditional power of the clan chieftains and the complete trust people placed in his judgments could, he was only too aware, arouse jealousy amongst those same chieftains. It is a measure of his diplomacy that he was so succesful during the years of 1755-1760. His methods are fascinatingly illustrated by the advice he gave later to some of his young administrators. 'You know our compatriots,' he wrote,

> are by nature talkative, lively and original. Listen patiently to them. If you interpret the majesty of the law too strongly, want to get on with the business and interrupt them brusquely they will immediately begin to doubt the nature of your justice. Amongst all their heat and fervour for a cause there is always mixed a good deal of cool calculation. There are few people in the world who know better how to colour their testimony or hide the real springs of their action. If they see the magistrate become impatient or bored they immediately take up an attitude of defiance – however impartial he may be in reality they distrust him. To inspire them with complete confidence the safest way is to hear them out. Have they finished at last? Then it is the magistrate's turn. Then he must expound the principles of justice and moderation, carefully pointing out to them their faults if they are guilty, quick to calm them if their consciousness of innocence leads them to make intem-perate threats, as it frequently does. You will find, if you do this, that Reason will not be slow to assume her empire and, if they are heard fairly, they will be quite satisfied with the audience they have obtained and wait calmly and carefully for the result of their case.

His patience and the steady emphasis which he always laid on the rule of law, his obvious devotion to his country, his disinterestedness and the force of his character gradually had an effect. So did the increasing efficiency of his administration. As early as February 1756, he wrote triumphantly: ' The vendetta is finished. The old, happy, carefree festivals of the villages which have been abandoned for so long can now be resumed.'

Figures in Corsica are hard to come by at this period, and need careful scrutinising when they are, but there is general agreement among authorities that, hard though it is to believe, since the outbreak of the revolt in 1729 some 900 Corsicans a year met their death through the operation of the vendetta. In the first four years after Paoli's advent the number dropped to a figure more like ten. Allowance has to be made, of course, for some unexplained accidents and unsolved disappearances but, this said, the measure of Paoli's success is impressive. The suppression of the vendetta must have made a not inconsiderable contribution to the rise in population which is another feature of his rule.

Pasquale Paoli's birthplace at Morosaglia in the *piave* of Rostino
19th century lithograph

Paoli's fort at Corte as it is today

4

THE SPRINGTIME OF
INDEPENDENCE

As Paoli's government steadily reduced lawlessness, so he moved
to build the island's economy; confident of the ability of his
forces to contain the Genoese, he devoted his best efforts to
putting into practice those principles of economy that derived
from Genovesi. One of his first tasks was to preach the virtues of
agriculture as against the excitements of the military life:
'Every Corsican,' he declared, 'should be a soldier enlisted in
the Militia, ready to defend his country: but outside these
duties he ought to cultivate the land.'

His organisation of the militia was intended to achieve just
this. Every month the military commander of the glen assembled
the men under his command and drilled them for a day. Since
there was always the danger of a Genoese attack, Paoli established a procedure whereby, on receipt of instructions from the
General, the men of the glen were to be called immediately to
the church square to receive the orders of their commander and
march where they were needed. But outside the monthly drilling
and the emergency mobilisations they were to be farmers.

He was very free with his advice and his encouragement to
achieve this end. To the inhabitants of the marshy region of
Casamatra, for instance, who, because of the unrewarding
nature of their land, had for generations been sunk in hopeless
indolence, he advised the planting of chestnuts and gave
detailed instructions on where they should be planted in order
that the trees could establish themselves, bind the soil together
and so return the region to cultivation. Again in dozens of glens
he encouraged, and was eager to help with, the laying out of
olive plantations. Understanding that nothing was so encouraging as example, he demonstrated the use of the onion in improving the soil of his native glen and, to encourage the
Corsicans to develop an alternative to the chestnut, he planted
potatoes extensively throughout Rostino; he further encouraged

and popularised the use of the potato by having potatoes served every day at the table, at which he entertained the chieftains and dignitaries of the island. Not of course, that the potato was unknown in the island, but before Paoli it had been little cultivated because of the easy return from the vast chestnut groves.

Nor was he slow in putting his reading, and the experience which he had gained in Elba, to use in improving the techniques of mining in the primitive lead and copper mines of the island, near Cervione. He made plans, too, for an increase in the local production of salt-petre for gunpowder: 'It is one of the sinews of war,' he said, 'and if we have the sinews we shall in time be able to grip the Genoese with an unbreakable grip'.

But from the very beginning of his rule Paoli realised that all the revivification of the island depended, in the last resort, on his finding markets for Corsican produce in the outside world. All the ports in the island were held by, or for, the enemy. He had no hope that the French would allow the use of the ports they occupied as outlets for Corsican produce and, even if they had done so, he had few ships in which the produce might be conveyed. When he had first offered advice to the Corsican leaders from Longone he had advised that they create a port in Corsica – a truly Corsican port; no sooner had his régime begun than he set to work to bring this end about. Isola Rossa, in the north of the island, was the place he had selected, where a sheltered bay of deep water provided the conditions he needed for the ships which would export Corsican produce. Primarily, he intended it as the port for the Balagna, that fertile region of olives, vineyards and fruit trees which would be its hinterland; but ultimately he meant that it should be the outlet for all the produce of the island until the main ports were re-taken.

The town was built about one of the round towers which had been constructed to preserve the population from the depredation of the Moors; this served to protect the first gangs of workmen and soldiers from the attacks of the Genoese. Isola Rossa was a well-planned little town, designed as a grid with the main streets running parallel to the side of the bay; one end of the town was marked by the natal tower, the other by a well-proportioned covered market space which gave on to a large open assembly square before the Church. As soon as the Genoese realised his plan they made desperate efforts to stop the building. By land, Paoli was secure but on the sea, the element from which the

Serene Republic had arisen, the Genoese were all-powerful; the building of Isola Rossa was accompanied by a series of battles, the Genoese strategy being to land forces from the sea and Paoli's to prevent them establishing any bridgehead. But the successes that the Genoese obtained, and the consequent slowness of the building of the port, brought home to him, once again, how very necessary it was for the Corsicans to have a navy.

With the same energy and thoroughness that he devoted to all his projects he gave instructions that, on every possible site, the Corsicans were to commence the building of a fleet. Every bay, every beach soon rang with the hammers of his shipwrights; day after day, axes went on busily in the woods, while the chisel, the plane and the adze shaped the timbers of his fleet in the numerous bays and inlets of the coast. There was no lack of land for improvised slipways, only the skilled designers and craftsmen were lacking and, after a time, even these became available in some quantity, for the fame of the Corsican revival began to bring back to the island craftsmen who, despairing under the Genoese, had left their homeland to seek their fortunes in other countries. Paoli had no building programme; what could be built was built; hulls floating in the water were what the General wanted; 'I want ships,' he wrote, 'many ships; and ships not only for Corsican produce but warships to harass the commerce of Genoa itself and revive the once-proud fame of the men of Capo Corso.'

Maddening as it was to the Genoese, his plans prospered. The great galleys of Genoa were well beyond his means, but a multitude of small craft soon carried the Corsican flag, first to the shores of Italy and then to the harbours of southern France. Already the English and the French were providing a steady stream of visitors to see this emergent republic. Now, as a result of the voyages of its seamen, the island began to figure again in the calculation of European Cabinets. Paoli's letters are full of exports at this time: 'I have arranged for the sale of a million barrels of olive oil'; 'We have a good market for our chestnuts'; 'I hope to interest Tuscany in our wine'; 'The vintage is very good this year'.

With the Genoese contained by land and increasingly threatened by sea and the economy of the island prospering Paoli's enthusiasm rose tremendously. His selflessness and his utter devotion to the cause of Corsica infected all the members of his administration. The disturbances caused by his innovations were compensated for to a large extent by the tranquillity he had brought to the islanders and the impartiality of the administration of his justice. But the old clan system was deep-rooted and was essentially divisive, while the Enlightened government, which he set up in the island, was new, and, in essence, centralising. The ever-present threat of the Genoese and his own tact and diplomacy did a great deal to avoid conflict, but they could not hope to be entirely successful. The two areas of the island in which Paoli's government was most strongly criticised and where, in the last resort, it had the least influence, were the districts of Capo Corso and the 'other side of the mountains'.

In Capo Corso, the opposition to Paoli came mainly from the chiefs of the clans and was due to the presence of Genoese troops, at the hands of which the Capo Corsan chiefs feared a bloody retribution if they should support Paoli too openly; but secretly, many of them harboured a great affection for the General, and certainly many of their clansmen were to be found fighting with his troops and contributing to his Exchequer.

The case of the 'other side of the mountains' was different. The west of the island had always enjoyed a high degree of independence because of its comparative remoteness. Here, too, were the most powerful clan chieftains in Corsica, many of them professing to trace their descent back to the semi-legendary Corsican nobility. At the head of these was the great Colonna clan which claimed to stem from the almost mythical founder of the Corsican nobility, Hugo Colonna himself. They were irked by the fact that under Paoli's administration they were treated, however courteously, as just another part of the island, and not as the separate entity they had always considered themselves to be. It was not surprising therefore that it was on the 'other side of the mountains' that the first serious split in the Paolist administration came.

In September 1757, Corsican separatism and Corsican pride, inflamed by some decisions in Paoli's courts, once more raised the standard of revolt under the leadership of Antonio Colonna. At an Assembly convoked by Antonio, many of the glens of the *Oltremonti* declared themselves independent of the rule of Paoli and his government. Paoli did not hesitate: he had been aware that trouble was threatening and he at once mobilised the militia in the north of the island. But he made no attempt to cross the mountain chain to attack Colonna; instead, he made overtures for a meeting. A few weeks later, a meeting having been arranged, he rode with a few followers to meet Colonna at the convent of Olmeto, near Ajaccio.

Colonna was already having second thoughts, for he found the enthusiasm of the chieftains for their independence was not shared to the same extent by many of their followers. Paoli and his advisors knew this too and the General was pressed by some to put an end to Colonna's pretensions, once for all, but he deeply feared a conflict which might tear the island in half and provide the Genoese gratuitously with the opportunity they had so often striven to create. His talks with Colonna went on for some days and out of them came a compromise. Paoli agreed to recognise the economic autonomy of the *Oltremonti* and offered the presidency of the new magistracy to Antonio Colonna (who would have been certain to obtain it if he had coveted it in any event); but, as a safeguard, every new proposal introduced was to be ratified by a free vote throughout the region.

It was a politic decision. With the 'other side of the mountains' divided, and Paoli quite capable of crushing the revolt militarily, he might have risked a confrontation. But in this crisis, as in all his dealing with the deeply-entrenched clan-structure of the island, he proceeded cautiously, willing to abandon the letter if he could preserve the spirit. Yet, nevertheless, the abortive rebellion was a warning to him, if he needed one, of the thorniness of the path to Corsican unity.

In this, as in his other conflicts, external and internal, he drew great advantages from the support of the clergy; this he attempted to repay by re-establishing the ecclesiastical organisation of the island on a new basis. It was not only gratitude to the clergy of course that inspired his action. Like most men of the Enlightenment, he had a far greater affection for Martha than for Mary and his ideal, like their ideal, was an ecclesiastical institution which was also a working-part in the State. The spiritual welfare of good citizens and the reproof of bad ones was its task; and this task did not necessitate that it should meddle in politics or make high and overriding claims for itself since spiritual welfare was seen in terms of the inculcation of ethics and the provision of solace for the inevitable disappointments and sorrows of man.

The Corsican bishops violated all these ideals; appointed by the Genoese they were deeply committed to the Genoese cause; they had been absent many years from their posts; yet they still continued to draw the revenues from their sees. Both by the standards of a Corsican patriot and a man of the Enlightenment they stood condemned. Paoli proceeded methodically to effect their replacement. Firstly, he wrote to them all individually to request that they return to Corsica and take up their episcopal duties. If they would do this he guaranteed them his protection in the island.

All Paoli's appeals were ignored. Finding that his offers had no result, he applied directly to the Pope, complaining that the Corsican bishops had abandoned their sees for all practical purposes and that they should accordingly be deprived of them. The Pope had his own quarrels with the Genoese Republic and, in any case, realised the lack of control by the bishops over the Corsican clergy threatened the very existence of the Church in the island. He, accordingly, sent an apostolic visitor, Crescentio de Angelis, the bishop of Segni, who was invested with authority to enquire into the abuses complained of and apply and remedy which he thought fit. The Genoese were infuriated. The Pope's action was tantamount to a recognition of the Corsican government and an insult to Genoese sovereignty. In Rome, the Genoese Ambassador protested that the Pope had no right to go over the head of the Republic in making any spiritual accommodations for the island. When the Pope ignored this protest, and the bishop was sent in spite of it, the Genoese prohibited his entry into Corsica and declared that he had no authority to exercise his ecclesiastical functions there. Relying on their power by sea, they sent ships to intercept the Papal visitor and offered rewards for anybody who should arrest him. A timely storm and the wrecking of some of the Genoese ships, naturally attributed by the Corsicans to the Divine intervention of Heaven, allowed the bishop to land in safety, to wild acclamation, on the east coast in April 1760.

Relations between the Holy See and the Genoese Republic were now at their worst. The Pope formally annulled the Genoese Proclamation, prohibiting the bishop's entry, and the Genoese replied by publicly tearing up his Annulment. The connection between the two powers was for some time at breaking point, but the Republic was too powerful in Italy for the Pope to risk the weapon of an interdict and the Genoese soon found that they had no opportunity of securing the person of the bishop. So a stalemate was reached.

After Crescentio had made his report, the Pope formally deprived the Corsican bishops of their sees; but he balked at appointing Corsican successors who would go unrecognised by the Genoese in the ports of the island. He therefore left the sees vacant, hoping that time and chance would enable him to resolve his dilemma. Paoli, however, at once sequestrated the revenues of the absent bishoprics. This policy dated back to his Neopolitan plans but it was something that surprisingly neither Pope nor clergy had anticipated and there was a great deal of complaint. Paoli, however, argued that: 'though the Altar should nourish its ministers, the tithes of those who fail to serve that Altar are the property of the poor'; he saw that it was to the poor the tithes went.

By the time the accommodation with Rome was made the French had finally quitted Corsica. The Corsicans were glad to see them go. The Comte de Vaux, who had succeeded the amiable Marquis de Castries, was of a far different disposition; suspicious and hypochondriacal, he was deeply prejudiced in favour of the Genoese; he had professed to see in Paoli's anxiety for good relations only Machiavellianism and an illustration of Corsican weakness; he had acted throughout his tenure of office as if the Corsicans were rebels and ignored their obvious allegiance to their own government. Paoli, for his part, had ignored de Vaux's provocations, but the Count had made the task of his administration all the more difficult. With the French gone and with the Genoese face to face with the Corsicans, he hoped that at last a settlement might be made.

For the Genoese too, it was a testing time. In this crisis in their history they made one of their most able citizens Doge. The election of the energetic and statesman-like Agostino Lomellino, in 1760, began a new and more dangerous era for the Corsicans in the attempt of the Serene Republic to bring its rebellious possession to heel. The Doge found the conditions in Corsica gave him some advantage. His elevation was marked by a stroke of good fortune for him by a demonstration of the limits of Paoli's power. With the agreement of Olmeto, in 1757, Capo Corso had remained the sole discordant voice in the spring madrigal of Corsican liberty. Its geographical position was the explanation. The Genoese held the ports of San Fiorenzo and of

Bastia and were thus in a position to seal off the Cape almost at will; moreover, they also held the towns of Rogliano, Macinaggio and Tomino, all strongly-fortified and garrisoned, and the island town of Centuri, which they could easily reinforce from the sea. There was, as has been said, no lack of popular enthusiasm in the Cape for the patriot cause; a steady stream of men, of money and of church plate had poured into Paoli's hands over the years. But the chieftains of Capo Corso wanted something more than the enthusiasm of their followers to make them openly adopt the national cause. They had, in that fertile region, prospered more than most of the islanders; relations between them and the Genoese had been easier; proximity had weakened their patriotism to an extent unknown in the west of the island. Moreover, they were open to fearful retribution from the Genoese if they dared to rebel. Paoli could only bring them under the Corsican flag by the defeat of the Genoese in the peninsula and in 1760, well aware of this, he moved north into the Cape to undertake the siege of the Genoese fortresses.

At first, all went well. His sea-borne forces stormed Centuri and Paoli immediately set about turning it into yet another of his shipyards, staffing it with workmen brought in from the Italian mainland. Then he invested Rogliano, Macinaggio and Tomino; time and again his troops stormed to the attack, but were driven back. At the same time, in an attempt to break the Genoese hold on the neck of the peninsula, he besieged San Fiorenzo. The Genoese fought back furiously. They knew that the loss of San Fiorenzo could easily result in their loss of the whole of the island. Moreover, they had the advantage that it could be reinforced from the sea. The fight for the town was excessively bloody. Paoli, leading a charge, was wounded in the leg. Determined to take the town, he directed operations from a litter. But still the town held out. Paoli became depressed: 'The patriots have shown great valour,' he said, 'but fortune sides always with the enemy'. Ugly streaks of despair, of bitterness and of uncharacteristic vengefulness against the chiefs who had refused to come to his aid in the peninsula began to colour his letters.

It was at this moment that the Doge Lomellino made his overtures for peace. It was a shrewd and statesmanlike move. On the one hand, the impetus of Paoli's attack had been spent and the idea of invincibility, which had come to be associated with him, dispelled; his wound, too, and his low spirits had led him into intemperate denunciations of the chiefs who refused to come to his assistance and this was resented by many other chieftains in the island. On the other hand, Genoa was eager for some sort of accommodation; the cost of military operations was steadily bleeding the Republic to death; the Doge had resolved on either a peace, or a last great effort to destroy Paoli and his followers.

The Genoese Senate, accordingly, sent a deputation of six Genoese dignitaries armed with plenipotentiary powers to meet the Corsicans at Bastia. The deputation, which was to go down in Corsican history as the Magnificent Deputation, was surrounded with all the pomp and panoply that the Republic could muster. Partly to impress, and partly to appease the susceptibilities of the Corsicans, the greatest galleys of Genoa were used to bring the majestic delegates and their most carefully and gorgeously-clad retinues to the Governor's Palace in Bastia which had been provided, in advance, with the most elaborate State furniture and the most impressive tapestries that the Republic could produce. The population of Bastia showed a proper awe and the delegates awaited the arrival of the Corsican deputation from Corte with confidence.

Paoli, meanwhile, realising the importance of the Genoese offer, and determined that it should be considered by the whole nation, convoked a Consulta at Vescovato, in the Casinca, on 10th May 1761 to discuss the action the Corsicans should take. The Consulta rapidly turned into a demonstration. In spite of their recent setbacks, Corsican spirits were high; economically, the island was going from strength to strength; by land and by sea the Corsicans had obtained startling victories over the Genoese. Full of self-confidence as a result, the Assembly would not even consider the drawing up of terms; they had only one demand to make of the Genoese and this was that the Genoese should completely evacuate the island. The Genoese delegates would not even consider meeting the Corsicans on these terms and the Magnificent Deputation returned as magnificently as it had come, without having exchanged one word with the Corsican leaders.

The Doge now resolved on pressing the war by every means at his disposal. He resorted to the time-honoured Genoese practice of bribery on a vast scale. In addition to money, honours and large grants of land were promised to all those Corsican chiefs who would take up arms against Paoli.

Paoli surprisingly played into the Doge's hands at this point; still suffering from the effects of his wound and deeply exasperated at the neutrality of the chiefs of Capo Corso, he announced the deposition of some three of those he considered most culpable. It was the first time that he had struck directly against the clan system of the Corsicans and the violent reaction showed how very necessary his caution had been in the past. Many chieftains saw their authority threatened; already there had been much criticism of the steadily increasing burden of taxes, caused by Paoli's necessity to find funds for the attack on Capo Corso; this added to the excitement caused by his deposition of the chiefs, produced a crisis in the administration. It was at this highly critical moment for Paoli's government that the Genoese launched their attack on the island.

This time, the attack was well-planned and adequately financed. Yet another of the great Matra clan, Antonuccio Matra, Emanuele's brother, was placed in command of a considerable force of Genoese soldiers; an experienced Genoese captain, Giacomo Martinetti, was his second-in-command and the Genoese troops were strongly backed by all those Corsican exiles who acknowledged the Matra as leaders. Four Genoese noblemen, all regular soldiers, were given commands under Matra and Martinetti. The way was well-prepared; before the expedition set sail emissaries were sent over to distribute money amongst those chiefs who had already shown themselves likely to prove hostile to the General. But in spite of the feeling of discontent with Paoli's government, the Corsicans drew together at this new threat from Genoa: only at Fiumorbo and Castello and the network of villages near them was there open insurrection against Paoli.

In May 1762, the Genoese forces landed at Aleria; they advanced immediately on Corte, directing their advance through the Matra country. At Zuani, they were met by Paoli's forces under the command of Clemente Paoli and Nicodemo Pasqualini. In Capo Corso Paoli himself refused to be panicked by the Genoese and continued his siege of Macinaggio. The Genoese and the Corsicans at Zuani were well-matched and the battle was very fierce, but Clemente was a great leader of men and his fire and example inspired his followers. The forces of

Matra soon broke off the engagement and retreated across the mountains to the elegant little village of Vivario which commanded the northern approaches to the mountain pass which linked the two great divisions of the island. That there was a strategic plan at work now became evident for, as Clemente and the main force of the Corsicans followed Matra in his retreat, the Genoese issued out of Bastia in force and Clemente, realising that Corte was threatened from the north, turned from the pursuit to meet them. Almost at the same time, a revolt broke out in Corte itself where there was a well-laid plot headed by one Pietro Cannocchiale, who by liberal use of Genoese gold raised a small force of traitors, broke into the prisons of the citadel, placed himself at the head of the prisoners held there and then quickly overran the garrison to capture the citadel itself.

With his capital threatened, the island cut in two and the very existence of Corsica in danger, Paoli at once broke up the siege of Macinaggio and headed south. By this time, the Genoese plan was clear. Holding Vivario with a small detachment, they could repulse any reinforcements which came from the *Oltremonti*. At the same time, Matra with the main body of his army had now an almost uninterrupted road, along the valley of the Vecchio and over the mountains, to Corte. Rapidly, his army crossed the valley between Vivario and Venaco; Venaco, perched on the mountainside at the other end of the valley, was a twin to Vivario and was the last important village on the road to the mountain passes from which the descent to Corte might by made. But now, when Paoli's forces had been completely outgeneralled, the fundamental strength of his position became clear, for with his army out-manoeuvred, it was the loyalty and bravery of the local militia which saved the day. Venaco lay high on the mountain up which the road from the valley tortuously wound. Beyond it were the two tiny villages of Lugo and San Pietro and it was between these on one of the steepest stretches of the twisting road that the militia of the district made its stand. The local inhabitants were commanded by Salvatore Carlotti and the local tax-collector, Gian Battista Jacobi. They positioned their men on the *macchia* and among the rocks which bordered the road. In that narrow place a few men could, for a time, hope to hold up an army. It was while the forces of Matra were fighting their way upwards from rock to rock that something totally unexpected took place. Giuseppina Jacobi, the wife of

Gian Battista, had ridden like an avenging fury through the nearby villages while her husband and his companions were making their way to the defile; everywhere, she called on the women to take up arms and join the men in their attack on the invaders. The response was immediate. The forces of Matra, checked on the mountainside by the militia, were suddenly attacked from below by a horde of black-clad Amazons. Disconcerted, uncertain of the strength of the forces which opposed him on the mountain, Matra gave up his attempt to fight his way through to Corte and retreated, still in good order, the way he had come.

Now his forces were increasingly on the defensive. From all the surrounding glens, Paoli's militia came flooding in to swell the ranks of the defenders of San Pietro. Others, at the head of whom was Edoardo Ciavaldini, one of Paoli's most trusted lieutenants, had as an aim to trap Matra between his own militia and the men of the victorious defenders of San Pietro. Ciavaldini's militia clashed with the Genoese on the banks of the river Vecchio near Noceta, but in an orthodox action the Genoese were easily the superior of the Corsicans; Ciavaldini was killed and his bands dispersed.

Matra, however, now decided to retreat to a strong-point and there re-group his forces. He, accordingly, made his way to Piedicorte, a village popularly regarded as impregnable since it was built on a jutting spur of rock high above the valley of the Tavignano. There he was soon joined by a troop led by Costa, a one-time captain of the *Royal Corse* and a chevalier of St Louis, who with his men had been detached from the main body of Genoese troops which had attempted to fight its way from Bastia to Corte from the north. The attack had failed for, harassed by the militia of the surrounding countryside and threatened by the junction of Paoli's forces with those of Clemente, the main Genoese force had withdrawn into Bastia. Costa, however, had been sent to provide additional support for Matra. Paoli and Clemente wasted no time but led their forces immediately to the attack of Piedicorte. It was essential that it was taken at once, for untaken it was a constant threat to the Corsicans. On the one hand, it provided a spring board from which Matra could attack Corte, and, on the other, it could easily be reinforced from Aleria by troops marching up the valley of the Tavignano. The fighting for the town was excessively bloody. Matra fortified the town competently and his trained troops fought well, but Paoli and Clemente, reinforced by the militia of the surrounding districts, attacked furiously with the consciousness that a failure to take Piedicorte could result in the disintegration of the Corsican realm.

The struggle lasted some days, and the price paid in lives was high, but the Paolists could not afford to count their losses; by sheer doggedness they fought their way into the town and took it at last, house by house. Matra himself, however, had by some means escaped and he soon sailed for the mainland.

5

THE CONSTITUTION

The invasion of Antonuccio Matra was a turning point in
Paoli's government of the island. His failure to carry Capo
Corso and the support, both overt and covert, that Matra had
obtained caused him to review all his actions. The flaw in his
policy was easy to see. In the whirl of daily business, in his
unceasing labours to establish the economy of the island, but
most of all, in the last few months, in the heat of battle, he had
forgotten his old caution when dealing with the clans and placed
his leadership above the democratic principles he had always
advocated. During his assault on the Cape, he had become,
whatever the excuses, something that looked perilously like a
despot. Paoli, over the years, had come to appreciate very clearly
the fears and susceptibilities of the Corsicans. It was now rare
for him to lose sight of them, even in the pursuit of his ideals
or through the exigencies of his policy. He realised that, in his
zeal to incorporate Capo Corso in his State, he had gone too far
and that there was a need to retreat, so that he could reforge
the links between himself and his countrymen. Immediately,
therefore, the danger from Matra was over he convoked a Consulta at Corte for 23rd May 1762. It was intended as an
assembly of reconciliation, and in his opening address he tried
to establish the mood in which he hoped it would be conducted:
'Gentlemen', he said,

> Your fellow citizens in electing you to represent them at this
> Consulta have placed their dearest interests in your hands.
> You know their needs, you share their sympathies, and their
> customs: so examine your consciences, enlighten each other
> by frank discussion, and be convinced that the resolutions you
> will take together will become the law of the land, because
> what they represent will be the sincere expression of the will
> of the country. Gentleman, let us search out our good to-

gether, and work hard to assure the well-being of our community; let us strive calmly and intelligently to undo our enemies' plans which, as you have already seen, count on our divisions to destroy us. We have never yet been defeated and now victory has once more alighted on our standard; but recent events reveal the need of all true patriots to be ever vigilant and ready to oppose the enemies of our State. Let each one of us remember what he owes to his country and resolve that he will seek his own good only in the good of all.

After this exhortatory address, Paoli and his counsellors offered a sop to his critics in the form of a change in the system of taxation. His reforms were all concessionary and, as such, were a measure of the weakness of his government, but so thriving had his economy become that he now felt he could face a reduction in taxes without endangering the welfare of the State. The increased Customs returns from the many exports of crops, wines and honey, when added to the flourishing revenues of the coral fisheries, where the government now drew substantial returns from its augmentations of the fleet and fishermen, had given Corsica a greatly increased revenue with which to offset tax concession.

Paoli, therefore, lowered the hearth-tax and revised it, on a basis of the total household income, thereby giving relief to the poor householders. At the same time, the most heavily-taxed of the clan chieftains were exempted from paying the tithes due to the sequestered bishoprics. All the widows and orphans of soldiers who had died in the defence of their country in the recent struggle were exempted from paying normal taxes for ten years and in exceptional cases for ever. When all these reforms had been made the total revenue of the State from taxation was cut by something in the region of five per cent.

To emphasise further the debt that the country owed to its defenders, the portraits of all the officers and clan chieftains who had fallen fighting Matra were to be exhibited in perpetuity in the hall of the Great Council.

At the same time, mindful of the fact that if he were to take the ports of the island he would almost certainly need help from within the towns themselves, Paoli abolished the law which forbade trading between the Corsicans of the interior and the Corsicans of the occupied ports.

The elections for the reforming Consulta incidentally pro-

duced, almost by accident as it were, a striking declaration of
religious tolerance in that very Catholic island. For a deputation
from Isola Rossa came to the General before the elections were
held in that town and demanded whether or not a Jew who
had settled in the port should be allowed to vote. 'My countrymen,' Paoli answered the deputation, 'Liberty does not go to
confession: we leave distinctions of that kind to the Inquisitors
of the Holy Office; we have a law here which says that any honest
man who lives on the soil of our country is able to take part in
the nomination of his magistrates and his representatives: you
should obey that law.'

The Consulta having completed its business, Paoli settled
down with his counsellors to consider what he believed the next
most necessary step – a Constitution for the island. But he was
interrupted by the descent of yet another Matra – the notorious
Alerio Francesco – who had left the service of the King of Sardinia
and who had been recruiting for the Serene Republic in
Sardinia. The divisions that were evident in Paoli's ranks in
May had struck the Genoese very forcibly and they hoped to
increase them. Accordingly, before he landed in the island with
his forces Matra went to Bastia and conducted a carefully-
planned propaganda campaign, which had for its avowed
object: 'to sow discord in the camp of the islanders and to
spread the story that Paoli was an ambitious betrayer of the
public good and aspired to the Crown.'

In order to place Paoli's opponent on an eminence com-
parable to that which the General himself occupied, the Genoese
invested Matra with the title of Grand Marshal and elevated
him to the ranks of the Genoese nobility. From Bastia he sent
letters to all the principal officers of the national militia in the
island to whom he promised money and commissions in his
army if they would support him. It was a carefully-planned
scheme aimed at what seemed the weakest point of Paoli's
State, but it came too late. Gian Carlo Saliceti, who received one
of the first letters, promptly sent it to the Supreme Council who
had it burnt in public. Paoli's reforms had had their effect and
the example of burning Matra's letters was widely followed up and
down the island.

The same Saliceti was instrumental in foiling this new attempt
to seize Corsica. Having done what he could to sow disaffection
among Paoli's followers, Matra chose to land at Aleria and once

again immediately advanced towards the Matra country to the northwest. But he was almost at once opposed by a strong force led by Giulio Serpentini. He thereupon retreated towards Antisanti with the intention of fortifying it, but, just outside the town, he encountered the combined forces of the local militia led by Saliceti, whose first impetuous charge shattered Matra's forces. Matra himself only just escaped capture by yet more of the militia who were hurrying to the scene of the battle.

The defeat of yet another expedition did not deter the Genoese. They realised how very close they had been in May to overthrowing Paoli and they were determined to strike yet again before he had a chance to reconsolidate his hold on the island. The General soon heard the news that they were recruiting intensively in Italy and that this time they were recruiting regular troops.

Paoli himself had always been opposed to the formation of a regular army. He had always placed his faith in the militia; 'When there is a standing army,' he wrote 'an *esprit de corps* is formed; men begin to speak of the bravery of such and such a regiment, of such and such a company; this can easily be a grave threat and I believe it wise to avoid it. I would much rather that men spoke of the bravery of this or of that family or praised the valour of a simple citizen; that sort of praise excites emulation among a free people. When the nation is at one with itself its militia will be invincible.' But the Council knew how close the country had been to defeat and they pressed upon Paoli the absolute necessity to oppose regular soldiers with regular soldiers. Paoli fought a delaying battle. 'In a country which values liberty,' he argued, 'every citizen ought to be a soldier and be ready to go to the defence of his rights.' 'Regular soldiers', he said again, 'have a stronger affinity for despotism than for liberty. Rome lost her liberty on the day that she created an army and the invincible Phalanxes of Sparta were formed of a *levée en masse*.' But a new invasion and more hard struggles were imminent and Paoli, in spite of his confidence in his own powers of military engineering and his belief in the islanders' fighting qualities, saw the force of the Council's argument. On 24th March 1762, the Council established two regiments, consisting of 400 men apiece. A former officer of the *Royal Corse*, Giacomo Baldassari, and Tito Buttafuoco, an able and successful leader of the patriot forces, were made its first colonels.

Paoli, with his Neapolitan experience, naturally gave advice on its training, but in the early months of 1762 the greater part of his endeavours were turned to quite a different object. The defeat of Matra and the tax concessions had drawn the islanders together. Now the lightening of the load of Paoli's military command gave him time to concentrate on an object much nearer his heart: the perfection of the political constitution of the island had always been one of his dearest aims and now he worked on it unceasingly. Considering the small number of trained administrators that he had to help him, the repeated calls that businesss of the island made on his attemtion and the need he had to consider the susceptibilities of the chiefs, his Constitution could never be, and indeed never was, a formal document; it was rather a body of law built up in the English manner; an *ad hoc* body of legislation. It was added to and altered at each Consulta in the light of experience; even on the eve of the final struggle with the French, amendments were being proposed to it. But that it was meant to be a whole, that it was meant to form a Constitution, that panacea for all the ills of eighteenth-century government, none of his associates for a moment doubted. For the ideals which informed it were the ideals of Paoli; partly derived from his knowledge of the government of Naples; partly from the experience of governing men for the last seven years; but most of all from the ideas of the Enlightenment which had coloured his thought since his youth in Calabria. All the democratic trends in the philosophy of the Enlightened; all the belief that men could, by the unfettered exercise of their natural reason, create a State whose government was the expression of their political and social desires shines through the clauses of Paoli's Constitution. With his love of his country and his faith in his countrymen he firmly believed that Corsica, enlightened by law and ennobled by her patriotic struggle, might serve as a model to the whole of Europe.

He was not to be disappointed, for the news of his Constitution – reaching England through Leghorn, Italy through the Tuscan ports, and France through the sea ports of Provence and the letters home of those soldiers who served at various times on the island – could be and was, taken as the practical symbol of many shadowy hopes. That wraith of the Enlightenment, the vast vague shadow of the 'Noble Savage', whose instincts were naturally good and whose relations with his fellow men were simple and reasonable, seemed to be printed black and clear in its clauses. The belief in men's ability to shape a wise and equitable social state; the refusal to rely on ecclesiastical sanction and superstition; the basic democracy towards which the Enlightenment, however unsteadily, always moved, all seemed embedded in its government. Corsica was near enough to be akin; it was also small enough to engender affection. It became, for thinking men entrapped in the rigid nation state of the *ancien régime*, a portent. In the early days of the Enlightenment, truly Enlightened governments had to be sought in the imagination, among the Persians of Montesquieu or the Chinese of Voltaire; now the ideal state had become real, embodied in the shape of the rocks, harbours, villages and forests and with the government of Paoli's Corsica.

There was more than a little self-deception in all this. Few of the islanders' most enthusiastic admirers knew Corsica at first hand; fewer still knew much of its customs or its society, its clan system or its intricate politics; and the measured diction of the eighteenth century, with its talk of assemblies and presidencies and magistracies, partly concealed the simple form of Corsican institutions. But if the reality were, at times, revealed to be more rude and simple than language would have it, this in itself became a source of affection and, in any event, the struggle of the Corsicans for their liberty excused much. At the very least, the Corsicans were seen to have created a constitutional state; who knew what, freed from their conflict with the Genoese, they might achieve?

The sovereign assembly established by the Constitution was the Consulta, composed of the representatives of the people and the clergy, and the presidents of the provincial magistracies. The representatives of the people were elected by universal male suffrage, the age of eligibility being twenty five and there was a representative on the average for every thousand men. To emphasise the great importance of the elections it was decided that, before the vote for the Consulta took place, the *Podesta*, or leader of the community, should receive a solemn oath from the assembled electors that they would name the man they believed would most sincerely serve the country.

The Assembly thus elected was the supreme authority. It alone had the right to impose taxes, make laws and decide the question of war or peace; a question which, however, in Corsica's condition, was usually decided for it by the march of events. There had to be a two-thirds majority to carry a resolution.

The executive power rested in the hands of nine members, each a former president of a province and of not less than thirty-five years in age who represented one of the nine provinces of the Nebbio, the Casinca, the Campoloro, the Balagna, Orezza, Alonia, Ornano, Vico and Cinarca. The General was the perpetual President of this body; but an inner Cabinet of three, in which by turns sat members of the nine, was responsible for the day to day work of governing the island. Major decisions affecting the future of this island had to be taken by the whole nine sitting in full conclave.

This Supreme Council had the duties of convoking the National Assembly, maintaining public security and presiding over foreign relations. It initiated and supervised public works, and in war it became the Supreme Junta; it could also issue free pardons, accord amnesties and suspend by veto any action of the Consulta until its next meeting.

The Council and the General attended the Consulta on the day of its opening, but afterwards left it so that it could make its own free decisions. The Consulta firstly elected a president to regulate business and an Orator, an important official, who presented a detailed report on the measures proposed before they were submitted to the Assembly. The representatives were elected for a single legislature and, before they dissolved, elected a new Council of nine. They also chose Inspectors of Agriculture and five Syndics or Censors.

The Syndics had the task of undertaking progresses through the provinces, to hear complaints on the taxes, on the maladministration of justice and on any other subject which affected the Corsicans. Its decrees were sovereign and the General himself formally submitted his conduct to its scrutiny. Not unnaturally, he was rarely questioned on his actions; but the possibility of censure always remained.

The General himself named the tax collectors and decided many other appointments, but they were all subject to the approval of the Consulta and subject also to the decisions of the Syndics. The Syndics also possessed the powers of being able to issue reprimands, and to censure the culpable, to decree amends, and to suspend certain political rights. In the last resort they had the authority to deprive any Corsican of his civic rights but this was without prejudice to his goods and chattels.

Justice was strictly regulated. In civil cases the *Podesta* decided all cases up to a fine of ten *livres;* for fines from ten *livres* to thirty *livres* the *Podesta* was assisted by two officials of the village named Fathers of the Commune. Cases of greater importance than this were decided by the Tribunal of the Province. This Tribunal was composed of a President and two assessors, nominated by the Consulta and an Advocate Fiscal who was nominated by the Supreme Council. This magistracy was elected for a year.

An appeal could be made from these to the Rota, which consisted of three Doctors of Law holding their appointments for life but subject to the Syndics.

In criminal cases the same tribunals dealt with all except homicidal cases. In these latter cases the public prosecutor arraigned the accused before a tribunal of three magistrates, cases being decided by a jury of six.

Political offenders were tried before the Supreme Council.

There were also extraordinary commissions called Juntas of War, or sometimes Juntas of Defence; these Juntas were invested with full powers at the time of a national emergency, the emergency itself being declared by the General.

The Juntas were formed of three, five, seven or more members and were composed of the most influential men of the district for which they were responsible. The President of each Junta was usually a member of the Council. These dictatorial commisions were still responsible for their actions to the Syndics.

This then was the famous Constitution of Paoli which commanded the admiration of his contemporaries throughout the whole of Europe. Voltaire summed up the general impression when he said: 'Europe regarded him as the legislator and the defender of his Fatherland.' What that legislation came to mean to the Corsicans is revealed in another comment of Voltaire's: 'The Corsicans,' he said, 'were seized with a violent enthusiasm for liberty and their General redoubled that natural passion until it became a species of fury'.

It was no paper Constitution as the Genoese, and later the French, were to allege. A stream of measures poured from the Corsican administration to give ample evidence of their industry. Most, of course, were concerned with the fostering of agriculture, but there were many others on a variety of matters proper to a nascent State: on the encouragement of industry for example, on the regulation of the medical profession; on the qualifications necessary for the practice of law, on the standardization and the inspection of weights and measures, Passports were issued, privateers licensed and safe conducts provided for the Genoese merchants who requested them. In 1761, by the government's decree, a Mint was set up at Murato, and Corsica provided yet another proof of her nationhood with the issue of a coinage, the most valuable coins of which bore the national symbol, the elegant head of a Moor.

Paoli's tax reforms and the nature of his Constitution led to a great renewal of his popularity on the island; his strength had always been great in the mountain glens but the good order and economic progressiveness of his régime, and perhaps more especially relaxation of the ban against trading with the Corsicans of the occupied ports, raised his popularity in the coastal towns to a new level. He had always been extremely popular with the humbler Corsicans in the ports; but Corsican merchants had viewed with mixed feelings a patriot who, in an attempt to starve the Genoese out, plundered their cargoes on the high seas and throttled their outlets to their countrymen. Trade was by no means unrestricted, in spite of Paoli's decrees, for the Genoese themselves had long banned trade with rebels. But since no Genoese dared to venture outside a narrow radius round the captive towns, rebels were hard to define and the Genoese ban had been far less effective then the Corsican one.

Paoli's lifting of the restrictions on trade led to a growth of conspiracy in the ports: at Ajaccio, San Fiorenzo and even in Capo Corso itself there was a great deal of plotting and preparing by the chief men of the towns.

The Genoese were all too aware of the growing momentum for Paoli and of the danger to their rule, for while discontent rose in the towns the Corsican navy was inflicting increasing damage on the Genoese merchantmen. Unless Paoli were stopped, and quickly, the Genoese could see the end of their rule in the island.

They therefore decided to launch a fourth Matra invasion. For the first time in their campaigns they used their command of the ports intelligently. They reinforced the garrisons of all the coastal ports and, at the same time, went to a great deal of trouble to spread the rumour that they would attack from all points simultaneously. This was strategically sensible, for it forced Paoli to split his forces; but he still, wisely, concentrated his regular army between Bastia and Aleria, the two ports from which his capital and the Matra glens could be most easily reached. While the Genoese waged their war of nerves they were recruiting heavily in Italy, in Provence and in Switzerland. On the eve of their invasion they had assembled an army of 2,000 well trained soldiers.

The Corsicans heard exaggerated rumours of what was brewing on the mainland; they became suspicious and apprehensive. In this atmosphere, small things could loom suddenly into something huge and threatening. Mere rumour caused the revolt of Abbatucci.

Giacomo Pietro Abbatucci was a clan leader from Zicavo on the 'other side of the mountains'. He was better educated, had a wider outlook and knew more of the outside world than the majority of the clan chieftains (although in his pride and his precipitancy he yielded nothing to them) for his clan had for long been associated with the Venetians; members of it had frequently served with the Venetian State, although it is not certain whether Giacomo Pietro had; he also had family connections with the Matra and this, being well known, made him suspect, although in spite of rumours there was no positive proof that he had ever supported, or indeed favoured, the Matra cause.

However, when the Junta organising the defence of the Mezzana heard rumours to the effect that Abbatucci had been in contact with the revolting Matra, they did not stop to investigate. They immediately summoned him to a tribunal to give an account of himself. The chiefs of the *Oltremonti* had always been concerned that their dignity be respected by Paoli's administrators. This summons was peremptory and its tone curt. Abbatucci considered that his honour had been offended. He therefore called on his clan to support him and answered the summons of the tribunal by appearing with large bands of followers at his back. The Junta was outraged and condemned his action outright, whereupon he immediately declared their authority abrogated and himself Paoli's lieutenant on the 'other side of the mountains'. The Genoese threat was too close for Paoli to temporize. He immediately crossed the mountains with large detachments of his army. Faced with the threat of civil war, Abbatucci, who had been determined to make a gesture but had had no thought of serious rebellion against the General, ordered his men to lay down their arms. But Paoli could not afford to take chances and Abbatucci was ordered to be confined at Corte until the emergency was over.

This time there were no repercussions as there had been in Capo Corso. Everywhere there was a general understanding that the Genoese were on the eve of making their greatest, perhaps their last, effort to carry the island by military force. Patriotic fervour in the island ran high. One incident was typical: Margherita Paccione of the Niolo came to Paoli's headquarters with a request: 'I had three sons, General,' she said, 'two have died fighting for their country. The magistrates say that the other boy is exempted from service and will not take him for your army. But I see our country threatened and I have walked fifteen miles to request his enlistment.'

The Genoese attack when it came was indeed formidable. Two thousand highly-trained soldiers commanded by Aleria Francesco Matra, with a Major Bustoro as his second-in-command, landed at Aleria; at the same time a large Genoese army moved out of Bastia. The pattern of events was familiar. The armies were to converge, cutting the island in two. Matra's forces naturally made for the Matra glens. But at Cervione they came face to face with two companies of Paoli's regular troops. supported by the militia of the Cervione clan.

The two armies faced each other in the plain outside the town. The islanders were determined not to allow the town and its vital powder-mill to be taken, but, in their eagerness to protect the town, they were inviting disaster. In the mountains, taking advantage of the terrain they knew so well, they were extremely difficult, perhaps even impossible, to overcome quickly. But against good troops in an open plain they threw away their advantages and risked a shattering defeat. They still retained, however, in the plain, as well as in the hills, that remarkably accurate fire-power which was so devastating to their enemies. It was this which saved them before Cervione. Gian Carlo Saliceti, the hero of Venaco, commanded the island's regular troops. He arranged his men in an extended line, so that he could bring the maximum number of muskets to bear, and waited. The invaders, confident in their numbers and in their discipline, moved to attack in good order. The islanders held their fire until the last moment, then they poured a withering hail of lead into the ranks of their opponents. The Matrans broke and were charged furiously by the Corsicans. Bustoro, who commanded the reserve, kept his head and counter-attacked through the ranks of the flying vanguard. The battle was hand to hand and savage, but in the *mêlée* the regular troops could not withstand the fury of the Corsicans. In their turn they retreated. The Corsican forces were being reinforced rapidly as reserves of the militia poured in from every district and the forces of Matra, overwhelmed by numbers, were driven back to Aleria itself. Many re-embarked and sailed back to Genoa: others took refuge in the tiny fort. But this time the Corsicans were in a mood of great elation and eager to settle accounts with the Matra for good; after a short pause they stormed the town itself. Thus fell the fort from which all the Genoese attacks had been launched.

In the meantime, the fighting in the north was once more concentrated on Furiani, although the Genoese also made sorties from the other towns of the west and north-west coast. The fighting for Furiani was furious. During the attack, the Genoese penetrated into the streets of the village, but were driven out again. In the fighting Gian-Andrea Ciavaldini, the brother of the hero of Noceta, fighting in command at the head of his troops, was killed. One of the Junta, Agostino Buonaccorsi, was mortally wounded and was succoured by two of his soldiers. He showed a Spartan fortitude. 'Pursue the enemy,' he cried, 'the wounded will await you'. The air was full of heroism. From San Fiorenzo Paoli received a letter from a sergeant named Massiani, mortally wounded in opposing a Genoese sally: 'My respects to you. Take care of my old father, for in two hours I will be dead and no longer able to look after him.'

The failure to take Furiani marked the effective end of the Genoese invasion. Isolated actions were still being fought some weeks later, but the Genoese had lost all hope of victory and soon withdrew all their forces into the ports again. The last and greatest of the Serene Republic's attempts to regain control of its rebellious possession was over.

6

A DARLING OF THE
ENLIGHTENMENT

The victory over the Genoese began a new phase in Corsica's struggle. In Bastia, in Calvi, in San Fiorenzo, but especially in Ajaccio, the Paolist faction grew stronger and stronger.

In Ajaccio, the leader of the Paolists was Masseria. Masseria was a man of some importance; he was also resolute and energetic. He had become convinced that the future of Corsica lay with Paoli, and, at a secret meeting with the General, it was arranged that he would lead a rising of trusted patriots within the town, while, at the same time, the General would launch his troops in a full-scale attack from without. Masseria laid an elaborate plot: the Paolists were to attack the citadel at a given signal, while the prisoners within, to whom arms had been smuggled, would rise at the same time, overpower their guards and join Masseria's followers. But the plot was discovered and Masseria compelled to give the signal for the rising before the time he had agreed with Paoli. Nevertheless, with his son at his side, he was successful in storming his way into the fortress, accompanied by a small body of his followers. He broke into the prison, overcame the guards and set the captives at liberty. This was all in accordance with the plan, and it seemed for a moment as though the attack had been completely successful, but the Genoese rallied while the prisoners, for the greater part, fled. Masseria's son, at the head of a few friends, stormed the tower of the citadel and, as a last proud gesture, planted high above the town the Corsican standard, but hardly had he done so than he fell, riddled with bullets from the Genoese soldiers. His father resolved that, since the attack had failed, he would destroy the fort as well as himself and he attacked the armoury with the intention of blowing up both fort and garrison. But he was shot down before he reached the door. Seriously wounded and dragged before the Genoese commander, he refused to answer any questions as to the names of his accomplices and died, declaring that his only regret was that he had failed. Paoli's attack, when it came, found the Genoese prepared and achieved nothing.

In spite of Paoli's failure to take Ajaccio the Genoese were close to desperation. They knew that plots had been hatched against them in every town that they occupied and relations between them and the Corsicans became more and more embittered; the pretence that their presence was anything more than a military occupation had long ago vanished. Moreover, their financing of the Matra invasions had cost them dearly in money and men and for all their efforts they had achieved less than nothing, for the islanders were bound together to defy them more closely then ever before.

But the success of the Corsican navy was perhaps an even greater drain on their resources. The Corsicans were still in no position to challenge the naval supremacy of the Genoese fleet, but their privateers, darting rapidly from their many harbours, had practically wiped out Genoese trade with the island. Mounting an expedition against their bases was useless; there were far too many of them and only in Capo Corso did the Genoese still possess enough command by land to have any hope of success in the amphibious operations that would be necessary to destroy them. As the Corsicans grew bolder and the number of their ships increased, they began to venture further afield. By 1764, from a nuisance they had become a threat to the very maintenance of the Genoese-Italian trade.

Paoli now mounted an amphibious operation, a kind of action which hitherto had been the monopoly of the Genoese. By land, the Paolists were hammering away repeatedly at the forts of Bastia, of San Fiorenzo and of Macinaggio. In order to supplement their efforts at San Fiorenzo, Paoli sent Rocca, who was famous for his brilliant seamanship and success against the Genoese, to command a specially assembled Corsican fleet and blockade the port. The Genoese, supremely confident of their ability to defeat the Corsicans in a sea-battle, sent a slightly larger fleet to disperse them. But Rocca, leading his ships with dash and daring, drove them off and took several prizes. Unfortunately, he was killed in the battle. His death was a heavy loss to Paoli, and a fruitless one, for the Genoese broke the blockade by sending still more ships into the Bay of San

Fiorenzo. It was a sharp reminder that the Serene Republic was still supreme in any orthodox sea-fight.

However, Rocca's pyrrhic victory had convinced Paoli that a regular Corsican navy might render the islanders important services. He therefore appointed the Comte de Perez admiral of his fleet. Perez was a Knight of Malta, a Frenchman who had professed enthusiasm for the islanders' cause and, having been granted letters of marque by Paoli, had preyed on the Genoese shipping with great success. The Council presented him with a brand-new brig to mark his new command. But the Count was by nature and by inclination, a privateer, and although he cost the Genoese a great deal in the way of shipping he did not contribute a good deal to the development of Paoli's navy. He was more interested in taking prizes than leading a fleet to victory and his opportunism was, at a later date, to nearly cost Paoli his life.

The Republic of Genoa was essentially a commercial one. 'When the Genoese find a cause costs them money,' said Paoli, 'they quickly become bored with it.' Corsica was costing the Genoese a great deal of money; a strong party grew up in the Republic which advocated the sale or the exchange of the island. One proposal made to the Senate was that the island should be ceded to the Grand Duke of Tuscany, but this was defeated on the grounds that Genoese trade might be damaged to the advantage of Leghorn. After much discussion, the Genoese resolved to turn again to France for help and Sorba, the Genoese Minister at the Court of Versailles, was instructed to request Louis for troops to 'preserve, reduce and pacify the island'. The request was seriously considered. Long ago, in 1735, Campredon, the French Minister at Genoa, had warned that, although the Genoese might hold the ports, they were incapable of ever subduing the interior of the island and that while the Corsicans disputed the overlordship of the Genoese the way was always open to intervention by a third Power. Naples was known to covet the island, so was Sardinia, but most dangerous of all was the interest of England, who had repossessed herself of Minorca by the Treaty of Paris in 1763 and who, with Minorca and Gibraltar, was already a dangerous presence in the Mediterranean. The French were very well aware that Paoli's cause was looked upon with sympathy by the English; they were also tired of sending troops to the island to hold the ports for the Genoese in an emergency and then withdrawing again without having gained any permanent advantage. They began to cast around for another policy. Informed, by his agents on the mainland, of the difficulties which Sorba's mission was meeting, Paoli, in December 1763, made a guarded offer to the French that he would agree to a placing of the island under a French Protectorate if certain conditions were granted respecting its autonomy. He offered, in return, to raise two Corsican regiments for France for which the French would pay an annual subsidy.

Unfortunately for Paoli, a French ex-army officer, Dumouriez (destined to immortal fame as the victor of Jemappes and to eternal infamy as the betrayer of the infant Republic) who was now on half-pay and seeking employment, led a raiding party to Corsica on behalf of the Genoese. He landed in the south of the island and his venture was short-lived, but not having seen the real centres of Paoli's strength, he became convinced that Paoli's government was not strongly founded and reported this to Paris.

Accordingly, the French decided to do their deal with Genoa rather than with Paoli and, at Compiègne, in August 1764, they signed a treaty with the Republic, by virtue of which France was to send three thousand men to Corsica for the protection of the seaports, three of which were to be held entirely by French troops; the Genoese were to evacuate these ports and would have no authority in them whatsoever; the French occupation was to last four years and during it French officers were to be allowed free intercourse with the Corsicans in order that they might use their influence to restore peace. At the same time, Genoa was confirmed by the French in her sovereignty of the island and the French agreed that, apart from the ports, the Genoese civil and ecclesiastical administration should be paramount. To Paoli the French wrote semi-officially that they would consider an unspecified subsidy at some unspecified time for some unspecified purpose; at the same time, they informed him that the French troops which were to be sent to Corsica had no hostile intent. The reply was couched in the most diplomatic terms: the General was requested to explain the position to the nation so that peace between Corsicans and French might prevail. All Paoli could do when faced with this *fait accompli* was to express his regret at the course of events, and hope that the French would communicate to him full details of the treaty they had concluded with Genoa. The Treaty of Compiègne bought the Genoese time and the hope that the French might be drawn into a conflict with Paoli. It brought the French one step nearer to the annexation of the island.

Commanded by the Comte de Marbeuf, the expedition appeared in the Gulf of San Fiorenzo on 17th October 1764. Their arrival was the first dangerous test for the Corsicans, for San Fiorenzo was at its last gasp and the Genoese were shut up in the fortress, part of which had already been stormed by the Paolists. Their attack was halted as the French fleet sailed into the wide bay. Marbeuf was a civilised and intelligent commander and, moreover, had instructions not to provoke the Corsicans. As his flagship entered the harbour, he saluted the Corsican flag which was flying triumphantly from a tower of the citadel. Then the waiting, silent Corsicans saw a boat pull away from the side of his flagship and make for the landing. When it reached the jetty a French officer stepped ashore with a letter addressed to General Paoli. In it Marbeuf stated formally what Paoli already knew: that the French troops had come for garrison duty only and that they had no intention of a conflict with the Corsicans. Paoli answered tactfully and the Corsicans then withdrew from the town. Marbeuf, impressed by the good order and the conciliatory spirit of the Corsicans, then arranged a formal truce with Paoli which was to last until 7th August 1768.

Paoli devoted a great deal of attention to establishing good relations with the French. He freely granted passports for the French officers to visit the interior of the island; he was eager that they should attend the Assembly itself so that they might observe how the Corsicans governed themselves. In order to impress them with the dignity of the Corsican government, he arranged for his Council to dress themselves in future in a uniform of green velvet with gold facings, the national colours of Corsica. At the same time, he introduced interpreters into the Council Chamber for the purpose of explaining to the French the methods of government. The French were delighted with their reception and amazed at the courtesy with which they were treated in the interior of the island; but the Corsicans remained a simple and unsophisticated people and not every French officer had the forbearance and the sensitivity to avoid giving offence; however, in spite of this, relations between the

Corsicans and the French were, on the whole, amicable and continued to be so for the period of the truce.

On 16th December 1764, Giacinto Paoli died at Naples. It
was the signal for a great outburst of sorrow. Masses were said
in every church of the island for the repose of Giacinto's soul,
and in every glen a solemn ceremony of commemoration was
carried out. At Corte crowds streamed in from every quarter of
the island to attend the ceremony. It was nine years since Paoli
had landed in the Gulf of the Golo and all his father's doubts
about his ability to rule the island were long past. Perhaps the
descent of the French might have reminded the old man that
history seemed to be repeating itself, but it was not very likely.
Always devout, he had, in his last years, occupied himself almost
completely with his devotions and had long given up any active
interest in Corsican politics. His last days were happy. His son
was famous throughout Europe and beloved in Italy. 'Our Paoli',
Genovesi, the great Italian savant, had called him proudly and
the words were echoed by Italians throughout the peninsula. It
was enough.

To Paoli, the event was sobering. He was a reflective man.
The French expedition had put an end to the progress of the
islander's conquest and no man now knew what the future
might hold. The memory of his youth and the years of his
father's exile must have been very much with him in those days.
It was evident that an era had come to an end.

He still had the reality of what he had done for the Corsicans
to contemplate. It is not too unreasonable to see in his foundation of the university of Corte, which took place a month after
his father's death, his determination to secure to his countrymen
lasting benefits, whatever might be his fate in the years to come.
Like the child of the Enlightenment that he was, the bringing
of the benefits of education to his countrymen was always one
of the most cherished of his ambitions.

Like all the *Philosophes*, Paoli had a very high opinion of the
value of education. And, like all the *Philosophes*, it was
education in its practical guise which fascinated him. 'Education,'
he said, 'should aim, not at producing a race of scholars, but a
society composed of educated men.' A man, he held, was
educated only if he could communicate useful ideas to his
fellow citizens. Moreover, education was the cement of the good
society. Education, said the General, 'reveals to men that they

95

have rights to exercise; it also reminds them that they have duties to perform.'

His university of Corsica was, however, not a revolutionary model. It could hardly be, for it was dependent upon the instructors he could gather together in Corsica, and in Corsica a professor needed an element of marksmanship as well as learning. But, apart from the Faculty of Medicine, it taught all that the universities of Europe taught.

Seven chairs were founded to establish the university and Paoli spent many hours with his advisers in the careful definition of their responsibilities. The first chair was to teach theology and ecclesiastical history. The establishment of the chair was part of Paoli's policy of ecclesiastical reform for the island. He intended the university, among a good many other things, to be a seminary for his priests, the learning of whom was not always at the same high level as their patriotism. To make sure that they all passed through the university he refused passports to any aspirant for holy orders who hoped to find more lenient instructors on the continent.

The second chair was to teach moral theology and the third civil and case law.

The fourth was that of ethics, the chair that Paoli held to be the most important of all. 'Young men,' he said, 'should early learn what they owe to themselves, to their country and to the Supreme Being'. The professor's duty was to instruct them in this knowledge.

The fifth chair was that of philosophy, which was to include mathematics, the sixth of rhetoric and the seventh of civil and commercial practice. Later, instruction was added in Latin, Greek, French, English and drawing.

The establishment of the university set the seal on Paoli's fame throughout Europe. Already Rousseau had surrounded it with the halo of his praise in his famous comment in 'The Social Contract': 'There is still in Europe a country capable of being given laws – Corsica. The valour and persistence with which that brave people has regained and defended its liberty well deserves that some wise man should teach it how to preserve what it has won. I have a feeling that some day that little island will astound Europe.' Rousseau's praise had led to an exchange of letters with Buttafuoco, after Buttafuoco, excited by such praise, had invited the Swiss philosopher to visit Corsica

Pasquale Paoli with some of his soldiers, and his dog, Cosacco,
painted by an unknown artist for the Earl of Pembroke on his visit to Corsica in 1769
18th century Italian school

The Invasion of Capraja by the Corsicans in 1767
19th century engraving

and play the part of the legislator. Rousseau accepted the invitation enthusiastically but then demurred. Paoli's added his invitation to Buttafuoco's. He had no intention, as he admitted later to Boswell, of submitting the island to the rule of Jean-Jacques, but he had a great respect for the genius of Rousseau and thought he might care to employ his talents for the good of the islanders. But the hope of a refuge closer at hand and probably, at bottom, doubts on the part he might play in Corsica, deterred the philosopher. His refusal, however, was elegant:

> My desire to dwell among you has not weakened; but my bodily strength is feeble, the tasks I must undertake, the cares I endure, the course of my life, have made me abandon, for the moment, my plan. It spite of all the difficulties which surround it my heart will not allow me to relinquish the design. But I grow older, my ambitions weaken, desire troubles me and hopes die.Whatever may be, give my most heartfelt thanks to General Paoli for the asylum he has offered me. The Corsicans are a brave and hospitable people. I shall never forget the period of my life when your hearts, your arms, your homes welcomed me, the only refuge I had in Europe.

Rousseau's affection for the island led to an indignant outburst in 1768, when war at last broke out between Corsica and France: 'The French are a very servile people, fondly reconciled to that tyranny which has taken away their liberty, cruel and predatory to those who are still free. If they knew that there was a free man living at the end of the world, they would go there, merely for the pleasure of destroying him.'

But Rousseau was only one of the admirers of Corsica. In France, Raynal and Voltaire soon added, each in his own fashion, their tributes to that of Rousseau, and while, on the domestic level, journals like the *Journal Encyclopédique* carried Paoli's name to every quarter of the country, correspondents like Frédéric-Melchior Grimm made it familiar and famous about the courts of Sweden, Poland and Russia. In Italy, Parini and Alfieri (who, in 1788, was to dedicate his tragedy of *Timoleone* to Paoli) were among the most illustrious of the generation of writers and poets who regarded Paoli as the Enlightened hero, not only of Corsica but of Italy also: 'our Paoli'. The Enlightened despots themselves swelled the chorus of praise; Joseph of

D

Austria, it was noted, frequently spoke of the General with admiration; so did Frederick the Great, whose admiration did not stop at words, but who sent Paoli a sword of honour with the words *'Patria, libertas'* inscribed on the blade. Grimm might indeed have held the pen of the Enlightenment itself, when he wrote of Paoli and his work in 1764: 'To bring under good government men such as the Corsicans, worthy men of spirit and ability, is without doubt the noblest task of the century. All Europe wishes the undertaking well for there is no man of principle who does not side with this brave people against the detestable government of the Genoese.'

Paoli had become the darling of the Enlightenment and from one end of Europe to the other his name resounded as the Enlightened trumpted forth their praise: he had brought to a proud, simple and courageous people the reality of a law freed from sectional interest and pettifogging precedent; his faith, deep and unshakable, went hand in hand with his desire for an Erastian Church staffed by an educated priesthood; his love for, and pride in, his country was tempered by an all-embracing tolerance to other creeds and nationalities; he was the founder of cities and the begetter of trade; to crown all, he did this consciously and deliberately in accordance with principles that all rational men accepted and in a language which all rational men understood. He had, indeed, made Corsica the cynosure of European eyes. Visitors began to arrive in order to survey at close quarters the model ruler and his realm. Most came from Italy, but France was well represented and there was the odd German. It was two Englishmen, however, who left behind the most lively record of Paoli's state at this time.

The Reverend Andrew Burnaby was chaplain to the British factory at Leghorn. He had many Corsican acquaintances, both among those who had settled in Leghorn and among the frequent visitors to the port from the island itself. In 1766, he made a visit to Paoli's State and afterwards wrote a short, but perceptive, account of that visit, some phrases of which were afterwards lifted for a far more famous work – Boswell's *An Account of Corsica*.

Boswell's visit was the most important Paoli ever received from a foreigner. From it stemmed many things: the long often-brilliant campaign that Boswell waged on, and in, England for the Corsican cause; the new surge of delighted enthusiasm for

Paoli which swept not only England but Europe after the publication of *An Account of Corsica* in February 1768; the aid in men and materials which subsequently flowed into Corsica from Britain during Paoli's struggle against the French; in some measure Paoli's decision to seek refuge in England, after the defeat of the islanders in 1769, and the General's subsequent cession of the island to George III after his return from exile on the outbreak of the French Revolution. Indeed, the whole of Paoli's life was to be altered in many ways by Boswell's visit. But in 1765, the visit seemed to Paoli no more than a pleasant interlude, the result of the whim of a singular but good, pleasant and cheerful young Scotsman.

To Boswell, of course, his trip was something more. His *Memoirs of Pascal Paoli* exists on two levels; on one level the visit was a lion-hunting one with the object of bagging a hero of the Enlightenment: 'One of those men who are no longer to be found except in the pages of Plutarch.' Fresh from his visit to Rousseau he intended to find in Paoli the legislator of that philosopher's dream, legislating selflessly for sentient but uncorrupted men. Gleefully, he noted down Corsican approximations to the 'Noble Savage' and played at being one himself: 'It was just like being for a little while one of the *"pisca gens mortalium*, the primitive race of men" who ran about in the woods, eating acorns and drinking water'; and in the same strain, at Corte, he thought himself 'sitting in the house of a Cincinnatus' when he visited the Great Chancellor. He warned the Corsicans against the perils of Euopean society: 'But I bid them remember, that they were much happier in their present state than in a state of refinement and vice; and that therefore they should beware of luxury.'

But on another level, Paoli was for Boswell what he was later to be for Napoleon, what every idealistic youth in every generation seeks for himself – the word made flesh, the lofty uncorrupted bearer of a noble standard who could serve as an example and inspiration. Since Boswell, however, was above all other things, even when he seems most innocent of art, an artist, his ideal man of action is contrasted for dramatic effect with a weaker vessel – Boswell himself, labouring after virtue, but all too often fatally diverted by the lusts of vanity and the flesh. Over and against Boswell as Everyman there is set the virtues of his Hero:

I saw from Paoli's example the great art of preserving young men of spirit from contagion of vice, in which there is often a species of sentiment, ingenuity and enterprise nearly allied to virtuous qualities.

Show a young man that there is more real merit in virtue than in vice, and you have a surer hold of him during his years of impetuosity and passion, than by convincing his judgement of all the rectitudes of ethics.

In more than one sense then, Boswell's *Corsica* was a work of propaganda. Paoli was not only a man of flesh and blood, but at the same time a symbol and a yardstick. But when the allowances have been made for this, the portrait of Paoli which arises from the *Memoirs* is a recognisable and endearing one. The point of view of the whole book is of course Paoli's and the gravity of Boswell's Augustan prose, with its talk of Senates and of Counsellors, and the heightened diction in which he always speaks of Paoli not only elevates the General, but gives a deceptively urbane, even majestic, air to the ideal Corsica Boswell saw him as creating. Even so, he was quick enough at times to notice the divergence between the aspiration and the reality, as when, for instance, he pointed out the essentially provisional nature of the Corsican university and set down the ugly story of the servant forced by legal torture to plead against his defiant mistress. But these are remarks in passing. Oddly enough, the only occasion on which he tends to be deliberately rather on the defensive about the General is when he defends Paoli's professed ability to divine the future in dreams against the charge that it was an act of policy. That Paoli's unconscious mind helped him to solve his political problems seems nowadays far less remarkable than it did to Boswell.

Boswell, by the end of his visit, had completely broken through Paoli's reserve and the friendship was secure. He returned to England as 'Corsica' Boswell and, for the next few years, worked heroically to whip up enthusiasm for the islanders' struggle. They were to need all the help they could get.

But for the moment all seemed to go well for Paoli. The presence of the French served as a buffer between Corsicans and Genoese and had brought a measure of peace to the island. The Genoese had lost their enthusiasm for the re-conquest of the island by force of arms. Meanwhile, the Corsican State grew increasingly strong. Success, popularity and the absence of a military threat, the flourishing economic condition of the country and the promise of a Corsican rule over the whole island when the period of French occupation should end raised Paoli's reputation to an unprecedented level everywhere, especially in the French-held ports. At Ajaccio, the most patriotic of the towns of the sea-coast, an event of some importance took place. In the Saline, about a mile from the walls of the town, a deputation, in the presence of a huge crowd of Ajaccians, solemnly prayed the General and his Counsellors that they might be represented in the Corsican State. As Paoli's Counsellors and the delegates from Ajaccio came face to face, all formalities suddenly broke down and, swept by a common emotion, they rushed into each other's arms. The crowds and the countrymen who had come to see the scene did likewise and, in a moment, they had formed a great, jostling crowd about the General, laughing and crying and swearing eternal friendship and fraternity. It was an event which deeply moved Paoli. He was to refer to it again and again during the years of his exile. In practice it resulted in the assimilation of the Ajaccians as part of the Corsican realm (*in partibus infidelium*).

Paoli received, at about this time, another and perhaps even more important addition to the strength of his cause in the west of the island by the acquisition of a new and powerful and most influential lieutenant. This was Giacomo Pietro Abbatucci, whom he had imprisoned for his rebellion before the last Matra invasion. After the invasion had failed and peace had been restored in the glens, Paoli had released Abbatucci from prison, but exiled him to Tuscany, on the condition that he should return to the island only with Paoli's express permission. Abbatucci passed some months in Tuscany, but he became bored in his exile and returned secretly to his glen, where he lived unobtrusively without making any attempt to exert the authority of a chief. Complete secrecy for any event was rarely possible in Corsica and, after he had been there some time, it was duly reported to Paoli that he had returned without permission from Tuscany. Paoli immediately sent an order to Zicavo that Abbatucci was to report to Corte and Abbatucci came at once without any demur. Questioned by Paoli, he said calmly that in Tuscany he was homesick for Corsica, so he had come back to the island. Paoli admired his *sang-froid* and, as a token punishment, sentenced him to one day in prison in the citadel at Corte. The day after he had been released, Paoli had several long conversations with him, during which he made great efforts to win his friendship. Abbatucci, for his part, although he could be proud and overbearing, greatly admired what Paoli had done in the island and had a great respect for the General. After some weeks as Paoli's guest at Corte, during which Paoli explained to him his aims, his methods and his hopes for Corsica, Abbatucci returned to his native glen. Paoli soon found him a position in his administration and Abbatucci's abilities made him a powerful influence for stability in west Corsica. By 1766, he had become Paoli's lieutenant on the 'other side of the mountains'.

While Paoli steadily strengthened his grip on the island, at sea his fleet became increasingly more venturesome. They were now ranging far into the Mediterranean, even to the shores of Liguria itself and already many Ligurian traders found it profitable to obtain passports from Paoli to safeguard them from Corsican privateers. The Corsican flag steadily became familiar in all the harbours of Provence and along the length of the coast of the Italian peninsula.

The only resource left to the Genoese was diplomacy, and throughout 1765, their representative at Paris, Sorba, worked incessantly to increase the amount of French help. Sorba was a typical eighteenth-century diplomat. Loquacious, hard-working and intriguing he cultivated any ally which might be helpful, from the Duchess of Gramont's maid to the Pope himself. Promises and presents flowed from him in an unceasing stream, but all his efforts had little effect. The French could see plainly enough what was evident to all Europe – that the Genoese had lost effective control of the island. The most that Sorba achieved was the sending of instructions to Marbeuf to use his influence in order to extract terms from the malcontents. Marbeuf, however, knew the drift of Choiseul's, the French Foreign Minister's, thinking and made a shrewd estimate of the value of the instructions. His advocacy consisted of a few conversations with Paoli and some regretful adjurations; his stay in Corsica was proving very pleasant to him and acceptable to both sides and, whatever the letter of the instructions received, he had no wish to stir up a hornet's nest in the vague hope of pleasing his Parisian masters; he made no attempt to do so.

Realising that all his diplomacy was achieving nothing, Sorba tried a new tack and petitioned the French to extend their stay in the island which was due to end in 1768. This was equally fruitless. It was to perpetuate a stalemate at the expense of the French. But his untiring efforts reminded the French diplomats that time was running out and now there was no solution in sight. They accordingly made unofficial overtures to Paoli. Paoli, for his part, was well aware of the Genoese predicament. He knew that, without French assistance, the Genoese could not possibly hold the island and he, therefore, proposed a solution that he hoped would satisfy the interests of both parties. In return for Corsican independence he offered compensation to the Genoese for the ports they vacated. But so humiliating an end to their Corsican suzerainty offended the pride of Genoa, and its counsellors carried on despairingly with their intrigues in the French Court.

7

CAPRAJA

The Genoese thought that the presence of the French in the ports at least guaranteed them peace. But it was in this period of deceptive calm that Paoli launched a daring and unexpected blow at the Republic. At the beginning of 1767, he received a report from Paulo Mattei, a citizen of his shipyard town of Centuri, a report that contained a very detailed assessment of the state of the island of Capraja; the island was a volcanic slab of rock, lying midway between Capo Corso and Tuscany and could be seen on a fine day from the Cape, a trapezoid, shimmering, faintly blue, on the horizon. It had long had close relations with Corsica and, like many of the Capo Corsans, its inhabitants were bold and hardy sailors for, since there was little to cultivate on the barren, craggy rocks of their island, they lived by fishing. They had been left in peace by the Corsican privateers, and throughout the whole of the Corsican struggle they continued, as they had always done, a simple primitive existence nominally ruled by the Genoese garrison which, however, had little contact with them.

Mattei had seen how weak the garrison was and how slackly it performed its duties; he also saw that the Corsican example was having its effect and that there was an undercurrent of resentment against the government of the Serene Republic. All this was contained in his report to Paoli. Paoli, for his part, was only too eager to find a new opportunity to harass the Republic. He knew of the intrigues of the Genoese in Paris; he knew how deadly weary they were of the struggle and he knew how willing they would be to quit it, if this could be done, without injury to their pride. He thought that a successful attack on Capraja might shatter their last scruples and break the last chain that bound Corsica. What he did not see was the consequences that were to stem from his success. For a success his invasion was, and of the most brilliant kind.

104

Carefully, methodically and as secretly as possible he assembled his forces. On the night of 15th February 1767, his fleet, which had been stealthily gathering in the Bay of Macinaggio, sailed for Capraja. The army of invasion consisted of two hundred of his regular troops, fifty or so Volunteers from Capo Corso and Capraja itself, and the militia of the valley of Tomino. They were commanded by two of his most trusted captains, Achille Murati and Gian Battista Ristori.

To create a diversion, Paoli had ordered attacks to be made on Genoese positions throughout the island but this feint was only partly successful. The harbour of Macinaggio was plainly visible from the church steps of Rogliano and as soon as the Genoese in the fortified town were aware that an unusual concentration of Corsican vessels was taking place in the crescent-shaped harbour, they sent a messenger, who, by skill and daring, possessed himself of a felucca and sailed swiftly to Capraja to warn the garrison of the impending attack.

The commander of the garrison was Baron Oltre. He called the Caprajans to his assistance and, leaving them to take the first thrust of the invasion, hurriedly began to provision and re-furbish the fortifications of the citadel. While the Caprajans were assembling their forces, the Corsican fleet sailed into the harbour of the Ceppo and quickly disembarked its troops. They were met with some opposition on the beaches, but the islanders who opposed the landing were quickly overborne and most of them made prisoners. The invaders then marched on the town, only to be met on the way by the Caprajan militia and both sides took up positions for a struggle. Then Gian Battista Ristori with a dramatic gesture, strangely prophetic of Napoleon at Grenoble so many years later, walked all unattended from the Corsican ranks and, standing before the levelled muskets of the Caprajans, he made a declaration: 'Friends,' he said, 'we do not come here as conquerors. We are your brothers and you know this. Why then have we come? We are free but you are still under the yoke of our common enemy. We come to share our liberty with you. Our cause is the same. Embrace us, march with us.'

The effect was immediate – the Caprajans threw down their arms and rushed to join the Corsicans. When day broke Baron Oltre, from the ramparts of the fortress, saw the Corsican flag flying everywhere and when he himself was seen by the Corsicans a roar of defiance rose to him from the village below. He at once sent a proclamation to the village which declared that, if the Caprajans helped the invaders in any way whatsoever, he would, after they had been defeated, raze the village to the ground; but his threats were thrown back in his teeth by his erstwhile subjects. While this scene was taking place at the fortress, the islanders were making themselves masters of the remainder of the Genoese strongpoints on the island. These consisted of three round towers; one at Sinipitio, one at Barbici and one at the entrance to the port; these, like the Corsican towers, had been erected long ago as a defence against the Moorish pirates; they were much decayed and were easily taken. In anticipation of a counter-attack from the sea the patriots stationed detachments in the towers and at all other parts of the island they thought might be menaced by a landing. A felucca, speeding back to Centuri, brought news to Paoli of the success of the enterprise. He immediately embarked a reserve of 300 men for the island, together with a great deal of munitions and provisions and several pieces of artillery. As soon as they had disembarked, the Corsicans and the Caprajans set about fortifying the island in accordance with Paoli's instructions.

In Genoa itself the news was quickly known and it spurred the Genoese into resolute action. Troops were mustered rapidly and embarked under the command of the senator Pinelli, an experienced and resolute Genoese admiral, and, within a few days, a whole flotilla lay off the island. Several times they attempted to disembark their troops from boats, but a hail of fire from the defenders caused the boats to put about on every occasion. Then a sudden storm drove the ships to shelter at Spezia.

Back in Genoa the Genoese worked incessantly to equip more ships for the attack. The sea-power of the Serene Republic was being insulted, the sea-power by which Genoa had risen and maintained herself; the deepest source of her pride, the very basis of her existence was being threatened; the nation rose magnificently to meet the challenge.

But before reinforcements had reached him Pirelli had launched his second attack against the island, only to be repulsed again. Reinforced by the galleys from Genoa, he tried once more. Once again the accurate fire of the Corsicans prevented the Genoese from coming ashore in strength; firing from the rocks they accounted for soldier after soldier as the Genoese desperately attempted to establish a bridgehead and the few invaders that scrambled ashore were at a desperate disadvantage, trying to take shelter while a hail of withering fire poured down from above. Pirelli threw in attack after attack. They were all beaten off and the fleet sailed away again at evening while the Corsicans settled down to the seige of the fort.

The Genoese were enraged. Their pride was exacerbated already by their inability, made plain before Europe, to overcome those they had called a rabble of peasants. Now the Corsicans had carried the initiative to a Genoese possession, and, in doing so, they had flouted the whole of the Genoese fleet. There were angry scenes and bitter recriminations in the Senate where men wept openly with rage and chagrin. But the senators were still full of spirit, and they systematically set about assembling the largest armada that Genoa had ever seen.

While they prepared their attack, Choiseul took a new initiative to settle the Corsican problem: after he had sounded Sorba and using Matteo Buttafuoco, the Corsican who had once invited Rousseau to Corsica and who was now a colonel in the *Royal Corse,* as his intermediary, he offered Paoli independence if the Genoese suzerainty were formally recognised and the Genoese were allowed control of the sea ports. But although Paoli listened, he had no intention of accepting the offer. He was demonstrating to Europe that the Genoese could not even control their dependencies. Paoli's attitude, on the verge as he was of establishing a much more favourable bargaining position, was, understandable, but it began a train of events which was ultimately to prove fatal to him, for Choiseul, aware that the Treaty of Compiègne had only one year to run, now began to consider the implication that, when the French retired, the Corsicans would almost certainly be masters in their own island.

The events of May confirmed him in this estimate of Corsican strength. On the 5th, the Genoese fleet, in all its splendour and power, appeared again off the coast of Capraja. This time they carried on board the transports all those Corsican exiles who were the irreconcilable opponents of Paoli: among them Antonuccio Matra himself. Some of them knew the island well and, as a result of their advice, the Genoese decided to concentrate the main weight of their attack on the Civita, a rocky, seemingly inaccessible position which the Corsicans, because of its unlikelihood as a landing-place, had only lightly fortified.

To make the main landing, simultaneous landings were to be threatened in several places and the great fleet split into flotillas for this purpose. To cover these landings the warships of the fleet sailed as close inshore as they dared to bombard the Corsican positions. It was a blue cloudless, Mediterranean day. Corsican observers saw with awe the great white ships sweeping towards them, suddenly blazing fire and shot and then seeming to glide leisurely and indifferently away, as if suddenly preoccupied with other matters. When the whole island was echoing with the sound of battle, like a huge sounding-board, the Genoese made their attempt on the Civita; they were successful. They landed a considerable force, among the leaders of which was Matra himself. Corsicans and Caprajans rushed together to the defence of the island and the fighting around the beach of the Civita was bitter. With other attacks threatened along the whole coast of the island the defenders could not concentrate their forces and Matra's troops maintained their ground. But the Genoese, too, were in a dilemma since they could not reinforce the invaders without uniting their transports; and once they were seen to do this the islanders and their allies combined to make a desperate assault on the bridgehead that the Genoese had established. In a few hours of savage fighting, and before more than a handful of reinforcements had been landed, the invaders were overcome and many were killed; some were captured and Matra himself was only taken off at the eleventh hour by a Genoese boat. As the day ended the admiral observed with despair the only result of all his efforts – dozens of bodies scattered among the rocks and smashed boats floating at the base of the cliffs. No more attacks were made. As the sun sank, the great Genoese fleet sailed east, its shattered woodwork and riddled sails an honourable apologia for all its unavailing efforts.

The news that the fleet had been unable to effect a landing caused many to despair at Genoa. But defeat brought out all that was most heroic in the city state and, after the first shock, the Senate was besieged by volunteers who wished to serve in the campaign against Corsica. The merchants vied with one another in donations to raise foreign mercenaries or equip new ships, and, within a few weeks, yet another expedition had been prepared with a new swarm of light craft to assist the landings. But patriotism was running remarkably high in the Corsicans too. Many of Paoli's opponents had sought refuge in Genoa and had in the course of time entered the Genoese army and navy. Many of these had taken part in the great attack on Capraja, but still others were left in the city itself and it was while they were being mustered to man the ships of the new invasion fleet that a mutiny broke out. Their renascent patriotism sparked by insults against Corsica, the exiles suddenly decided that they would no longer fight against their brothers, and with typical Corsican fortitude they stolidly endured the taunts, the threats and the violence of the Genoese crowds. The reaction spread upwards; one of the most respected officers in the Genoese Service, Major Quenzi, resigned his commission rather than lead men against his countrymen.

Re-equipped and refurbished, the Genoese fleet sailed again to the attack. Forty warships, together with an immense attendant flotilla of shalloops and barks, bore down upon Capraja on 18th May 1767. The battle raged all day. The very rocks vomited flames, said a Corsican observer later. Attack after attack was repulsed as Paoli's well-placed artillery hammered away relentlessly against the Genoese galleys and when night fell the rocks below the island's crags were once again littered with dead men and smoking wood. But, in spite of all its efforts, the fleet was unable to force a landing. The great attack had failed. The Genoese fort of Capraja was now at its last gasp and, some days later, Baron Oltre surrendered it on honourable terms.

If the Genoese were in despair, the Corsicans were in a mood of exaltation and Paoli immediately sent one of his Commissioners to Capraja to organise the island as a glen. The sensation that the Corsican occupation caused was immense. There was astonishment and rejoicing throught the length of Italy. But the implications of the success were far wider than the mere capture of the Genoese island. Capraja lay athwart the Genoese sealanes to the Levant, and whoever held it could throttle Genoese trade which was condemned, if denied the Tuscan seaway, to make the long exposed haul around Corsica itself.

But it was not only the Genoese trade which was threatened; it was the French, and for the same reason. Paoli understood this; what he does not seem to have appreciated is the length to which the Corsican occupation of Capraja might drive the French.

The conquest of Capraja meant that the solution of the Corsican problem was now of the first importance to French diplomacy. The French were under no illusion about the Genoese position in Corsica; they knew that Genoese rule was a fiction; they knew that only their own troops stood between the Corsicans and independence, and the reports that Chauvelin had received from Dumouriez led him to believe that an independent Corsica might be as weak in the face of a foreign enemy as the Genoese were in the face of the Corsicans. France could not tolerate that the island might pass into the possession of a hostile Power and this led to the French minister to consider the courses he could pursue: he could use French troops to overthrow Paoli and put Genoa firmly in possession of the island; he could involve Paoli in a three-cornered agreement with Genoa and France; he could ally with Paoli himself; or he could annex Corsica to France, either with or without Genoese concurrence. There was a great deal to be said for the last course. To annex Corsica was to cut the Gordian knot: to settle at one blow all the doubts raised by the weaknesses of the Genoese or of Paoli's young Republic. It was a policy with an ancestry; there was a long-standing opinion in France that an annexation of Corsica was a simple way to resolve all the problems associated with it: this had been Campredon's position in 1735. Corsica was to be a French counterpart to the English possession of Gibraltar and Minorca. There were also political benefits to be derived from an annexation of Corsica. France had been humiliated by the loss of Canada in the Seven Years' War and Choiseul, as the French Minister for Foreign Affairs, looked for some new theatre in which to demonstrate the power of French arms; some new conquest to reassure French pride.

Paoli was not well enough informed about Choiseul to guess the way in which the French Minister's mind was working. The conquest of Capraja had elated him as it had elated all the Corsicans. Everything he knew made him believe that a happy outcome of the long insurrection was now close. He knew that Corsica was admired throughout the whole of Europe. He knew that the Enlightened principles he was putting into action in Corsica aroused admiration in many of the French themselves. Moreover, his relations with the French on the island were excellent and he had some reason to believe the inactivity of the French during his conquest of Capraja was deliberate policy,

as indeed it might have been, although rather on the part of
Marbeuf than through any direction of the central government.
He had made offers to the French which he considered to be
reasonable; he knew that the French would not support the
Genoese for ever. He believed that the reports which were
reaching France from the island demonstrated just how powerful he was in the island itself. Moreover, he knew that the
English had an interest in Corsica, and in his diplomacy there
was perhaps just a hint of a threat.

Of all this, only the threat of an English intervention carried
any weight with Choiseul. He could not be sure of the decision
of England in the event of a struggle with Corsica and it was
this, and the problem of displacing Genoa without antagonising
her and her allies, which made him hesitant about the policy of
annexation. He had long conversations with Sorba.

At the end of these he informed Paoli that he was willing to
guarantee peace between Genoese and Corsicans on the basis
of Genoese suzerainty and possession of some coastal forts. Not
unexpectedly, the anticipated rejection came from Paoli on 3rd
June. Choiseul subsequently proposed that Genoa should
recognise Corsican independence, but should maintain garrisons
in Bastia, San Fiorenzo and the strongpoints of Capo Corso.
This, too, Paoli rejected.

These negotiations took place against a European imbroglio,
which in August exploded into Corsica itself: this was the
expulsion of the Jesuits from Spain. A reforming ministry had
forced this course upon the King of Spain, but the king was
personally unwilling to see the Jesuit Fathers wandering homeless in Europe and he, therefore, requested the Genoese Senate
to allow them to set up a home in Corsica. The request was not
only a sop to Genoese pride, but appeared to be a hostage for
the future and the Senate, therefore, readily assented. France,
however, which had already expelled the Jesuits, was angry that
the Genoese had so quickly and readily agreed to give them
succour. As a mark of displeasure, on the day that the Jesuit
Fathers landed in Ajaccio, the French retired from the town,
although since they were concerned to make a gesture rather
than upset the balance of power in the island, they surrendered
the fort to a Genoese garrison before they left. The town was
immediately occupied by the Paolists and the fort besieged. The
Genoese, who were soon in desperate straits, sent urgent cries

for help to Marbeuf, who immediately wrote to Paoli, requesting him to lift the siege and this Paoli did, anxious as ever to prove his respect to the French throne.

But the outcome of the attempt by the Genoese to provide succour for the Jesuits was fatal to their control of the island. The incident led to bitter recriminations between the French and the Genoese Courts and, in the exchange Choiseul wrote haughtily to Sorba that the Genoese were completely at the mercy of the Corsicans in the island and that without French protection, they would have to accept any terms which Paoli chose to make. This was true and the Genoese knew it. Already news had come to them that Paoli was preparing a fresh expedition and it was rumoured that this was intended to effect a landing in Liguria itself. But more important even than this threat was the steady drain on the Genoese exchequer. The defence of Capraja had cost the Republic 3,000,000 *livres* and all of this expenditure had been lost. Many Genoese merchants saw in renewed struggles against the Corsicans only ceaseless expense without any return. Yet the pride of the Republic in its Corsican possession, however tenuous the hold it had on it, was very strong and a peace party in the Senate, led by G. B. Brignole, at first made no headway at all, all its financial arguments being countered by the defiant cry that eventually Genoa's forces would prevail. As time passed, they looked less and less like prevailing, and at length Brignole obtained reluctant assent to his plan for leaving the island by means of some accommodation with the French. The solution that was worked out was diplomatically ingenious. Genoa did not relinquish her suzerainty over the island. Instead, formally recognising that the sea-ports which had been leased to France in 1764 could not be reoccupied by the Genoese without dangerous results to peace in the island, the Genoese consented to the French retaining the ports they occupied and using them as bases for the occupation of those other parts of the island which they thought necessary for the safety of the French troops. The French possession of the island was to be security for the repayment of the expenses incurred by the French during the occupation. By the terms of the Treaty Genoa could, at any time, exercise her right to turn the French out by paying the cost to date of the occupation. For ten years France was to pay the Republic 200,000 *livres* a year for the advantages of the occupation and, in the meantime, the

French would free the island of Capraja and return it to Genoa as well as protecting the Genoese trade from the attacks of the Corsicans. It was, in effect, to cede the island to France.

Sorba worked hard in his usual fashion to obtain the Treaty. Up to the very signature there was a great deal of wrangling and the Genoese were doubtful as to the sincerity of the French attitude. It was cynically said in the Genoese Senate that any country might be glad to escape the honour of the ownership of Corsica. But the French were sincere and, on 15th May 1768, Sorba and Choiseul finally negotiated the Treaty.

It was, in effect, power politics as naked and unashamed as power politics are able to be. Voltaire's ironic comment was just: 'Perhaps men have no right to sell their fellows; but that is a question which treaties do not enter into.'

Almost immediately the Treaty was signed Marbeuf requested that Paoli should quit the town of Ajaccio. Paoli knew of the negotiations which had been going on in France, even though he did not know of the conclusion of the Treaty, and the request seemed ominous. Relying on the good relations which existed between his government and Marbeuf's forces, he asked Marbeuf point-blank for an explanation of the request and Marbeuf lied brazenly, or diplomatically, according to the point of view. He said that the evacuation was requested so that the French could terminate the Treaty of 1764 without an legal quibbles for the Genoese, and that this in no way affected either the Treaty or the determination of the French not to alter the status of the island.

Paoli was doubtful, but he had committed the Corsicans to a policy of appeasing the French. With the end of the occupation so near, he was determined to do nothing which might injure the amicable *de facto* relations which existed between the French and Corsicans. However, the threat was clear. He, accordingly, convoked a Consulta of the Corsicans at Corte for 22nd May. On the 19th, the Corsican forces having withdrawn, the French occupied the town of Ajaccio. On the 22nd, as the representatives were gathering for the Consulta, news was brought that transports were arriving in the harbour at Ajaccio and disembarking French troops; rumour was rife, but nothing definite was known. The Assembly was unnaturally quiet when Paolo entered, surrounded by the members of his Council. The universal feeling was that the fate of the island was being decided and this made the tension palpable as Paoli rose to speak. After a few opening words, he launched into a detailed explanation of the negotiations of the previous months. 'We had reached,' he said, 'a position that I hoped would soon enable me to declare to the nation that our long labour was on the point of being crowned by an honourable peace. On the contrary, all is now doubtful, dark and confused. Peace now appears farther away from our shores. Our enemies sound more menacing. Our very existence may now be in danger.' He recalled the negotiations that he had undertaken: 'The French assured me,' he said, 'that if we suspended our operations against the ports that they had occupied, they would retire at the end of the four years' agreement and would be free to assert our rights. I sacrificed all the manifold advantages which we had because I honoured the French King's intentions.'

Throughout the four years, he said, the Corsicans had always been willing to come to an agreement with Genoa and, because of this, they had willingly accepted French mediation; but they had insisted that any such agreement should guarantee Corsica independence and the unity of the island. When it was quite clear that the Genoese would not come to any agreement of this kind the Corsicans were indeed entitled to expect that the French troops, in accordance with their undertaking, would retire from the island and leave the islanders free to settle their differences with the Republic.

'We had regarded the rumours which had reached the island of some sort of dubious provisional cession of Corsica, by the Genoese to the French, as baseless and indeed incredible. Yet the French have just disembarked troops. Other arrivals of French troops are expected. We are completely ignorant of the motives behind this landing and of the end for which the expedition is intended. But, naturally enough, this event alarms the whole nation. You have gathered here for the purpose of considering the French action and of adopting the measures that you judge will be the most efficacious in the preservation of our liberty and our independence. I have no doubt the measures that you undertake today will be worthy of the people who have chosen you for their representatives.'

The Assembly was in a mood to give Paoli carte-blanche and he made no ado about accepting the powers which it willingly yielded up to him. He wrote immediately to the French government, pointing out the disquiet which the arrival of new detachments of troops in the island had aroused. At the same time, he issued instructions to all the detachments of militia in the island to hold themselves in readiness. But, while he still preached and practised moderation, the anger of the Corsicans was rising. An incident at the university was typical.

It was the custom for the students at the university to be publicly examined at the end of a session by members of the Assembly and the government. One of the students seized the opportunity that the custom afforded and, beginning with a general disquisition on liberty, he rapidly turned his exercise into a patriotic oration:

'I have no words for the faint-hearted, but I have words for all true Corsicans. We, the young men of the island, will answer the first call to arms. How else can we show our worth? If foreigners land on our shores to sustain the pretensions of their allies we will face them. We will be ready to undertake any necessary tasks. If necessary, we will lay down our lives. For we are fighting, not only for ourselves, but for the lives of our children, for the defence of our country, for the maintenance of all that our fathers have built up. My valiant fellow-citizens, liberty is our end and throughout Europe generous souls will see us, will sympathise with us, will pray for the triumph of our cause. May our resolution never fail and may our enemies, whatever may be their name, learn by experience that the conquest of Corsica is not an easy task. There are in this country free men and free men know how to die.'

The feeling at the university was typical of the mood of the island. In Ajaccio, after a review of the troops had been carried out before a small and silent crowd of onlookers by the Comte de Narbonne, the Comte, to provoke some show of support, threw a handful of gold pieces among the crowd, crying gaily, '*Vive le roi!*' There was no answering cry. Silently and coldly the crowd dispersed, leaving the gold pieces lying on the ground. A French officer, accustomed to call on Corsican friends on that day of the week, met only Frenchmen as he walked through the streets to pay his visit. In the place of a hospitable welcome he found a locked door and a silent house. Thinking gloomily over the events of the day, he walked down on to the quay. The Corsicans had vanished. All he heard were

French voices rising above the slap of the waves and the sucking of the sea at the shingle.

Yet, in spite of this and other incidents, which demonstrated the islanders' loyalty to their government, Paoli was deeply worried and disturbed over the conflict which now loomed. The tide of success had been running very fast for him in the last few years and it had carried everything with it; the cause of the Genoese had been a lost cause; the future had appeared to be brilliant. But with a new and powerful enemy in the field, and moreover a very wealthy enemy, one well able to begin again, and on a much greater scale, the old Genoese arts of bribery and corruption, Paoli had to face the old threat of Corsican separatism. In the glens of the interior he was sure that his government would hold. But in the sea-ports, where there had always been a strong Genoese element, especially among the merchants, he was not so sure. Their patriotism was of a late date and the advent of the French promised a new and enhanced prosperity for them.

Bastia showed the way things might go. When the *fleur-de-lys* broke out over the citadel, replacing the Genoese flag, there were cries of, '*Vive le roi!*' in the streets. The French openly encouraged celebrations to mark the event, and not without some success. At night, part of the town was illuminated and there was some dancing in the streets.

Yet still the French, in spite of these incidents, professed neutrality and friendship for the government of the General. It seemed to Paoli too widespread and sincere a sentiment to be the result of a conspiracy among the French. It was hardly possible that deceit could have been practised successfuly on such a scale. The true intention of the French government was known probably only to a few, and certain of the French officers, placing their own interpretation on events, respresented their increasing readiness for war as merely a diversion to give satisfaction to the Genoese. The Marquis de Tilly repeatedly assured Salvatore Carlotti, with whom he was friendly and who was one of Paoli's Council, that: 'The government of the King had no wish at all to fight the Corsicans.' The General was uneasy but prepared to hold his forces in check until the truce between French and Corsicans expired on 7th August. Until the French actually attacked he estimated that the Corsicans could still retain a hope of liberty.

At this juncture, by one of the ironies of history, Paoli's government was accorded full diplomatic recognition by a foreign Power. As an additional turn of the screw the recognition was given by a heathen Power. The occasion dated back some months. At that time, a Tunisian ship had been wrecked on the rocky coast of the Balagna and the inhabitants of the region had swarmed to the wreck, plundered the ship and left the shipwrecked sailors to fend for themselves. When Paoli heard of this he gave immediate instructions that the sailors were to be succoured and the goods returned. His order was obeyed at once, for in the Balagna the founder of Isola Rossa had a status near divine. Paoli then ordered the ship to be repaired and re-provisioned and he had it provided with a new set of sails before he sent it on its way with gifts for the Bey of Tunis. The Bey was astounded. This kind of conduct by Christians was outside his experience. He repaid it in kind. One of his suite, accompanied by two secretaries and a small army of servants, soldiers, slaves and a great deal of impedimenta, landed at Isola Rossa, and at the end of July arrived at Corte. Paoli formally received them on the steps of the National Palace. The Tunisian Ambassador bowed and said loudly in Italian so that all could hear: 'The Bey salutes you and wishes you well.' Paoli immediately shook him by the hand, and catching him by the arm, conducted him into the Palace. There followed a series of talks and gifts. Paoli was presented with an Arab horse, two ostriches, a tiger, a pair of pistols and diamond-encrusted sword. The Ambassador attended Paoli's Council of State to see the way in which it worked.

It was a picturesque interlude. Reality broke in again with the request made by the commander of the *Soubise* Regiment of Cavalry, which had recently disembarked at San Fiorenzo, to be allowed to proceed to Bastia. Paoli, diplomatic as ever, agreed provided that the regiment proceeded with unloaded weapons. The condition was agreed to by the French and the regiment passed unmolested between the two towns. But all Paoli's diplomacy was unavailing. The French had decided on war; all they sought now was a pretext. Paoli, accordingly, received a dispatch from Marbeuf which informed him that the Marquis de Chauvelin was on his way to the island to explain to the General the intentions of the Duc de Choiseul, and with this dispatch came a request from Marbeuf that free passage should be allowed to his troops in future between San Fiorenzo and Bastia without specific instructions from Paoli, and that as a pledge of Paoli's good faith Isola Rossa and some villages of the interior should admit French troops. The demand was designed to provoke the breach. Paoli, indeed, felt that the time for diplomacy was over and that a stand must be made, but before he even had time to reply to Marbeuf's request the French launched the first attack.

8

FROM NONZA TO BORGO

The attack that the French made on the Corsicans' positions was an act of cynical treachery. Marbeuf and his officers had repeatedly insisted on their peaceful attitude; the truce with the Corsicans was not due to expire until 7th August and Marbeuf had not yet had an answer to his last request. Yet on 30th July, having received instructions from his Court to occupy any necessary post before Chauvelin arrived to conduct the final campaign, Marbeuf moved out of Bastia at the head of five thousand men, along the San Fiorenzo road, at the same time as the commander of the garrison at San Fiorenzo launched a flying column against the Pass of Santa Maria.

Their initial strategy was simple : their aim was to cut off Capo Corso from the rest of the island by holding the strongpoints of the San Fiorenzo–Bastia road and then to reduce the garrisons of the Cape at leisure. It was a brilliant success. In the Pass the flying columns soon ran into trouble. The surprise was not complete, the Corsicans rallied and, as the day wore on, reinforcements seemed to spring out of the gound as the inhabitants of the surrounding glens swarmed in. The French retreated back to San Fiorenzo, after having suffered heavy losses. But Marbeuf's weightier attack overwhelmed the Corsican forces. They fought furiously, but at the end of the day French troops were established in the two key villages of Patrimonio and Barbaggio and the Cape cut off from the rest of the island.

Paoli's adherents were quick to blame this reverse on the perfidy of the French and the unexpectedness of the attack, coming as it did after so many professions of friendship, but, when all the excuses have been made, it is a fact that in this initial clash Paoli was out-generalled. Patrimonio and Barbaggio were the keys to Capo Corso. Their absolute importance had already been demonstrated in Paoli's former campaigns against the Genoese. With a cordon across the neck of the Cape, Paoli's forces in the rocky peninsula were isolated, and Marbeuf, with his vastly superior forces, could easily overrun them. Even if Paoli's garrisons had held Patrimonio and Barbaggio against these initial attacks it could be argued that, in the long run, the peninsula was untenable. In a few weeks, the French would command the seas around the Cape and, with their vastly superior numbers, they would then be in a position to launch attacks by sea and land from the two seaports whenever they wished. Then Capo Corso would have become a trap for any Corsican troops billeted there. Yet Paoli had left, under the command of Barbaggi, locked up in the Cape, fully half of his regular troops.

The second part of the French plan now got under way as Marbeuf levelled all the weight of his forces against the Corsicans in Capo Corso. Barbaggi, realising he faced impossible odds, retreated along the shores of the peninsula towards Rogliano, which he intended to hold long enough for his troops to embark for Capraja. But the impetus of the French attack was too great and the town was stormed before they had time to take up defensive positions. The Corsicans were completely overrun. Dispersed and confused, the majority of them had in a few days surrendered to the French. Only a few troops managed to set sail for the island before the French occupied all the peninsula. Thus the campaign opened with a devastating defeat for the Corsicans.

Only one incident redeemed the French conquest of the Cape : the dramatic defence of the tower of Nonza became a legend in Corsican history. One of Paoli's captains, Giacomo Casella, an ancient veteran of the Wars of Independence, had been given command of the tower of Nonza, a dark menacing, round tower which frowned down upon the village of the same name. It was protected on three sides by the sea, and commanded the road north from San Fiorenzo. On the news that the French were attacking the defenders of the east coast Casella sent most of the garrison of the tower to the aid of Barbaggi retaining only a few men as a garrison. Those he sent were soon caught up in the great catastrophe and killed or captured, and the next day the sentinels in the tower saw French troops approaching their strongpoint. News had already come to them that the cause of Corsica in the peninsula was irretrievably lost. A feeling of defeat was sweeping the villages of Capo Corso and Casella's men wished him to surrender without more ado. The old man was furious. 'We have cannon, muskets, provisions and ammunition,' he said, 'and you talk of the impossibility of resistance. We will hold out to the last bullet and then we will jump out of the tower.' His sanguinity was not shared and in the night most of his soldiers fled. The veteran was not dismayed. Barring all the doors to the tower, he loaded his cannon, carefully disposed his muskets along the parapet and waited.

In the morning, as the French advanced, he fired off the cannon and blazed away with musket after musket, at the same time shouting out orders as though he were in command of a strong garrison. The French had instructions to make their conquest as bloodless as possible and General Grand-Maison, who was in command of the French troops in the peninsula, believed that he was on the verge of being forced to fight a bloody action. He, accordingly sent forward a man with a white flag to announce that the rest of the peninsula had surrendered and that resistance was useless; he demanded to know if Casella would surrender the tower. Cassella demanded time to consult his fellows and soon returned with the conditions of the capitulation, which were that the garrison should march out with the full honours of war and that the French should furnish horses to draw away the cannon. Grand-Maison, believing that the conquest of Capo Corso was the prelude to the complete overrunning of the rest of the island, that this would be completed in the very short time, and that any reasonable conditions were acceptable, consented. Accordingly, with the documents of capitulation exchanged, a company of French grenadiers lined up at the foot of the tower to render the honours due to the garrison. The door opened and out came the old man, musket on shoulder, pistols in his cummerbund, a sword at his waist. With great dignity, he advanced towards the French while the French waited for the rest of the garrison to follow. Then the French captain in command of the guard went up to the old man. 'Commander,' he said, 'where is the rest of the garrison?' 'I am the garrison,' said Casella. Believing that the Corsican intended some treachery, the captain drew his sword. At that moment, Grand-Maison came up and demanded the reason for the delay, whereupon Casella explained the situation. Grand-Maison began to laugh, shook the old man by the hand and give instructions for the terms of the capitulation to be scrupulously observed. He also gave orders that Casella was to be conducted to the outpost of Paoli's troops, and he gave him a letter to the General explaining the bravery of the old patriot.

Casella's action gave the Corsicans something to be proud of, but it did nothing to redeem the heavy blow they had suffered. However, if Capo Corso had fallen quickly, in the Nebbio Clemente's rapid action in occupying Oletta at the head of four thousand Volunteers, and hence blocking the way through the passes from the Nebbio to the interior of the island, effectively checked the French attempt to move south from San Fiorenzo.

The deliberate treachery of the French had roused the islanders to a fury and, once again, the clergy were preaching a Holy War in the glens; men women and children everywhere demanded the opportunity to strike at the hated invaders; patriotic fervour rose to the highest pitch it had ever reached in the island. But, for the moment, operations were broken off. After his first tentative attempt to break out of the Nebbio through the mountain passes had been repulsed by Clemente, Marbeuf proceeded to consolidate his positions and awaited the arrival of the Marquis de Chauvelin, who had sailed from the ports of Provence with a new army.

The Marquis brought some nine thousand additional troops with him; with the troops now on the island he had a force of some thirteen thousand men to take the field against the islanders, among them some of the finest troops in the French army. The arrival of the troops was the measure of the French determination to achieve a rapid victory. But the arrival of Chauvelin had another significance: it spelt the end of those hopes which had been aroused in Paoli by the news he had received from England. The General was always kept reasonably well-informed of European, and particularly of English, affairs by his correspondents in Leghorn; moreover, he had other informants scattered throughout Italy; foremost among them was Raimondo Cocchi, the professor of the unlikely twin subjects of Anatomy and Roman Antiquities at the University of Pisa and the friend of Sir Horace Mann, the English Ambassador to the Tuscan Court. From Cocchi and from Boswell's enthusiastic letters, Paoli heard of the widespread English support for Corsica and of strong opposition to any suggestion of French interference with the islanders; this opposition was particularly marked, he was told, in the City of London and in the ports, and it had been raised to a new pitch of intensity by the publication of Boswell's *Account of Corsica* in February 1768. He learnt, too, that opposition to the French was strong, not only in civilian life but also in the navy itself, where many admirals and captains were saying openly that the French possession of the island, which was repeatedly rumoured, would confer upon France a great strategical advantage, indeed that the possession of Corsica's harbours might threaten the whole of England's command of the Mediterranean. Burke spoke for no small part of English opinion when he pronounced that: 'Corsica naked, I do not dread; but Corsica a province of France, is terrible to me.'

Paoli had high hopes of the result of this support, but unfortunately for those hopes the English government itself was as divided on the Corsican question as on its other problems and unfortunately for Paoli, the strongest group clustered round the Bedford Whigs, led by Weymouth who consistently advocated a pacific policy towards France. Opposed to them were the Chathamites, led by the Prime Minister, Grafton, the Lord Chancellor and Lord Shelburne; but their opposition to the Bedford Whigs was not firm. Their original inspiration, Chatham, was a doubtful guide, for although he had told Boswell at the beginning of 1767 that: 'I see not the least ground at present for this country to interfere with any justice in the affairs of Corsica'. this was before his mental breakdown had taken place and rendered him incapable of leading his party, as Choiseul's policy became bolder and more minatory. It could, too, be taken as a counter-weight to his first declaration that, in the days of his vigour, he assured Boswell that: 'I should be sorry that in any corner of the world, however distant, or however small, it should be supected that I could ever be indifferent to the cause of liberty.' This, and even more, of course, the vigorous policy that he had always advocated with respect to the French, might have been expected to provide the real model for the Chathamites' policy. Certainly, Shelburne showed no sign of weakness when news of the Treaty of May 15th reached England. Sweeping aside the French Ambassador, the Comte de Châtelet's, flagrantly untrue denials that any such Treaty had been signed, he instructed his Ambassador in France, Rochfort, to demand a full explanation from Chauvelin and dispatched an observer, an able and talented linguist named John Stewart, on a fact-finding mission to France and Corsica. In the face of this, Choiseul temporised; Rochfort reported to Shelburne that the French seemed to be having second thoughts about Corsican policy. On 18th June, Shelburne laid before the Cabinet a draft copy of the treaty which he had just received, and subsequently instructed Rochfort to represent most strongly to the French Minister the opposition of the British government to any projected French invasion of the island. Chauvelin professed to regard this as an ultimatum, and although he declared France was now too deeply committed to her Corsican policy to turn back, Rochfort believed that, dismayed by the opposition that he encountered on all sides, Chauvelin would do anything rather than bring about a war with England. Indeed, the Minister's advisers were not slow to point out to him the military dangers the French ran and the vulnerability of a French force if the English chose to blockade the Corsican ports and left the French troops without supplies at the mercy of the islanders.

But all Shelburne's efforts were defeated by Weymouth and the Bedford Whigs. They, overborne in the Cabinet, carried on their struggle outside. They assured the foreign ambassadors with whom they had connections that, no matter what Shelburne might say, England would not, under any circumstances, go to war for Corsica. The report caused great excitement in Italy and Germany. When the news reached Frederick the Great he said, sourly and prophetically, that England's weakness towards the French would, in the end, bring about that very war it sought to avoid. De Châtelet, on his part, was quick to realise the importance of Bedford's opposition and set off immediately for Paris to assure Chauvelin that he could safely pursue his plans. Hardly had he explained the position to Chauvelin when Lord Chief Justice Mansfield, who was also in Paris at that time, declared at a dinner that 'The English Ministry was too weak and the nation too wise to enter into a war for the sake of Corsica.' Reassured, Choiseul decided that he could safely risk the possibility of English intervention, and instructed Chauvelin to press forward the attack on the Corsicans without delay.

Paoli had been reasonably well-informed of the course of these events, but the sudden *dénouement* was unexpected.

Chauvelin's arrival was the visible evidence of it. It received an appropriate classical quotation from the General: 'While Rome deliberates, Saguntum is lost.'

Along with the troops, Chauvelin brought a proclamation. It was, however, to the embittered Corsicans nothing more than a mockery. It coolly instructed the Corsicans to obey their legitimate rulers, and forbade any Corsican ship to sail under the national flag. Paoli sent a reply: it was proud and dignified. It did not concern itself with details, but set out the Corsican case, simply and defiantly:

> Already our nation has shown how little claim the Genoese had to our island. All the powers of Europe, especially France, have recognised us in practice as a free and independent people. So France has treated us, until the last few years. Even if Genoa had possessed the sovereignty she falsely claimed would she now be able to transfer it to another nation without the consent of those she professed to govern? She has no right to do so, for the basis of sovereignty is the people.

With this flourish of the Social Contract in the face of the French there came a few contemptuous reflections on the great nation which could wage war on a small and insignificant people in such a cause.

Together with this reply Paoli issued a call to all the islanders to keep the ranks they had closed against the invaders. For already the French had taken over an old Genoese tactic and were assuring the Corsicans that the King of France intended nothing but good to Corsica, which had been led astray by Paoli, and that they would pardon and reward handsomely all those chiefs who deserted the General and submitted to the King of France. Those chiefs who submitted, and they were few, were paid handsomely for their submission. At the same time, Buttafuoco who, like many, although by no means all, Corsicans with the *Royal Corse* had thrown in his lot with the French, was now a battalion commander in the French forces, sounded all his kindred in the island to see if the united ranks behind Paoli could be divided. Paoli aimed to counter the French blandishments with his appeal to the islanders' pride and patriotism. His ringing proclamation said:

> Let each take up his appointed position. We will show them

that we are not to be treated like a flock of old sheep bought in a market place, for that is what they are trying to do. Always there have been strangers between ourselves and the Genoese, preventing us from a decision by negotiating or by the force of our arms, and always, as a result, Justice and Honour have been trampled in the mud. Now we are face to face with our last enemy. Citizens, I know the danger is great but I know, too, we are not accustomed to count the number of our foes.

All the French efforts at subversion produced very little effect. There were some submissions and a few traitors but, on the whole, it became very evident that the Corsicans could not yet be divided and intended to fight. Chauvelin quickly realised this and prepared to launch a full scale attack to crush them.

It was directed against the densely-populated Castagniccia, Paoli's own country and one of the most wealthy and prosperous parts of the island. But first, the French had to secure their lines of communication. While one column attempted to fight its way through the passes of the Nebbio, another struck at Paoli's strategic hill town of Furiani, which had halted so many Genoese attacks.

The French had been reconnoitering the island for four years. They had no illusions about Furiani: they knew that it must be taken, or the way south along the coastal plain would always be open to an attack, as would the road between Bastia and San Fiorenzo. Thus, taking Furiani was, from the first, one of the most important objectives in the French plan for conquest. For Paoli, too, it was one of the keys to the island and he was determined to retain it if it were humanly possible. When the French attacked, it had been provided with a garrison of two hundred picked men, commanded by the famous captains, Gian Carlo Saliceti and Ristori. The French had brought with them all the necessary weapons for an attack and they disposed their batteries carefully. Then a hail of shells, bombs and bullets fell on the little village. The town was soon reduced to ruins. Before long, the houses were set alight and a column of smoke rose, like a staff, in the still, summer air. The French continued their bombardment steadily through the day, and, when night fell, the little town could be picked out on the hill top by the flames flickering in the shells of its shattered houses.

On the morning of the next day, French columns wound up the twisting roads to occupy the ruins. As they approached there was no sign of life: only wisps of blue smoke and the howling of some dogs. Then, as the French reached the outskirts of the town, the rocks above them became alive with men, and a hail of bullets shattered the head of the French column which sought to enter the village. The French, suprised, confused and thrown into disorder in the narrow paths, broke and ran, followed by the jeers of the Corsicans.

For a week Furiani held the French immobilized. Time and again it was shelled. Time and again the French attempted to storm the heights. Each time they were repulsed with loss. Then the garrison began to run out of ammunition and treated for surrender. The French were willing to grant an honourable capitulation, but they were unable to stomach the conditions the Corsicans demanded. In reality, these were no more than Casella's conditions at Nonza, but since then it had become only too evident to the French that they had a stiff fight on their hands and they, accordingly, refused to accept the Corsicans' terms. Ristori then came to talk with Arcambal, the French General in charge of the besieging troops, and, while the conversations were being held, Gian Carlo Saliceti, taking a leaf from the French book, rushed down the hill at the head of his garrison, broke through the French lines and, relying on his knowledge of the country, wheeled to by-pass the French along the coast. So Furiani fell, the vigour of its defence and the cost of its capture an ill omen for the French commanders

The French were even less successful in their attempts to storm the passes of the Nebbio. Indeed, they had a very hard task. In the narrow ways the French were at a disadvantage. They were unable to bring the full weight of their forces against the Corsicans and they soon realised that their trained soldiers were not the equals of the islanders as marksmen. Effectively pinned down by Clemente's troops, they could make no progress.

Along the plain of the east coast, however, the French, with Furiani taken, could bring all the advantage of their superior numbers to bear and they, accordingly advanced to the bridge across the Golo. But there, their advance was stayed, for Paoli had again positioned his defenders with great skill and in depth. The French commander, however, was experienced and resourceful. Advised by Buttafuoco, Chauvelin used French warships and transports to effect a landing in the rear of the defenders of the Golo and, commanded by Arcambal, the French amphibious force landed with the intention of marching across the eastern plain to the Casinca, that densely-wooded region which lay between the plain and the heartlands of Paoli's power in the Castagniccia. The landing was a complete success. Two thousand men came ashore, completely unopposed and as soon as the French to the north had heard that their forces had landed they launched an all-out attack on the bridge of the Golo. Three attacks were driven back but the fourth was successful and the Corsicans, who in the last stage of the battle had fought from behind a rampart of their dead, streamed back in disorder from the lost bridgehead. The whole of Paoli's forces now looked like being defeated. Buttafuoco at the head of his troops, sweeping inland, occupied his native village of Vescovato, where he announced to all his relatives and their clansmen that the cause of Paoli was irretrievably lost.

It was at this point that Paoli's system of defence and the widespread enthusiasm that his government everywhere aroused proved their worth. The Junta of the Casinca, established at the Convent of San Antonio della Casabianca, began the counter-attack by appealing to every man of the surrounding glens to rally to the patriot cause. As a rallying place, the convent itself had a great symbolic significance; elegant and austere, lying high in the pass between two wooded valleys, it had long been the seat of the region's Councils, and, in 1750, it had been the place where Paoli's Generalship was inaugurated.

As soon as he heard of the gathering of the clans, Clemente Paoli, vigorous in war as he was retiring in peace, rode rapidly back from the mountains of Nebbio to take command of the forces of the Casinca. Hardly had he been invested as their leader, when messengers came from Vescovato, declaring that the French were everywhere, that they were irresistible and that all the Corsicans could do was to plead for terms. Clemente, in a fury, ordered them to be shot. Then the other side of that strange division in his nature, between the warrior and the monk, came uppermost and he turned them over to the Fathers of the Commune for punishment. Immediately afterwards, completely undaunted by the stories of French strength, he launched a furious attack on Vescovato itself. The fighting around the town was excessively bloody, for Vescovato lay surrounded by groves of

Pasquale Paoli, painted for James Boswell in 1768 by Henry Bembridge

S. Wale del.   J. Miller Sc.

JAMES BOSWELL Esqr.

*In the Dress of an Armed Corsican Chief, as he appear'd at
Shakespeare's Jubilee, at Stratford upon Avon September 1769.*

Engraving by J. Miller after S. Wale

olives and chestnuts and there was little opportunity for the deployment of troops; bitter hand-to-hand fighting took place for hours among the olive groves and chestnut woods. The French, with victory and the conquest of the island almost within their grasp, fought desperately, but they were overwhelmed by the onrush of the Corsican militia. Vescovato itself fell and the French army split and, fighting in separate units, retreated towards Penta. But, with their coherence as an army lost, reduced to fighting among unfamiliar rocks, woods and groves and opposed by a race of marksmen who knew every inch of the terrain, they suffered heavy losses. Clemente Paoli wasted no time and, without stopping to overcome isolated French units, he pushed on with his detachments and stormed Penta where the French were trying to rally.

As soon as Paoli heard of his brother's brilliant tactical successes he gave orders to the Corsican commanders on every front to launch an all-out attack on the French positions. The fury with which they were assailed by the Corsicans disconcerted the French. Detachments of their army were driven back along the valley of the Golo, through which they had been advancing, and fortified themselves in Vignale, a little village which, perched on the side of the mountain, seemed to them impregnable. But a body of Paoli's regular troops, led by Pietro Colle, stormed the village to a wild cry of: 'Victory! Victory!' and the Royal troops, driven out of their positions, retreated in disorder, a great many being captured. Having taken the French advance position Colle, reinforced by yet more of Paoli's militia, continued his advance to Murato, where General Grand-Maison had established his headquarters. Without pausing, he threw his troops against the town. The French were unused to such furious and impetuous attacks, nor in their confidence had they fortified the town. They were driven from it, after suffering heavy losses in the narrow streets, leaving the munitions and provisions for a whole division in the hands of the Corsicans. Colle then pursued their broken forces across the *macchia* of the Nebbio.

Meanwhile, Clemente Paoli, reinforced now by yet more regiments of militia, led by the famous Serpentini, continued to mop of the French forces in the Casinca. The French had now lost half the troops they had disembarked for their amphibious expedition, but the fight was not yet over, for the survivors, led

E

by General Arcambal, had regrouped at Loreto. They fought bravely, determined to sell their lives dearly, and fighting went on for seven hours while they survived fifteen Corsican attacks. But finally, the Corsicans broke into the town. The French troops with Arcambal at their head, fought their way through the Corsican lines and made for the Golo. They were retreating through a completely hostile countryside, where every tree and every rock became a threat to the stragglers who were picked off in great numbers by snipers. In the meantime, Clemente detached his best troops to cross the mountains and seize the bridge over the Golo on which the French were retreating. The French, worn out and decimated, arrived at last at Lagobenetto only to find the bridge occupied by the patriots. They made several desperate attacks on the Corsican positions, but they were repulsed time and time again. At every moment, their position grew more dangerous as more and more Corsican forces arrived from the interior. At last, Arcambal, in desperation, ordered them to swim or ford the river. This the remainder of his troops did, attempting to cross through a hail of Corsican lead. Of the 2,000 invaders only 500 made the far bank and sought refuge in the hill village of Borgo.

In Borgo they believed that they were safe. The village, strung along the side of the mountain, overlooked a deep valley to the west and steep slopes to the east; it was connected by rough roads along the spurs of the mountain to the villages of Nebbio and by a rocky, difficult road to the plain. Well-provisioned, and with a French armoury already established there, it seemed a good rallying point and General Arcambal, confident that it could be easily held, made his way up the east coast to Bastia, leaving in the village, under the command of Colonel de Ludre, the remnant of his troops and the 200 men which originally comprised the garrison. But Paoli, knowing that the French were completely disconcerted by the failure of their attack on the Casinca, saw an opportunity here to deliver them a yet more damaging blow. On the night of 7th October, he issued orders to all his commanders in the east to gather under the walls of Borgo, and there he held a Council of War with them, at which unanimously they decided to attack the village and attempt to destroy completely the army of the Casinca. Clemente Paoli undertood to occupy the position which commanded the tracks to Nebbio and so frustrate any attempt to relieve Borgo which

General Grand-Maison might make from Oletta. Four of Paoli's most trusted captains, Pietro Colle, Giocante Grimaldi, Carlo Raffaelli and Ferdinando Agostino with 500 men were given the task of making the most difficult attack from the valley, while Serpentini with the same number of men was given the task of attacking the village from the east. Carlo Saliceti and Achillo Murati, leading the greater part of the troops, were to hold the road which led to the plain, and Paoli himself, with the reserve of about 600 men, occupied Luciana. Hardly had he taken his dispositions when he received unexpected reinforcements. As at Venaco, at another critical moment of the island's history, the women of the district, headed by Rosanna Serpentini, came armed for the struggle to Luciana to reinforce the General's troops.

At day break, on 9th October, the attack began. Well-entrenched, the defenders inflicted heavy losses on the Corsicans before the sheer fury and weight of the attack forced them to withdraw to a second line of defences. The withdrawal was orderly and well-prepared, for Colonel de Ludre had already seen from a tower in the town that a large force from Bastia was marching along the east coast to his assistance. The relieving force was, indeed, impressive. The French committed the whole of their reserve to the relief of Borgo; 4,000 infantry, 300 cavalry and nine pieces of artillery commanded by the Marquis de Chauvelin had been allotted to the attack. At the same time, General Grand-Maison, with 1,500 men, attempted to advance from Oletta across the mountains.

Seeing help so near at hand, the defenders of the village sallied out and bitter fighting ensued between them and the troops of Saliceti. Paoli, in the meantime, threw all his reserve in to oppose the French from Bastia and fierce fighting took place at the approaches to the town. Saliceti was victorious and drove the troops of the garrison back into Borgo while Paoli's reserve, taking every advantage that they could of the rocks of the *macchia,* held the forces of Chauvelin pinned down on the hillside. At midday, Narbonne-Fritzlar, commanding the Grenadiers of the Saxon and Rovergue Regiments, ordered a suicidal bayonet charge. The courage of his men and the sheer audacity of the action almost won the day. His troops sliced through the Corsicans and some of them reached the trenches of the besieged, but their losses were appallingly heavy. The

Corsicans, although overrun, held firm and, once the initial shock was over, the Grenadiers were unable to maintain themselves and retreated in disorder, many being cut down as they made their way down the hillside. Through their retreating ranks Chauvelin launched his cavalry, followed by the remainder of his infantry. The battle now became general. Every bush and every rock was ferociously contended for. At the same time, from the east and from the west the Paolists pressed upon the besieged garrison. Fighting went on through the afternoon. But, in spite of their discipline and bravery, the French could not penetrate the Corsican ranks before Borgo and, in the late afternoon, after having suffered extremely heavy losses, they retreated. Colonel de Ludre, short of water and convinced that any attempt to resistance was no longer possible, surrendered his garrison and, before nightfall, the French suffered the humiliation of seeing the Corsican flag flying from the ramparts of the town.

9

THE LAST DAYS OF
FREEDOM

For the regular troops of France, the most splendid of military nations, to have suffered such a defeat astonished all Europe. There was wild enthusiasm in England, where interest in the Corsican cause had been spreading, much aided by the growing fame of Boswell's *Account of Corsica*; additional impetus was given to the subscriptions which were being, organized, not only in England, but in Ireland and Scotland as well to provide aid for the 'brave Corsicans'. In the City, and in the main sea-ports of the kingdom, there was especial activity and letters rained upon the London journals demanding that the government take action to oppose the aggression of France. Already, 'Corsica' Boswell himself was throwing the greater part of his considerable energy into the struggle; pouring out appeals and exhortations; organising committees; and methodically arranging for the shipment of cannon to the island from the Carron ironworks in Stirlingshire. His tireless efforts and complete lack of inhibitions did something, indeed, to embarrass the government and drew from Lord Holland the sour remark : 'Foolish as we are we cannot be so foolish as to go to war because Mr Boswell has been in Corsica.'

But without action on the part of the government, not all the efforts of idealistic individuals and enthusiastic groups of 'Corsicans' were likely to be sufficient seriously to affect the final issue, limited as was the assistance that they could possibly give, and opposed as the islanders were by the full strength of France.

The French, however, aware of the English enthusiasm for the Corsican cause, but unaware of how ineffectual it really was, were seriously worried. They realised that the conquest of the island would mean a hard struggle, the length of which now appeared very uncertain; and for the duration of such a struggle they were well aware that they would lie exposed to a sea-borne

English attack. Any rumour of English preparations, therefore, caused a flutter at Versailles, and in this atmosphere phrases from a letter of Paoli which he had written to one of his captains – Ristori – then in captivity at Bastia, caused them a degree of concern altogether incommensurate with their content.

After a general resumé of all the efforts the Corsicans had made to placate the French during the few years of truce, Paoli wrote:

> Against their own best interests the French today make war against a people which had always delighted to be on good terms with them. And now they complain that I am seeking assistance from a foreign Power, as if that were a crime. Indeed, if I were the master of thunder I would use it for the defence of the liberty and independence of my country. On the other hand, I would not, however, refuse any proposal of the King of France which might spare us our national identity. We would readily respond to any overtures of that nature, but, if they do not come, I know where my duty lies and be assured I will do it.

These ambigious words reported to Paris suggested to the French government that Paoli was in full negotiation with another European Power, almost certainly England, for support.

But although Paoli's letter suggested this, and was perhaps phrased to make a covert threat that might startle the French into negotiation, badly confused and depressed as they were after their defeat at Borgo, the implication it contained was sadly untrue. Chauvelin's gamble that the English Cabinet would remain supine in the face of a French attack was all too successful and nothing effective was thereafter done by Grafton's government to help the Corsicans.

But the government was not as unconcerned about Corsica as might be supposed from Lord Holland's remark. Grafton, indeed, was extremely anxious to do something for the islanders, short of going to war, but he had no idea what. After some thought, he produced a scheme to aid the Corsicans secretly with arms taken from the stock held in the Tower of London. Shelburne was contemptuous of the idea, arguing that such a scheme could not be kept secret and that, when news of it was known, it would merely antagonise the French without being of very great help to the Corsicans. If the government wished to give qualified support to Paoli, Shelburne argued the logical thing to do was to recognise Corsica as a belligerent; but he himself had doubts about this step, for he knew that Paoli was not without a great deal of skill in negotiation, and he feared that if England attempted to give Corsica the shadow of support, rather than the substance, Paoli might use the English action to come to some agreement with the French and leave England with two enemies in the Mediterranean instead of one. The Cabinet was irritated with Shelburne's attitude, but aware that it was not without a certain logic; the only positive action they took was to dispatch another observer, Captain Dunant, a native of Geneva, to Corsica on a second fact-finding mission.

The sole consolation the supporters of the Corsicans in England had from their rulers was the tacit suspension of the Volunteers Act of 1763.

When the reports of Stewart and Dunant arrived they were found to be greatly enthusiastic about Paoli's abilities and the Corsican's warlike attitude and Grafton wretchedly complained of 'the unfortunate ignorance he had been in as to the disposition of the Corsicans, as well as their power to resist the attacks preparing against them by the French'. But, he regretfully decided, the time for a vigorous policy had passed and the last hope for positive action by the British government disappeared in the middle of November 1768, when, in the first division of the new Parliament, a 'Corsican' motion was defeated by 230 votes to 84.

For the moment, French disquiet was partly allayed by the news that French money had accomplished what French arms could not. Capraja, the island whose heroic defence had demonstrated to all Europe that the Genoese were no longer the masters of Corsica, was treacherously surrendered to the French navy by its commandant, Astolfi. Paoli had reinforced it heavily as soon as hostilities between France and Corsica had broken out, and it was plentifully supplied with ammunition and provisions. But Chauvelin's agents accomplished what the Genoese navy could not do. When the French fleet entered the Bay, Astolfi made no attempt at resistance and the island surrendered without a shot being fired. It was a heavy blow to Paoli.

Corsican honour was somewhat redeemed by the action of one of his sea captains, Angelo di Franceschi, who, on the point of sailing into the island's harbour with additional provisions and ammunition, saw the French flag flying from the citadel and immediately turned and sailed for the Italian coast. He was closely pursued by three French ships. His little vessel outgunned but not outsailed, fought a heroic running battle with them until he, at length, attained the shelter of Leghorn. In that town, he and his crew were offered substantial sums by French agents to desert to France, but to the suggestion that they could, by a simple shift of allegiances, become the favoured subjects of a King, they answered proudly that they were already the subjects of a Queen whose name was Liberty. Paoli was proud of their retort and prouder still of the spirit they had shown; he congratulated them gaily on their allegiance to Queen Liberty.

But the betrayal of Capraja deeply disturbed him. The loss of the island was a hard blow, but even harder was the knowledge that among his most trusted commanders there were those who would sell their country for money. He had always thought, and preached, that Corsica's greatest danger lay, not in an external enemy, but in an age-old tendency to sacrifice national unity for the sake of self-interest or clan; now the fear had become reality. The Council was even more enraged by the betrayal. They demanded that action be taken against the families of all those Corsicans who served with the French army or gave any form of aid to the French. Paoli threw all his weight against the proposal: he would not, he said, sacrifice the many innocent for the sake of a few guilty. His arguments carred the day, but there were many who said that he was being unduly quixotic at a time when the nation was struggling for its very existence. That he could carry the day, at such a time and in such circumstances, was a tribute to the love and affection in which he was held among the vast majority of Corsicans: 'We do not believe that he can be deceived or that he will ever deceive us,' his friend, the Abbé Rostino, had once said, and the Abbé's confidence was widely shared by the islanders whose adulation of the General had been raised to fever pitch by the victory of Borgo. They were willing to follow Paoli wherever he led.

Paoli resolved to make another effort to obtain some sort of agreement with the French. Unlike the more sanguine of his countrymen, he was under no illusions about the strength of the enemy that Corsica faced. He had a just appreciation of the strength of France, both militarily and financially, and he knew that, if nothing intervened, Corsica would grow relatively weaker with the passage of time as the French grew stronger. Accordingly, he wrote to the Duc de Choiseul, outlining a plan which he hoped might satisfy both countries. This plan proposed that the Royal Authority would be recognised in Corsica, but Corsica would have the right to manage her internal affairs and be responsible for her own law and order. France would protect Corsica against any exterior attack, and Corsica would supply troops to France if France became involved with any other power. Corsica would agree to pay an indemnity to Genoa equal to the value of the goods possessed in Corsica by Genoese subjects on the Continent at the beginning of the rebellion, and this indemnity would be payable in annuities. There was to be complete liberty of commerce between Corsica and France for the exchange of their manufactured or natural goods. One, or several, of the seaports would admit a French garrison and an equal number of Corsicans would serve France in any possession she might stipulate on the continent. But Choiseul made no reply. Any agreement, such as Paoli suggested, was too damaging to French pride. Besides the French had already seen what money could buy and they were now prepared to make more purchases.

While he awaited a reply, Paoli went, at the beginning of November, on a visit to the Balagna which had shown itself once more to be one of the most patriotic and courageous parts of the island, the French having had no success at all with their attempts to penetrate into the province. At the port of Isola Rossa Paoli found two Englishmen, Fawkener and Menzies, awaiting him, delegates from the patriotic committees of London, which had subscribed £8,000 for the Corsican cause. They told him that Corsican sympathisers in England had given an undertaking to supply this sum annually to Corsica until the conclusion of the war. Paoli was deeply moved by the gesture and especially by the story of one of the contributors, a merchant of the City of London, an old man called Trimmer, who had, in his will, left 'his little fortune to Liberty in its struggle with Royal despotism in the island of Corsica'. The old man regretted that the legacy was so small. He gave it, he said, 'to that Liberty for which heroes shed their blood and sacrifice their lives'. Paoli requested the Englishmen to stay with him and see something of the Corsican campaign, and it was while he was explaining affairs in Corsica to them that news was brought to him of two emissaries from the French who wished to see him. The emissaries were the renegade priests, Guasco and Morazzini, and Paoli met them in company with Fawkener and Menzies at the convent of Santa Raparata on 13th November. Guasco and Morazzini conveyed to him Chauvelin's proposals for an armistice of twenty days, in order that both sides might make arrangements for their winter quarters. Paoli retorted sardonically that, if the Royal troops would return to the positions they had occupied during the four years' truce he would agree to an armistice, but if they would not, well he was entrusted by his nation with the defence of its liberty and its independence and was not really concerned with the convenience of his nation's enemies: 'As for us,' he added, 'it is a matter of indifference to us whether we die in one season, or another.'

Chauvelin took the news philosophically; he knew that a well-laid plot was just about to be hatched. It had been proposed by Dumouriez, that soldier of fortune who had already been involved once in the affairs of Corsica. Dumouriez had, through the agency of two Corsicans in the French army, Giulo Peraldi and Fillippo Banconi, made contact with the Abbé Fabbiani, a member of one of the most influential families of the province, and Fabbiani, seduced by the promise of ecclesiastical promotion in the event of a French victory, undertook to subvert one of his nephews who was an officer in the garrison of Isola Rossa. When he sounded out his nephew, however, he found that the young man was utterly committed to Paoli and the Corsican national cause. Undeterred, Dumouriez proposed a far more elaborate plan. Acting under his instructions, the Abbé made contact with Comte de Perez, the admiral of Paoli's fleet, whose flagship lay at that time in the Bay of Isola Rossa; by large bribes and the promise of still greater rewards in cash and promotion he thus led Perez to betray his adopted country. An elaborate plot was prepared between them, and Perez then confided the plan to all the members of his Maltese crew that he could trust.

On the night appointed for the attempt on the town some boatloads of French from Algajola boarded his brig and, together with his followers, overcame all the Paolists. He then hoisted a lantern aloft as a signal to the French warship *La Provence* which was cruising off-shore and *La Provence* rapidly landed French troops just outside the town and then sailed into the harbour to open fire on the citadel. At the same time, Perez went ashore with the French soldiers from Algajola and made an attack on the house where the General was known to be lodging. Paoli was awakened by shots and the noise of fighting between his guard and the attackers; he rushed out of the house, followed by the two Englishmen who were staying with him and a short, savage fight took place in the street. Paoli's guard was outnumbered, but at every instant Paoli's followers were arriving from the surrounding houses and the attackers, fearing for their lives if they remained, dashed back through the streets to their boats. Dumouriez and Perez escaped, but the Abbé Fabbiani, who had been one of their company, was drowned when one of the boats overturned.

In the meantime, the attack by the French from outside the town had failed and the guns of the port were engaged in a duel with the French man-of-war. Learning that their surprise attack had miscarried, the French landing party withdrew.

Perez knew that his credit with the French was exhausted after the unsuccessful attack on the Isola Rossa. Hardly had he landed the survivors of his ill-fated expedition at Ajaccio, therefore, than he was proposing a new scheme to the Comte de Narbonne, who commanded the French troops in the west of the island. On the day before he had attempted to betray the Isola Rossa, he had heard the news that Abbatucci, who commanded Paoli's forces in the west of the island, was ill at Zicavo. During his spells ashore, while he was the Admiral of Paoli's navy, he had made many friends and got to know the glens around Ajaccio extremely well. He assured the Comte de Narbonne that there was a great deal of disaffection for the government of Paoli in the glens of the west of the island, and that only Abbatucci's dominating character, military talents and powerful clan had kept it in check. Moreover, he said the French had in Ajaccio itself a body of men who would, if they were enlisted, be loyal to France since they had long harboured resentment at their treatment by the patriots. These were the Corsican Greeks, the descendants of a Greek colony from the Peloponnesos which the Genoese had settled in the *Oltremonti* in 1676. Hated by the Corsicans as the allies of the Genoese, their settlement had been overrun soon after the outbreak of the rebellion in 1729 and since then they had been forced to seek shelter in Ajaccio itself. He assured Narbonne that he could easily recruit a powerful force from the Greeks and the Ajaccians themselves. These he would combine with the survivors of the expedition and, if Narbonne could furnish him with French troops, he would guarantee to conquer the western part of the island within weeks. Narbonne was convinced and Perez thereupon fulfilled the first part of his bargain by quickly recruiting most of the Greeks who were able to carry arms. With these, the survivors of the expedition and two battalions of French troops, he had advanced into the interior.

It seemed as if he were to be right on all counts. At first, he met with little but token resistance and penetrated rapidly into the Mezzana. There, however, there was hard fighting with the local militia, and within a few days, Abbatucci himself, that lion-headed, lion-hearted patriot who had dragged himself from a sick-bed to lead his countrymen, opposed him. The fighting was hard and bloody, and both sides suffered heavy losses. But Abbatucci's personality, and the knowledge his troops had of the terrain in which they fought, proved decisive and Perez and his company were driven back the way they had come and forced to seek refuge within the walls of Ajaccio itself. It was the end of Perez's career. After his defeat he was ashamed to show his face, even in the streets of Ajaccio. He, accordingly, took ship for France as quickly as possible.

The French had, up to now, been far more successful in bribing Corsicans than in fighting them. Once again they tried their luck with subversion, and once again the traitor was very close to the General. This was the son of the Grand Chancellor, the young Matteo Massesi, whose crime was all the more heinous in that Paoli had, for some time, admired young Matteo's ability and prophesied that he would be one of the future leaders of a free Corsica. By means of Corsican intermediaries a French officer offered Matteo a large reward if he would betray Paoli to the French troops; more than this, he informed Matteo that he was empowered to offer him ennoblement in the new Corsica that would be set up. A great deal of incriminating correspondence passed between the two, which was discovered, oddly enough, by a letter falling out of Matteo's pocket and being picked up by one of Paoli's followers. Sent to Corte to be tried, the young man confessed everything and was condemned by the Council to be executed. Even more menacing than Matteo's treason was the inference in some of the captured correspondence that the

Grand Chancellor himself would accept a French victory without a great deal of repining. The Chancellor denied this furiously but, some weeks later, he was deprived of his office by the command of the Council.

10

PONTENUOVO

Throughout the island the French troops were now very much on the defensive. The arrival of reinforcements in the shape of ten new battalions of infantry and two squadrons of cavalry, however, restored their confidence and that of their commander. Thus reinforced, Chauvelin planned a concerted attack throughout the island. Accordingly, columns of his troops attacked the Corsicans from Calvi and Ajaccio and feints were also made from Bastia and Algajola, but the main weight of the attack came from San Fiorenzo and was designed to conquer the whole of the Nebbio. The French troops, taking the roads and the paths through the mountains that encircled the valley, converged rapidly on Murato in two well-planned thrusts. The Corsicans fought furiously and stubbornly as they retreated through the mountains of the Nebbio and then, massing, they attempted to make a stand at Murato, but the French were not to be denied and, after a short siege, the town was occupied. Elated by his success and determined to give the Corsicans no time to rally, Chauvelin ordered his forces to storm the passes which led through the mountains and advance into the interior of the island, but, advancing incautiously in unfamiliar country and opposed by two of Paoli's most able captains, Colle and Pelone, they suffered heavy losses from the accuracy of the Corsican fire and the clever disposition of the Corsican marksmen among the rocky defiles. Retreating from the passes, they were counter-attacked as they straggled back into Murato and something like a rout resulted as, abandoning the town, they retreated in disorder the way they had come. The Corsicans, raised to new heights of boldness and daring by their success, gave them no time to re-form; they pursued them relentlessly; within a week they had swept the French out of almost all the valley and, at the last, they stormed back took the strategic village of Barbaggio and so severed the connection between Bastia and San Fiorenzo.

When the news of their latest defeat reached the French at Versailles, it was accompanied by the considered opinion of Chauvelin that the conquest of Corsica was not worth the expense in men and money that would be necessary to achieve it. There was agitated discussion in the Court and it was widely rumoured that the King himself thought seriously of accepting the proposals that Paoli had made. But Choiseul considered that the credit of his administration depended on his prosecuting the war to a successful conclusion and so, on 28th December 1768, Chauvelin was recalled to Paris to be replaced by a new commander. Until that commander was appointed, the Comte de Marbeuf was promoted to the grade of lieutenant-general and placed provisionally at the head of the troops. The recall of Chauvelin was a painful reminder that all the greatest military nation in Europe had achieved after a six months' struggle against an island of peasants was the occupation of a few villages.

Paoli resolved to strike quickly against the French before the new commander arrived. The object of his campaign was to clear the French completely from the Nebbio and to take San Fiorenzo. The key to the upper part of the Nebbio was Oletta, a large village of 900 inhabitants perched in the mountain pass which commanded the approaches to Murato and the way to the eastern plain; it was dominated by its huge, dark church hanging threateningly above the traveller as he made his way up from the valley into the mountains. It was held for the French by General Grand-Maison, one of the ablest and also, incidentally, one of the most amiable of the French commanders, who had surrounded it with a complex system of trenches and strongpoints. Inside the town, a garrison of some 1,500 French soldiers lived uneasily; many were quartered in the great church which had been turned into a barracks; others were billeted in the houses of the town. There was a general hatred of the garrison, for the Nebbio had always been one of the most patriotic parts of the island and Oletta one of the most enthusiastically Paolist of towns. In spite of Grand-Maison's personal amiability, he was well aware of the detestation that the villagers had for his soldiers and he governed the village by a deliberate system of terror and repression. Any Corsican who went into the surrounding countryside had first to be granted a pass by a French officer. If he did not return within the appointed time his family was immediately imprisoned. If it became known that he had communicated with any of Paoli's forces he was, if taken, immediately shot. The inhabitants, who had been disarmed by the French, bore all this sullenly and resentfully. Paoli was, of course, aware of the situation and hoped to profit by the village's disaffection, but several executions, for having patriot connections and the knowledge that there was an informer, or informers, at work, inhibited the villagers from action.

It was at this point that a boy named Giulio Saliceti managed to leave the village unnoticed by the French. His escapade had no purpose, being merely done in a fit of boyish bravado. When he attempted to steal back into the town, later in the day, he was seized by the French and taken before the commander, Grand-Maison, who, after closely questioning him and realising that this was merely a prank, threatened him with death if he should do the like in future and set him free. Welcomed home enthusiastically as a hero by his friends, he was overheard by a passing French officer to make ribald remarks about the commander. The officer immediately seized him and gave him a beating. This took place outside the house of the Abbé Saliceti, his uncle, who saw the whole affair from a window. The Abbé, a little round man called Peverino, because he was said to remind people of a little pear, was greatly esteemed in the town and was one of the most enthusiastic Paolists. He was also very proud, with a truly Corsican pride in his relatives, and Giulio was his favourite nephew. The incident stung him into preparing a plot for the subversion of the town, no matter what the cost to the townspeople might be.

His plot was to dig a tunnel from a house neighbouring the church which would come up in an unused part of the vault. The tunnel would be used to place enough ammunition to blow both church and soldiers sky high. Although the Corsicans in the town had been deprived of their arms, there was still a great store of powder hidden away in their houses and more was soon smuggled in from the surrounding countryside. The Abbé planned the explosion for the night of 13th February 1769 and, while the tunnel was being dug, he organised, with the greatest caution, all those in the town whom he could trust. To them he confided the plan to blow up the church and arranged the aftermath; at a given signal on the night of the 13th, when the charge was fired, all the Frenchmen in private houses were to be overpowered. Contact was established with Paoli's commanders in the surrounding countryside. warning them to be ready to storm the town as soon as a signal was given.

The Abbé kept the details of his plot to blow up the church restricted to those who were actually engaged in the enterprise, for he knew that it might have grave dangers for the towns-people in the surrounding houses.

But some of the relatives of these working in the tunnel lived close to that side of the church under which the charge was to be placed and on the day of the 13th, on one pretext or another, they brought their relatives to stay in houses which they thought would be safe. The French in the town were always on edge. One or two of them became suspicious at this unusual movement which was taking place among the Corsicans and reported the matter to Grand-Maison, who immediately ordered anyone who seemed to act suspiciously to be arrested and their houses to be searched. At this, the Abbé Saliceti, realising that the whole plot was on the verge of being discovered, gathered to-gether a band of his adherents and fought his way out of the town. Grand-Maison immediately ordered martial law to be proclaimed, the tunnel was discovered and summary executions were made. So ended in disaster the plot to betray Oletta.

The Corsican commanders in the surrounding countryside had been eagerly awaiting the Abbé's signal, but, on his appearance at the head of his band, they realised that the plot had miscarried and immediately launched a heavy attack on the village; bitter fighting went on for the trenches and strongpoints in which the French were embattled.

The attack on Oletta was the signal for Paoli's forces to attack San Fiorenzo, both by land and by sea. The occupation of Barbaggio had cut the town off from the main French forces at Bastia; but the garrison was still kept supplied by sea and Paoli planned to stop those supplies by an ingenious feint. This demanded the use of his navy, which had quickly recovered from the disarray into which it had been thrown after the defection of Perez. It was too small and too light to be other than brushed aside by the French fleet in the Mediterranean in any general action, but with each captain acting as a privateer, preying on the French shipping in the Ligurian Sea, the Corsicans had caused the French a great deal of bother and expense. Two of Paoli's captains, Paciola di Calvi and Lazaro

Costa, had been especially successful. Lazaro in particular, a tiny man of great bravery and superb seamanship, captured prize after prize and the French reckoned that since the beginning of hostilities his 'piracy' had cost them 2,000,000 francs. In the first fortnight of December 1769, he had considerably embarrassed the French in Corsica by making prizes of the two ships which brought them long-awaited muskets, ammunition and clothing; the French estimated that his daring attack had cost them 340 barrels of powder, 3,000 muskets and 160,000 francs worth of uniforms and miscellaneous stores. Paoli, hearing of this, wrote to him enthusiastically: 'If all our commanders were as zealous and successful as you, my brave captain, the cause of Liberty would soon be won.'

Before he began his attack on the Nebbio, Paoli gave instructions to his captains that they were to carry out diversionary attacks even farther afield, raiding along the coast of France itself, while secretly gathering together as many ships as they possibly could and sailing suddenly to the blockade of San Fiorenzo, while the Corsicans threw all their forces in the Nebbio into an all-out attack on the port. At the same time, Abbatucci, who had brilliantly defeated all the French attempts to break out of Ajaccio, suddenly launched an attack on the environs of the western sea-port and, after heavy fighting, a body of his troops, led by the priest of Guagno, Giulio Foata, occupied the Jesuit convent at the gates of the town itself.

Once more, Paoli's well-laid plans were defeated, not by French military skill or bravery, but by French money. Just before the blockade of San Fiorenzo began, the French had landed fresh troops there, which, in the form of a flying column, made their way up the valley to revictual Oletta. Attacked by the men of the Nebbio, unable to fight their way through the Corsicans to the relief of the village and equally unable to return to San Fiorenzo (since Paoli's forces now surrounded the town in depth), they were saved from destruction by having the Corsican fortified village of Olmeta rendered up to them by one of Paoli's most trusted captains, Ferdinando Agostini, one of the heroes of the battle of Borgo. He had, for some time, been in communication with General Grand-Maison and he now sold all his honour and his reputation for French gold (admittedly a great deal of it) and the promise of employment in a victorious French army. The possession of Olmeta at once enabled the

French to cut Paoli's lines of communication with Murato, the Casinca and the Castagniccia and effectively hamstrung his attempt to recapture the Nebbio. It was the first of two blows, for in Ajaccio the French had a more honourable victory, retaking the Jesuit convent after some days of bitter fighting.

Although Paoli's attack on the Nebbio had failed, the French were still deeply worried about their war with the islanders. In a year of fighting they had hardly anything to show for their pains and it was still widely rumoured, and widely believed, that the English were on the point of intervening. It was known for a fact that English observers were with Paoli's army and that money was being provided by many subscribers throughout England to enable him to buy arms and ammunition. In the circumstances, therefore, the new French commander in the island, the Comte de Vaux, was able to obtain all the forces he asked for. De Vaux was a good choice to lead the French troops. He had won himself a fine reputation as a soldier and he had a good knowledge of Corsica, having fought there formerly in the army of Maillebois. He knew the islanders' fighting qualities and he had the recent defeats of Chauvelin to remind him of just how capable Paoli was of using the islanders' bravery wisely. He, accordingly, demanded a large increase in the French forces in Corsica before he undertook his command. There were already 30 battalions of infantry in the island and he requested that they be increased to 45 and that all the battalions which had suffered losses should be made up to full strength. At the same time, he requested that the three regiments of cavalry, which were already at Bastia, should be brought up to strength, and that a fourth should be added. He requested that a great deal more artillery should be provided and, bearing in mind his knowledge of Paoli's skill in military engineering, provided himself with several companies of military engineers, sappers and pioneers. His force was completed by a body of Corsican Volunteers, recruited in Corsica by Buttafuoco, Agostini and Angelo Matra; Volunteers who were called derisively by the Paolists the 'corps of Vittoli', after the murderers of Sampiero in 1765.

Paoli had expected the French to reinforce their forces in the island for a summer campaign, but not to the extent which now became evident. For, with every day, shiploads of French soldiers were being disembarked at all the French-held ports around the island. Information, too, soon came back to Paoli from France, warning him that the French intended to prosecute the war on an unprecedented scale. He realised that the climacteric moment of the war had come. He knew that the war would, even if it ended in a victory, claim many Corsican lives and devastate families and he determined to obtain the assent of the nation to the continuation of the struggle. Accordingly, on 15th April 1769, he convoked an Extraordinary Consulta at San Antonio della Casabianca in the Casinca, that scene of so many fateful decisions for the Corsican people. Delegates came from every part of the island. As soon as the Consulta was opened, a resolution was proposed that the Corsicans would defend their native soil and their national institutions to the last ditch and it was passed unanimously amid wild cheering. Resolutions were then carried for a *levée en masse*. Every Corsican from six to sixty was to be placed immediately at the disposition of the General: 'Since all Corsicans enjoy the same advantage of liberty it is just that they all take part in its defence.'

The prosecution of the war, and the number of men it would be necessary to call immediately to the colours, was left entirely to the discretion of the General. He immediately stated that, in order to offer effective opposition to the French, he would need, on a permanent footing, a third of all the able-bodied men in Corsica. The Assembly then passed a resolution that the inhabitants of all those places which had been taken, or might be taken, by the French would continue to be regarded as subjects of Corsica and treated as such by the Corsican law and the Corsican people.

The delegates returned to their glens glowing with enthusiasm, only to find that, in their absence, national spirit had risen to their own level. Paoli's popularity was at an unprecedented height; everywhere, the priests and monks preached a Holy War against the invader; every glen and village sent declarations of loyalty and affection to Paoli; his name rang like a battle-cry up and down the island.

Of Paoli's innermost thoughts during these days there is no record. He was too good a soldier not to know he was facing almost impossible odds. He estimated that the French had in the island, at the commencement of de Vaux's attack, as many men as there were able-bodied Corsicans in Corsica, and de Vaux's men were well-trained and experienced soldiers. The young Napoleon, dreaming of Corsican greatness at Brienne, said that if he had been in Paoli's position he would have broken up the Corsican army into small units and fought a guerilla war and certainly such a war would have given Paoli a far better chance of survival. But the Corsicans had already achieved wonders. Perhaps he hoped in his innermost heart for miracles. The most likely explanation, though, is the political one. With an army of guerillas he might indeed have been able to hold out in the *macchia* for many years, but the French could have then presented the patriots to the eyes of Europe as a mere band of rebels. Above all, Paoli intended that Corsica should retain her national identity. If Corsica were defeated he meant it should be defeated as a nation; its overthrow would be the overthrow of a nation. He believed, too, and always believed, in the ultimate victory of justice. He was sure that, even if it were not to be under him, in the fullness of time Corsica would achieve her freedom.

On 26th April, Paoli reviewed his assembled troops in the Casinca in the presence of Lord Pembroke and Admiral Smith, two Englishmen whose presence in the island, although allegedly in an unofficial capacity, increased the French eagerness for a quick victory. Indeed, the hauteur of Lord Pembroke who had reached the General by way of Bastia was particularly worrying to them : 'He has,' it was reported to Paris, 'the reserve of an ambassador extraordinary'. In the grand manner of an eighteenth-century nobleman, he had included in his train two noble Italian partisans of Paoli, the Marchése Fagnani and the Cavalière Tancredo and a portrait painter to paint the General's portrait. Paoli's troops consisted, for the greater part, of Corsican militia and his own regular regiments, but there were also two companies of Swiss and Prussian volunteers who had come to the island in the first place to fight for the Genoese, but, on the Genoese withdrawal, elected to fight for Corsica. There were, too, much to Paoli's delight, a corps of Tuscan volunteers. These came, as their name implied, mainly from Tuscany but they numbered among their ranks Italians from all over the peninsula. Twenty years later, Paoli was to recall his pride on seeing the Tuscans among the ranks of Corsicans.

By 30th April both sides were taking up their positions. Paoli, leaving the reserve of his troops in the Casinca under the command of Saliceti, Serpentini and Cottoni, established his headquarters in the Nebbio. While he did this, de Vaux marched out of San Fiorenzo with 24 infantry battalions and several squadrons of cavalry and occupied the village of San Pietro di Tenda. Marbeuf, with six infantry battalions and a regiment of cavalry, then advanced along the eastern plain to the river Bevinco; at the same time, Grand-Maison, in Oletta, was reinforced with a fourth battalion of infantry.

The Nebbio was swarming with soldiers. The newly-arrived French troops seeing the rough dress and undisciplined movements of their opponents, were in high feather, saying that it would not take them long to defeat an army of peasants, such as the Corsicans. The more experienced Frenchmen said grimly that the Corsicans fought much better than they looked.

On 3rd May, as the sun rose, de Vaux gave the instructions for a great bombardment of the Corsican positions to begin. The Corsicans had never seen such masses of artillery in action; all day long, the French cannon thundered against their positions; the air seemed to rain metal. But, if they were amazed at the French strength, they were not awed. They resolutely guarded their positions and waited. The day ended with nothing more than a few skirmishes having taken place. De Vaux, indeed, had not hoped for more. He had intended, mainly, a display; to demonstrate to his own troops the power that they represented and to the Corsicans the power against which they contended.

On the morning of the 4th, de Vaux's troops, in great numbers, moved against the village of Rapale, which guarded the approaches to Murato. If the new arrivals among the French had any doubts of the Corsican capacity to fight they were rapidly dispelled. Taking advantage of every bush and rock, the Corsicans caused them extremely heavy losses. However, in spite of being severely mauled, the French pushed forward until they entered the town itself. The Corsicans contested every house. Then, reinforced by Paoli's reserves sent from Murato, they, in their turn, steadily pushed the French backwards. Colle and Pelone were in the forefront of their men, inspiring all by their bravery and fire. By the end of the day the French had not been successful in retaining a single house. But on the 4th, de Vaux, deploying his forces on a wide front, managed to break through the Corsican lines and, turning the flank of the Corsicans, he drove them rapidly back into Murato itself. The fighting for the little town was savage. Paoli, seeing it would be impossible to hold it against such odds, gave instructions that the bulk of the Corsican army should retreat to the right bank of the Golo. He himself made his way over the mountains and re-established his headquarters south of the Golo in the mountains of Rostino, where he could observe the French as they crossed the mountain passes to occupy the opposing heights. To fortify the line of the river Golo in this way was a completely orthodox tactic although, considering his inferiority in numbers, a doubtful one. But his troops held the strategic villages of Lento and Canavaggia on the left bank of the Golo, and he hoped that, by holding Lento, he would be able to threaten the French lines of communication and inhibit the French from attempting to cross the Golo into the Castagniccia, while by holding Canavaggia he would be able to deter them from attempting to wheel to the passes which led to the Balagna. Two trusted captains were intended for the command of these vital villages: Captain Gaffori was to have command of the troops in Lento and Giocante Grimaldi was to hold Canavaggia.

Paoli gave instructions to his troops that the line of the Golo was to be held at all costs. His scouts soon brought him information that the French were concentrating their troops on the heights near Lento and he accordingly sent 1,000 extra men under Saliceti to guard the bridge of Pontenuovo; the bridge was already protected by about 15,000 of his troops, supported by the militia of Rostino.

Part of the Corsican strength had always lain in the eagerness of the troops to rush to the scene of any possible conflict. This readiness time and again enabled the commanders to practise the classic maxim of being first on the battlefield with the most men. But it was a dangerous virtue unless it was controlled wisely and not all their leaders controlled it wisely.

The troops at Pontenuovo were thirsting for action. Hearing heavy musket fire coming from the top of the hills near Lento large numbers swarmed enthusiastically up the tracks of the hillside in the Corsican fashion, convinced that they were coming to the help of their comrades who still disputed the French passage through the mountains from Murato. But Gaffori, either through negligence or because he had been bought by the French (which was never determined) had neglected to well-fortify Lento. The musket fire which the Corsicans in the valley had heard was only the evidence of a token resistance put up by Paoli's defenders in, and near, the town as the French troops, who had massed before the village in great numbers, stormed through the streets. Elated by their easy victory, the French swept away the last defenders and, without a pause, hurled themselves upon the scattered ranks of the advancing Corsicans. Crying, 'Treachery!' the Corsicans rushed pell-mell back down the hillside, streaming towards the safety of their camp. But a good many Corsicans had now crossed the bridge with the intention of following the advance guard up the slopes and into the mountains. Retreat turned into a rout, with scenes of hopeless confusion as the Corsicans sought to seek safety, across the bridge, from the advancing French columns. The brigadier, Gentili, who was on the spot, desperately tried to restore order and instructed a company of Swiss and of Prussians, who were nearest to the bridge, to hold its southern side, while the Corsicans re-formed on the north to take the first shock of the French troops. But many of the retreating Corsicans, panic-stricken, attacked the Prussians and these, to try and restore order, fired on them. There were cries of 'Treachery!' everywhere. The struggle became confused. The advancing French columns easily swept away the Corsican defenders at the head of the bridge and, after a bloody combat, crossed the river. As the French spread out, some Corsicans ran, while others hurled themselves bravely upon their enemies. But de Vaux's commanders, seeing the advantage they had obtained, sent their men swarming down the slopes to consolidate their victory. The Corsicans fought bravely to contain the French bridgehead, but a detachment of French soldiers made their way to their rear and poured in on them a withering fire from a neighbouring hill. The Corsicans put up a desperate resistance until nightfall, but on the banks of the river they had lost the advantage they possessed in the mountain passes. Their losses were very heavy. The Corsican annalist who reported the battle wrote that the Golo 'ran red with the blood of the defenders of Pontenuovo'. But their heroic struggle was in vain. The French seemed to have limitless numbers of reinforcements. At nightfall, the Corsicans gave it up and retreated into the protecting woods.

Pontenuovo was the decisive battle of the campaign. It was not so much that the defeat was militarily irredeemable as that its unexpectedness, and the treachery which had caused it, filled the islanders with foreboding and sapped their will to resist. Accounts of treason at the bridge, greatly exaggerated in the telling, flew up and down the island in the days after the

defeat, and the despair they caused was increased when it became known that Cavanaggia had been betrayed by Grimaldi,
and that French troops had already reached Pietralba and were
advancing into the glens of the Balagna. At the other end of the
valley, Serpentini, at the bridge of Golo, was repeating the heroic
resistance of the previous year, but, with the defeat at
Pontenuovo, his flank was turned by the French, and, when he
retreated through the interior of the Casinca and the Castagniccia, he found that many inhabitants had already lost heart and
were unwilling to continue the struggle.

De Vaux was lavish with promises and money as his troops
penetrated into the villages of the interior. But along with the
blandishments went intimidation. The houses of known patriots
were razed to the ground and a proclamation was issued to the
effect that any Corsican found in arms against the French
would be sent to the galleys.

In the Balagna Paoli's forces had been contending furiously
against the French army of 4,000 which had marched out of
Calvi. But, threatened with de Vaux's troops advancing from the
south, the Corsican troops were forced to retreat to Isola Rossa,
where as many of them as possible embarked on an English
ship and were taken to Ajaccio. The rest surrendered.

Paoli shifted his headquarters again, this time across the
mountains to Vivario. From this village he strove to rally his
followers in the north and west of the island, while Serpentini
and Clemente, who had made their way to the 'other side of the
mountains', joined Abbatucci, who was successfully holding the
French troops who had attempted to sally out of Ajaccio. Paoli
seems to have had some idea of a counter-attack against the
French at this time, using the forces of the western glens, but
Clemente informed him that the 'other side of the mountains'
had no troops to spare and that it would take all their men and
resources to prevent the French from advancing from Ajaccio.

Throughout the glens of the Casinca and the Castagniccia
there was still a great deal of opposition to the French. Hamlets
and villages were furiously contended for and the Corsicans,
fighting in the country they knew best, in the familiar woods and
rocks of their own glens, caused the French disproportionate losses.
A guerilla war was still possible, as indeed it had been from the
beginning. But Paoli was profoundly discouraged. His talents
were not those of a guerilla commander and he dreaded the

miseries that such a war would impose on his fellow country-men with only the prospect of delaying the French victory as the result. From Vivario, therefore, he gave orders that the majority of the islanders were to make their peace with the French and only continue fighting for long enough to enable the most deeply compromised of their leaders to make their way to the 'other side of the mountains' or, if this were impossible, to some place on the coast where they might embark for Tuscany. He himself waited, entrenched in Vivario, until he was sure that this had been done and then he made his way to Porto-Vecchio, where, on 12th June, he embarked in an English ship which had been placed at his disposal by Admiral Smith. With him went 300 of the most distinguished of his followers. It was estimated that about 300 others made their escape at various times to Leghorn.

He advised those who remained to make their peace with the French authorities, since they were uncompromised by his rule. Not everyone obeyed his orders, of course. The French still had many bitter isolated actions on their hands before they eventually pacified the island. Indeed, some of Paoli's followers, taking to the hills and protected by the connivance of their fellow countrymen, were never conquered and their bands re-mained to greet him 20 years later when he sailed back from exile. But the majority of the Corsicans made their peace as best they could with their French conquerors. As for Paoli, when he sailed out of the bay of Ajaccio on 12th June, he was convinced that it would not be a permanent exile. He could not believe that the cause of Corsican liberty had been lost forever. Already in his mind was the resolution that he would go to England and there try and enlist aid for his defeated country.

PART II

Paoli in England

THE APOTHEOSIS OF AN ENLIGHTENED HERO

Paoli and the other refugees disembarked from the English ship at Leghorn. Paoli was determined to make his way to England, for in England, where there was widespread, wealthy and powerful support for the Corsican cause, he hoped to find some way of re-opening the struggle against the French. Indeed, he had hopes that England itself might, in a short space of time, become an open ally, for Fawkener and Menzies, Lord Pembroke and Admiral Smith, as well as Raimondo Cocchi and the network of informants that he had established in Italy, all led him to believe that the English might be on the point of actively taking up the struggle against France; he knew that Grafton's government, which had been so pusillanimous in the face of French aggression, was disordered and discredited, not only by the Corsican affair but also by its inability to deal effectively with the problems of America and Wilkes; he knew that it was moving towards its inevitable dissolution and he knew, too, in the City and in the country there was active sympathy for the Corsican cause, with men eager for an opportunity to make that sympathy effective.

But his first task was to see to the well-being of his fellow-refugees. This was not too difficult. Their arrival at Leghorn had been an occasion of almost frenetic enthusiasm. The Corsicans were widely popular in Tuscany and opportunities of employment, both in the army and in civil life, were many in those early days. Some, in the traditional Corsican fashion for refugees, retired to convents; one of these was Pasquale's brother, Clemente, who made his way to Vallombrosa. But Paoli himself, eager to continue the fight with France, stayed only long enough to make sure that most of his companions were settled before he set off for England with a few followers.

His progress through Europe was a triumphant one. In Milan, when it was learnt that he was in the town, great crowds gathered before his lodgings to cheer him. In his short stay there, he made firm and lasting friendships with the Marchése Fagnani, a distinguished Tuscan statesman, and with the poet, Verri, whose *Notturne Romani* was to be a harbinger of the Italian Romantic movement. His reception at Mantua was even more enthusiastic. Crowds cheered him wherever he went, songs were composed in his honour, and on his visiting the theatre, the whole audience stood to applaud him when he appeared in a box. It was at Mantua, too, that he made the acquaintance of Joseph II, the Emperor of Austria, who afterwards praised him as freely in public as he had been doing for some years in private (according, at least to the English Ambassador, Sir Horace Mann). In Vienna, similar scenes took place. The populace greeted him with great enthusiasm and, Joseph having shown the way, he was welcomed cordially at Court.

In Holland, Paoli was the centre, once again, of scenes of wild enthusiasm, and shortly after his arrival he was entertained by the Stadtholder at a dinner, at which it was recorded twenty-eight of the most eminent men in the States were present. He did not stay in Holland long. After a brief visit to Sir Joseph York at the Hague, in order to bring himself up-to-date with English affairs, he set sail for England and arrived at Harwich at two o'clock on 18th September 1769. His arrival with Aubanis Gentili, Gueffacci, the Baron Grothous and a retinue of humbler followers, caused a sensation. He almost immediately took the post for London, but so great was the excitement when he made a stop at Ingratestone that he decided to stay there and write to Burnaby (who seems, as Boswell later guessed, to have been his link with the British government), requesting him to find lodgings for himself and his friends in order that they might not be embarrassed on their arrival in the capital by having to look for somewhere to stay in the midst of a demonstration for the Corsican cause. It was not until the 20th that he, at last, entered London to the great enthusiasm of the people who had anticipated his arrival and who followed him, cheering wildly, to the magnificent lodgings which Burnaby had arranged for him in Old Bond Street. On the next day, Boswell visited him. The account bears repeating:

A footman who opened the door said he was not well and could not see company and made a great many difficulties.

'Stay,' said I. 'Get me a bit of paper and pen and ink, and I'll write a note to him.' His *valet de chambre* came down. Seeing something about him like what I had been used to see in Corsica, I asked him in Italian, if he was a Corsican. He answered, 'Yes Sir.' 'Oh then,' said I, 'there is no occasion to write. My name is Boswell.' No sooner had I said this then Giuseppe (for that was his name) gave a jump, catched hold of my hand and kissed it, and clapped his hand several times upon my shoulders with such a natural joy and fondness as flattered me exceedingly. Then he ran upstairs before me like an Italian harlequin, being a very little fellow, and, opening the door of the General's bedchamber, called out, 'Mr Boswell.' I heard the General give a shout before I saw him. When I entered he was in his night-gown and night-cap. He ran to me, took me all in his arms, and held me there for some time. I cannot describe my feelings on meeting him again. We sat down, and instantly were just as when we parted.

The next few days were very crowded. Boswell eagerly directed well-wishers to the General's lodgings, among the first of whom was the Duke of Queensberry. Paoli's appearance in the streets was enthusiastically cheered and reported upon sedulously by the journals. Within a few days, the King's desire to see him privately was conveyed to him and, as a result, Paoli had a very lengthy conversation with the monarch in the Queen's Palace. Paoli was eager to outline the Corsican case to as many people as he could meet and knowing that there was great enthusiasm for him in the ports, he arranged to visit them next.

But, just before he sailed, on his first visit to Portsmouth, he had been a party to one of the most famous meetings in English literature. On 10th October 1769, Boswell had taken Johnson to Paoli's lodgings to present the Doctor to Paoli. The auguries for the meeting were not auspicious. Four days before, Johnson, provoked perhaps by Boswell's unceasing praise for the Corsicans, had belaboured them unmercifully: 'Sir,' said he, 'what is all this rout about the Corsicans? They have been at war with the Genoese for upwards of twenty years, and have never yet taken their fortified towns. They might have battered down their walls and reduced them to powder in twenty years. They might have pulled the walls in pieces, and cracked the stones with their teeth in twenty years.' But on 10th October, when Johnson was presented to Paoli, all reservations vanished:

They met with a manly ease, mutually conscious of their own abilities, and of the abilities of each other. The General spoke Italian, and Dr Johnson English, and understood one another very well, with a little aid of interpretation from me, in which I compared myself to an isthmus which joins two great continents. Upon Johnson's approach, the General said, 'From what I have read of your work, Sir, and from what Mr Boswell has told me of you, I have long held you in great veneration.' The General talked of languages being formed on the particular notions and manners of a people, without knowing which, we cannot know the language. We may know the direct signification of single words; but by these no beauty of expression, no sally of genius, no wit is conveyed to the mind. All this must be by allusion to other ideas. 'Sir, (said Johnson) you talk of language, as if you had never done anything else but study it, instead of governing a nation.' The General said, '*Questo e un troppo gran complimento;*' this is too great a compliment. Johnson answered. 'I should have thought so, Sir, if I had not heard you talk.' The General asked him, what he thought of the spirit of infidelity which was so prevalent. Johnson. 'Sir, this gloom of infidelity, I hope, is only a transient cloud passing through the hemisphere, which will soon be dissipated, and the sun break forth with his usual splendour.' 'You think then, (said the General), that they will change their principles like their clothes.' Johnson. 'Why, Sir, if they bestow no more thought on principles than a dress, it must be so.' The General said, that 'a great part of the fashionable infidelity was owing to a desire of shewing courage. Men who have no opportunities of shewing it as to things in this life, take death and futurity as objects on which to display it.' Johnson. 'That is mighty foolish affectation. Fear is one of the passions of human nature, of which it is impossible to divest it. You remember that the Emperor Charles V, when he read upon the tomb-stone of a Spanish nobleman, 'Here lies one who never knew fear,' wittily said, 'Then he never snuffed a candle with his fingers.'

He talked a few words of French to the General; but finding

160

The Battle of Pontenuovo which ended Corsican independence, 1769
19th century engraving

A gold medallion struck in 1770
to commemorate Corsica's reunion with France

he did not do it with facility, he asked for pen, ink and paper and wrote the following note:

'*J'ai lu dans la geographie de Lucas de Linda un Paternoster écrit dans une langue tout à-fait differente de l'Italienne, et de toutes autres lesquelles se derivent du Latin. L'auteur l'appelle* linguam Corsicae rusticam; *elle a peut-être passé, peu à peu; mais elle a certainement prevalue autre fois dans les montagnes et dans la campagne. Le même auteur dit la même chose en parlant de Sardaigne; qu'il y a deux langues dans l'Isle, une des villes, l'autre de la campagne.*'

The General immediately informed him that the *lingua rustica* was only in Sardinia.

Dr Johnson went home with me, and drank tea till late in the night. He said, 'General Paoli, had the loftiest port of any man he had ever seen.' He denied that military men were always the best bred men. 'Perfect good breeding, he observed, consists in having no particular mark of any profession, but a general elegance of manners; whereas, in a military man, you can commonly distinguish the brand of a soldiers, *l'homme d'épée*.'

Paoli arrived at Portsmouth on 13th October 1769 and his arrival there was marked by an entry in John Wesley's diary: 'I very narrowly missed meeting the great Pascal Paoli. He landed in the dock but a very few minutes after I left the waterside. Surely He who hath been with him from his youth up hath not sent him into England for nothing. Lord, show him what is Thy will concerning him, and give him a Kingdom that cannot be moved.' Wesley's admiration of Paoli was widely shared wherever Paoli went. At the opposite extreme to Wesley, Horace Walpole, with his special knowledge and interest which dated from the time of King Theodore, had been following the Corsican struggle enthusiastically. Often in his letters he seems less concerned that Paoli might be preserved than with the piquancy that he might be preserved through the agency of Madame du Barry, the inveterate enemy of Choiseul. But his outburst, when the news of Pontenuovo reached England, seems sincere enough: 'Poor brave Paoli! – but he's not disgraced. We, that have sat still and seen him overwhelmed must answer it to History.' In between these two extremes was everywhere, and in every walk of life, great enthusiasm for the

General and the Corsicans; many felt they had a personal
stake in Corsican freedom for, since the French invasion began,
over £20,000 had been contributed for the islanders by various
enthusiasts for Corsican liberty. The fact that the English government had nothing to be proud of in its relations with Corsica
did nothing to diminish the enthusiasm for Paoli, for Grafton's
government was widely despised and Grafton himself very unpopular. The Prime Minister, flaunting Nancy Parsons in his
box at the theatre and paying far more attention to her, and to
Newmarket, than to Westminster, had roused the anger of even
such a tolerant class as the English eighteenth-century
politicians. And he was incorrigible: when taken to task for his
behaviour he sulked. While the character of the Prime Minister
invoked derision, the Ministry itself showed little ability to deal
with the thorny questions of Wilkes and America. The question
of Wilkes was the most pressing. Under the banner of 'Wilkes and
Liberty' the witty, loose-living tribune had gathered all the
forces opposed to the Crown and to the governing Whig
aristocracy. Indeed, the riots which followed in the wake of
Wilkes' agitation bid fair to split the nation into two. This, in
the course of time, was to strengthen the hand of the government, as gradually the great landlords and the wealthier merchants drew together to oppose the threat to their position. But
this division of interests came later. At the time of Paoli's arrival
the government was hard put to find supporters, and on the
other side, the middle and lower parts of the population, and
especially many of those merchants who were not of the very
first rank in the City and who had so willingly provided subscriptions for arms for Paoli, had rallied behind the ebullient
Wilkes. Wilkes was very conscious of such links. It was not for
nothing that he had given it out, on his return from France to
face trial, that he had been offered a commission in the army of
General Paoli. It was not only in England that Paoli and
Liberty were joined in men's minds. It was a measure of the
underlying unity of the libertarian movement that, even as the
American colonists had identified Wilkes with the liberty they so
greatly desired, so they identified Paoli.

In Pennsylvania one town was named after him and another
after Corsica. Throughout the colony, and especially in the west
in those territories which were to become the States of Missouri
and Texas, settlements were named either Corsica or Corsicana.

162

Years later, it was noted at least one American, an officer in the United States navy, bore the Christian name, Pascalpaoli.

Paoli then, so closely identified with the opposition to Grafton, could, if he had wished, have become a focus for this opposition. But he did not wish it. He was determined that he would not be caught up in a faction. His attitude was summed up in some words he wrote later in his exile: 'I am not English but Corsican; my sole and only political interest is the interest of Corsica; if you wish to do me a favour, if indeed you wish to establish common ground with me this is the assumption you must make. But I know how difficult it is for men to make it and how difficult it is for me to remain neutral to faction.' In pursuance of his attitude, he carefully avoided any utterance or activity at this time which would have identified him in any way with either the government or the Opposition.

But with Boswell he had no need to tread the razor edge of neutrality. Indeed, on the question of Corsica all Boswell's generosity, good nature, warm-heartedness and idealism came to the fore and provided many evidences, even before Paoli arrived in England, of how deeply the young Scotsman was committed to the Corsican cause. Paoli was what Boswell needed at intervals throughout his life – a virtuous, stable, unchanging character to which he could refer his own confused whirl of emotion and sentiment. It was as such he had portrayed Paoli to the English public, and to Europe at large, in his *Journal of a Tour to Corsica*. The book had been a terrific success and had in its wake a rash of poems praising Paoli and Liberty. Lord Lyttelton, Horace Walpole, Mrs Macaulay and David Garrick all wrote enthusiastic letters to the author, while Gray, the poet, who unkindly described it as a dialogue between a green goose and a hero, declared that Paoli was a man born 2,000 years after his time. Even Dr Johnson was enthusiastic, although his praise was typically measured : 'Your History,' he wrote to Boswell on 9th September 1769, 'is like other histories, but your Journal is in a very high degree curious and delightful.' Boswell became overnight 'Corsica' Boswell and he laboured hard to preserve the distinction. The uproar caused, in 1768, by the French attack on Paoli, and the enthusiasm which the General's heroic resistance subsequently aroused, raised Boswell's enthusiasm for the Corsicans and their General to new heights and, at the same time, excited his passion for display to

greater splendour. He was indefatigable, both in England and in
Scotland, in helping to raise subscriptions in order to send arms
and money to the Corsicans. In December 1768 had appeared
under his editorship *Essays in favour of the brave Corsicans,* in
which a whole cross-section of the community – merchants,
lawyers, financiers, politicians and patriots – all emphasised how
closely the Corsican cause was related to the welfare of Great
Britain. And, just as one side of his character was expressed in
these labours for the Corsican cause, so the other was shown, to
Horace Walpole's shrill delight, at Shakespeare's Jubilee which
took place at Stratford-on-Avon from 6th to 8th September
1769, where Boswell appeared 'in a Corsican habit, with pistols
in his belt, and a musket at his back, and on the front of his cap,
in gilt letters, these words, PAOLI AND LIBERTY'. Boswell had
written a poem for recitation for the Shakespeare celebrations
but the crowd refused to hear it, so that, resourceful as ever, he
took it with him to London and had it published in the news-
papers. A month later, Paoli himself arrived in the island and the
friendship was sealed by Johnson's acceptance and admiration
of Boswell's hero.

With friendship with Johnson came an introduction into the
literary and artistic society that surrounded him, the luminaries
of which were Sir Joshua Reynolds, Goldsmith and Burke. But,
although he was honoured and deeply grateful for such friendship and affection, Paoli's labours during the first months of his
arrival in England were essentially political ones. His aim was,
above all, to arouse enthusiasm and perhaps obtain active help
for his island: at least, to keep Corsica in the public eye until
Choiseul's aggressive policy produced, as Paoli thought it eventually must, a conflict between France and England. He adhered
scrupulously to his policy of making no distinction between
parties. His detachment was frequently remarked upon, not
always favourably, and indeed, with his attitude of friendliness
slightly mixed with reserve, he conveyed at times the impression,
ironically enough, of being less the personification of democracy
than of being a sovereign in exile. He was frequently to be
found at Court: 'I found him last week at Court,' Horace
Walpole recorded,

> and could not believe it when I was told who he was. I had
> stood close by him for some minutes, taking him for an

English, or at least a Scottish, officer. Nobody sure ever had an air so little foreign! He was dressed in scarlet and gold, and the simplicity of his whole appearance had not given me the slightest suspicion of anything remarkable in him. Afterwards in the circle, as he again stood by me, he asked me some very indifferent question, without knowing me . . . the King and Queen both took great notice of him.

Some were distressed that he accepted so readily a pension – a not unhandsome one of £1,200 a year – from the English government. But he had little choice. He had not brought much money with him from Corsica. He had with him, in England, a body of dependants, and in Italy, followers who turned to him in every emergency for funds. Moreover, he made it clear that he accepted the pension from the King as the representative of the English people and certainly not from any political party. Indeed, a letter he wrote to Burnaby and which seems, like a good many of his letters to the clergyman, to be aimed less at, than through, Burnaby, to those he represented, leaves it in no doubt that England was not his only refuge and that he was prepared to leave it should it become necessary. Of the pension he wrote:

I, confident in the security which it suggested to me, wrote to my representative in Leghorn and told him to furnish my brother with the money he had requested last November and December to assist my countrymen in Tuscany, for I had no money of my own to send him at that moment. Now, in the accounts which he has rendered to me I find both myself and Count Gentili, who also authorised payment in his name, owing considerable debts and without any possession in Leghorn by means of which we might settle those debts. I thus find myself in a situation of great embarrassment. . . . I have no funds in Tuscany, far fewer in London, where I indeed incurred considerable debts. The promise of a pension is well enough for a man who has not urgent need of it. But I am not able to live on promises. I say more: these promises are useless to me and I will have to betake myself to other expedients if I am not paid the pension promptly. Reproaches of this nature I find extremely distasteful, but I have too much confidence in the affection and the generous sensibility which has been shown towards my cause to fear appearing importunate in the matter so critical.

The other expedient which he mentions in his letter was the acceptance of a refuge at St Petersburg, which had been offered to him by one of the most celebrated of the Enlightened despots in the whole of Europe, Catherine the Great of Russia. Besides the offer of a refuge, she had written to say that he would be paid a pension of 6,000 roubles if he came. But the real attraction of the offer was the hope she held out that he might have Russian assistance, at some future time, to regain Corsica, the use of whose harbours appeared to the Russians a very desirable asset in the Mediterranean.

He certainly did not allow the pension to affect his relations with the Opposition and, indeed, he was enthusiastically welcomed by the government opponents at Oxford and Bath when he made journeys there to publicise the Corsican cause. On the other hand, if he avoided being too closely associated with the government he, at the same time, avoided the political embraces of the more furious opponents of the King, such as Mrs Macaulay (Burke's 'Republician Virago'), the attractive authoress of a Republican History of England and the sister of the most zealous of the City's Radicals, Alderman Sawbridge. He regularly attended the debates of English Parliament, committed to none by his attendance but serving, but his presence, to remind the English politicians of the continued existence of the Corsican question.

THE LONG YEARS OF EXILE

But, for all his efforts, the climacteric moment of the Corsican question in England had passed in 1768.

In one thing his informants had been right; Grafton's government, formed in the first place by Chatham, but having since shed most of the principles for which he stood, and now hoplessly discredited, was destroyed, in January 1770 by the emergence of Chatham himself from his long, dark madness. But the administration which succeeded it, headed by Lord North, although it was far more stable, was equally devoted to a policy of peace. No more capable of solving the problems that beset the country than Grafton's administration had been, it could count upon a great deal more support, for reaction had set in; the violence of the riots triggered off by Wilkes and his followers had been increasingly alarming to the propertied classes, and the continuing complaints of the American colonists increasingly irritating. North, therefore, found a great deal of support for his government. He himself – indolent, good-natured and unpretentious – was as popular with the Commons as Grafton had been unpopular; he had the further advantage that the King doted on him.

Abroad his policy was quite simple: it was that, it was the 'first duty of a Foreign Minister to preserve peace with honour'. Even so, in the face of Choiseul's ambition for France and his determination to force the issue over the question of the Falkland Islands (where France backed Spanish claims) might have made North's duty very difficult. But Louis XVI, dismayed by the implications of Choiseul's restlessness, and moved perhaps even more by the ever-present persuasions of Madame du Barry, took fright at his Minister's policy and dismissed him in December 1770. So, on both counts, Paoli's hopes of Corsican alliance being forced on England by necessity were disappointed.

Though Paoli's own hopes never wavered, the idea of Corsica

being a separate Sovereign Power, treating with England, became with the passage of time less and less of a political reality. The General drew some comfort from his visit to Scotland, in September 1771, with the Polish Ambassador, Count Burzynski. The General was everywhere treated with great affection and respect. At the great Carron Iron Foundry 'General Paoli had a peculiar pleasure in viewing the forge, where was formed the cannon and warlike stores which a society of gentlemen in Scotland sent to the aid of the brave Corsicans. They were elegantly entertained at dinner by Charles Gascoigne Esq. of the Carron Company and while they sat at table all the vessels at Carron-shore, which was just in their view, had all their flags displayed, a circumstance which led the General to speak with his usual esteem of the British hearts of oak.' But by 1772, there are unmistakable signs things had changed, both with and towards Paoli. This is noted in Boswell's *Journal* for 31st March 1772:

> Mr Johnson . . . said he thought General Paoli had lost somewhat of that grandeur in his air and manner which he had when he came first to England. The observation is just, and the fact is easily accounted for. When he first came here, he was just arrived from being at the head of a nation. Wherever he had passed, and even here, he was addressed in that high character. But after having been near three years just in the style of a private gentleman, much of the majesty of his deportment must insensibly be lost.

Just before this, on 19th March 1772, Boswell had refused an invitation to lodge at Paoli's house, partly on the grounds that Paoli already had one lodger, Count Gentili, with him, and partly because it might give the Grub-Street writers an opportunity for low abuse of the General, on the ground that he was pensioned by British generosity, yet nevertheless kept a Scotsman for nothing in his house. Three years later, in 1775, Boswell reports outspoken criticism of the General when he was dining at the house of the bookseller Edward Dilly. A clergyman there criticised Paoli for doing nothing but eat English beef. Boswell defended him: 'He is a game-cock, ready to fight wherever there is a Main. In the meantime he must be fed – George III, feeder.' In the natural course of things Corsica had not remained in the forefront of fashion for long. Paoli seems soon to have lost what hold he had on popular memory. On 19th March 1772, Boswell reports: 'I asked a chairman which was General Paoli's. "What", said he, "the General who is married to Lady – – ?" (I did not hear what). "No," said his companion, "the foreign gentleman." So little is the great Paoli known to some.'

But if with the passage of the years he faded from the memory of many and became a subject of criticism for some, yet those who knew him most intimately found their admiration, respect and affection increased manifold the better they knew him. When he realised the English were not likely to dispute the French control of his island, he did not go overmuch into Society and Boswell found that Paoli's coach was at his disposal on most days. He lived quietly with his Corsican dependants and servants at his lodgings, first in Old Bond Street, then in Albermarle Street and Jermyn Street. But he was certainly no recluse. He mixed freely with the literary and artistic society which revolved around Johnson. Both Reynolds and Goldsmith esteemed him and valued his friendship. Comparatively wealthy by virtue of his pension, good-mannered, dignified, kindly, well-read in the classics, and moving with a certain English reserve, he fitted easily into eighteenth-century society. In Italian or French, which he spoke in preference to English he could, when the occasion arrived, turn a pretty compliment : as, for instance, when, protecting Goldsmith from Boswell's teasing over *She Stoops to Conquer* he said in French that 'Goldsmith's talent is as carelessly profuse with its treasures as the cornucopian sea' – a comment which drew a delightful exclamation from the playwright. It is in the writings of Boswell, of course, both in the *Life of Johnson* and in the *Journals*, that he appears most frequently in these years: often it is very characteristically as when, for instance, he rebuked Johnson for his quotation from Dryden:

> For colleges on bounteous Kings depend,
> And never rebel was to Arts a friend,

by pointing out that successful rebels might patronise the arts and retorting to Goldsmith's comment that in England there is no such phrase as a 'happy rebel': 'But you have the thing, have you not?'; or when his Rousseauish assumption received rather a mauling at the hands of Dr Johnson:

JOHNSON. 'Sir, it is so far from being natural for a man and woman to live in a state of marriage, that we find all the motives which they have for remaining in that connection, and the restraints which civilised society imposes to prevent separation, are hardly sufficient to keep them together.' The General said that, in a state of nature a man and a woman uniting together would form a strong and constant affection, by the mutual pleasure each would receive; and that the same causes of dissention would not arise between them, as occur between husband and wife in a civilised state.

JOHNSON. 'Sir, they would have dissentions enough, though of another kind. One would choose to go a hunting, when the other would choose to go a fishing; and so they would part. Besides, Sir, a savage man and a savage woman meet by chance; and when the man sees another woman that pleases him better, he will leave the first'.

Or, on the same occasion as the former, when the General in opposition to Dr Johnson, but very much in accordance with his Enlightened principles, maintained that there was no beauty independent of utility.

There are also some highly uncharacteristic comments recorded; when for instance the earnest reader and the founder of Corsica's university argued against the art of printing (which had hurt learning by disseminating idle writings) and the diffusion of knowledge.

But in spite of Boswell's affection for Paoli, Boswell is an artist and his portrait of Paoli, like his portrait of Johnson, is an artistic composition, even when sketched in the rough form of a Journal. Paoli becomes in contradistinction to Boswell's plunges into the depths and heady exhilarations on the heights, a pillar of unshakeable virtue and integrity, his humanity emphasised by the slightly ridiculous air in which he sometimes appears as a foil to Johnson.

Another account of him, one which shows his warmth and humanity in a new light and which rescues his tone of voice for a moment from the formal diction of the eighteenth century is given in Fanny Burney's letter to Mr Crisp of 15th October 1782.

You would have been much pleased, I am sure, by meeting with General Paoli, who spent the day there, and was extremely communicative and agreeable. I had seen him in large companies, but was never made known to him before; nevertheless, he conversed with me as if well acquainted not only with myself, but my connections, – inquiring of me when I had last seen Mrs Montagu? And calling Sir Joshua Reynolds, when he spoke of him, my friend. He is a very pleasing man, tall and genteel in his person, remarkably well bred and very mild and soft in his manners.

I will try to give you a little specimen of his conversation, because I know you love to hear particulars of all out-of-the-way persons. His English is blundering, but not unpretty. Speaking of his first acquaintance with Mr Boswell,

'He came,' he said, 'to my country, and he fetched me some letter of recommending him; but I was of the belief he might be an imposter, and I supposed, in my minte, he was an espy; for I look away from him, and in a moment I look to him again, and I behold his tablets. Oh! he was to the work of writing down all I say! Indeed I was angry. But soon I discover he was no imposter and no espy; and I only find I was myself the monster he had come to discern. Oh, – is a very good man; I love him indeed; so cheerful! so gay! so pleasant! but at the first, oh I was indeed angry.'

After this, he told us a story of an expectation he had of being robbed, and of the protection he found from a very large dog that he is very fond of.

'I walk out,' he said, 'in the night; I go towards the field; I behold a man – oh, ugly one! I proceed – he follow; I go on – he address me, 'You have one dog,' he says; 'is he fiery?' 'Yes,' reply I, 'he can bite.' 'I would not attack in the night,' says he, 'a house to have such dog in it.' Then I conclude he was a breaker; so I turn to him – oh, very rough! not gentle – and I say, very fierce, 'He shall destroy you, if you are ten!'

Afterwards, speaking of the Irish giant, who is now shown in town, he said, 'He is so large I am as a baby! I look at him – oh! I find myself so little as a child! Indeed, my indignation it rises when I see him hold up his hand so high. I am as nothing; and I find myself in the power of a man who fetches from me half a crown.'

This language, which is all spoke very pompously by him, sounds comical from himself, though I know not how it may read.

The liking and respect that Fanny Burney shows for Paoli was widely shared, and by all manner of men. Paoli was as welcome at Wilton, the great house of the sophisticated, cultured, amoral Lord Pembroke as he was among the scholars of the Royal Society who showed their respect for him by electing him to membership on 3rd March 1774. This circle of distinguished friends and acquaintances was very large; it included Johan Christian Bach, the composer; Zoffany and Cipriani the painters; Bartolozzi the engraver and Carlini the sculptor. He was a prominent member of the fashionable Masonic Lodge of the Nine Muses, which numbered among its members some of the most distinguished Italians in London, including the Venetian Ambassador and the Chevalier Ruspini who was famous both for his pioneering studies in dentistry and his philanthropy.

Glancing references to the General occur again and again in the diaries and memoirs of the age: visiting Sir Thomas Wynn in Wales; arousing, during the winter of 1782, the interest, perhaps even the passion, of Hannah More; spending an evening drinking with Fox, Sheridan and the sculptor Nollekins; taking a part in rout and ball.

The friendship and recognition that Paoli found in England was of great assistance to him in helping him to bear his exile easily. Certainly, he had lost the two things which mattered most to him in life: his country and his ability to put his Enlightened principles into practice. Religion in the shape of the Church, the chief solace of so many of his countrymen in their exile, appears to have sat as easily on him in England as John Stewart, Grafton's emissary in 1768, said it had in Corsica. He performed the duties of a Catholic conscientiously at the Polish Ambassador's Chapel or at the Sardinian Minister's Chapel in Lincoln's Inn Fields. But a letter of 1st August 1787 shows that his attitude towards the unenlightened aspects of the Catholic Church had not softened and, indeed, that he saw more than a little virtue in countries that were nominally Protestant: 'The countryside of France is cultivated but the masses there have no return from their labours. There are more cooking pots and kitchen spits in England, Switzerland and Holland than in all the rest of Europe. In these places you do not see a ragged man or an emaciated countenance. The miracles of Liberty are more frequent, more grand and more useful than those of Saint Anthony of Padua.' But in spite of the fact that he had established religious toleration (and what for all intents and purposes was an Erastian Church in Corsica) he had no undue respect for the state of religion in England; as is evidenced by his rather tart remark, when Boswell and Johnson dined with him on 31st March 1772, that a great variety of oaths was to be expected among a people with a great variety of religions.

Corsica was never far from his thoughts; he kept up a constant correspondence with, and was extremely generous with financial aid to, the Corsican exiles in Leghorn and he drew other information about Corsica and the European scene from a variety of correspondents in various countries. When he returned to Corsica, on the outbreak of the Revolution, he showed himself, to the surprise of many, very well informed about the events that occured in the island during his absence.

Like all political exiles, he was subject to fits of irrational enthusiasm and of unfounded hopes. Although he does not appear to have been implicated in the planning of the Great Rising of 1774, he followed its rapid progress with great attention; in 1776, as Boswell reports, he was full of mysterious hints about great events which were taking place in Corsica, but nothing came of them.

The event that was to return Paoli in triumph to the island was not the result of an English alliance, nor was it due, in the first instance at least, to the Corsican rebels; it was the outbreak of the French Revolution when those Enlightened principles which he had advocated all his life seemed to have triumphed and the world, for a moment, seemed about to be made new. Paoli had not foreseen the French Revolution. When it came, it was a bolt from the blue but it did not take him long to realise its great significance for Corsica. For once the influence of the Revolution had reached the island, it became clear that only the return of Paoli himself was a guarantee of peace.

CORSICA WITHOUT PAOLI
1769-1789

By 1789, Corsica, and more particularly its government, had altered a great deal since Paoli had first sailed into exile, for the French were, in intention at least, very different masters from the Genoese. From the conquest to the Revolution the French administrators in Paris and in the island sought, in the main, to make Corsica a model state within the framework of the *ancien régime*. Marbeuf, who stayed in the island to command the French troops after the conquest and in 1772 became the commander-in-chief there, made it plain from the first that he intended all French scores against particular Corsicans to be forgotten and that he would welcome without reservation any Corsican who was now willing to co-operate with the French authorities. In the first months of his rule he showed himself friendly, indeed, affable and forgiving. His attitude was well illustrated by the anecdote (which he took care to have widely circulated) of Domenici de Luri, an inhabitant of Capo Corso, who had hidden Pasqualini, one of Paoli's unrepentant guerillas, in his house while the French troops were searching for him. When Domenici was brought before Marbeuf the French general demanded to know why he had sheltered a rebel. When Domenici answered boldly that he would never close his door to anyone who demanded asylum of him, Marbeuf, instead of imprisoning him, shook him warmly by the hand and said loudly that Corsica could be proud of such men.

On the other hand, honours were showered on those Corsicans who had supported the French in the conflict with Paoli. Buttafuoco was made brigadier, count and inspector of the Corsican Provincial Regiment, and, at the same time, he received the monopoly of fishing in the Etang de Bigulia, together with the exclusive right of hunting in his own glen. Ottavio Colonna d'Istria was likewise made a count. Petriconi was made a lieutenant-colonel of the Corsican Legion and

Raffaello Casabianca a lieutenant-colonel of the Provincial Corsican Regiment, while others were liberally rewarded with money and distinctions.

But these were in the minority. The French hoped to obtain widespread Corsican support in the long term by the organisation of a society based on the French model and drawing its inspiration from France. Corsica, after the conquest, was made a *pays d'Etat,* which meant that it was granted a measure of self-government in the shape of its own Estates which were to meet whenever there was a necessity for them to meet. Which, of course, in practice, meant very infrequently. But the privilege, if unimportant in practice, was very important as a symbol of the special status which the island was meant to enjoy. A *pays d'Etat* had to have a social organisation in order to function. The French were shrewd enough not to risk a head-on clash with the clan chieftains and the clergy. They planned to mould Corsican society to a French shape by attempting to create an aristocracy, a clergy and a third Estate on the French pattern.

The Corsican nobility thus created was decreed to consist of four Orders – proved, avowed, created and foreign. The proved were those who could produce documentary evidence of the grant of their title, which to count must have been in existence for at least two hundred years. The avowed were those who could produce a certificate on which twelve noblemen had declared that the applicant was himself noble. The created nobility consisted of those whom the French themselves had ennobled, and the foreign nobility were those whose titles had been granted by other sovereigns. The documents of the proved nobility were not scrutinised too closely but, even so, and not unnaturally, as Paoli's hard-core supporters bitterly remarked, the avowed nobility soon outnumbered all the other classes. To show what nobility meant in political terms the new nobility was given the right to send twenty-three members to the Estates.

But to grant the shadow of political power was not the only, and certainly not the main, way in which the French hoped to secure the loyalty of the new nobility. Great emphasis was placed on education. The religious teaching orders set up schools on the island, staffed by Frenchmen, and, as a further inducement to the Corsicans to place their children's culture in the hands of their new rulers, places were provided for fifty children in the schools at Paris. Noble families might send their children in the course of time to the Mazarin College, to a Seminary at Aix, to Saint-Cyr or to the Royal Military Schools and they were encouraged to do this by example and by exhortation. So, incidentally, the way was paved for the education of France's most brilliant and successful soldier. It was arranged, too, that Corsican girls of noble family might be sent to French homes on the mainland in order to acquire French manners and polish; in Corsica itself Marbeuf encouraged first his mistress and later his wife to hold open house for the ladies of Corsican aristocratic families so that they might come to model themselves, sartorially at least, on the French.

As the French example demanded, it was decreed that the clergy, too, would send twenty-three members to the Estates. These consisted of the five bishops of the island and eighteen higher clergy who were elected by the appropriate ecclesiastical body. The monks on the island were allowed to vote for their representatives but not to be candidates for election; the French had little affection for them for they remembered clearly how enthusiastically the monks had supported Paoli and they were all too well aware that the monasteries still kept the General's memory green. De Vaux, in the early days of the occupation, irritated by the number of times the springs of opposition and conspiracy went underground in the vicinity of a monastery, openly called the monks 'leeches' and said that, for men who had renounced the world, they still retained an uncommonly lively interest in its doings.

Thought was taken, too, for the Third Estate. Those humbler Corsicans who sought a release for their energies and a way to fame and honour were permitted to enlist in any of the regiments of France. They also had their own regiment in the *Royal Corse* and, after the dissolution of the *Royal Corse* in 1778, in two battalions of Corsican light infantry. There were also two Corsican Provincial Regiments which they could join. All of which showed that the French had well learnt the traditional Genoese tactic of drawing off hot blood by encouraging the young men to take a musket and go to the wars.

The civil constitution for the island was designed to appease those who, for whatever reason, stayed behind. It did not deviate too radically from Paoli's system of government. The village was the basic element in which the *Podesta* and two Fathers of the Commune were responsible for the local administration and the maintenance of public order. The electorate consisted of all the heads of families who had reached the age of twenty-five years. Each glen had its own administration presided over by the *Podestat Major*, who was chosen from among the wealthiest and most distinguished men of his glen (whenever possible of course a clan chieftain) and the glens formed groups from which provinces were created, each province being supervised by an Inspector drawn from the nobility.

Most of the money needed to bring about this reorganisation and the administrative cost of maintaining it came from France. The French indeed took great care to have their régime associated with concessions: the taxes imposed by the French on the Corsicans after the conquest were meant to be reassuringly light. The French were very conscious of their forbearance and in illustration of this there is a well-known Corsican story. Just before the French Revolution a French soldier is represented as having said to a Corsican shepherd: 'Why is the island so unquiet? We have treated you well. In the time of your Paoli you would have paid double what you pay now.' To which the shepherd replied, 'Yes that is true, but we gave it to Paoli, you take it from us.'

The French had reason to wonder, for the island was indeed unquiet throughout all the twenty years of French rule; the shepherd's retort summed up why, in a sentence. The Corsicans regarded themselves, not as a conquered people, but as a defeated nation. The French attempt at a new model of society had a limited success, and that success only with a very few. The Corsicans of the generation after Paoli grew up with a simple attitude to the conquest, an attitude learnt somewhat before and rather better than their catechism: their clan system had been slighted, their chosen leader driven into exile, their liberty lost. They and their elders showed their resentment in many ways, but the factor common to all was distaste for, and a resentment of, everything French. More than one Frenchman garrisoned in the island was to comment indignantly in his letters home on the sullen hostility with which the Corsicans regarded the French in spite of all French attempts at friendliness. The resistance began with pinpricks. The French King's birthday was pointedly ignored by the islanders; fêtes in honour of St Louis met the same fate (for, after all, Louis was a French saint). When Corsican ships were out of sight of the mainland they ran up at their mast-head the old flag, bearing the head of a Moor, but now the head had bandaged eyes, symbolising that Corsica's emblem had no wish to look upon Corsica's bondage.

At first there were few disturbances, but as the French proceeded with the reorganisation of government and as their supporters and nominees began to take over the positions of authority from the Corsican chiefs the islanders' hostility became more and more marked. All this time, groups of armed men, the remnants of Paoli's regiments, still roamed the hills obtaining a great deal of support from the Corsican villages, scattering and dispersing like smoke when the French mounted operations against them. Trouble soon took a familiar shape for the garrisons : a murder would be reported from a village, a French detachment would make its way to the scene of the crime as quickly as possible. All they ever met with was silence and unseeing eyes. No one had seen the crime committed, no one could be found to talk. The French were never quite sure whether these attacks were due to the complicated operation of the vendetta or to secret plots against their rule; they were never quite certain whether the frequently blamed bandits were real or imaginary. They noted grimly that all too often it was a suspected sympathiser who was cut down.

Enmeshed in the dark, sullen villages the nerves of the French troops and commanders became more and more frayed as the months wore on. The deterioration of the relations between the two peoples may be traced from the progress of the penal legislation of the French.

The French began with the intention of being not only conciliatory but firm. In May 1769, a law was passed forbidding any Corsican to carry arms and ordering all citizens to deliver their arms to depots which were specially set up to receive them. The response was not encouraging and, in May 1770, new legislation was passed against the carrying of arms. In August 1771, as opposition grew, harsh legislation was passed against anyone manufacturing, selling or possessing a dagger or a pointed knife. Yet still attacks on French soldiers continued and outside the village a French soldier on his own took his life in his hands. In June 1770, more penal legislation was passed and any Corsican found guilty of an attack on a French soldier was automatically stigmatised a bandit and could be hung from the nearest tree without any form of trial. In September 1770, in an attempt to eliminate some of the more obvious centres of opposition, the families of those Corsicans who had gone into exile with Paoli were deported. On 20th April 1771, it was decreed that any person who had given help to the bandits, or who had any contact with them or who had even written to a Corsican exile was to be immediately arrested and imprisoned. On 12th May 1771, the *Podestat Majors* were provided with very detailed instructions: they were to enter into the closest collaboration with the French troops; they were to report any suspicious movements immediately and they were to provide lists of all those in their villages whom they suspected of being disaffected; they were to make known to the shepherds that the French would regard very seriously the lighting of any fires when French troops were in their vicinity, or indeed any other action which could be constructed as a signal to the bandits lurking in the hills.

Yet still the attacks on the French went on and in August 1772, the French resorted to the most Draconian measures: all Corsicans were to be enrolled in the village where they lived and no Corsican was to absent himself from his village without specific permission from the French authorities; shepherds and other itinerants were to be enrolled on a parish register and the parish authorities were to be responsible for knowledge of their whereabouts at any particular time; if any Corsican left his village without permission, and had not returned within a month he was to be registered and proclaimed a fugitive; if he had not returned at the end of six months he was to be declared a criminal and all his goods and chattels were to be sold with the proceeds given to charity. Four territorial Juntas were set up in which Corsican Commissioners were instructed to co-operate with French troops in the maintenance of peace and order and a force of mounted police which was to ride immediately to the scene of any trouble, was established at Bastia. Regulations against rebels were made even more savage. Any political assassin, anyone found to be involved in an ambush was to be broken on the wheel and if anyone was found guilty of pursuing a vendetta, no matter on what pretext, his house was to be burnt to the ground and all his posterity debarred from any public office.

In 1774, the pressure which had been building up for some time under the weight of this legislation suddenly exploded the island into revolt. The history of the revolt was obscure and the amount of the planning that went into it uncertain. It seems certain that Paoli had no part in whatever planning there was, but it was his name that was used as the inspiration and the rallying cry of the islanders. Pasqualini, that Pasqualini who had been protected by Domenici, was the prime mover in the revolt and the acknowledged leader once it was under way. Appearing in the Niolo he, in a few days, had gathered to him a little army. In a short while the whole island was aflame. Many of the Corsicans had arms hidden away; and more arms were obtained from the French garrisons they rapidly overran. But even when they had only scythes and spades with which to attack the French the Corsicans were brought out by the mere utterance of Paoli's name.

Having possessed himself of the glen of the Niolo, Pasqualini led his army through the passes of the mountains on to the eastern plain and thence to Aleria. As he went, so men swarmed in to join him from every village and glen in his path. What he intended to do in Aleria was uncertain. It seems that he expected to hold it as a base to which reinforcements might be sent from Italy. But the speed with which the French reacted destroyed any hope he might have had of outside help.

For the French were not taken by surprise. They had long expected that some concerted opposition to their rule would be organised and their forces rallied quickly. A brigadier, Sionville, marched out in force from Bastia a few days after the taking of Aleria and, without much difficulty, led his army along the eastern plain to the siege of the tiny fortress. Pasqualini, seeing the force arraigned against him and unsupported by any help from the sea, decided that his cause was lost and took ship for Italy. He left in the nick of time, for Sionville, on being reinforced, stormed and overran the fortress.

The aftermath was terrible. Sionville spent some weeks gathering information about those who had supported Pasqualini. He began an ugly and bloody progress backwards over the line of the rebels' march. There was no attempt at justice. In every village his troops entered, men were dragged out of their habitations; 'that looks a good branch for three or four,' he would say and up on the branches of the nearest chestnut would go three or four of his captives. But what was so hideous about his vengeance, and remained so long in Corsican popular memory, was the degree to which it was pursued. He had been invested with full powers to quell the rebellion; he shamelessly and cynically abused them. Since many of the rebels had taken to the hills and the woods before his arrival, he found at his drum-head tribunals that his quota of victims in each village was disappointingly small, and he accordingly seized upon and hanged any relatives of the rebels he could find. No one, even to the second degree of cousinhood, was safe; even a similarity of names could be a death warrant. Nor did he stop at persons. Vines were grubbed up, olives were cut down and the houses of the proscribed and their kin were razed to the ground. To increase the number of his victims he had recourse to trickery. He caused the news to be spread that he held many hostages for each rebel, but that he would spare them if the rebels returned from their hiding places and gave themselves up. He promised in these cases the rebels would be sent into exile and no further action would be taken against them or their kindred. To those who surrendered, however, he did not keep his word. Some were strangled on the spot, others were sent to rot in the dungeons at Toulon. His cynicism, brutality and arbitrariness sunk deep into Corsican consciousness; twenty years later, villagers would excuse their unrelenting hatred of the French by telling Paoli of the horrors inflicted by the march of the brigadier.

Narbonne-Fritzlar was hated almost as much as Sionville. He was responsible for the government of the island from August 1774 to May 1755 during a visit of Marbeuf to Paris and he aspired to win a reputation for himself by governing Corsica ruthlessly during Marbeuf's absence. His year of office was a smoky, bloody year, full of trampling troops, savage examples, blazing cabins and files of prisoners passing through the streets of Bastia to embark on ships which took them to a loathsome imprisonment in the great tower of Toulon.

In spite of Marbeuf's unpopularity the Corsicans were glad of his return. He might show himself arbitrary and unjust, but at least he was capable and could, on occasion, display charm and generosity as readers of Boswell who remember his appearance in the pages of the Corsican Journal will know. Indeed, there were some things that could be said to explain, if not to excuse, his all too frequent outbreaks of pride and vanity. He had begun his rule with good intentions and a pacific policy towards Corsica and the progressive collapse of good relations between Corsicans

and French had become for him a personal tragedy; the em-
bitterment of his nature was deepened by his being pent up in
Bastia (where alone he was safe) and entrained in the quarrels
and intrigues of his bold and domineering mistress, Madame de
Varese. His misery was increased by struggles to maintain his
position, for from 1775 until his death he had to contend not
only with the Corsicans, towards whom, at the beginning of his
régime, he had made so many fruitless overtures, but also with
constant intriguing against him at the Court of Versailles. Whoever aimed to injure the reputation of Marbeuf at Versailles
had much material ready at hand, for he could easily draw on the
fund of Corsican stories and a cloud of Corsican witnesses; both
were zealously deployed by his enemies. However, he had his
own friends and his own channels of influence at Court and he
beat off all the attempts to replace him that were launched in
his period of government.

The Corsicans, of course, had no wish or desire to make
allowances for his personal difficulties. Coldly, and with no
attempt at extenuation, they recorded his injustices, his follies,
his vanity and his pride. Foremost among the injustices for
which he was responsible, and for which he became infamous,
was the notorious condemnation to the galleys of Giacomo Pietro
Abbatucci, Paoli's former lieutenant in the *Oltremonti*. He had
fought on in 1769 until Paoli sailed for Leghorn and then
surrendered to the French. Amnestied, he had joined the
Provincial Corsican Regiment and soon became a lieutenant-
general. The condemnation of Abbatucci was very typical of
Marbeuf's splenetic reactions. The crime of which Abbatucci
was accused was that he had suborned two witnesses in a trial,
but the actions for which, in reality, Marbeuf condemned him
were that even though he served as lieutenant-colonel in the
French forces, he had retained the respect and liking of even the
most intransigent of the Corsicans by his moderation and his
good sense and, in addition, the most damaging crime
of all in Marbeuf's eyes, that he was suspected to be the author
of a pamphlet which arraigned Marbeuf's government.

Among the follies which were most often recounted as evidences of Marbeuf's pride, vanity and bad judgment were the
attempts he made to establish foreign colonies in Corsica. At
Poretto, he attempted to found a colony of German Lorrainers,
and at Chiavari and at Galeria he tried, most unwisely of all, to

182

settle colonies of Genoese. The islanders, with their national pride already raw, were infuriated by these attempts to turn foreigners into Corsicans. These colonies had very little hope of survival; surrounded by hostile Corsicans and composed of colonists who were ignorant, both of the climate and the crops of Corsica, the odds were heavily weighted against them from the day of their foundation. Only Marbeuf was surprised when they soon collapsed miserably. Only at Cargese, where in 1774 he established those Corsican Greeks who for so many years had been refugees in Ajaccio, was he successful.

If Marbeuf had any illusions about his standing with the Corsicans they were sharply dispelled when a sycophantic proposal to erect his statue in the square at Bastia nearly caused another uprising. That the dislike was not short-lived was amply demonstrated when, on the outbreak of the Revolution, one of the first acts of the citizens of Bastia was to dash into the cathedral to smash into pieces with their hammers the marble tomb of their former master.

Marbeuf was succeeded on his death in 1784 by the Vicomte de Barrin. Barrin was a good-natured, kindly, well-meaning man who had a great respect for Paoli. He himself was one of the Enlightened nobility and passed easily in the course of time into the service of the Revolutionary governments. The years of his rule in Corsica, if they did nothing to alleviate the resentment of the Corsicans towards the French did nothing to increase it either. His period of rule was not without disturbances, but it was nevertheless, compared with the last years of Marbeuf's rule, a time of relative tranquillity. But the calm remained a menacing calm until the Revolution came to set a torch to the powder keg.

Yet there is still something to be accounted for when trying to assess why the French had such scant success in coming to terms with the Corsicans. For, as has been said, the rule of the French in the twenty years from 1769 to 1789 was intended by the statesmen at Paris to be a just one. And, if the loss of liberty was the factor which, as both the French and the Corsicans agreed, caused Corsican opposition, nevertheless it is a fairly common observation that men can be reconciled even to the loss of liberty and to labour for an alien master, in the event or even in the hope of their own personal gain. Why then, given the fact that the French were obviously militarily masters of the island and seemed likely to remain so and that their policy was intended to be a generous and conciliatory one, did the situation in the island deteriorate so badly? And why were so relatively few Corsicans loyal to the French cause when the testing time came? The answer almost certainly lies in the inability of the administrators in Paris to have their intentions intelligently carried out in Corsica. Or rather in the corruption and inefficiency which was inherent in the machinery of the *ancien régime*.

Paoli, who kept a close watch on affairs in Corsica through his numerous informants, summed up the situation of the Corsicans very succintly in some comments he made just before the Revolution: 'What has depressed their spirits beyond all else is clear,' he wrote of his fellow countrymen. 'When they were deprived of the pleasure of considering and contributing to the common good, when they no longer saw any connection between their own and the general interest, when they saw all the most patriotic honourable and inspiring labours monopolised by Frenchmen whose only talent consisted in being able to add up figures and write letters, then their souls knew final despair.' As usual, where the Corsicans were concerned, he made a shrewd judgement. For the Corsicans were in practice, in spite of all the French government's intentions and plans, excluded from everything that concerned the management of the welfare of the island.

Controlled at first by the Ministry of War, Corsica was, in 1773, placed for financial matters under the control of the Abbé Terany, the Controller-General, who thus became completely responsible for the financial administration of the whole island. He had, it is true, to pay the expenses of the military, but once this was done he had complete control of all civil finances. His agents, reckoned among the blackest of all the island's oppressors were two Lorrainers, the Coster brothers. The brothers prudently remained at Versailles, but they sent into the island as their representatives a horde of relatives and clients who battened ruthlessly on the Corsican economy. Without the approval of the Coster brothers few had a chance of obtaining employment in the government service, and so few Corsicans did in fact penetrate into the administration that it became a common Corsican jibe that to obtain office under the French it was necessary to come from Lorraine or be related to a Lorrainer. The reign of the Costers indeed gave rise to a whole set of sour Corsican jibes, the one which most frequently found its way into print being that

French investment in the island was like a tennis ball, which the agents of the Costers volleyed back to France without it ever having touched the ground.

No matter what the statesmen at Versailles might decree, or Marbeuf advise, or the wiser of his administrators practise the fact remained that the greater part of the French civil administration in the island professed a contempt for all things Corsican as rude, rustic and uncivilised. Almost everything that they used was imported from France : their dress, their drink, their food, even their furniture in a country which abounded in trees and whose craftsmen, if their work was rough, were intelligent and open to instruction.

The failure of the French to develop the island's resources was, Paoli considered, one of the most damaging criticisms which could be made of them, and again, this was the fault of the endemic corruption rather than the result of a lack of thought. It was one thing to legislate at Versailles, another to make the legislation fruitful in Corsica: to quote one example among many – although there was an Inspector of Agriculture he did nothing but draw his pay. Paoli said, that in spite of the Inspector's post, the Corsicans during the twenty years of French rule received no benefits at all from the knowledge and skills in agriculture and husbandry which the French had at their disposal; they were given no advice at all on the cultivation of their crops, on the grafting of fruit trees, on the development of irrigation, on the provision of pasture land, on the importation of new strains of sheep. In 1789 Paoli noted that they had neither ploughs nor stables nor dairies.

The development of their vineyards and the production of wine, always one of Paoli's most cherished objectives and the subject of some of his most striking economic successes, were neglected. Not only was no help given to the development of the island's resources but French customs dues as relatively heavy as their taxes were light, crippled Corsican attempts to send what surplus they had for export to the Italian mainland. What was even worse was that the French suppressed the one industry which continued to flourish. The Corsican coral fisheries, which in the heyday of Paoli's administration had numbered some 140 craft and employed over 1,000 men, were forbidden to fish by order of the French Royal African Company which feared their competition.

Nor did the Corsicans receive any benefit from the skills of French craftsmen and engineers. Some public works were indeed carried out in the island: two main roads were built, one from Bastia to San Fiorenzo, another from Bastia to Corte; but both these roads were badly constructed and the one to Corte badly aligned. Moreover, their construction highlighted the fact that the French did nothing at all with the other roads of the island so that communication by road, which Paoli in spite of his other labours had somewhat improved before 1768, became as bad as ever it had been in Corsican history, and the Corsicans had to make their way from village to village in winter by their old tracks across the hills and mountains. As for the other public works undertaken in the towns by the French, they were executed by a swarm of *entrepreneurs* whom the Corsicans likened to a swarm of locusts. Few of them had experience in what they undertook and all had obtained their position by influence. Wig-makers ex-soldiers and farm bailiffs, many of them of very doubtful financial standing, hastened to Corsica after the conquest pellmell, to make or recoup their fortunes. The Corsicans noted cynically that a new and badly-constructed fountain in Ajaccio had cost twenty-four thousand *livres,* while the old one which it had replaced cost eleven thousand *livres* and held water. The Hôtel de Ville at Ajaccio was extended; the Ajaccio masons commented sardonically that the *entrepreneur* who undertook the work had been paid at least three times the amount which the most rapacious Corsican workmen would have asked. The list of follies was very long. In various parts of the island plant nurseries were created. But little care was given to their management and once more it became the common joke throughout the island that the French were paying high rates for brambles. A wall was built around Corte which enclosed a great deal of ground reserved for future building, but the future building never materialised. It was no wonder that the Corsicans treated the oft-repeated French complaint that the island cost the French Crown a great deal of money with ribaldry.

What caused them less amusement was the French introduction of the system of monopolies. The right of buying and slaughtering cattle granted to one monopolist sent the price of meat in Bastia rocketing to eight *sols* the pound. To peasants who complained that they had to sell their cattle too cheaply, a monopolist retorted coolly that he had set himself the target of obtaining a thousand *livres* a year and could not be bothered with questions of cheap or dear. At Ajaccio, on another occasion, a monopolist cornered the corn and the chestnut crops and in years of scarcity ransomed the population. In one year when the harvest failed, some monopolists bought barge-loads of grain at Leghorn, but were swindled by the sellers who provided them with only the sweepings of the granaries. Nevertheless, the monopolists used their powers to force a sale on those Corsicans who lived in the interior, extracting from them the promise that they would repay their borrowings in kind at the next harvest. At the next harvest, however, with their own agents managing the accounts, the monopolists managed to secure something like a crop and a quarter of good corn from the indignant farmers.

But what caused the Corsicans more anger than perhaps any other failure of the French government of the island was the malfunction of justice. Paoli had long ago said that if anyone wished to govern the island he must convince the Corsicans of the impartiality of the judges. Marbeuf himself said that if a Corsican felt himself guilty he rarely complained of the severity of the penalty exacted. But justice on the island under the French was slow, costly and uncertain. The action of the Juntas overriding the courts was onerous and oppressive. The Supreme Council of the island was staffed by men who inspired neither respect nor confidence. Many of them were not legally qualified nor had they any legal experience. To the Corsicans, whom Paoli had taught to respect and honour the law-giver as being one of the noblest of mankind, the French law officers appeared to be an incompetent and even dangerous crew.

PART III

The Hero's Return

THE OUTBREAK OF THE FRENCH
REVOLUTION IN CORSICA

Early in April 1789, the Vicomte de Barrin, as Governor of
Corsica, received instructions from Versailles dated 22nd March,
to assemble the three Estates of the island for the purpose of
electing representatives to the Estates General. Corsica was to
have four representatives, one for the clergy, one for the
nobility and two for the Third Estate. Almost immediately the
Estates, which whatever they represented in France, represented
in Corsica acceptance of, or covert hostility to, French rule, split
into two camps. One, the nobility, elected Buttafuoco, the head
of the anti-Paolists on the island and the soul of French collaboration, as its representative. The other, composed of the
clergy and the Third Estate, elected three representatives, the
Abbé Peretti, Colonna Cesari and Saliceti; none of these had
participated in the affairs of the island formerly. Peretti was the
Vicar-General of Aleria; Saliceti was a lawyer and assessor of a
tribunal at Sartene; Colonna Cesari, a captain in the Provincial
Corsican Regiment, had the most important qualification –
he was a friend of Paoli.

Once in Paris the Deputies regrouped themselves in a slightly
different way. Buttafuoco naturally luxuriated in the circles
of the aristocracy at the Châtelet, at Cazales and Espréméril.
Saliceti and Cesari mixed with the humbler and more radical
Deputies. But the Abbé Peretti, by virtue of his office, found that
he was entitled to a place among the high clergy of the *ancien
régime* and he accepted his due very willingly, all the more so
since it was pleasant and had very little connection with the sort
of life he had known in Corsica.

The defection of the Abbé Peretti confused many of the
clergy in the island, for in Corsica the interests of the different
divisions of Society which existed in France had, in spite of all
the French efforts, no meaning. In the island there was a single
division – those who had done well out of the French occupation

and those who, through principle or lack of opportunity, had not. The defection was, however, symptomatic, for once Corsicans had dwelt for a time in metropolitan France of the Revolution they learned how to regroup themselves in the French manner and to identify themselves with the mainlanders. The criss-cross pattern which ensued was to produce in the future very strange results.

While the Deputies in Paris made themselves acquainted with the French scene, in Corsica there was a constant expectation of great events. A French officer who returned to the island in 1789, after a year in France, reported that since his absence the mood of the Corsicans had completely changed. Always sober, he wrote, they were now grim. But whereas before, the sobriety when it cracked had revealed a hollow hopelessness, it now revealed menace and a determination to prevail that threatened the continuance of French rule. Hundreds of eyes, said the officer, daily scanned the horizon for the boats which brought news from France; in public places groups gathered and talked animatedly in a way which he had not known before; in a short time societies had sprung up to discuss the principles of the Revolution and the meaning of the events which were taking place in Paris.

But the French observer saw only the Corsicans of the seaports. In the interior, where the strength of Paoli had always lain, the situation became every day more dangerous. The Vicomte de Barrin, who had a good understanding of the position in the island, reported that, if disturbances should break out in the interior, French rule would rapidly crumble and the French would in a few weeks be shut up in the fortresses of the sea coast.

The number of French troops in the island was, he pointed out, not large. There were 900 at Bastia, 600 at Ajaccio, 210 at Calvi, 40 at Isola Rossa, 30 at San Fiorenzo and a regiment of 500 Swiss, the *Salis Grison* regiment, at Corte; Barrin, seeing the way events were shaping, demanded additional troops. But the Minister of War had no intention of denuding the garrisons of the Midi to protect a highly vulnerable French possession in the middle of the Mediterranean. Barrin must, he was told, practise indulgence and rely on diplomacy. The essential thing was to be sure of the fortresses. Barrin was an amiable man, tactful and well-meaning but he was no diplomat.

The only diplomacy he knew how to practise was delay, and that became steadily harder. Presented with a tricolour by Peretti, the mayor of Bastia, on 1st August 1790, he accepted it gaily and wrote immediately to La Ferandière, the commander of the garrison at Ajaccio, to do the same. But things were becoming too heated for gestures to suffice, and shortly after this relatively aimable clash there was an ugly disturbance in Ajaccio, in which the pro-French bishop, Doria, was roughly handled. A few days later, there was an even more menacing incident: royal property on the outskirts of Ajaccio was seized by a body of sailors who quoted the tricolour as their warrant. Even worse followed: the agitation against French taxes, which had been steadily increasing, culminated suddenly in an invasion of the town by groups from the neighbouring glens. Barrin now decided that the Corsicans had overreached themselves; he threatened that, unless order was restored, he would unleash his troops on the town and, to give body to his threat, pointedly positioned his cannon to cover the main streets. Overawed by this display of French force, the invaders withdrew and the Municipality, fearing for the future of public order, set up a committee of 36, which raised a militia for the purpose of collaborating with the French in the preservation of peace.

These disturbances at Ajaccio were paralleled by outbreaks in Bastia. On 14th August, there was a meeting in the church of the Conception of representatives of the French government, of many of the pro-French nobility, of merchants and of representatives of the clergy. These quietly and, as they thought, unobtrusively, elected a new Municipality. As soon as this news became known, however, it produced uproar in the town. Rapidly convened committees of Corsicans accused the new Council of having connived at an injustice; they went on to demand that Frenchmen in public office should be replaced by Corsicans. Overnight, posters appeared on the walls of the town, demanding that the magistrates should leave the island and go to France so that their places might be filled by patriots.

On 7th September, Cherrier, the Inspector-General of domains, who was a bold, impetuous and tactless man, refused to authorise a French contribution to a new market which had been proposed, saying in passing that he would rather be hanged than give money to the enemies of France. Within a few hours this comment had been transmogrified into a threat to hang

A Tavern Scene. Waxwork by Samuel Percy (possibly an early 19th century reconstruction) l. to r.: servant, Johnson, Reynolds, an unidentified man, Gainsborough, Paoli, Fox, Boswell, the landlord, and Nollekens.

Cristoforo Saliceti
(1757–1809)
from an engraving
by Vicart

Carlo Andrea
Pozzo di Borgo
(1764–1842)
19th century engraving

all the Corsicans in the island and when Cherrier next left his house he was attacked and insulted in the street. Things looked more and more menacing. It was evident that the French and their allies would not be able to preserve order for very long and many French and pro-French families prudently took ship for Provence. Their example was soon followed at Ajaccio by all those who were French or closely allied with the French.

At Corte and at Sartene, as well as at Bonifacio, there were similar disturbances on various pretexts. But the most menacing occurrences took place in Paoli's former strongholds, the villages of the interior. There, the French government completely collapsed. In glen after glen, committees were elected and took over government from French-appointed officials. The only yardstick was patriotism, and patriotism in Corsican terms meant being a Paolist. The revolution produced its own religious settlement. Priests who had been known to support, or to be favourable to, the General's cause went unmolested. Priests who had collaborated with the French were hunted down and replaced by vicars.

Soon the Paolists passed to the attack. The peasants of the glens of Frasseto, Zicavo, Quasquara and Campo united into an armed band and, with the old Corsican flag waving at their head, they ravaged the possessions of the Comte de Rossi; his crops were set on fire and his olive trees were hacked down. At Vico, the inhabitants launched an attack on the much-hated Greek colony which had been founded by Marbeuf in 1774.

But worse was in store for the French administration. Throughout August, bands of Paolists, veterans of the struggle for independence, began to land in the bays and on the beaches of north Corsica. They came in groups of twenty-five to thirty and as soon as they had landed, they began to wage an active guerilla warfare, striking rapidly at villages which were believed to be pro-French, and then retreating into the all-embracing *macchia* before French troops could arrive.

Barrin, faced with the total collapse of French rule in the interior, resorted to a time-honoured expedient: he distributed arms and money to all those Corsican leaders he believed would support France. So, first the Fabiani, then the Boccheciampi, and then all the members of the clans of the Twelve were provided with arms and ammunition. This led to more and more incidents, and before long something like civil war was raging in many parts of the island.

When news of the disastrous way in which things were going arrived at Paris, the Corsican Deputies joined together to discuss how the pacification of the island might be effected. But the points of view of Buttafuoco and Peretti were already far from those of Saliceti and Cesari, and their meeting dissolved in accusation and recrimination. Saliceti and Cesari thereupon devised a plan on their own account. This was to set up a National Committee, composed of twenty-two members from the different parts of of the island. The Committee would have as its executive an inspector in each of twelve jurisdictions and a commissioner in each glen. The Committee would be responsible to the executive for the decrees of the French National Assembly and might, by special request, enlist the aid of the French government. At the same time, it was proposed to set up a national militia in each of the towns of the island.

Not unnaturally, this proposal which would have given the Corsicans a large measure of autonomy was enthusiastically received by the Paolists and immediately rejected by the French and their supporters on the island. Barrin in particular had no illusions: 'If you arm these Corsicans,' he said, 'they will turn their arms against us. Farewell then to all idea of peace and industry. Their only desire will be to enact vengeance.' He recommended that French troops should be sent to keep order and that sterner measures should be taken and in this he was supported by the Twelve and those Frenchmen who had the greatest knowledge of the island, such as Rossi and Wargemont. Their view accorded well with the view that the French government was beginning to take, and just after the disturbances in Ajaccio had died down, Gaffori landed in the island with a regiment of French regulars who were, for the most part, Corsicans, and who were intended especially for the purpose of putting down the risings in the interior of the island. Gaffori was not only a capable and able soldier; even more important was the name he bore, for he was the son of Paoli's predecessor, General Gaffori, who had once united the Corsicans and whose memory was still revered in the island.

Gaffori, immediately he had landed, issued a proclamation, declaring that he had not come as the agent of tyranny, which he freely acknowledged to have been exerted by the French in the past; he had one wish, he declared, to lead the Corsicans peacefully from servitude to liberty. Peace and order, he said, and repeated again and again, were the corner-stones of his policy.

He acted rapidly. He united his own troops with the Swiss at Bastia and marched at once on Ajaccio. There he reviewed his assembled forces. Immediately afterwards he closed the more active of the Revolutionary Clubs and dissolved the municipal militia. He assembled the Municipality and then assured them in emphatic terms that, in the future, order would be preserved, tranquillity would reign and that Ajaccio would reassume its normal peaceful life. The town was divided. His detachment from party in the island, the name he bore, his assurance of freedom and the goodwill of the governing French towards him gained him a great deal of support among many who dreaded the increasing anarchy. The French, and the pro-French particularly, hoped and expected a great deal of him. But the more ardent patriots regarded Gaffori's arrival with disquiet, for out of the difficulties of the French they had hoped to pluck who knows what degree of independence, and they saw that he would be a strong support to the *status quo*. Among these was the young Napoleon Buonaparte, now twenty years old and an Artillery lieutenant, who had recently returned to the island from France and was hopeful of employment. Still, although he was opposed to Gaffori and denounced his coming he was clear-sighted enough to see that the French commander had had a striking initial success.

Gaffori's example was infectious. At Bastia, Barrin, relieved at finding that his council was at last being accepted on the mainland, acted vigorously in his turn. The citadel was reinforced; Colonel Rully, a firebrand who, in season and out, had been advocating repressive action against the Corsicans, was given his head, and ostentatiously prepared to put down any rebellion to the accompaniment of a great deal of loud talking. Contrary to the patriots' expectations there were no repercussions; the island looked on the way to pacification.

Paoli, in London, had been kept well-informed of the progress of the agitation in the island. But he could do very little. France was at peace with England. To the English, indeed to Europe as a whole, the Corsicans who were opposing the French in the island were rebels, and, moreover, rebels against a government which was committed to redressing their grievances. Paoli himself had at first believed that the Constituent Assembly would freely grant Corsica her liberty and he wrote in this strain to Turgot. Although this expectation was disappointed, he seems to have done little to encourage those partisans who had roused the interior in his name. Nevertheless, he could hardly disown them, for their cause had been his cause and his Enlightened principles, however much they might lead him to expect from the French, had little part in the simple patriotism and desire for revenge that drove forward his adherents in the island.

He sent Masseria, his friend and follower, on two missions to the French in those early months of the Revolution, to sound out the views of the leading French statesmen. Masseria talked with Bailly, Lafayette, Mirabeau, Volney, Lameth and a good many other leaders of the Popular Party. There were many assurances of good intentions towards the General and the island, but there was also doubt expressed, partly of his ability to restrain his fellow-countrymen, partly of the ability of Corsica to remain free, even if liberty were granted to it by France. Corsica, it was emphasised, was still strategically important, still a tempting possession for an English fleet, and Paoli himself, with his English connections, was suspect in some quarters.

In October, Paoli tried again to break the stalemate which existed by sending his trusted friend and secretary, Antonio Gentili, to Paris, where Gentili had several conversations with Lafayette and La Tour du Pin. Gentili, in these talks, emphasised Paoli's joy in the regeneration of the monarchy. He explained that Paoli had given up all idea of a free and independent Corsica, but hoped to see Corsica as free as the other provinces of France with a government formed in accordance with the ancient character and institutions of the island and not so slavishly based on the French model as it had been in the past. He mentioned that Paoli had recalled the happy days of Monsieur de Cursay, a Frenchman who because of his knowledge of, and attention to, Corsican customs, had ruled happily and with only a handful of men. Paoli wished, he said, to make what contribution he could to bring about a similar happy state of affairs.

Was Paoli sincere? Possibly he had other hopes at the back of his mind. Possibly not. His principles, the principles of the Enlightenment, were, after all, those of the men he addressed and all the Enlightened believed, in the early happy days of the

Revolution, that the fruits of their principles would soon be plucked by all men. There was nothing very extraordinary in the hopes he had of the French. Certainly Gentili, who was to break with Paoli, and whose future was to lie with the French, never subsequently questioned Paoli's sincerity at this time.

La Tour du Pin and Lafayette, however, had doubts of any collaboration with Paoli. Already, they hoped much of Gaffori's operations in the island; they urged Paoli to second them by supporting Gaffori and the French with his influence. They held out to him the hope of an amnesty if he would thus aid them in restoring tranquillity to the island. It seemed a sensible policy. But the peace that Gaffori had established was not enduring. The manifesto of the Twelve, rejecting the proposed national Committee of Saliceti and Cesari as 'dangerous and impracticable', and prophesying financial and economic disaster for the Corsicans if they were allowed to create a paid national militia, shattered the deceptive peace that Gaffori had established. On 31st October, the Ajaccians burst into print against the Twelve and by the hand of the young Buonaparte drew up a savage manifesto, in which Gaffori was personally attacked as the betrayer of the traditions of his family. Rumours were spread at the same time that Narbonne, accompanied by 50,000 troops, had been orded to relieve Gaffori and reassert French tyranny. While Ajaccio thus seethed, Bastia burst into open rebellion.

The occasion was the demand of the Municipality to be allowed to form a National Guard. Characteristically delaying, Barrin offered to consider the request and to deliver his answer at midday on 5th March. But at midday, officers who were in the town noticed that everywhere swords were being sharpened and arms distributed, and believing that the town was on the verge of a rising, they rushed back to the citadel to inform the governor. He immediately had the gates closed and armed the garrison.

A tragi-comedy then ensued, brought about by the different attitudes to the situation of the commander and his troops. The garrison itself was only too eager for a fight; they despised the Bastians as 'beggars and Italians' and they were eager to force a confrontation. But Barrin was confused. He had believed that the actions of Gaffori had restored the initiative to him. Now, suddenly and from nowhere, the old threat of civil war loomed again. Falling back on his old policy, he decided to wait on events. When the Corsicans, in the person of Morelli, the President of the Council, demanded a prompt reply to their request to be allowed to form the militia, Barrin, as usual, temporised. He wrote to Morelli that, although he could not authorise the formation of the militia, he believed that before long the French would see its advantages and order its creation, and in anticipation of this he told the Council to draw up a list of the proposed commanders of this militia. At this moment, news was brought to him that fighting had broken out in the streets and Barrin, in a panic and urged on by the fire-eating Colonel Rully, declared martial law. No sooner had Rully set his excited troops in motion than word was brought to Barrin that his advice had been accepted and that the Bastians were meeting in an orderly fashion in the church of St Jean. In a thorough panic, Barrin injudiciously made his way to the church accompanied by the bringers of the news from the Council, to reinforce in person the expected good effect of his letter. He found that he had walked into a lion's den. As soon as he entered the church, pistols were levelled at him and daggers were flourished in his face. Urged to restore order by giving responsible citizens weapons he signed an order for the distribution of 200 rifles to the Municipality and another for the retreat of his troops. While he was thus engaged in the church of St Jean furious fighting was going on in the streets between Rully's soldiers and the Bastians. Barrin's order caused Rully to retire within the citadel, and in the confusion the Bastians armed with Barrin's warrant, entered the citadel with the retreating troops and pillaged the armoury. Barrin then gave way completely and making the best of an impossible situation, he gave the Corsicans permission to establish a militia, an exercise which, by the time his decree reached them, was already almost complete.

Rully was furious. 'The Corsicans have always hated us,' he said, 'and if reinforcements are not forthcoming the French will, in a very few months, have the task of reconquering the whole island.' He demanded that Barrin should allow him to resign his commission. Barrin agreed. A few days later, Rully embarked, supposedly secretly, for Provence. But secrecy in the Corsican beehive was not possible. As Rully's ship sailed out of the harbour, it was accompanied by a shoal of small craft, from which issued the derisive, sinister bleating of the conch, the old Corsican war trumpet.

But the damage had been done, for the risings triggered off a series of new attacks on the French and their sympathisers. Almost at once the Corsicans at Cervione forced similar concessions from the commander of the Limousin Regiment that garrisoned the town; and insurrection at Vico followed with the same results; and here the newly-armed militia immediately turned its weapons against the hated Greeks. These risings did not go unopposed. For, while La Ferandière sent an amphibious expedition which was intended to succour the Greeks, Gaffori marched at the head of his troops to pacify Cervione. But the damage had been done. In Paris, Rully's bitter recriminations against the Corsicans and the almost daily news of the Corsican trouble demonstrated sufficiently for the leaders of the parties that the French hold on the island was weakening.

A further heavy blow was given to French authority when, on 14th March 1790, Bartolomeo Arena arrived in Isola Rossa. He had gone to London on a special mission to Paoli and had just returned via Paris. The nature of his mission, and what exactly Paoli said to him, is unrecorded, but whatever passed between them in London did nothing to moderate the revolutionary ardour of Arena which, even when it was restrained, rarely sank below fever pitch. Nor does Paoli's partiality for the furious young advocate after his return to the island suggest that he found Arena's enthusiasm displeasing.

Within a few days of Bartolomeo's arrival, Isola Rossa was in rebellion; a rebellion sparked off by the fire of Bartolomeo's advocacy, and spread rapidly among the tinder of his many relations. The Fabiani, the pro-French party which had been armed by Barrin, were overthrown and Arena set up a committee which tactfully appointed him president, a brother, Giuseppe Mario, mayor, and another brother, Filippo Antonio, colonel of the National Guard. The French in the town were placed under house arrest and Arena formally demanded the keys of the citadel from the French commander. His action was perfectly legal he maintained, since it was carried out in obedience with the will of the National Assembly. But this deceived no one. The hand might look like the hand of the National Assembly, but the voice was uncommonly like that of Paoli.

It was now plainly written, by events, that if France were to retain Corsica, new and important measures must be taken. On 30th November, in the National Assembly, Saliceti formally delivered a letter from Galeazziani, Murati and Guasco, three captains of the National Guard of Bastia, which explained in detail the uprising of 5th November. The letter bears all the marks of having been inspired by Saliceti himself. It ended with an appeal for the assimiliation of Corsica as a part of France. As soon as he had read the letter, Saliceti formally proposed that Corsica be recognised as an integral part of French territory.

It seems that Saliceti must have done some preparatory work with the popular party, for immediately he sat down, Mirabeau rose and proposed that: 'those citizens who had fought for liberty and accepted exile when their island had been conquered, if they were guiltless of any legal crime, should have the right to return immediately to their country, and receive the rights due to French citizens'.

A heated debate ensued. The purpose of the motion was obvious. Its primary concern was evidently to arrange for the recall of Paoli. But it was also implicitly a condemnation of the royal conquest and, as such, the Royalists strongly opposed it. They brought upon themselves the powerful rhetoric of Mirabeau : 'My youth,' he cried,

> was sullied by a participation in the conquest of Corsica; all the more reason then that I should attempt to make amends by the abolition of a law which my reason, in any case, tells me is an unjust law. For those Corsicans who formerly defended their native hearths, those men whose love of liberty drove them into exile, now stand condemned to death for their virtues if they should return to their homeland. Will your sense of justice permit this? Will your knowledge of the King's goodness allow you to retain unaltered legislation which severed men from the land of their birth, and which punishes them with death if they return? Let us have this decree; let us after long years give justice and humanity a voice; let us do honour to the first days of French liberty.

His eloquence swept away the opposition and the motion was passed by a huge majority.

All was now ready for the return of Paoli. The streets of the island's towns were soon full of banners : *'Viva Paoli!'* *'Viva Mirabeau!'* *'Vive la nazione!'* Everywhere there was rejoicing.

At a solemn fête on 27th December in Bastia a marriage ceremony was conducted, which was meant to symbolise the union
of Corsica with France. The Bishop of Bastia preached an eloquent and patriotic sermon, which ended with the words: ' . . .
The Corsicans are now part of France. The heritage of Abraham
and Isaac is assured them. May God bestow His Grace on this
marriage.' At this, all the bells in the town began pealing, soldiers
fired volleys into the air, cannon thundered the ramparts, the
ships in the harbour broke their flags at their mast-heads and the
standard of France was unfurled on the citadel. In the evening,
as a climax to the celebrations, a huge bonfire was set alight. As
the flames rose into the air, there came two great cries from the
crowd: *'Viva Paoli!' 'Viva la liberta!'*

It was indeed time for Paoli's return, for the victory of his
party in the island threatened to get out of hand and the
country was fast slipping into anarchy. It was evident that everywhere the Paolists' cause was to be victorious and his supporters
were quick to settle accounts. At Isola Rossa, Arena demanded
again that the French should quit the citadel and Barrin recalled
the garrison to Bastia. Gaffori and La Ferandière were furious,
but could do nothing. Gaffori was becoming an object of
vilification; he was openly pointed out everywhere as 'the enemy
of the nation'; Bastia, Sartene and Corte sent resolutions pro-
testing against his employment. Only in Ajaccio, ably seconded
by La Ferandière, did he still command respect. But the
orders he issued did not run outside the town. Everywhere
the Paolists prepared to take over the government of the island.
Bastia led the way. In the church of the Conception in the
eight days from 22nd February to 1st March, a National
Committee was set up under the celebrated Clemente Paoli,
who had returned to the island after the decree of 30th
November. But Clemente was now an old and a tired man and
his Presidency was really only nominal. The work was done by
the eager young Paolists of the new generation. Their first resolution declared that the first General Assembly of the nation
would await the arrival of Paoli, the nation's leader: 'The best
guide'. It then ordered Gaffori to come and aid it in its work.
Gaffori realised that the National Assembly, whatever might be
its legal position, was the *de facto* authority. He was a straightforward, honest soldier, rather than a politician. The Council
promised at least a backing for some sort of law and order and

so he made the journey to his secular Canossa. In the presence of the Assembly he promised that he would provide the Council with soldiers and would help them with the recruitment of their militia. He then recommended that Corte be made the permanent seat of the Committee and to this the Council agreed. Ominously for his hopes that the Council might have a tranquilising effect on the nation, his agreement was made in the shadow of Colonel Rully's murder at Bastia.

Rully, colonel of the Maine regiment, after his ignominious self-exile from Corsica, carried his hatred of the Corsicans into the Council Chambers of Paris with the same furious energy that he had shown on the island. He was a wealthy man and, to show the extent of his contempt for the Corsicans and his affection for his soldiers, he offered to defray the expenses of the transfer of his regiment from Corsica to the mainland. Having obtained the authority to do this, he landed at Bastia on 18th April while the Council deliberated. Petriconi, the commander of the militia and the best guarantee of order, was away. Intercepted by men of the local militia before he reached the citadel and threatened with death, Rully retreated to a local barracks where (the news of his arrival having been spread) he was beseiged by the National Guard. Ironically, Rully whose return had been, at least in part, occasioned by his affection for his troops, found the soldiers he was among too cowardly to face the wrath of the populace. They demanded that he leave the barracks. Rully was a brave man. Coolly he strolled out of the barracks: 'Behold,' he cried, as he walked to confront the Corsicans, 'the colonel of the Maine!' Hardly had the words left his lips when he died, riddled with bullets.

It was an ill-omened start to the rule of the Council. Worse was to come. In June, the authority of the King's representatives at Bastia was flouted and they were relentlessly harried by the Municipality – one Cadenol, being imprisoned on a trumped-up charge of corruption and the others forced to seek refuge in France, while Gaffori was again pilloried in print as a despot in league with them. But even before this, it had become obvious that the work of the Council had meaning only in the seaports. The interior of the island was in a state of complete anarchy. The round of the agricultural day, that the French had striven, even if fitfully and ineffectually, to establish, had stopped.

An older, bloodier order had returned to take its place.

Everywhere, the traveller saw signs of destruction: the olives of the Boccheciampe had been systematically hacked down; the vineyards of the Matra were a mass of smouldering ash, and the bodies of the clansmen lay dead among them. The former good-will of the French was a death-warrant. In most glens of French sympathisers, cattle wandered aimlessly through deserted fields or were found seeking shelter in the shells of burnt-out houses. In some of the Matra and Fabiana glens, which were united and strong, the Francophile Corsicans held out, the road to the outside world blocked, the passes held by armed men, the villages in the glens embattled.

— 15 —

PAOLI'S RETURN

While confusion reigned in Corsica Paoli was making a triumphal
return to the island. He showed considerable emotion on leaving
England. Corsica was always first in his affections and rarely
absent from his thoughts, but he had spent the greater part of
his mature life in England; almost all his daily companions, and
many of his dearest friends, for the last twenty years had been
English. However, the good wishes for his future that were
showered on him, and the knowledge that the France through
which he was to pass was Enlightened France, was both a
consolation and an encouragement to him. When he reached
France, the welcome that he experienced was so tremendous
that it, for a time at least, swept away the restraint that he was
usually accustomed to practise in his public utterances. In a
letter to Tomaso Arrighi, written on 10th April 1790, he tells of
his enthusiastic reception at the Bar of the Assembly and how
fervently he expressed his gratitude to the French: 'I have already
welcomed the Constitution which you have established. Now I
demand from the National Assembly the honour of serving the
French nation and its King. I swear obedience and fidelity to
the French people, to the King and to the decrees of the National
Assembly.' With such words on his lips the vestigial opposition to
his return vanished. The Duc de Biron presented him to the King
on 9th April and Paoli found Louis 'charming and gracious'. All
the principal politicians of France flocked to see him. It reminded
him he said, apparently without a trace of irony, of the way in
which he had been received in England twenty years before.

Everywhere, he was received with enthusiasm. Invited to
attend a meeting of the Societé des Amis de la Constitution,
he was placed at the right hand of the President and made
the subject of a fulsome oration. At a banquet given by the
Societé de 1789 for the purpose of commemorating the foundation of the National Assembly, Bailly, the mayor of Paris, paid

204

him a glowing tribute in a toast; the words repeated to citizens who were vicariously participating in the streets outside, aroused such enthusiasm that Paoli, flanked by Sieyés, Lafayette and Mirabeau, had to come to the window to answer the ringing cheers. He had, indeed, come at an auspicious time for his cause. He was filled with pleasure at all he saw in France, and the French reacted eagerly to the admiration of such an admirer, for to them his presence restored some brightness to visions that had begun to fade. The first, heady days of the Revolution were over, the first transports past, and it was evident that the millenium had not yet dawned; intrigue had begun again; food prices were high; the division was already taking shape between those who believed that the work of regeneration had just begun, and those who wished to call a halt and consolidate their gains in the face of what they believed was a dangerous disorder. But with all this, enthusiasm was by no means dead; the great slogans still rolled through the streets, giving confidence and echoing the hopes that men still dreamed that they might realise. Paoli, fresh from England, the martyr of the Enlightenment, completely unsmirched by politics and untouched by ambition, his habitual reticence calling forth repeated demonstrations of affection, was the incarnation of the ideals of the Revolution and an incarnation that those principles had called into being.

Paoli was much impressed by the Deputies who supported his cause. Cesari, he found brave and forthright, Saliceti, a bundle of energy and ideas: few reservations about them can be detected in his correspondence. The apotheosis of liberty covered all. Yet all his new-found happiness could hardly have concealed from him that there were fundamental differences between himself and Saliceti, the driving force of Paoli's cause in the Assembly. They were, indeed, destined to become the most famous opponents of the Revolutionary years in Corsica. And Paoli was always a perceptive man. 'Old Paoli misses very little', as Napoleon was to say a little later. Perhaps they rejoiced in what they had in common, for they were both idealists and both, initially at least, idealists of the Enlightenment. Both believed that men were rational and capable of determining their own fate when superstition and tradition had ceased to oppress them. Neither had an undue reverence for Kings. Both, too, were practical politicians and were quite ready in an emergency in the high Rousseauist fashion to use force to keep the freedom they believed necessary to men. These were large areas on which they could agree. Their difference was a temperamental difference. Saliceti's portrait reflects his being: dark, cavernous, eager, his head thrust forward like a beak, ready to strike, his face burning above a thin, meagre body. He was the revolutionary *par excellence*. He believed passionately in revolutionary action. Those who hesitated or doubted were little better than the enemies he struck at so furiously. He was the natural follower of Robespierre with whom indeed he had much in common. Revolutionary virtue was his eternal cry. But, unlike Robespierre, the virtue he embraced was strictly limited by the adjective revolutionary. In his personal affairs, he was as grasping as any legendary lawyer and a Corsican lawyer at that.

Paoli was something quite other than this. Essentially a reflective man and slow to anger, he had to convince himself of the necessity of force before he could use it. And where Saliceti was quick to destroy, Paoli was naturally magnanimous. At one bound, Saliceti could easily reach the stage of terror, whereas Paoli habitually tried to counter folly by opposing good example. Saliceti was often to threaten a cause by precipitate action. Paoli's fault was procrastination. Yet, in spite of their differences, the likenesses were there; Saliceti was to show himself capable of as great a patience in his dealing with Paoli's caution, which was so foreign to him, as Paoli himself displayed understanding about Saliceti's precipitancy, which he so deplored.

However no dissension between them appeared at this stage. Paoli was the hero of the hour and adulation showed itself in many ways. He stood beside Lafayette when the hero of the American War reviewed the National Guard at the end of March and drew from the *Moniteur* the obvious comparison of the young warrior, his laurels fresh from victory, to the old martyr, with his noble head erect and his face seamed with the years of exile. His portrait was sold everywhere on the streets. He had only to appear to be surrounded by a cheering crowd, eager to pat him on the back and press his hand.

But what was more important to him than all these demonstrations was the French government's realisation that there could be no peace in Corsica without him. They knew that the sooner he arrived in the island the more hope there would be for the restoration of order and consequently, in the discussions on the future government of Corsica, his advice was accepted eagerly and almost without question in the effort to get him back to the island.

He advised that the King should appoint Commissioners to execute in Corsica the decrees of the Assembly; he advised that taxes should continue unchanged until they could be reconsidered as part of the general reconstruction of the island; he advised that the Duc de Biron, whom he trusted, should be sent as the commander of the troops in Corsica (the fact that Biron was a Deputy and *ipso facto* forbidden this sort of command was quietly overlooked); a proposal to divide the island into two Departments was quietly burked by Paoli's advice. By a twist of fortune's wheel he had become once more, and, ironically enough in France itself, the legislator of the island.

Paoli's journey to the coast at the beginning of July was a triumphal procession. As he descended the valley of the Rhône every village was *en fête* to receive him; everywhere there were flowers and triumphal arches and cries of '*Vive Paoli!*' At Aix, he was met by Joseph Buonaparte and Pozzo di Borgo, who brought him the official welcome of the Council and he was delighted with them. Educated in Italy, they were the representatives of the younger generation of the Enlightened on the island. Both had been born under his rule, but both had been educated with the expectation of a career under the French. Nevertheless, they assured him that they had always been ardent Paolists and in this they said they were merely representative of most men of their generation and training. They accompanied him gaily, volubly answering all the way his eager questions about affairs in the island, to Toulon where they set sail for Corsica.

If the reception Paoli had received in France was enthusiastic, then the reception in Corsica was delirious. On 17th July, he sailed into Centuri. The bells of the little church rang madly, but they were drowned by the crash of cannon and the rattle of *feux de joie*. From every quarter of the island, but perhaps most of all from his beloved Castagniccia, men had come swarming into the peninsula to be among the first to greet him and they now went mad with joy. So great was the noise that it seemed to some that the very rocks were shouting his name. As the General stepped ashore he fell upon his knees and kissed the soil of his native land. He was weeping unashamedly. After he had received the congratulations of the townspeople, he reboarded the ship and sailed for Bastia. The ship sailed close to the coast and from the deck he saw crowds of islanders gathered everywhere to cheer him. Indeed, the sound of cheering hardly stopped from Centuri to Bastia, except when it was drowned by volleys of musketry.

The reception at Bastia, if more formal, was none the less enthusiastic. On the jetty, Paoli was met by the chief of the Municipality and all the officials of the town. His way from harbour to palace was lined with the men of the National Guard. Paoli walked slowly through the cheering streets, preceded by a band of the National Guard whose music vied with the pealing of church bells and the discharge of cannon. In the palace he met his brother Clemente. It was a very different homecoming from that first humble landing in the Bay of Golo. A Corsican rebel, an ex-Neopolitan officer, had become the idol of Europe and America and was now the representative of an Enlightened republic. But things were sadder in other ways. Then he had been in the full glory of his manhood. Now he was older, older than his sixty-four years. The English climate had not been good to him and he suffered greatly from arthritis. Clemente was even more enfeebled. His post was merely nominal. He had long since ceased to weigh the things of this world heavily. It was evident that he had returned to die among his countrymen, not to play a part in his country's government.

The meeting of the brothers was touching to all who saw it and many thought, seeing Paoli's slow and painful movements, that he too would be little concerned in future with the affairs of the island. They were mistaken. The next day, Paoli received visits from Barrin, the Supreme Council, the Intendant, the bishops, the officers of the garrison and various military and civil dignataries. To all these, he was his old affable, shrewd self. To the Tuscans, who were at Bastia, he was especially gracious, recalling how often they had succoured Corsican exiles and assuring them that their good offices would always be borne in mind by the Corsicans.

During the next few days, he was no less active. From every quarter of the island delegates came to assure him of their good wishes and loyalty. In every church of the island, they assured him, services of thanksgiving were being held. In Corte, Calvi, Bonifaccio, San Fiorenzo, Tollano, Bastelica, Olmeto, Calenzara Cervione and La Platta the Municipality held unprecedented fêtes.

In Ajaccio, a bust of the General commissioned in Marseilles, arrived and was installed in the hall of the municipal palace with the verse written underneath:

> Time and misfortune have not overcome him,
> Hero of a free people, he defended their rights,
> Love of his country and of liberty moved him,
> A rebel to tyrants, he now serves the law.

But in the general rejoicing, the old strain of Corsican separation was heard again. Paoli, as a mark of honour to his native glen, gave his personal guard to the militia of Rostino. Almost immediately, the story began to circulate through the streets of Bastia that the General only trusted his own clan and was ungraciously wary of the Bastians.

Any suspicions of him, however, were for the moment soon shelved, for Paoli declared often and to everyone in those early days that he had not come to rule, but to retire. Far from displaying vindictiveness, he behaved with great tact towards those who had been forced by necessity into some sort of collaboration with the French (and in the capital they were fairly numerous). He always acted as though the French occupation of the island had never taken place and that his countrymen had steadily developed their own institutions in their own way; in this scheme of things he was but a traveller returned after a long voyage abroad. Naturally, his advice was much sought after. He was as easy of access as ever and just as willing as he had always been to give advice, but always his refrain was that obedience was due above all to the civil magistrates. He spent a good deal of time bringing himself up to date on the affairs of the island. The days of his peregrinations through the glens were over, but he wrote unceasingly to the chiefs of the clans, weighing and balancing their replies so that when they asked him for advice he could speak with some sort of authority. In a way, his extensive correspondence served as a substitute for his old journeys on horseback, but his inability to see for himself was to be, in the future, a dangerous handicap.

Certainly, in spite of his arrival, the persecution of French sympathisers went on unabated. Perhaps the reports, which after all came mainly from his supporters, hid from him the extent to which anarchy reigned in the interior. Or perhaps he realised how impossible it was to enforce tolerance by men exasperated beyond forbearance by years of French oppression. Certainly, in spite of his exhortations, most of the families that had been anti-Paolist soon left the island for exile in France or Tuscany. There was little future for them in the new scheme of things. For one thing, they had been deprived of the protection of Gaffori. That commander, disillusioned by the failure of the French government to support him, disabused by the politic transfer to Paoli of what allegiance remained to him of any idea that he might still command and distressed by the complete loss of confidence shown by his closest collaborators after Paoli's arrival, retired to Corte and shut himself up there with the regiment of the *Salis Grison*. To him there rallied the wreck of the Royalist supporters and Corte became for a time an armed island of Royalists in the middle of a sea of Paolists.

Paoli could not allow this threat to his government to continue and he began systematically to organise an expedition to take Corte. The Paolists throughout the island were only too ready. From every quarter of the country, men converged on Corte. Gaffori knew that the position was hopeless. In response to an invitation from Paoli, he went to see the General at Bastia. What passed between them is not known, but not hard to guess. Gaffori was too deeply involved with the Royalists to give any allegiance to Paoli. Paoli was determined that the Corsicans should decide their own fate and feared the presence of a French regiment, commanded by an avowed Royalist which moreover held a strong position in the old capital of the island. As Gaffori left the audience, Paoli ordered his arrest. He was immediately embarked for the mainland. With his final eclipse there was a panic exodus from the island of all the old supporters of the French. However much the harrying of the Royalists might have been hidden from him before, Paoli could not now avoid seeing the extent of their emigration from the island. He did what he could to ameliorate the position of the fugitives. He emphasised repeatedly to his followers there would be in future no distinctions between Corsicans and Frenchmen. Indeed, he advised the Corsicans to select Frenchmen as judges as they would be more likely to be impartial and unswayed by family ties. But this advice was too late and too early. It had little effect. It was all too easy to cover the attack on French sympathisers as an attack on reactionary aristocrats. The accusations would be well received in France and Paoli, in spite of his strong position in the island, was hardly in a position to override such accusations. From every harbour in the island the old anti-Paolist families set out: the Boccheciampe, the Cuttoli, the Fabiana, the Figarelli, the Matra, the Sansonetti. Everywhere, they were treated to displays of hatred and contempt on their way to the ports. But the worst excesses were avoided. Paoli's prompt use of the National Guard saved them from anything more dangerous than man-handling. Naturally enough, their arrival in France produced a hail of execration of the General by the French Royalists. Buttafuoco launched a bitter, personal attack on Paoli which compared him, among other things, to Tiberius and Sulla. But these fulminations had little effect in France, for the French believed they had righted a wrong, they believed that the exiles were another proof of this and they now awaited confidently the proofs of their virtue.

They had little effect either in Corsica. For with the going of Paoli's opponents, the state of near civil war, which had been raging in the interior, ceased. Paoli had become indisputably the master of the island. He thereupon decided to convene a Congress to demonstrate that a new era was beginning and to set the island's affairs on an orderly course. He was confident that, in a little while, it would be possible to restore complete peace and tranquillity to towns and glens. He had been greatly impressed by the quality of the new men that he saw everywhere. Anomalies existed. In Isola Rossa the Arena brothers practised a vendetta as bloody, as unrelenting as any in Corsican history. Zampaglino, who had fought on in Paoli's name long after 1769, but without Paoli's moderation and magnanimity, was, though unable to read or write, administering Ajaccio in a very rough and ready fashion. But Paoli was confident that a reorganised administration would soon clear up all these anomalies. He placed his belief in the triumphant spirit of the Enlightenment, which he now saw everywhere. Things, however, were not to be so simple.

Paoli had not yet found out the full limitations of his position. He had been, before 1769, the soul of Corsican freedom. In an emergency he had *been* Corsica and his voice had been the voice of a nation. But Corsica was now linked to France: her fate was decided in Paris. Indeed, Paoli's return had been decided by the government of France, however much its hand had been forced by events in Corsica. Paoli himself realised this. He knew that the mission on which the French government had sent him was that of a dove and not that of an eagle. Yet, because of his past, men everywhere, and particularly in the interior of the island where the French writ had never run powerfully, looked to him for guidance. Indeed, they looked to him for more than guidance; they looked to him for authority. And authority was what Paoli did not, in the last resort, have. Authority lay with the administration in the island and Paoli, not only because of his age and infirmities, but also because he believed that it was wise and necessary for the younger generation to undertake the burden of government, was determined to have only a nominal role in the administration. He made two mistakes: he did not make allowance enough for youthful impatience and ambition; nor did he realise that to the younger generation the Enlightenment was not the same thing that it had been to him.

The Directory, which was about to be set up, was to be composed of much younger men than Paoli. Moreover, although they were enthusiastic Corsican patriots, they had been educated and had begun their careers under the French. Their enemy had thus been, not so much France as the *ancien régime* in France to which they were, in the last resort, upstart peasants with their path to the highest office blocked. But with the *ancien régime* swept away and the careers now open to the talents, and, moreover, with themselves the rulers of the island, their feelings against the French were considerably ameliorated. It was the survivals of the old order which they really disliked and it was all too easy for them, especially those who came from the seaports, to confound the old order with the old Corsican system of clans. There was an element of truth in their assessment. Some chiefs had indeed exercised their function under the French by cloaking it in their acceptance of office. But many more had emerged again during the period of anarchy, and believed that with Paoli back they were sure of their old authority. Temperament and experience had left Paoli in the past to placate the clan chieftains, even at the expense of the speed of his reforms. The advice of his father and of his brother, his own temperament and the bitter shock of Capo Corso had produced a policy of great flexibility. The new Directory, however, saw no room for his manoeuvring. They were determined to recognise only their own authority and Paoli was soon forced into the position of a mediator between them and the clansmen. But a mediator without power: apart, that is, from his own considerable reputation which, in the early stages at least, concealed the conflict.

As a mediator, Paoli had certain advantages: he had a natural sympathy with the clan chieftains of the island; he also found, or thought he had found, in the early stages of his return to the island that he shared the Enlightenment in common with his young compatriots. To a large extent, of course, he did. Pozzo di Borgo was to recollect years later that among the young men of his generation and education in the island there was everywhere, at the outbreak of the Revolution, earnest discussion of the writings and ideas of the *Philosophes*. The new men in the island were as much children of the Enlightenment in their day as Paoli had been in his, when he prepared himself in Elba for his Generalship by reading Montesquieu. But whereas an amiable Deism had informed its first promotors, its later adherents were increasingly inclined to profess a pugnacious atheism. In France, faced by a rich and often Laodicean Church, this attitude was more understandable than in Corsica, where the clergy were as poor as their lay fellows. But the French bishops and the French organisation enabled the Corsican anti-clericals to treat the Church as a French one. Paoli could never do this. The religious in the island had always been in the past among his most loyal and enthusiastic supporters. He could not, even if he would, during the wars for Corsican independence, have attempted to destroy the Corsican Church and his alliance with the Corsican clergy had proved fruitful, indeed essential, to his success. The trappings of religion had never mattered much to him. Like the Deists in the early years of the Enlightenment, he believed in a beneficent Creator and was content that men should make their own way towards Him. It was this amiable Deism which had enabled him to enter into a useful working alliance with the Corsican priests and monks. But now, faced with threatened persecution from the new men, the clergy looked to Paoli for support and, he, mindful of his obligations towards them, was forced increasingly into the position of protecting them against the fury of the more anti-clerical of the new Directory and this, too, was to call his position into question.

Indeed, his role was as a mediator threatened from the start by the persistence of another old Corsican custom. For, if the clan system had been eroded, the vendetta had not. In many parts of the island the new Directory pursued the vendetta with the same ferocity as had existed before the arrival of Paoli in 1755, but now, branding their opponents as Royalists and reactionaries and obscurantist clergy, the vendetta could be waged using the terms of the Enlightenment itself. Thus Paoli could be attacked by the Directory on two counts; that he supported an ancient social system and that he supported a reactionary Church. Neither was true; he had not abandoned his early principles, he preserved them to the end, but for him, as for Goya's 'Sleeper', monsters had begun to spring from the Dream of Reason.

But this was for the future. At first, no dissension about principle arose between Paoli and the younger generations. The first troubles, indeed, rose from an old source: the friction between the *Oltremonti* and the rest of the island. Paoli believed that the sooner a National Congress was held to regulate the government of the island, the sooner tranquillity would reign.

16

THE REVOLT IN BASTIA

In September, therefore, the Congress of Orezza took place. It was held deep in the Castagniccia, in the great convent of Orezzo, standing stark on its hill above the valley, a site of great symbolic importance in Corsican history, for it had been the meeting-place for Corsican Consultas as far back as there were records.

Paoli's journey there for the opening, on 9th September 1790, provided another lively demonstration of the affection in which he was held. Every village which bordered his way sent out deputations to hail him in sonorous Latin or Italian as the 'liberator of his country and the apostle of liberty'. Then, as his cortège wound along the road towards the convent they joined it, until, at length, it turned into a great procession stretching back miles through the countryside. At Pontenuovo, the Ajaccian delegation, amongst whom were Napoleon and Joseph Buonaparte, met him. The relations of Paoli with Napoleon produced a great crop of legends in Corsica, very few of which are verifiable. It was said, for instance, that at Pontenuovo Paoli was offended by the young lieutenant's ready criticism of his dispositions on the fatal day of 9th May. But, like a good deal of the Napoleonic hagiography, the story is very hard to believe, for Napoleon was, when he wished, nothing if not tactful, and at this point in his career he was very eager for the favour of the General.

The procession made its way to Orezza by a roundabout way through Morosaglia and there the General saw with emotion his old home and was greatly moved when he remembered his arrival there to begin the struggle for Corsican freedom so many years before. On overhearing it said that it was a humble habitation for the founder of the Corsican nation he murmured reflectively: 'I did not need a magnificent home. In those days all the island was my home.'

At the first session on 9th September, he was unanimously

elected President. A tussle between Paoli and the Assembly then developed, which was not without comedy, for the Assembly as eagerly tried to confer honours on the General as the General attempted to avoid them. The first resolution proposed was that Paoli should himself designate two Commissioners who would carry to Paris the thanks of the National Assembly for the freedom and the institutions that the French had granted them. Paoli was very determined that he should not find himself placed in the position of dictator of the island. He therefore immediately opposed the resolution in a speech which turned into a homily: 'This nomination belongs to you, gentlemen. Are you eager so soon to give up your privileges? If I do not abuse the confidence with which you honour me today, someone else will abuse it tomorrow. Nature has provided you with abundant reason and good sense and you would be wise always to use them and look with a certain suspicion on power vested in a single individual.' However, after issuing his warning, the Assembly persisting, he chose Antonio Gentili, his former secretary, and the young Carlo Andrea Pozzo di Borgo as the Commissioners. Emboldened by their success, and not taking his advice to heart, the Assembly next proposed to raise a statue to him 'which should recall to posterity the memory of that illustrious citizen who had won the esteem and admiration of all the world'.

This time Paoli made a far fiercer speech, coloured again with his old irony, which ended: 'The most honourable monument for me is the one you have consecrated to me in your hearts. Believe me, gentlemen, you are unwise to be so prodigal with your praise and veneration to a citizen who, after all, is still a public man. Who knows? The last days of my life may arouse in you very different sentiments from the ones you show at this moment. In the nature of things, the course of my life should not have very far to run. Wait until it is finished before you make your judgement on the services I have rendered to our Fatherland. Besides, you will then be able to express your opinions with a great deal more freedom.' Deprived of their statue, the Assembly took fresh thought and came forward with a proposal to provide an annual pension for the General of 50,000 francs. Paoli would not accept it: 'It's not because I am proud, gentlemen, that I refuse your generous offer. But the state of your finances forbids you to be so free with your money. The public good always comes before private interest'.

However, in spite of his rejection of honours Paoli was by no means purely a nominal President. He allowed himself to be elected a commander of the militia in the island and he vigorously opposed a proposal made by the Ajaccians to split the island into two Departments. A flood of resolutions were then passed, redressing the wrongs that the French government had done to Corsican patriots and revoking many of the ordinances that dated from the days of Marbeuf.

Just before the Assembly had gathered, the new administrative system for French Departments, for which the Assembly had rendered thanks, had been promulgated in the island. Each Department was to have an administrative Council composed of 36 members and a Directory, composed of 5; Departments were split into Districts organised in the same manner but with smaller councils. Districts were divided into Cantons and in Corsica these were made equivalent to the glens. Towns and glens elected representatives in proportion to their population and were governed by a Council with a mayor at its head. A criminal tribunal was established in each Department, a civil tribunal in each District and a judge of the peace in each Canton. The head of the Department's Directory was the Procurator General Syndic. Saliceti was made an honorary Procurator General Syndic in appreciation of his services and Gentili, for the same reason, was made the honorary second-in-command of the island's militia. But in practice the first administration was headed by the fiery Bartolomeo Arena. The rest of the Directory consisted of Mattei, Multedo, Pietri, Pompei Paoli and Taddei. Paoli was very pleased with the conference and its appointments. After it had dissolved he wrote that everything had been done with goodwill and perfect tranquillity and in decorous order. The Corsicans, he added cheerfully, were becoming good Frenchmen and he did not think that the French King would find more loyal citizens in any part in his domain.

When the new Council met at Bastia, on 1st October, Paoli was formally elected as President. He intended his Presidency to be, for the future, purely nominal. He placed his reliance on the Directory which was young and enthusiastic and apparently shared the principles that he had professed for so long, The enthusiasm that the Congress of Orezzo had shown for him, and particularly the respect which he had been shown by the young Directors, led him to hope that he might exercise the function of a benevolent adviser while they learnt the business of government (the role that he had always hoped that he might one day play in Corsica).

The two Commissioners, Pozzo and Gentili, scored a great success on their arrival at the Assembly at Paris; Pozzo particularly in a brilliant denunciatory speech against Peretti and Buttafuoco. Both representatives were then elected to reinforce Saliceti and Cesare in the Assembly. Pozzo's brilliance soon won him the close friendship of Mirabeau who was extremely pleased with the action that he had initiated, for Pozzo assured him that, with Paoli in the island peace and tranquility were now assured. He was a little too sanguine, as he was to discover when he returned to the island after some five months to become a member of the island's governing Directory.

For as the months wore on, relations between Paoli and the Directory became cool. The Directory, headed by the enthusiastic Arena, showed none of the moderation that Paoli had hoped for. They contrived to find opponents for themselves everywhere and hounded them gleefully in the name of Paoli. Paoli rested at Rostino and made few journeys to other parts of the island, but the journeys he did make and his extensive correspondence soon convinced him that all his hopes for a tolerant and liberal administration were disappointed. He was not slow to express his disappointment. For one thing, he disliked the virulent anticlericalism of the Directory. At first, as a man of the Enlightenment, he regarded the harrying of the clergy with a certain amount of amusement, knowing how strong they were fundamentally in the island, and thinking it but natural that the enthusiastic young Directors should come into conflict with the more conservative of the priests. He had little affection for the French bishops and he thought at first that it was the Directory's conflict with these that was provoking clashes between Church and State in the island, but it soon became clear that Arena and, still more, his Eminence Grise, the Florentine journalist Fillipo Buonarotti, who edited in Bastia the atheistic *Giornale Pattrioto,* had no restraint. Though he had little respect for bishops, Paoli knew that the clergy of the island were no threat to the Revolution. They were as poor and as unpretending as the peasants they served, honest, simple patriots, loyal and courageous in the national struggle. But Buonarotti had little knowledge of, and no affection for, them and a positive hatred of the God they served. Paoli become worried and distressed at the bitter fury with which Buonarotti raged, dividing the nation with his too readily accepted counsel.

But it was not only the intolerance and lack of judgement on the religious question that caused Paoli concern. From the very beginning, a taint of fiscal corruption hung about the Directory. During the elections for the Districts and the Cantons, there were strong suspicions of widespread bribery. Paoli, whose correspondence was extensive and whose visitors legion, had no doubt that many elections were rigged: 'Votes are all too often given to him who pays,' he said bluntly.

It soon became evident that the Councils elected thus inauspiciously were lax and inefficient in their control of the public funds. The accounts of the majority were appallingly badly kept. The Directory of the Department was equally at fault in this respect and Paoli soon discovered two flagrant instances. In the first, he found to his chagrin (since he had been so proud of Corsica's exports during his former rule) that no systematic account of any kind was kept of customs dues. Close enquiry revealed the distinct possibility that a good many of the dues went into the pockets of the administrations. In the second case, he learnt that monks who should have been paid pensions from 1st January 1791, on the dissolution of the monasteries, were left begging on the road; the money due to them having unaccountably vanished. There were many less striking, but no less dubious, cases. What particularly aroused his fury was that when money and prompt action were needed for an emergency they were not forthcoming; he said hard things when an epidemic broke out at Ghisoni and the Directory took no measures to attenuate or allay it. The malfunction of justice was another source of constant worry to him. The Council soon became notorious for its partiality. Case after case was reported to Paoli of violence and chicanery going unpunished because of the connivance of the delinquents' relatives and friends who held positions of power in the local Directories or Councils. The worst abuses of justice meant that men began to take the law into their own hands and the vendetta began to spread once again. Saliceti himself, when at a later date he became the chief defender of the Directory's actions, when indeed his very life depended on his justifiying the Directory's policy, past as well as present, had to admit that they had been a 'little partial', inclined to place the interest of their side foremost.

Not all the faults of the island's administration were due to the chicanery or dishonesty of the administrators. More than a little was due to their youth and inexperience. Inexperienced, they procrastinated rather than reveal their ignorance of administration. When they struck, they struck far too hard: 'They lack moderation,' said Paoli. 'They lack prudence, they are partial judges and do not even cloak their partiality. They certainly need more tact and they need a great deal more disinterestedness.' These remarks were made in confidence to his friends, but he certainly did not cease to criticise the Directory and the administration publicly in specific cases, and if his public remarks were more tactfully worded, the criticisms were nevertheless pointed.

The Directory was, at first, astonished and apologetic and endeavoured to mend its ways, but gradually as the volume of complaint continued they began to be irritable at Paoli's continual criticism. Finding that they were all criticised, with no exception, they began among themselves to criticise Paoli in turn, accusing him of lukewarmness towards the Revolution, of a covert Royalism, or of ambition for absolute power. But his steady refusal to issue from his semi-retirement and his great reputation inhibited his opponents. Besides, at Paris, Saliceti was still fervently Paolist and his influence was reinforced for a few months by that of the brilliant Pozzo di Borgo, who, partly from calculation and partly from conviction, portrayed Paoli everywhere as the source and font of Corsican republicanism.

Indeed, in the island itself Paoli's embryo opponents were soon to be glad to have his ubiquitous power on their side, for they were by no means in complete control of the Corsican State; just how shallow were the roots of their power was dramatically shown by an insurrection at Bastia on 2nd June 1791. The insurrection was, above all, a religious one, but it had other overtones. For, like Paoli, the Municipality of Bastia was bitterly critical of the Directory led by Arena; like Paoli, the Municipality detested Arena's arbitrary exercise of power. But, at Bastia, with its Genoese and *ancien régime* connections, Paoli was mentally linked with the Directory and the support he might have given to the Municipality was never invoked. As

for Arena, he used the powers with which he had been invested
to override the decrees of the Municipality on the least provocation. When the Municipality became critical of his actions, he
ruthlessly pressed its members into service with the National
Guard. The Municipality said, bitterly, that he had turned the
Commission that had been set up to assess the redress due to
exiled Corsicans into a Commission of vengeance. Driven to
desperation by the Procurator General Syndic's continued attack
on their rights, they contrived to have a placard attached to the
house of the Directory: *'Haec domus inimica tyrannis'* (This is
the hated house of Tyranny).

But, although the Municipality had many grievances against
the Directory, the occasion of the rebellion at Bastia was a
religious one. Until the advent of the Directory to power, the
Church in the island had not been particularly harried. The
confiscation of Church property, instituted on 10th November
1789, had little effect on the island, for the Corsican clergy had
few wordly goods; they were as poor as the islanders themselves.
In the same way, the suppression of religious houses which
followed in February 1790 was largely tacitly ignored in Corsica
where the monks were on extremely good terms with their
neighbours. But, once the Directory had obtained power,
things changed. Convents were closed everywhere and in
Bastia, led by Arena, encouraged by the fulminating Buonarotti,
the authorities dissolved not only the religious houses but even
those religious educational establishments which had been exempted from the general decree. The suppression of the educational establishments roused the Municipality to action. The
town contacted the Corsican respresentatives in Paris and the
representatives threw their weight against Arena. The Directory
was thereupon instructed by the Assembly to re-open the religious educational establishments at once. This trial of strength
excited both sides.

The civil constitution of the clergy was the charge which exploded Bastia. By it, the five Corsican bishoprics were reduced
to one, Mariana-Accia, whereupon the incumbent Monseigneur
de Verclos, who was deeply venerated in the town, refused to
take the oath to uphold the Constitution decreed by the National
Assembly. On 8th May 1791, in accordance with the civil constitution, the Abbé Guasco, an old friend of Paoli's, was elected
in his place. On the 12th, the Directory peremptorily ordered

Monseigneur de Verclos out of the island. The Pope had already condemned the oath. With the departure of the bishop, Buonarotti enthusiastically poured oil on the flames by a denunici-ation of the Papacy, the bishoprics, the priests and finally the papal institution itself. On Rogation Day, 1st June, the faithful of the sea-port registered their protest by marching in solemn procession through the town. It was an impressive occasion. The priests, simply robed, openly weeping as they walked through the streets, followed a crucifix. The monks and the re-ligious brotherhoods marched with bare feet; some with halters around their necks, others whipping themselves as they went, while still others trailed chains. Behind them came a great crowd of women, weeping and wailing. The procession passed off peacefully, but the next day, in the great dusky church of St John the Baptist, the Bastians held an Extraordinary Assembly which drew up a solemn resolution, declaring that although they were proud to be French and had a proper respect for the National Assembly, they also respected the Pope and the Church and wished to retain their bishop. At the same time they con-demned the bitter tirades of Buonarotti and proclaimed that he was a menace to peace and order in the island. They de-manded his deportation. As night fell, a great crowd of citizens stormed the citadel, forced the gates, dragged out Arena from the headquarters of the Directory and threw him into a boat, together with the Secretary-General Panattieri and Buonarotti himself, giving instructions to the captain that he was to take them at once to Italy.

The next day, the women of the town attacked the Free-masonic Lodges in Bastia, gutted them and burnt their spoils in a great *auto-da-fé* by the seashore.

Paoli was at Ajaccio when the rebellion broke out. As soon as he heard the news he set out with a band of soldiers for Bastia, taking the shortest route through the valleys to the east coast plain. As he went, his original band grew with every village that he passed. From the villages by the way, as the news pene-trated into the glens, more men poured out to follow him; they came, exultant and joyful, in the spirit of a crusade, for Bastia had long been an object of hatred to the Corsicans of the interior, both under the Genoese and the French govern-ments; now word spread that Paoli was marching to revenge the hills against the city of the plain.

The Bastians offered no resistance. Indeed, before Paoli reached the town, as soon as they heard of the forces being mustered against them, they sent frantic appeals to him, praying him not to enter the port with an indisciplined army, but to hold talks in which they were sure they could justify the recent conduct of the citizens. But Paoli was not to be deflected. Whatever his reflections on the intemperance of the Directory, the fact was that the Bastians had humiliated the civil power and insulted Paoli's old friend, Guasco. Mixed with his determination to secure order might have been the reflection that Bastia had always been an adherent of his enemies, and that the Bastians were the first to criticise him on his return. However, within a short time, the General, who had come with the intention of putting down a rebellion and punishing the rebels, found himself being forced into the position of being their protector. For the Directory was in a malignant mood, especially the humiliated Arena; he and the propagandist Buonarotti had escaped their captors and returned to join Paoli's troops on their entry into the capital. They were determined to make an example of Bastia that would long be remembered in the rest of the island. They therefore made no attempt at all to punish the licence of the troops who, particularly the detachments of the National Guard, seized the opportunity given to them for looting with no little enthusiasm. Arena ordered that the troops should be billeted among the citizens and Arena's agents let it be known that here was a heaven-sent opportunity for them to settle old grievances and despoil their despoilers. Paoli quickly found that their officers, whom he instructed to bring them to some sort of order, were unable to control them. His own mountaineers were far more orderly, but many of the appointments of the officers of the National Guard had been managed by the Directory and their men had neither respect nor affection for them. Later in the month, Paoli showed how dangerous he thought their unbridled licence by requesting the French government to provide him with a fourth regiment of infantry to help in preserving order on the island.

In the month that the occupation lasted, the Corsicans coined the word *cuccagna,* or season of unbridled licence, or month in the land of cockaigne – to express their feelings about the operations of the soldiery. But Arena was not finished. Not content with the *cuccagna,* as a further punishment for the rebellion he ordered that the wealthier citizens should all be heavily taxed to pay for the expenses of the troops. At the same time it was arranged that Saliceti and Cesari at the National Assembly should exert their influence to have a decree passed transferring the capital of the island and the seat of the Archbishopric from Bastia to Corte, a task they quickly accomplished.

Lt-Col. John Moore
(1761–1809)
by Thomas Lawrence

Sir Gilbert Elliot
(1751–1814)
by James Atkinson

Pasquale Paoli as an old man, by George Dance

17

SALICETI

The rebellion in Bastia widened the breach between Paoli and the Directory, but there was still no open split. However, Paoli now began to sound his friends in various quarters of the island to find the full extent of the Directory's malpractices. The Directory itself learnt nothing by its mistakes. If anything, its victory in Bastia, such as it was, whetted its appetite for power. But criticism of it became far more widespread. Its justice was mocked and the Judges of Peace whom it nominated for office were cynically described by the Corsicans as Judges for War, since they so frequently antagonised men by their open favour to their own families and the families of those who were related to the members of the Directory.

One result of their abuse of power was that the vendetta went on merrily. In April 1792, Monestier, a French agent sent to report on the condition of the island, related as an instance of a common practice that, after a murder had taken place in Isola Rossa, no enquiries, depositions or interviews of any kind were carried out to discover the murderer. In the eighteen months before this, he wrote, there had been in four districts alone, Corte, Ajaccio, Cervione and Tallano, thirty-nine murders and six serious woundings which were directly attributable to the vendetta. Yet not one execution had taken place. The partiality of many of the administrators was, he noted, scandalous in many other ways; nepotism was rife everywhere; on the other hand the judges of the tribunal at Bastia who were not favoured by the Directory simply received no pay; despite grants the roads in the island went unrepaired and during the winter of 1791-2, the way from Bastia to Corte, the main route through the island, was again and again reported impassible; the Royal forests were demolished quite haphazardly by peasants seeking ash to manure their fields and their destruction went unpunished; the 80,000 francs which were voted

225

for the reclamation of the marshes at San Fiorenzo and Aleria were swallowed up, not by the marsh, but by the pockets of the administration.

Monestier's report on the island was one of almost unmitigated condemnation; he did not spare the Directory any detail of its maladministration; nor, for that matter, did he spare Paoli whom he unjustly identified with the Directors. It might indeed be argued that Paoli was slow to exert the immense authority he possessed. Certainly he was aware that there was widespread mismanagement, for every week brought to him new instances of corruption and maladministration. But the General was inhibited by his principles from interfering with the government other than by advice and rebuke. The administrators might be inefficient and more aware of their power than their responsibility but, in extenuation, they were young; they were, Paoli thought, corrigible and moreover they represented the civil power to which, Paoli had never ceased to preach, the obedience of the islanders was due. Yet, in spite of his reluctance to interfere in the island's affairs, in spite of his age, the state of his health and his desire for a peaceful retirement, Paoli became increasingly convinced that he must intervene. His chance to dramatically and decisively affect the course of events came with the elections to the French Legislative Assembly in September 1791. By this time, he had come to believe that it was necessary both to administer a public rebuke to the Directory for its past errors, and to reshape it in such a way that it might be of use to the Corsicans. To do this, he realised that it was necessary to organise a party to contest the elections. There were other reasons for his decision to oppose the Directors at the polls.

Since the attempted flight of Louis in June, Republicanism in France was gaining ground rapidly and every visitor who came to the island from France bore witness to the fact that the Monarchy itself was becoming suspect and unpopular. By the self-denying ordinance of the Constituent Assembly, the Deputies of that body enacted that they should be ineligible for re-election. The Legislative Assembly, which was to succeed the Constitutional Assembly, would evidently be made up of new men in a rapidly changing political climate. It was essential for Paoli that he be represented there. The Directory, or elements of it, such as Mattei and Pompei Paoli, were rumoured to be planning to pack the Assembly which would nominate the deputies. Paoli, therefore, threw himself into a campaign to ensure that their efforts would prove fruitless. By letter and by word of mouth he gathered in names from every part of the island and chose his representatives. It was the fundamental weakness of his position that he was in this way restricted to hearsay evidence. His age, by limiting his movements and hence his first-hand knowledge of men, and his long absence from Corsica which had rendered a part of his minute knowledge of the affairs of particular glens out of date, were exacting a heavy price. In the necessary confusion and faced with a far more efficient local organisation of the Directory, the support he commanded was by no means so powerful as he could have hoped for; again his determination not to call into question the authority of the civil power also imposed limits on the power of his campaign, although this was in some measure paid back by the reluctance of many of the Directory's adherents openly to criticise the actions of a Corsican for whom they had a deep-seated respect. However, the resultant Assembly which gathered at Corte was a sufficiently powerful instrument to achieve what he intended. He was determined that the whole affair should be legal with no suspicion of the influence of military power, but at the same time he knew Corsican habits too well to leave anything to chance. He arrived at Corte, accompanied by a detachment of his personal guard, and it was rumoured that, after the delegates had assembled in Corte, the passes through the mountains to the capital were occupied by detachments of his trusted mountaineers. In the town itself election fever ran high. In spite of all their efforts to disguise the breach which had arisen between them Paoli's displeasure with the Directory was pretty widely known and there was a general feeling that a time to redress grievances had come.

The General's influence, and perhaps his guards too, kept good order in the town until the day of the election itself. In the Corsican fashion the hall of a convent was selected for the voting. The Directory attempted to introduce far more than its fair share of representatives into the convent by means of a signed pass, which was given to all those in the town whom they thought would support it, even though they were not delegates. This was detected. Nevertheless, the Directory had more than its legitimate share of delegates in the hall when the proceedings opened. Its adherents were well organised. As soon as discussions began, a *claque* which had been formed began operations. The Abbé Coti, a huge formidable man, with a stentorian voice, began in his address to state the case against the Directory. Immediately howls, whistles and stamping feet broke out. The Abbé was quite used to raising his voice; he began to roar furiously. His opponents retaliated in kind. This contest went on for some time; every time criticism was levelled against the Directory the hall became a bearpit. Paoli watched all this with grim amusement, interested to see who would break the deadlock. It proved to be Mario Falacci, who suddenly leapt up on a bench at a break in the noisy contest with a noose around his neck: 'If the people's delegates are made dumb,' he cried, holding up the end of the halter rope for all to see, 'then slavery will soon be imposed on us again'. This of course caused a fresh outburst, but it was followed by a comparative calm. The leaders of the *claque* realised that they were really digging the grave of their cause. A more or less restrained debate followed in which accusations and counter-accusations were hurled around the hall without any result being achieved. The business of the elections then began. The debate had revealed, however, that the Directory's adherents were in a minority and that changes would be made. The first contest was between Bartholomeo Arena, the Procurator General Syndic, and Paoli's nephew, Leonetti. Paoli made no secret of his support for Leonetti: 'Are you a candidate for the National Assembly?' he called out to Leonetti loudly. 'I wish to serve Corsica as I have always served her,' Leonetti said in answer, 'Bravo,' said Paoli, 'service should always be the object of a candidate for office.'

If there were any doubts, this little scene resolved them. Leonetti was elected by a huge majority. The Paolist candidate who contested the second seat was Pietri Fozzoro. He was opposed by a member of the great Casabianca clan. Once again the election was a foregone conclusion. Paoli's candidate was overwhelmingly elected. The next candidate of the Directory to stand was Pozzo di Borgo. His record as a Director was not unblemished, but he had impressed Paoli by the energy which he had shown on many occasions and besides this he had been absent in Paris for the first five months of the Directory's operations. Moreover, Paoli had marked Pozzo from the very first as one of the young men whose abilities would be of great importance to the island's welfare. Pozzo was certainly able and he was also ambitious. His stay in Paris had whetted his appetite for the real seat of power. He was determined to leave nothing to chance. Realising that his being lumped with the rest of the Directory threatened his ambitions, he went to Paoli and said to him: 'What chance has any member of the Directory to be elected? Even now, your nephew Leonetti is openly lobbying against us in your name. These elections will become a farce'.

Paoli saw in Pozzo's action the first split in the united front of the Directory. He gave instructions to Leonetti that his name was not to be used to influence voters. Pozzo, he said, could take his chance. Pozzo, in return, largely dissociated himself from a great deal of the actions of the other Directors. Each member of the Directory should stand on his own feet, he said, and not be held accountable for the actions of the others. Without Paoli's opposition the election was much closer. Pozzo's eloquence and his record won him the third Deputyship after a very close contest. The objectives of Paoli at the Conference had now been largely achieved. The Directory had been split apart by Pozzo's defection and admission of error. His going led to bitter recriminations amongst the other Directors. Bartholomeo Arena coveted the Deputyship and the opportunity to make a career in Paris above all else. It was now slipping from him. He changed his tactics. Standing again for the fourth Deputyship, he was prepared to admit that mistakes had been made and that the Directory had, in some instances, acted unlawfully. He pleaded that the pressure of office and the necessity to govern in difficult circumstances was in some measure an extenuation. Paoli markedly stood aloof, and after a bitter and closely fought contest Arena was elected after two recounts. With two unsullied Paolists, Peraldi and Biron, the six chosen to represent Corsica in the new National Assembly was complete.

Paoli had demonstrated that, in the last resort, power in the island lay in his hands; he had split the unity of the Directory and he had obtained public admissions that they had fallen into error; at the same time, he had shown a measure of magnanimity and had left some room for a reconciliation, if the Directory and its associates so wished. Above all, everything had been done legally and he had refrained from using the military power that he undoubtedly commanded. He had great hope that, with the return of Saliceti to be Procurator General Syndic and the reconstitution of the administration of the island (half of which, in accordance with a decree of the National Assembly, had been renewed after the elections for the Legislative and with much the same result for the Directory's candidates), the island would begin a new and more fruitful period of its history.

But he also knew that the national unity he had made so many sacrifices for, was, for the time, lost. The old Corsican spirit of vendetta and clan had been roused against him, in spite of the comparatively mild way in which he had handled the faction of the Directory. In the island, in the future, he was to have open enemies and critics. His emergence from his semi-retirement had demonstrated just how powerful he was, but at the cost of shattering the assumption that loyalty to Paoli was necessarily loyalty to Corsica.

He lacked, too, one of the most essential requirements of a man in his position – that of having collaborators of his own ability and temper. During the wars of liberation against the Genoese, nationalism had bound all the followers together and the Enlightenment had provided the driving force of all his policy. But now the nationalism of the clansmen in the hills hindered the actions of any administrator who displayed too openly that he drew his authority, or even his inspiration, from France. The young French-educated Corsicans were however, proud of their authority; they did not consider themselves any the less Corsican for it. No small proportion of Paoli's time was given up to sweetening the relations between the representatives of the two different kinds of society. Paoli's advice to particular chieftains to obey the decree of the Directory was often listened to grumblingly, but, backed by his past and his years and expressed, as it unfailingly was, in terms that took due account of the pride of the chieftains, it was never ignored and rarely rejected. But from their ranks he obtained few recruits for posts in the administration. On the other hand, the young administrators, drawn mainly from the ports, many of whom shared his ideas, planned to sweep away without consideration or remorse the authority of those who alone could ensure the unity and good order of Corsica. Their aims were often Paoli's aims; what he opposed was their precipitancy and their reluctance to count the cost of their haste. When Paoli offered them advice it was carefully considered, especially after the elections of 1791, but the consideration was increasingly accompanied by complaints about his excessive caution. With the enthusiasm of youth they had, in the last resort, more respect for Paoli's latent power than for his past and his experience, and this was true even of the new members of the Directory, who soon adopted the attitude of the survivors of the first Directory, Mattei and Pompei Paoli. When they wished to criticise him an instrument lay ready in the shape of party.

For in Bastia and in Ajaccio particularly, but in Calvi and San Fiorenzo too, allegiance to a political party had more meaning than allegiance to country, with which it was often confused, not surprisingly since 'country' in some contexts meant Corsica and in others, France. By a profession of allegiance to party Paoli's opponents could take on the appearance of the upholders of a principle that the General was held to have violated. So Paoli after his return was by turns and by pamphlet transmogrified into a blood-thirsty republican, a hypocritical devotee, a covert Royalist, an English agent and, increasingly, an aristocrat. The irony was that the charge of the General's aristocratic sympathies was superficially plausible and was accepted by many, especially in France. Paoli had attempted to put the principles of the Enlightenment into effect gradually, and to be gradual was, in France, the badge of reaction. He had never been extreme in his opinions; now he was being forced to walk, like the wayfarer on Slieve League, a narrow path between two precipices; reaction lay on one side, anarchy on the other.

Saliceti had become for Paoli the hope of such a policy of balance. But Paoli was doomed to disappointment. Saliceti was certainly Enlightened and he was politically astute, but his Enlightenment and his politics were those of the Jacobins. During his time in Paris, he had become one of their most enthusiastic members; he was trusted greatly by Robespierre and he had, in no small measure, modelled himself on the 'Great Incorruptible'. Small and insignificant, his long, thin nose dominated a stern and severe lawyer's face. He had a great deal in common with Paoli, perhaps even more with the young Paoli. He shared Paoli's reserve, but he had none of the charm Paoli now showed in company. In company, he acted more as the young Paoli in his Neopolitan days had done, loudly scorning brilliant conversation and being, a trifle over-conspicuously, stern and taciturn. Yet again, like the young Paoli, he had a sharp intelligence and a ruthless and direct political instinct. His political creed, though, was something new in Corsican politics. It was inspired by a revolutionary pride which, in the manner of the Jacobins, despised Kings and Princes as a matter of principle, finding always the authority for its actions in the name of the people of France.

Saliceti's return to Corsica seemed, at first, to be of extremely good augury for Paoli. Both looked forward to their collaboration in the island: 'Your will', Saliceti wrote enthusiastically to Paoli, 'will be mine', while Paoli, for his part, highly and frequently praised the actions of Saliceti in the National Assembly. He was especially grateful for the steady support that Saliceti had given him, especially in the days before his return to Corsica. Over the years they had vied in the exchange of compliments. Paoli had always declared that Saliceti was the man who could sing the litany of liberty confidently. Saliceti declared again and again that Paoli was the incarnation of public spirit; he praised the General's past and his present equally.

Alas for all their hopes of co-operation! Saliceti, for all his similarities to Robespierre, had one great and fatal difference: 'Before all else', said Joseph Buonaparte sardonically, 'he loves money'. Joseph was unjust; he loved power even more. Whatever the balance, the combination was fatal to his relations with Paoli.

He had made sure that, when he was a member of the Constitutional Assembly, he had been paid the three salaries of the posts he could claim: that of a Deputy, that of the Procurator General Syndic and that of an Assessor of the Tribunal of Sartene. Hardly had he arrived in the island than he employed the gains he had made to buy up a property near Aleria which cost 70,000 *livres*. Ominously, it was a pistol point bargain, for Saliceti exiled the possessors of the property he coveted on a charge of disloyalty and took possession of his land with a troop of soldiers. It was not to be the only instance of his use of power for profit. But his urge to acquire was only a by-product of his desire for power. Power was really the God in the inner shrine of his being. In that, he was a true Jacobin. His writings, as well as his actions, proved it: 'It is necessary to govern men by force', he wrote, 'the words they understand best are short and final'. The Corsicans, he said, were too fond of independence. It would do them good to learn obedience. These, and like phrases, and there were plenty of them, might have been very impressive in Paris, but they were of a nature to cause great trouble in Corsica. Opposition, however, did not at all deter Saliceti. He used all the authority of his office and all the troops he could command to crush it. Whenever he lacked legal authority he assumed it. Everywhere he professed to see counter-revolution. His dominating personality swept the new Directory along with him, for his methods, brutal and insensitive as they were, certainly achieved a measure of success and at first his rapid and decisive actions produced a stunned reaction that looked like the beginning of peace. Paoli was not slow to show his displeasure at some of Saliceti's actions. But Saliceti disregarded Paoli's warnings. He was determined to brook no opposition and was confident that he could override it if it came. He was wrong. He thought that Paoli's caution was due to the timidity of age but the outbreak in Isola Rossa on 1st March 1792 showed on what hollow foundations his power rested. It demonstrated to him what he had not wished to know, or perhaps ever been aware of; that the power of the Directory in the island, no matter who the Directors were, depended in the last resort upon Paoli.

Since 14th November 1789, the Arena brothers had ruled Isola Rossa. Filippo Antonio, a brother of Bartolomeo, the newly elected member of the Convention, was the mayor of the town and his followers and relations, in very typical Corsican fashion, dominated the Municipality. They disputed power in the little sea-port with another clan, the Savelli, who, defeated in their attempts to control the Municipality, had found consolation in obtaining control of the Directory of the District. Relations between the Savelli and the Arena became increasingly embittered over the months and, not unnaturally, the Arena had prohibited the carrying of arms in the town. When Franceschi, a district official, defiantly entered the town, carrying a musket, he was immediately arrested by the Municipal officials. The local Directory peremptorily ordered him to be released. Filippo Antonio referred the question to the Municipality, and the Municipality procrastinated happily. The Directory of the District, deciding that the delay was intolerable, sent in the National Guard they commanded to surround Arena's house and take the mayor into custody. Eleven days later, when he was released, there was a violent uprising among the citizens of the town. It had probably been instigated by the Savelli, but it nevertheless found ready enough grievances in the arbitrary actions which had been carried out at various times by the brothers. The insurgent citizens threatened the life of the mayor, and he and his brother, after some hair-breadth adventures, eventually made their escape from the port by boat. His mother and niece were compelled to seek safety in the house of the Judge of the Tribunal and their family home was then gutted. The citizens next set about demolishing the walls of the sea-port at the gates of which Arena had in the past levelled what they considered to be exhorbitant customs dues.

As soon as they had found safety the brothers immediately appealed to Paoli for help. Paoli sent in the National Guard of Monticello, but only after a delay of some days, to restore order in the town. Saliceti, in his capacity of Procurator General Syndic, ordered a full investigation to be made and, as a result of the report made by the Commissioners, the Savelli brothers were deposed from all their offices. But in spite of their vindication the Arena's power in the town was destroyed and for this they blamed Paoli who, they said bitterly, had delayed far too long before he came to their assistance. They wrote angrily to their brother Bartolomeo in Paris that this delay on Paoli's part was deliberate. They might have been right, for Paoli certainly said in public that it was good for the Arena to learn that their power was dependent upon Corte: 'I had a great partiality for the enthusiasm of that young advocate', he said, speaking of Bartolomeo, 'but the actions of the family in the Balagna have long become insufferable'. Certainly the breach which had been created between Bartolomeo and Paoli at the elections for the National Assembly now widened and deepened. The Arena, in future, were to become Paoli's most bitter opponents in the island, while Bartolomeo became an arch-critic of Paoli in the Assembly. Paoli was distressed, but resigned: 'This quarrel could not have been avoided', he said 'the Balagna was no longer able to endure the Arena'.

But it was not only the Arena whose pride had been injured, but the pride of Saliceti, and Saliceti was not the man to brook easily affronts to his pride. Relations between the Procurator General Syndic and the General became strained. But they still respected one another and, still more important, they still needed one another. For, as war fever spread in Paris, Republicanism grew with it. The two were by no means in cahoots, but because of their spread the Royal troops in the island presented a problem. If war were declared upon Revolutionary France by European powers pledged to restore the *ancien régime,* would the garrisons obey the government or would they hold the sea-ports for a foreign power? Both Paoli and Saliceti saw the potential danger and worked for the introduction of detachments of the recently-recruited battalions of Volunteers into the citadels of the key towns in order that they might share the garrison duties. The official commander-in-chief of the island, Paoli's friend Biron, who, although he possessed the command, still remained in France, was more concerned with the Alpine front than he was with Corsica. His song, said Cesari, is always the same one – tomorrow I shall come – but tomorrow never comes. Antonio Rossi, his second-in-command, was a good soldier but an un-certain politician, in a position where a good politician was of infinitely more use than a good soldier.

Rossi was tired and weary of all the intrigue and chicanery that went on in the island. He hoped that, by keeping as aloof as possible, he would avoid becoming embroiled. But to be above the battle in Corsica was, as Paoli had already found, almost an impossibility. Rossi was a Corsican who hailed originally from Ajaccio and the Corsicans were not slow to play on his family loyalties and remind him that his refusal to have the Volunteers guarding the citadels of the sea-ports was an affront to his Corsican fellows. But Rossi was well aware of the Volunteers' reason for wishing to share the garrison duties and he stolidly repelled all requests; not all Paoli's polite diplomacy or Saliceti's veiled menace had any effect on him. Paoli had a certain sympathy with him, although he regarded it as of the first importance that the Volunteers should obtain a foothold in the citadels. What irked Paoli even more than Rossi's continued refusals was the fact that in Calvi and in Ajaccio and in Bastia the Municipality were very content that Rossi should hold the citadel and refused to make any of the representations to Rossi that the Directory and the General requested. But Paoli had no illusions about the quality of the battalions of Corsican Volunteers that had just been created. He was only too well aware that the Directory had been at work again, that many of the officers had been selected by local intrigues and that the Volunteers were often less interested in service than in the pickings they hoped to enjoy. In a private letter and in a fit of exasperation he delivered a scathing condemnation of them: 'In some detachments', he said, 'the officers are not even able to control their men and this is because they have obtained their rank, not because of any qualities they possess, but because of intrigue and corruption; they have no idea of service and they are prepared to steal anything that falls in their way. I would rather have a battalion of *gendarmes* than these four battalions of Volunteers recruited with so much irregularity and indecency'.

With all their faults the Volunteers were Corsicans and in the event of a conflict would be loyal to Corsica and to the Republican cause, while the French in the garrison might not. Paoli believed that chance and tact would eventually carry the day and he believed the best policy was to woo the Municipalities and preserve good relations with the French. It was the policy he had always pursued. But while he sought to conciliate, Saliceti was in the way to provoke another explosion.

18

THE VOLUNTEERS AT AJACCIO

Ajaccio, like Bastia, had a great affection for its religious. This was especially irritating of course to the anti-clerical Directors. At first it was merely an affair of words, with the Ajaccian faithful having to ignore taunts like that of the young Napoleon who remarked apropos of the respect of the townsmen for their priests that: 'a population which consists of sailors is, above all, extremely superstitious'. As well as being superstitious they were loyal. At the end of 1791, there had been an impressive demonstration in the sea-port, when hundreds of the faithful had converged on the municipal hall, after having heard the rumour that the well-beloved monastery of the Capucins was to be closed. The Directory of the District had sent very full reports about this to the General Council of the Department, pointing out how undesirable it was to needlessly agitate the population and Paoli, who deplored the provocations of the Directory, also sought in his way to pour oil on the waters: 'The old ladies of Bastia are very fond of their venerable beards,' he said, 'Why cause trouble needlessly?'

But the Directory was implacable. On 28th February 1792, the order was given by Saliceti for the suppression of the convents of Ajaccio, Bastia, Bonifacio and Corte. The pattern of events at Bastia began to shape itself again. In Ajaccio, on 25th March, the Capucins gave Easter communion to most of the inhabitants, those who received it loudly declaring that they received it from religious men and not from the bought priests of the Directory. On the same day, the Municipality, which had met in the church of San Francesco, sent a delegation to petition for a stay in the execution of the Directory's orders. The representative of the Directory in Ajaccio was Joseph Buonaparte. His reply to the petitioners was hardly helpful: 'Go home', he said, 'if the Procurator Saliceti should find you here you will be sent immediately to the prisons of the citadel and after you, those who sent you. Go home quickly and stop making useless demands'. The delegates realised that what he said was all too true. They dispersed quietly but resentfully. The fires were being stoked.

While this was going on, Joseph's younger brother, Napoleon, was thirsty for action. Because of his future, Napoleon bulks very large during this period in the histories of the island, and the glorious future that was to be his was so enormous that all too many historians afterwards found it tempting, not only to see the seeds of greatness in all his actions but, when the record was deficient, to draw heavily on anecdote and legend. There is very little ground for most of the stories that concern him; for instance, the most famous of all Corsican injunctions, that of Paoli to the young soldier to: 'go forth and be the successor of Alexander' is highly unlikely to have ever been uttered, given the nature of their relations. Napoleon was certainly not an unimportant figure, especially in Ajaccio, but the truth is that he appeared to Paoli, and to many others, as an ambitious and restless, if talented, young man.

In spite of the misgivings that his obvious ambitions raised, however, he was in a position to make a brilliant career for himself in Corsica, for Paoli had returned from exile favourably disposed towards the Buonapartes; he knew the family well, had close personal links with them and deemed them good patriots. Carlo, the father of the Buonaparte clan, had been Paoli's secretary during the years of his rule at Corte and Paoli had been instrumental in effecting the marriage of Carlo with Laetitia Ramolino, the mother of the clan. They, for their part, quickly joined themselves to the General's party. Joseph had, at Aix, been one of the first Corsicans to welcome the General back to the island; Napoleon, an admirer of Paoli from his boyhood, early in 1791 requested Paoli to provide him with documents, in order that he could write a history of the Corsican struggle for liberty (a request which, incidentally, Paoli had rather unkindly refused, saying that he had not the time to have copies made of all his documents, and in any case the writing of history was not the occupation of young men). But although Paoli was initially disposed to look favourably upon the Buonapartes, he had been very annoyed by the circumstances of Napoleon's election to the lieutenant-colonelcy of the Fourth Battalion of Corsican Volunteers.

Napoleon was, at that time, a second-lieutenant in the Artillery and on leave from France. The formation of the battalions of Volunteers, in the early part of 1792, led him to hope that he could better himself by exploiting all the local Buonapartist connections. Two lieutenant-colonels were to be elected for each battalion, and of all the candidates for the battalion of Ajaccio and Tallano only two, Quenza and Pozzo di Borgo's younger brother, Matteo, were serious rivals. Quenza, who had commanded the National Guard in Bastia wisely and moderately after the uprising, had won Paoli's approbation for his conduct and was almost certain to be elected. Napoleon, therefore, made a deal with him that each should support the other's candidature. He then kept open house for the Volunteers from the country districts, who were in Ajaccio for the purpose of the election, spending, much to his mother's despair, an inheritance from his uncle, the Abbé Fesche, quite recklessly for this purpose. But he was still not sure of success and determined to leave nothing to chance. Nervous and impatient, he was foolhardy enough, on the eve of the election, to descend with a group of Volunteers upon the house of Peraldi and kidnap a guest, Maroti, one of the three Commissioners sent to supervise the elections. He had his prisoner taken back to the Buonaparte mansion. He seems to have had some confused idea that the Volunteers (many of them from remote glens and inclined to judge a man's standing in his community by the simplest tests) would be impressed by the fact that one of the Commissioners had stayed at his house. But Napoleon's intrigues had not finished yet. When, next day, the vote for the lieutenant-colonels was due to be taken in the church of San Francesco, his supporters gathered, heavily armed with pistols and daggers. On Matteo Pozzo di Borgo's protestations to the Commissioners that violence had been used the evening before, he was howled down and threatened by Napoleon's followers. On his persisting that an enquiry should be made into his allegations, Napoleon's partisans promptly dragged him from the platform. The election developed into farce; Quenza and Napoleon were elected the lieutenant-colonels by main force, their opponents being afraid to declare themselves and risk the violence of Napoleon's adherents. Paoli was furious when he heard of the mock election and remonstrated with the Directory, but the Buonapartes were strongly backed by Saliceti and no enquiry was held. For Paoli, however, after this Napoleon became a typical instance of those officers who had obtained their position by, as he scathingly said, 'Corruption and intrigue.'

Napoleon was quite unperturbed by any criticism of his conduct and, far from allowing the storms his action aroused to die down, he began at once, armed with his new authority, to advocate action against the supporters of 'reactionaries and obscurantists'. He repeatedly remonstrated to Joseph about the unchecked 'progress of fanaticism'; his ready pen quickly earned him some notoriety and he was probably responsible for the drafting of Joseph's forceful letter to Rossi of 1st March, in which Joseph, speaking for the Directory, said that since it was necessary to guard against an outbreak of violence at Ajaccio, the four companies of Volunteers in the District would be moved into the town as a safeguard. A few days later, Saliceti came to Ajaccio to arrange for the entry of the Volunteers. It was a month later, however, before the Directory was finally successful in calming the fears of the Municipality and of Rossi; it was not until 2nd April 1792, that the Volunteers made a formal entry into the town to be reviewed by Colonel Maillard, the French commander of the garrison. Immediately after this, on Rossi's instructions, Maillard demanded that Quenza should detach part of his troops and sent them to guard the valleys of the interior, where, Rossi said, there was growing danger of insurrection. Quenza temporised and demanded until the 11th to organise the companies which could depart for the valleys. While this was being done, the Municipality informed him that only part of the Volunteers might be quartered in the town. The Municipality said that accommodation could not be found for the others; but it arranged for them to be billeted in a new barracks just outside the walls.

The next few days, after the reception of the troops, were full of trouble. In the port fighting broke out on several occasions between the Volunteers and Ajaccian sailors. The severity of the brawls led several families who feared the future to take ship for Italy.

On Easter Day the nonjuring priests offered mass at the convent of San Francesco. The more zealous of the enthusiasts who accompanied them openly announced that the next day there would be a procession of the faithful, which, by implication, meant all the opponents of the Directory.

The procession accordingly took place on 9th April. The day

passed quietly, until five o'clock in the afternoon when a bloody affray broke out between some sailors and the Volunteers. Napoleon led a group of his officers to the scene of the disturbance, but hardly had he arrived there than one of this lieutenants, Rocco-Serra, was shot dead at his side and Napoleon and the others only just escaped by passing through the Ternano mansion, which abutted the Cathedral Square, and gaining the shelter of the seminary where the rest of his troops were quartered. Both Napoleon and Quenza were raging at the affront which had been offered to the battalions, but they saw that an advantage might be drawn from it; they sent a messenger to Colonel Maillard, demanding that they be admitted immediately within the citadel for their own safety since the Municipality could not apparently control its citizens. Maillard retorted that this could not be. He could not admit anyone into the citadel without the express orders of his King. Quenza and Buonaparte then demanded to be given munitions of war for their defence, but the Colonel retorted that they had already had their due allowance. However, he promised that he would use all his influence with the Municipality to bring those guilty of the murder of Rocco-Serra to justice.

On the next day. a Justice of the Peace, Drago, went to the seminary to enquire if there were any wounded soldiers there, as had been reported. Quenza retorted that he had no wounded soldiers at the seminary and then, to Drago's amazement, ordered his arrest. Almost at the same time a party of the Volunteers smashed down the door of the tower of St George at the seminary and ascending the staircase to the top of the tower they began to fire on the inhabitants who were coming out of the Cathedral at the end of Mass. They killed a widow, a little girl of 13 years and the Abbé Santo Peraldi. Infuriated by this, the citizens banded themselves together under the Abbé's father, Mario Battista Peraldi, and attacked the seminary. The Volunteers heavily counter-attacked; some quickly occupied the houses which commanded the nearby streets and other stormed the ancient church of the Jesuits. The Municipality thereupon declared that the Volunteers were carrying out a full-scale campaign against them, and demanded that Colonel Millard should provide the town with pieces of cannon in order they might protect themselves. The colonel refused to do this, but, realising the situation was getting out of hand, he declared martial law. He then called Quenza to him and told him that he, Maillard, was responsible for law and order in the town, and that he would use the French troops in the garrison to attack the Volunteers if they did not immediately withdraw from the positions they had occupied.

Quenza and Napoleon, resorting to politics, now used their influence with Abbé Coti, the Procurator Syndic of the District, demanding of him that he annul the Municipality's request to Maillard. Coti, closely related to the Buonapartes, was willing to do this. Acting on his own authority, and without consulting the rest of the Directory of the District, he demanded of Colonel Maillard that he should take all necessary measures to secure the safety of the Volunteers and that they should be allowed to retain the positions they already occupied. Maillard answered Coti that he could not revoke the orders that he had given. Napoleon and Quenza then went to Maillard and assured him that, if they were allowed to retain the positions they had occupied, they would answer for the good order of the Volunteers. Maillard, seeing in this an opportunity to bring about a peace, agreed.

But that very night, Napoleon ordered his troops to attack the Benielli mansion, one of the strongest and easiest to fortify in the town. At the same time, his troops occupied yet more houses in the surrounding streets. Maillard immediately called an emergency meeting for 10th April and presided over a meeting between the magistrates of the town, Quenza, Buonaparte and some officers of his own battalion. These managed to draw up an armistice.

However, on the morning of the next day, it was reported to Maillard that the armistice was not being obeyed, that the Volunteers were preventing the citizens who wished to draw water from reaching the fountains and that they were numerous incidents in which the Volunteers had manhandled innocent people in the streets and damaged property. At the same time, Maillard was infuriated to learn that Napoleon had been attempting to organise a conspiracy against him among the soldiers of the French garrison. Napoleon's plans were revealed to Maillard by those very soldiers whom he had hoped to subvert, by means of an appeal to their revolutionary ardour and the condemnation of Maillard as an aristocrat. When, that afternoon, the citizens demanded that he should provide them with cannon and soldiers, so that they might restore some sort of order in the town and save the citizens from dying of hunger and thirst, he was disposed to listen. At a conference of war held in the citadel on the night of the 11th, he agreed that he would give the Municipality help. The next day detachments of his garrison marched out of the citadel and trained two cannon, one on the seminary and the other on the Ternano mansion. Quenza and Naploeon were then instructed by the Municipality to retire immediately from the positions they had occupied in the town. Napoleon, in his reply, played a trump card. He had just been informed that the Directory of the Department was to send two Commissioners, Cesari and Bartolomeo Arrighi, to Ajaccio to conduct an enquiry and to undertake the command of all the local forces. In informing the Municipality of this, Napoleon also added some completely false information of his own, writing that he had received express instructions from Paoli to retain the positions that the Volunteers had occupied, that Quenza had been given the command of the National Guards in the surrounding districts and that, in consequence of this, if the cannon were not immediately retired, Quenza would give the order for the invasion of the town. The Municipality, in a panic, requested Maillard to withdraw his troops and his cannon, and this the Colonel accordingly did.

The next few days were a time of comparative quiet. On 16th April, Arrighi and Cesari entered Ajaccio. They met on the way, they reported, crowds of peasants with empty sacks who hoped to join them with the intention of filling their sacks when the *cuccagna* of Ajaccio took place. When the Commissioners arrived, they peremptorily ordered the battalion of Quenza to Corte. Napoleon furiously opposed this measure and only Arrighi's threat of force and Joseph's insistence made him give way. An enquiry was set up (which produced a balanced report some time later); but the Directory was determined to assert its authority at once and thirty-four of the leading citizens of the town who had been most active against the Volunteers were imprisoned. But this time there was to be no *cuccagna*. Paoli was incensed with the way in which Napoleon had recklessly used his own name and compromised his honour.

The Municipality, too, once it realised that Napoleon had resorted to outright lying to make it relinquish its favourable

243

position, behaved with outraged indignation. At its instigation, the Directory of the District demanded that Coti be suspended from all his functions and imprisoned. The Directory of the Department immediately annulled this. When Coti was called to Corte for an explanation of his conduct, he was immediately dismissed by the Directory of the District. The Directory of the Department immediately reinstated him. In its turn it demanded that the Municipality receive heavy punishment for all the troubles it had caused.

But the Directory was on the defensive. Throughout Corsica it was known that Paoli looked upon its actions in Ajaccio with anger. From Paris, Pozzo and Peraldi wrote indignantly, condeming the action that the Volunteers had taken, criticising the Directory and demanding that order and justice should prevail in Ajaccio. The rebuke was weighty, for Carlo Andrea Pozzo had become a man of importance in France, having been made one of the four Commissioners for War. By letters to the Ministry of Justice, he attacked the Directory and all its judges. Ceaselessly, but with the furious energy so characteristic of him, he intrigued to obtain a public condemnation of their actions. In the whirl of accusation and counter-accusation contained in the reports the French government had to read on the situation, it became increasingly plain that Paoli was the one sure centre in the island and the only one who could guarantee its security.

Paoli used his enhanced authority with his usual moderation. With all his large reservations about Saliceti and the Directory he recognised the energy and ability of the Procurator General Syndic and believed it could be turned to good account. Saliceti, for his part, deplored Paoli's caution, but realised that the General had been extremely forbearing towards him and, although he feared his influence as a misplaced brake upon effective government, he still believed that a fruitful alliance was possible. But Paoli had quite strong feelings about the part that Napoleon had played in the Ajaccian revolt. When Napoleon came to Corte with his battalion in May, he went immediately to see Paoli. He was quite unimpressed by the censure that had been generally passed on his conduct and blithely unconcerned at having taken Paoli's name in vain. He offered no apologies to Paoli, only new proposals. He proposed that a new battalion should be formed to replace the old one, which was evidently undisciplined and that he should command it. On 13th May, Paoli had a talk with Joseph about Napoleon's proposals.

Immediately afterwards Joseph had, in his turn, a short talk with his young brother: 'It seems to me', said Joseph, 'that your most prudent course of action would be to leave the island immediately and return to France'. Napoleon took his advice.

As the summer wore on, Paoli's influence was in the ascendant. Saliceti took great care to secure his advice on most measures. The island returned to something like tranquillity. Paoli's reproaches became less frequent. When they did come, they produced extremely quick reactions. But while Corsica became calmer, in France the combination of widespread hardship and national danger enabled the Jacobins to pluck more and more power from the hands of the government. On 10th August, an attack on the Tuileries led to the suspension of the Royal power and the resolution to set up a National Convention. However, so great was the respect that Paoli now commanded in Paris as a result of the tranquillity that had settled on the island, now that his influence was predominant, that when Rossi seized the period of comparative calm to retire, it was Paoli who was appointed on 11th September 1792, even while the elections for the National Convention were taking place, as commander of the twenty-third Division and hence as the military head of all the troops in the island.

It was at the elections in the island for this Convention that the conflict between the General and the Directory, which had been concealed in the aftermath of the Ajaccian revolt, burst once more into the open. If it had been essential for Paoli to be faithfully represented the year before, it was even more essential now that the war fever in Paris and the struggle of the Jacobins with their opponents created a climate of unhealthy suspicion. Paoli anticipated no trouble with elections. Trusted in Paris, idolised in Corsica, with the Directory efficiently checked at the centre of the island's government, he could advocate that the Corsicans exercise their franchise wisely, secure in the knowledge that the electors would provide him with an adequate majority. Saliceti and his associates exerted every scrap of influence that they possessed in the glens to drum up support for themselves. But all their skill and energy, all their threats and promises were of little avail against the simple loaded advice of the General. The weakness of Saliceti's position was clearly shown by his manoeuvrings on the eve of the elections at Corte. As the electors assembled, Saliceti went to see his former fellow Deputy, Cesari, who was staying at Paoli's house. Cesari was no politician, in spite of the fact that he had been elected a Deputy in 1789; he was, at bottom, a straightforward soldier who was determined to do his duty as he saw it. Saliceti appealed to him to leave Paoli's house and take appartments in the town. He inferred that Paoli had been secretly plotting to destroy the French administration: 'Paoli', he said to Cesari, 'hates France and the Revolution, but he professes patriotism and outwits us all by his diplomacy'. Cesari indignantly replied that he admired and esteemed Paoli. Paoli, he said, was too old to dream of despotism; his only love was for his country. He said to Saliceti that it would be a sad thing if the General had been called from his exile in London, only to be repudiated and betrayed by his fellow countrymen. Saliceti returned to the Directory, terribly gloomy about the probable outcome of the elections.

But here, chance took a hand. Before the electors convened, Paoli was struck down by typhus. While he lay close to death in the convent, Saliceti made a supreme effort. His ability was undoubted and well known and it seemed as if he would be, on the death of Paoli and by right of possession, the new ruler in the island. He extracted every scrap of possible menace and promise from this. He appealed to all true patriots to rally around him in this decisive hour. Saliceti had a great deal of experience in political organisation which he had gained in France and he used it well. He hamstrung Cesari by the accusation that Cesari was plotting to usurp supreme power for himself. That honest soldier was in no position to deal with Saliceti's insinuations. Saliceti juggled groups and interests furiously, dividing clan against clan with all the skill and élan that he had acquired in the clubs and assemblies of Paris. He distributed the Directory's money lavishly and recklessly in bribes. He employed every procedural device to exclude his opponents and include his supporters.

When it came to the elections it was seen just how successful his manoeuvres had been. His own election, of course, was quite secure, but if Paoli had been well the election of the Directory's candidates which ensued would never have taken place. Even so, even with Paoli on a sick bed and Saliceti using every electoral tactic at his command, the candidates of the Directory only just scraped home – Chiappe, an ex-Director, only by seventeen votes, Casabianca only after two recounts, Moltedo only after three; and in both these two latter cases there were bitter accusations of a rigged count. But only two of Paoli's supporters, Andrei and Bozio, were returned.

As quickly as possible, Saliceti and his group set sail for France. By a freak of chance he had obtained his object. The devoted follower of Robespierre, he could rely on being a power in the Convention and thus being able to greatly affect events in Corsica. He knew that if he and the party he had created in Corsica were one day to control the island, it was the only course he could follow, for it had become evident to him that it was only from France that he could hope to checkmate Paoli.

As for Paoli, the fundamental weakness in his position had again been demonstrated. He had hoped from the moment of his return from exile that the new men of the Enlightenment would rely on his judgement and experience in their government. But the most able and energetic of those new men were also the most extreme and implaccable. To them the principles of liberty and equality counted for far more than that of fraternity, and together with their new ideas they carried the old hatreds of the vendetta with which they all too often confused their zeal for revolutionary activity. In the last resort, power in the island lay in the hands of Paoli, for his past always justified his present discretion and moderation. But while he held himself aloof, the Directors could reasonably allege that he reserved for himself only the praise attached to governing, while they bore most of the blame. In a crisis, such as occurred in 1791, he could always defeat them, but when his own influence was temporarily removed, as it had been, by illness, for the elections for the Convention, his lieutenants were not able or strong enough to stand up to his opponents.

For the immediate future, his way seemed easier with the return of Pozzo and Peraldi: he was assured of having two able and experienced, and comparatively young, men at the head of his government. But he had lost control of a vital position. From now on, his actions in the island would be remorselessly misrepresented in Paris. He knew that a life and death struggle was beginning. He knew that he could no longer stand aloof, but that, in spite of his age and infirmities, he had to participate far more directly in the island's government.

His recovery from the typhus was marked by a resurgence of his energy. With Pozzo and Peraldi at his side, he rapidly made concrete his always potential control of the island. By the law of 22nd September 1792, all the administrators, Municipalities and justices of the island had to be re-elected. Paoli was determined to leave no links in Corsica through which Saliceti could operate. The supporters of the Directory were swept away at the elections All the old members of the Directory were defeated. The new Directory consisted entirely of Paolists. So began for a space of a few brief weeks a halcyon period in the island, with the administrators taking Paoli's advice and consulting him on every occasion. Peace and order were rapidly restored. The enthusiasts of the old Directors had always been a small body, creating a party as much as by what they promised as by the ideas they possessed. With Saliceti in Paris, the mainspring of this party in the island was broken.

An uneasy equipoise had been reached. In Corsica, Paoli and his followers had complete control. In Paris, Saliceti and his three lieutenants counter-balanced them. It was a stalemate. The expedition against Sardinia broke it.

19

THE INVASION OF SARDINIA

The desire of the revolutionary government to spread the revolution to Sardinia had a history which went back to February 1791. In that month Buttafuoco, hoping to save the pro-French faction by the time-honoured expedient of putting them at the head of a war against an external enemy, suggested that, in the event of a war with the Kingdom of Piedmont, its island possession of Sardinia was ripe for revolution, and that Gaffori was the ideal leader to lead a combination of French regulars and Corsican Volunteers to an easy victory against the Royal troops.

When, over a year later, in May 1792, the same plan was put forward by Constantini, a Corsican Jacobin who had, in his capacity as a dealer in grain, obtained a knowledge of the Sardinian seaports, Saliceti had enthusiastically supported the plan and assured his fellow Jacobins in Paris that the Sardinians awaited freedom and that the island would rise enthusiastically if the French landed.

In September, the Provisional Council at Paris, planning the Austrian invasion, accepted the Jacobin idea and named Bartolomeo Arena and Mario Peraldi as Commissioners to the armies of invasion. Arena, not unnaturally considering his bitter feud with Paoli, avoided Corsica and made for Nice, which had just been occupied bloodlessly by Anselme, in order to organise the troops of invasion. Peraldi, being the ally of Paoli, made for Corsica by way of Toulon. In Toulon, he had long conversations with Pache, the Minister of War. His advice was that Paoli should direct the Sardinian campaign and that Ajaccio should be the port for the projected invasion. Pache agreed that Ajaccio should be the port but he told Peraldi what the Executive Council in Paris had already decided: that Paoli was necessary to carry on his already immensely succesful efforts to pacify the island. Accordingly, they had designated Anselme to lead the expedition. He was to embark part of his Army of the Midi, together with six battalions of Marseillais Volunteers, on the ships of Rear-Admiral Truguet, who would sail to Ajaccio by way of Bastia and Calvi, at which ports he would embark additional soldiers for the invasion. At Ajaccio, 3,000 men drawn both from the garrisons of the island and the Corsican Volunteers would join him. Bartolomeo Arena would accompany them as Commissioner and would afford assistance as a liaison officer; Anselme (or any deputy he might employ) and Truguet were invested with plenipotentiary powers for the expedition. Anselme was already fully occupied with the problems of the Midi; Raffaello Casabianca, the second in command of the troops in the island, was finally appointed the leader of the military expedition.

Peraldi arrived in Ajaccio on 1st October and went immediately to Corte with his news. Paoli welcomed him and made him adjutant-general on the spot. The army of invasion was some time assembling, and from the beginning there was an air of defeat in all that touched the expedition. The troops themselves were in a fine disorder. This was hardly surprising for the detachments of the army of the Midi detailed for the Sardinian expedition were composed of six battalions of inexperienced National Guards, while the *phalange marseillaise*, famous for its bloody participation on 10th August 1792 in the storming of the Tuileries, numbered among its volatile and enthusiastic ranks many who were little more than children: boys of thirteen to fourteen years old – 'without a smattering of military instruction, turbulent and ferocious'; reluctant to obey orders, prone to outbursts of violence, they were the despair of their officers and a threat to good order wherever they went.

At last, on 5th December, two squadrons set sail from Nice. One, under La Touche-Tréville, sailed for Naples with the intention of awing the King of that country into neutrality. The other sailed for Ajaccio to prepare the way for the troops which would follow later. They were to rendezvous in the Sardinian Bay of Palmos to concert an attack on Cagliari.

On 15th December, Truguet reached Ajaccio and he and his officers immediately embarked on the organisation of the expedition and on the social life of the town. They could hardly have been sorry to exchange their cabins for the drawing-rooms of the sea-port, for each ship was a floating club, the sailors gathered from the ports of the Midi which was already in the full flower of revolutionary agitation. They brought on board ship a passion for politics; they seemed to a harassed Truguet more intent on drawing up petitions and debating the affairs of the country than in sailing their ships. Nevertheless, he admitted they were good sailors. It was the insolence that they habitually displayed that distressed their captains. At the least suspicion of censure, said Truguet, they formed committees to assert their right and to reprimand their officers. It was an explosive situation and Truguet and his fellows were only to pleased to have some relaxation ashore for a few days.

But being away from his troublesome crews brought Truguet no respite from politics. Almost as soon as he landed he heard of Paoli's objections to the demands of his forces. Paoli declared that he could not spare the 3,000 men that Anselme requested; he needed them to govern the island and protect the ports. Even with all the economies that he could possibly make he could supply little more than half of that number – 1,000 from the French garrison on the island and 800 from the Volunteers. Even so, he believed that Truguet was having the best of the bargain. He had not yet completed his reorganisation of the battalions of Volunteers. Many of them were badly led and indisciplined and, added to this, they were not as all eager to attack Sardinia, with whom the Corsicans, especially those in the south of the island, had a good many links. Paoli pointed out that there had been a great deal of jobbery in the appointment of their officers. He also warned Truguet that he had grave doubts of their discipline when removed from their native soil and of their ability to face seasoned troops. Time was to justify his doubts. Indeed, hardly had Truguet made his first round of social calls when there was bloody fighting in the streets of the port between the sailors and the Volunteers. The Volunteers were already, of course, notorious in Ajaccio for their disorder, but this time they seemed to have been guiltlesss of provocation. Indeed, they were out-Heroded. For, from the moment the sea-men of Truguet's fleet stepped ashore, they paraded the streets calling for the execution of all aristocrats (of whom there were not, by this date, a great many in Corsica). The Volunteers, fresh from the hills and having no French, caught the meaning, if they did not understand actual words. Indeed, they could hardly fail to do so when the sailors brandished knives and nooses everywhere. Moreover, the sailors had a form of insult the Corsicans could not stomach. The Arena and their friends had already a strong footing in the Revolutionary clubs of the Midi where they had vilified Paoli freely. The sailors, following the example, mixed their calls for a holocaust of aristocrats with denunciations of the General and again the significance of the name, chanted with considerable venom, needed no interpreter. Some of the Volunteers were ardent Paolists who had replaced part of those who had caused such trouble in Ajaccio in September; others were veterans of the battle and were resentful of the part that Paoli had played in their uprising; but both were prepared to support a Corsican against a crowd of free-booting French sailors. Quarrels soon broke out and the sailors, very prone to action, hacked two Volunteers to pieces and paraded their bloody fragments up and down the streets. Infuriated, two battalions of Volunteers rushed from their barracks with the intention of shooting down the murderers. Only the naval officers and the commanders of the Volunteers, interposing themselves between their followers, managed to pacify the infuriated warriors and restore some sort of peace on the quays. But the damage had been done. It was no longer possible to mix sailors and Volunteers together safely. Paoli, with Truguet's agreement, decided to keep the Volunteers together and to draw all the invasion contingent from the Royal garrison troops. The whole of the Forty-Second Regiment and detachments of the Twenty-Sixth and the Fifty-Second were to be used. The Corsicans would, he thought, be best used in creating a diversionary attack on the isles of La Maddalena, off the north of Sardinia, for which the sailors accompanying the transports from Nice would also be used. The remaining two weeks before the fleet set sail were tense. Nevertheless, Truguet had time to flirt gaily with Elisa with the amiable approval of the Buonaparte family. In later years, re-collecting the time that he had spent in the island, and observing the regiments of Buonapartist nobility that had been created under the First Empire, Truguet was to say ruefully that in his failure to carry off Elisa he lost his fortune.

On 9th January 1793, he sailed to his rendezvous with La Touche-Tréville. He had not waited for the Marseillais Volunteers who should have been with him by that time, but who had been detained in the ports of the Midi by contrary winds; he expected them to follow in a few days. Nine days later, on the

18th they landed on the Corsican coast at San Fiorenzo. Their propensity to violence and their indiscipline were terrifying. 'They are not an army,' said Paoli, 'they are a horde'. The little port was too insignificant to detain them. Nightfall saw long columns of Marseillais winding up the mountainside to the passes which led to the eastern plain. By the 15th, they were at the gates of Bastia. The Revolutionary Clubs in Bastia, who had already heard, from the astounded citizens of San Fiorenzo and the inhabitants of the villages on their way, of the character of their visitors, united in the face of this sudden danger. They agreed to meet the Marseillais hospitably, but with dignity, and to leave them in no doubt that they wanted no 10th August in Bastia. For the first day all went well and the day closed in what seemed harmony. But on the second day, groups of Marseillias appeared in the streets of the town shouting: '*A la lanterne!*' and '*A bas les aristocrats!*' No aristocrats being available, they hanged a carpenter as the next best thing: Gian Pietri, the lieutenant-colonel of the Volunteers in the town, was rescued from them just as he was about to be hoisted up on the *lanterne*. In the struggle to free him a Volunteer was shot down and several Marseillais wounded. Only the prompt joint action of their officers and the commander of the French garrison in the town, who threatened to attack them with his soldiers, saved the town from being sacked. At Ajaccio, where they then sailed, the pattern was repeated. In a new demonstration they attacked Raffaello Casabianca himself and shot down a Volunteer at his side in the ensuing mêlée; afterwards they gleefully pressed Ajaccians into their ranks. There was only one way to ensure peace and that was to put them to sea as quickly as possible. On the 25th, the transports sailed out to join Truguet. Paoli saw them go with relief and foreboding: 'I can see nothing but disaster coming from their indiscipline,' he said.

His prophecy quickly came true. On 14th January 1793, 800 regulars and 2,000 Marseillais went ashore on the so-called 'Spanish beach', a few hours march from Cagliari; while the rest of the fleet sailed on to create a diversion closer to the town which was already being systematically bombarded by Truguet. The invaders bivouacked close to their landing place, and the next morning they marched out towards Cagliari and encamped some distance from the fort of Sant' Elia, which protected the Sardinian capital on the landward side. Casabianca who led the expedition, hoping to draw an advantage from the fiery spirits of his eager young Volunteers, intended to use them as his advance guard, and, with this object, he led them as close to the fort as he dared and instructed their officers to make camp and be ready for a morning attack. He then returned to the main body of his troops who had made their dispositions for the night some six miles away.

The silence and the menace of an enemy almost within gunshot told on the febrile young Marseillais. A sudden fear, the cause of which was never ascertained, suddenly swept through their ranks. Crying out that they were attacked and betrayed, they broke camp and rushed for safety towards the main body of the army. Coming suddenly out of the night, shouting wildly that they were betrayed, they were taken for the enemy by Casabianca's guard who shot down the first-comers before they realised their mistake. The rest of the night was catastrophic; some faced Casabianca and accused him of treason; some rushed into the countryside to die or surrender weeks later to the Sardinians; some brawled with the regular troops who jeered at them that they were better at crying and hanging than at fighting.

What was evident by daybreak was that the army of invasion was in no position to attack Cagliari. Word was sent to Truguet that the expedition was in disarray.

The weather, in the meantime, worsened. When the fleet at last sailed to pick up the disheartened survivors from the Spanish beach, it sailed through bitter, pouring rain under ever-darkening skies. But when they stood opposite the beach, Truguet realised that to embark an army in those conditions was impossible; as the strength of the gale increased, he decided to put supplies ashore for the army and sail for a safer anchorage in order to ride out the storm. The most disastrous part of the whole adventure followed. The Marseillais, when they realised the admiral's intention, cried out that they were being betrayed to their enemies. Wild scenes followed on the beach. Some of the boats bringing supplies were rushed and their sailors shot down; elsewhere bitter fighting took place between soldiers and sailors in the shallow water, with the Marseillais trying to possess the boats and the sailors desperately struggling to get them back into deeper water and escape. Truguet, in despair, decided that he would try to ride out the storm in the exposed bay to give his compatriots assurance of his good faith. It was a gallant, but unwise decision; before long, some of his light craft were dashed on the rocks. To his disgust, the sailors were shot down by Sardinian troops, in sight of the Marseillais who refused to go to their aid.

On 19th February, the weather improved and Truguet quickly took off what remained of the invaders and sailed for France, leaving only a token force of regulars behind. Their fate was sad: those who had not died of exposure surrendered a few weeks later to the Sardinians.

Some ships of Truguet's fleet sailed back directly to Provence; others put into Bastia. The unrepentant Marseillais were looking for scapegoats. Around the sea-port they loudly asserted that Paoli had betrayed them. They demanded his head. They were treated coldly. Sailing again for Provence, they brought to the Revolutionary Clubs of the mainland the story that Corsica had been betrayed and that the revolution there was destroyed by reaction.

As Truguet sailed for Corsica the diversionary expedition led by Pier Paulo Colonna di Cesari Rocca, or as he was more commonly known, Cesari, left Corsica. The Volunteer contingents were commanded by Quenza and by Napoleon. Napoleon had returned to Corsica early in September to close the ranks of the clan in support of his brother Joseph, who had expected to be far more important in the island under the Convention than he actually became. Napoleon was as ambitious and questing as ever; he was placed in charge of the artillery. Napoleon later called Cesari, not perhaps without a dash of jealousy, a 'clothes horse', because his fine military bearing was unaccompanied by any laurels won in the field. But Cesari had the voices of Pozzo, of Peraldi and most telling of all, Paoli, and indeed he had already won a reputation of sorts as a politician and a soldier. His polititical talents were not extensive and based chiefly on experience gained as a Deputy to the Constitutional Assembly: his military knowledge commanded more respect, for he had been successively and successfully a captain in the former Provincial Corsican Regiment, the second in command of the island's National Guard and, latterly, a colonel of *gendarmerie*.

Cestri was much less sanguine than his subordinate about the Sardinian expedition and had doubts about assuming its command. He knew Sardinia. He was aware indeed that there was discontent with the government in Turin, but he also knew that local patriotism, local leaders and the exhortations of the clergy would count for a great deal in the face of a foreign invasion. Money and good troops, both in large measure, were, he believed, necessary to reduce Sardinia. In spite of his doubts, ambition and the fear of being condemned for incivism, combined with the exhortations of Truguet, led him to the sticking point.

On 22nd February 1793, after having been detained for some time by contrary winds and bad weather, the little armada sailed out of the bay of Bonifacio, led by the *Fauvette*, a corvette of twenty-two guns. That very evening, Cesari's forces made a landing on the island of San Stefano, the southern-most of the three islands (the other two being La Maddalena and Caprera) which together with the mainland, made up a sheltered, bay one of the most magnificent and coveted anchorages in the Mediterranean. The three islands of the group were separated one from the other by only about 800 metres.

As it landed the expedition met some opposition, but by night-fall on the 23rd San Stefano had been occupied and during the night Naploeon placed his cannon so that they could fire across the strait between San Stefano and La Maddalena. His first cannonade did considerable damage. On the evening of the 24th Cesari held a Council of War and it was decided that, at dawn the next day, an attack would be made by the Volunteers on the batteries which protected the island of La Maddalena, and that the transports which ferried them to the attack would, as they crossed the narrow strait, be covered by the *Fauvette*.

But aboard the *Fauvette* all was not well. Its crew was made up, not of the experienced sailors of Truguet's fleet, but of peasants pressed into service in Provence. If they lacked naval experience, they had the same revolutionary ardour. The *Fauvette* had already been damaged by a chance shot from the Volunteers' cannon. The sailors, as a result, professed a distrust of the Volunteers' reliability, but they were even more apprehensive of the two light galleys which the Sardinians commanded and which, although they were lightly armed, were very manoeuvrable and armed with rams. They were also disconcerted by the very war-like appearance of the Sardinians who thronged the shore and showed no inclination at all to welcome their liberators. Realising their temper and declaring that the whole enterprise was hopeless, the captain of the *Fauvette,* Goyetche, made ready to depart. Cesari, seeing the whole expedition endangered, immediately went on board and was untruthfully assured by the Captain that he had no intention of sailing and that Cesari was misled by his lack of knowledge of naval matters. Cesari, nevertheless, decided to sleep on board, and, at seven o'clock in the morning, he was warned that the sailors were about to rig their sails. He rushed on deck and, seconded by the Captain and the officers, pleaded with them not to abandon their comrades. A rapid vote was taken among the sailors, the majority being for departing immediately; orders had no effect, nor did appeals. Cesari could not afford to leave the transports at the mercy of the Sardinian light galleys. Indeed, without the *Fauvette,* the whole expedition was at once rendered highly vulnerable. The only thing Cesari could do for his troops was to order the immediate evacuation of San Stefano. Quenza and Napoleon received the order with incredulity, which rapidly turned into fury. But they had no choice. The expedition sailed back to Corsica, with the Volunteers and the sailors almost at each other's throats.

20

THE RIFT WITH THE
CONVENTION

While the Sardinian campaign was coming to its inglorious conclusion, another campaign was being pushed to a successful
end. Saliceti had, in the winter of 1792, confirmed the golden
opinions the Jacobins already held of him. His republicanism
was awe-inspiring, a pure flame which shrivelled up humanity
and compassion alike and left only a blackened core of self-
interest untouched. That indestructible core made him suspect,
to some of the Republican enthusiasts, of venality, but there
were few to deny that his rhetoric against kings and priests,
aristocrats and emperors, was sincere. Time was, indeed, to show
its sincerity, for all his career was to bear witness to the fact
that his Jacobinism was not superficial, but was the expression
of his deepest convictions. Twice threatened with death, once
after the fall of Robespierre and once after the 18th of
Brumaire, for his intransigent republicanism he twice escaped
through the operation of Napoleon's sense of gratitude to him.
He lived to serve two Kings – Joseph and Murat – at Naples,
and his enemies were quick to point out that this showed his
republicanism had been very short-lived, but his Jacobin principles, inconveniently displayed, did him as much harm with
the newly-installed monarchs as his relentless energy and ability
did him service. When he died suddenly in 1809 it was widely
rumoured that he had been poisoned, since he was too able to
be passed over and too unyielding to be used.

But in 1793, all this was hidden in the future, and in the
heady months of increasing Jacobin power he was in his
element. The Jacobins, for their part, rejoiced in the return of
such a devoted adherent to aid their cause. He had declared
himself irrevocably by being the only one of the Corsican
Deputies to vote for the death of the King, giving his reasons
briefly and brutally: 'You have judged Louis a traitor. The
law decrees death for traitors. I vote for the death of Louis

Capet.' It was only natural that with such *bona fides* he should become the Jacobin expert on Corsica. His Corsican policy was very simple for his fellow Jacobins to comprehend. Without Paoli, all opposition in Corsica, he said and reiterated, would fall to the ground. Paoli, he maintained, was sincere but he was jealous of his power and too able to exercise it. His republican virtue was clouded by the excessive caution of old age and of old friendships with men of the *ancient régime*. The best course was obviously to remove Paoli painlessly from office, whereupon the government of the island would assume its rightful course. On 17th January 1793, Saliceti's policy began to bear fruit, when Paoli was placed under the command of Biron by attaching the Twenty-Third Division to the army of Italy. A good and reasoned case could be made for this step and it was a case which appealed to a wider public than just the Jacobins and their sympathisers. The King had been condemned on 17th January and war with England loomed. It was true Paoli had been no upholder of royal power. Indeed, all his ideals, all his endeavours had shown him to be a republican at heart. But, both in the Clubs of the Mediterranean coast and in the halls of the Jacobins, the idea had been spread of Paoli's growing lukewarmness towards France. Moreover, Paoli was widely know to have been the pensioner of the English and a resident in England for twenty years. He was known, too, often to speak warmly of the English and still to maintain many English connections. Biron saw that a dangerous burden was being laid on him. Known to be an old friend of Paoli, he realised the haze of suspicion which surrounded the General could be a menace to his own position if he did not at once elicit from Paris some clear statement of what his relationship with the General should be. Should he, he wrote to Pache, the War Minister, leave Paoli in command in Corsica or should he recall him to Nice? While he waited for an answer, Saliceti made a shrewd move against Paoli. On 29th January, after a meeting with the Committee of General Defence and after long conversations with one of its members, Barbaroux, the Deputy for Marseilles, Saliceti launched an attack from the Tribune of the Chamber on refractory priests who, he held, were misleading and deluding the people in Corsica. Supported by another furiously anti-clerical Deputy, Goupilleau, he succeeded in having a decree passed to deport all the non-juring priests from the island. It was a shrewd attempt to make Paoli show his hand. Tacitly, the General had protected the non-juring priests whenever he could, from the full rigour of the old Directory's anti-clerical policy. His attitude had been evident for a long time: with the civil power in the hands of republicans the priests were, at the worst, harmless in their hostility; at the best, and with tactful handling they might even become useful; and, above all, they were Corsican. Saliceti calculated confidently that Paoli would use all his powers of manoeuvre to spare them the deportations and thus show plainly before the world how opposed he was to Jacobin policies.

The declaration of war on England by the Convention on 1st February 1793, and the passion for positive action that was rife in France, gave him another chance. With the potential threat of English sea-power facing them, the government could afford to take no chances with their island exposed in the middle of the Mediterranean. On 1st and 5th February, two measures were passed which placed power directly in Saliceti's hands. By the 1st, the four battalions of Corsican Volunteers were to be disbanded and four battalions of light infantry formed in their place; the officers were to be selected by the Executive Council, together with the Corsican Deputies. The second measure enacted that three Commissioners were to be appointed to go to Corsica and assist in putting the sea-ports in the state of maximum readiness; they were to survey fortified sites and they were invested with plenipotentiary powers for the accomplishment of their mission. The Commissioners were to be Saliceti himself, Delcher (a member of the Committee of General Defence) and Lacombe St Michel, a former artillery captain. Of these, only Saliceti had any knowledge of Corsica.

He had played his game well. His following among the Corsican Deputies outnumbered the Paolists four to two, and he was infinitely the Paolists' superior in tactics, so he could count on the Corsican battalions being substantially officered by his own followers. He knew that the regular troops in the island would, in a crisis, obey Paris and not Paoli. Thus, armed with legal authority and backed by a powerful military force, he was sure that, in any case of conflict, he would be able to outface the General. Moreover, all this could be represented to Paoli with some plausibility as being precautionary, for, with the English fleet in the Mediterranean, it was evident that the French coast, and particularly an island of many fine harbours like Corsica, would be threatened.

When Paoli first heard the news of the Committee's decree, it lacked the details of the identity of the Commissioners and he was not unduly concerned. He had himself complained often enough about the formation of the battalions of Volunteers, of the irregularity of their elections and of the indiscipline and inexperience of their officers. But he had recommended that they be reorganised, rather than disbanded and had indeed proceeded some way with the reorganisation. It was, however, obvious, that the new officers would depend greatly on Paris and Paoli was sceptical of any improvement in the regiments if this were to be the case. As for the Commissioners, he was sure that if they had open minds he would be able to dispel any idea they might have of his disloyalty to France. He knew very well just how bitter was the campaign being waged against him in the Clubs of Provence by the Arena: 'Some have called me a tyrant,' he said at this time, 'Well, if they come here they will find that, far from Corsica being a despotism, we have a governemnt here which would serve as a model for any Department in France. Those who call me despot are those who fear me as an obstacle to their partisan and privy projects.' But the news that Saliceti was one of the Commissioners damped his spirits. He realised that the situation was for more serious than it had at first seemed, and that a life and death struggle was about to begin.

From Paris, Pache had replied to Biron that he should take immediate steps to call Paoli to his side and employ his talents on the mainland. Almost at the same time he was informed that the Commissioners of the Mediterranean coast, Royeur, Letoumer and Brunel, had written to Paoli inviting him to the mainland. The invitation, however, inspired by the feeling against Paoli along the Mediterranean littoral, was phrased more as a command than a request. They had not the time, the Commissioners wrote, to go to Corsica and see the General personally but they awaited his return with impatience. They requested him to embark at once in the *Flêche*, the frigate which brought him the invitation. Paoli's reply was tactful, but devious. He was, he said, old and infirm; he suffered from sea-sickness and feared the voyage in his weakened state. Besides, the country was in peril and without a General would be helpless. Borin received much the same reply. Paoli was polite and courteous, but he could not come.

February and March saw a gradual hardening of the attitudes of both sides. The Minister of Finance, Clavière, who had many friends and informants in the Midi, added fuel to the flames by issuing a report which stated that Corsica, of all the Departments of France, contributed least to the national good. Yet, he wrote, it was the island which would not accept the revolutionary *assignat* currency as legal, the island which sheltered fanatical retrograde priests, the island which hindered the sales of national goods, the island which was ruled by a mendacious agent who abused his ascendancy for his own interest, an interest which was contrary to that of the Republic.

When this report reached the island, Paoli was stung to a reply. Up to this time, he had been very careful with his comments and guarded in his letters. Now he burst out in words which, Corsica being Corsica, soon ran up and down the island. He knew, he said, that his calumniators came largely from the Clubs of the Mediterranean coast and that Arena stood at the back of them: 'But what is Arena,' he wrote, 'but a four-day patriot? I drank in liberty with my mother's milk, but they and their connections whirl about with every wind. My patrotism is of long standing. I have been a patriot for 65 years. I am hardly likely to submit to the censure of slaves who have known liberty for only three.' His whole defence had a nationalistic ring which had been missing from all his pronouncements since he returned to the island in 1790.

In Paris, Bozio and Andrei did their best to put Paoli's case. But on 1st March 1793, the critics of Paoli were reinforced by Volney who had just arrived back from Corsica and who attacked Paoli furiously in the Convention. Constantin, Comte de Volney, was one of the most celebrated authors of his day. The author of *Ruins* and *A voyage to Syria and Egypt*, he had aroused the enthusiasm of the younger generation for his egalitarian and liberal opinions. On his arrival in the island, the young Napoleon had hurried to see him and Paoli had openly praised him and rejoiced in his friendship. But his hopes for his life in Corsica were pitched too high. In Corsica he had hoped to find an approximation to a society of 'Noble Savages' and, since he brought knowledge to them, wealth. He found, instead, a great deal of anarchy and on his newly-acquired land a back-breaking toil. Furthermore, he had counted on his reputation and his abilities to procure him either the Presidency of the Corsican Assembly or the Procurator General Syndicship. He obtained neither, although Paoli did offer to procure him a post in the administration as some compensation. Volney soon became disillusioned with the Corsicans and his disillusion advanced with the years. Bitterness against Paoli, who he felt might have done more for him, became mixed with that disillusion and he returned from Corsica full of resentment. At the Bar of the Convention, after his return, he accused Paoli roundly of being a despot: 'He is an adept,' he cried, 'at delay. Always he clouds judgement by manoeuvring and by fine words. But he loves neither France nor our Republic. He is an egotist who, at bottom, despises you, me and all the world.' Andrei and Bozio leapt to the General's defence. Casabianca and Moltedo supported Volney. But the support was short and embarrassed and Casabianca betrayed his mixed feelings when he declared that without Paoli the island would long ago have gone up in flames.

Volney followed up his verbal attack three weeks later by publishing a report on the island. He renewed his attack on Paoli: 'He is an astute Machiavel,' he wrote, 'a King in the trappings of liberty'. But at the same time in his report he censured Saliceti. Saliceti, he said, used the Directory to place his agents in power and line his pockets at the expense of the State. But the criticism of Saliceti aroused far less notice than the criticism of Paoli. For by now the news of the Sardinian débâcles had reached Paris, together with the loud complaints of the *phalange* that Paoli had been at the back of their failure. From the coast of the Mediterranean they brought the news, too, that everywhere, not only the Clubs but the whole population were raging against Paoli. Paoli, said their informants, had replaced the regular troops in every strategic position with Corsican Volunteers; batteries which commanded the most important parts of the island were now manned entirely by Corsicans; Corte was being fortified and the national funds were being systematically transferred to the island capital. The volume and the detail of the criticism began to worry even Saliceti (detained at Toulon by contrary winds) who was in a better position than most on the mainland to make allowances for rumours: 'I fear,' he said, 'that I shall find the island in a state of

263

rebellion'. He was fretfully impatient to begin his work in Corsica.

He was not to know how near he had been to a victory. For Paoli was tired of the long stream of reports that were coming to him from every quarter concerning the campaign which was being conducted against him in France: 'I am tired,' he said, 'of trying to be a General with four bad battalions, and of trying to direct affairs on the island when I am attacked by my peers on the mainland and insulted by the public they lead.' He wanted to retire and leave the Directory to manage affairs without him in the hope that the criticism would then die down. But the General Council of the island indignantly refused to contemplate his resignation. They wrote angrily to the Ministry of the Interior that his going would be a public calamity: 'The rule of law will pass from our mountains and our *macchia* if he goes,' they wrote. 'The role of the General in Corsica is indispensable. Nothing can replace his personal influence.' Paoli's depression was short. 'He has recovered his spirits,' wrote Terrami from the island to Andrei at Paris, 'His friends have assured him again and again that they depend on his council and respect his reputation.'

The General Council of the island did more than defend Paoli; they attacked his traducers furiously. They censured Arena as a disturber of public peace and a spreader of falsehoods. They condemned the selection of officers for the Corsican battalions in Paris: 'We are Republican and French,' they wrote, 'and true to the principles of the Revolution. We have sworn to uphold liberty and equality. We fight against fanaticism and aristocracy, but we will not be oppressed by anyone.' They accused Saliceti, Chiappe and Moltedo of doing nothing to hinder the spread of lying rumours about Corsica.

The Council on the island also wrote pointedly to the Commissioners, who were still delayed at Toulon, that when they came to the island they would soon be ashamed of the lies which had been spread about Paoli. Pozzo di Borgo, rapidly emerging as the most talented of Paoli's followers, was also the most outspoken and indeed menacing: 'We are,' he declared at one point, 'strong enough to impose respect for our power'. Paoli, though he was more guarded in his correspondence with Saliceti, was by no means placatory: 'We are brothers and not subjects,' Paoli wrote, 'If our loyalty is proved the Commissioners ought not to arraign themselves against us. Certainly our people will not suffer arbitrary power and the abuse of authority under a Republican constitution. The Corsican people cannot be reconciled to despotism.'

But it was evident that, over and above all the words, a trial of strength was about to take place. Paoli began to sound out his potential supporters in the island. There were many who refused to contemplate the possibility of a final choice between the French government and Paoli. Gentili was one such. Paoli's old comrade-in-arms bluntly said 'that Paoli would ever be a traitor is unthinkable,' and left it at that. But there were many who let it be known that they would only support Paoli part of the way. They would not support him if he ever broke with the French government. Among these were many of those who were linked to him by close ties and had always been his supporters.

Amongst these were the Buonapartes, Saliceti having come to friendship and an understanding with Napoleon in France before Napoleon returned to Corsica.

It was the Buonapartes in the person of Napoleon's younger brother, Lucien, who were to be instrumental in the final break between the General and France. Lucien had, at one time, been employed among the General's secretariat, but he had left to rejoin the clan in Ajaccio. Lucien was intelligent but hair-brained. When he returned home from Corte he was one of the General's most unabashed adulators, but back in the clan he soon fell into line with the family attitude and, finding life dull in the seaport, he set off for France. In the Clubs of the Mediterranean coast, as a Buonaparte and, moreover, as a Buonaparte who knew a great deal about Paoli's government, he found a willing audience for any condemnation of the General. He became an authority overnight. The Republican Society of Toulon received the full flow of his oratory. Paoli was, Lucien thundered, a despot who provided himself with regiments recruited with French money; Paoli hated true Republicans; Paoli imprisoned good citizens; Paoli was a monstrous tyrant, oppressing all Corsica. Who would free the Corsicans from their oppressor?

The Club relished the task of being the island's champion. On 2nd April 1793, its address to the Convention was read in that Assembly by Escudier, a Deputy of the Vaar. All the usual charges against Paoli were reiterated, together with a round condemnation of Pozzo for good measure. The denunciation fell on willing ears. The Convention had just heard of the defection of their General, Paoli's old enemy, Dumouriez, to the Austrians. Suspicion was rife and traitors were seen everywhere. The demand of Andrei, that the report of the Commissioners be awaited before anything be done, was ignored. On 2nd April, the Convention issued instructions that Paoli and Pozzo were to be seized by any means. It was a call to civil war.

Before the news arrived on the Mediterranean coast, Saliceti and his followers had landed at San Fiorenzo. They soon made their way to Bastia which had always been pro-French and was now a stronghold of the Clubs. Saliceti was welcomed, as he afterwards wrote, with goodwill and dignity. He sent a courier to Paoli asking him to join him in Bastia for an Assembly which would reorganise the government of the island.

This time, Paoli was suffering from an inflammation of the chest that would not even allow him to mount a horse. Some manoeuvring tinged with comedy then followed. Saliceti invited the Directory to come and meet him in Bastia. The Directory replied that they had not yet received his credentials, that Bastia was not a suitable place and that to convince the Corsicans of his *bona fides* he himself should come to Corte and then visit the other parts of the island to show that he was properly empowered. The presence of Bartolomeo Arena in Saliceti's suite irritated the Directory immensely. They knew he was the source of most of the vilifications of Paoli which had so incensed public opinion against the General on the Mediterranean coast. They were aware that Paoli had written to the Minister of War to protest at his presence in the island. Accordingly, by a message to Rossi, the commander of the French garrison at Bastia, they issued an order for his arrest. When they learned of this, the Commissioners immediately countermanded the order. Undeterred by this flouting of their authority, the Directory sent an order that the 36 Corsican *gendarmes* who had come with Saliceti from Toulon should immediately proceed to the capital. Saliceti promptly countered this by saying that he had work to do for them in Bastia. At the same time, he proclaimed that he had arranged that, on 18th and 20th April, the battalions of light infantry would be established and the list of their officers announced.

In anticipation of this event, he forbade the issue of any

more supplies to the Volunteers who, he said, would soon be disbanded. The speed with which he had acted in this matter was a clear threat and the Directory recognised it as such. They accordingly issued a proclamation, announcing to the island that the Commissioners had arrived and exhorting their countrymen to range themselves loyally behind the tricolour. But at the same time they condemned all those who might mislead the Commissioners to suppose there was any opposition to the French in the island. The ambiguous tone of this proclamation, and another command of the Directory that the ships which had brought the Commissioners from Toulon should sail from Bastia to ports on the west coast, made Saliceti determined to avert what was beginning to look like the prelude to civil war. He forbade the ships to sail and then immediately set out for Corte to see Paoli. Hardly had he set out than he began to send back messages to his fellow Commissioners, warning them to be on their guard against surprise, for everywhere along his route he saw armed men gathering and everywhere he heard and experienced hostility towards France. From Bastia, Lacombe and Delcher wrote to Paris that Paoli seemed to have taken over the interior of the island. They listed the old familiar charges against him.

At Corte, Saliceti stayed three days. The only surviving account of his meeting with Paoli is his. Paoli, he said, was enfeebled; Pozzo and his henchmen were the real governors. Saliceti says that he enjoined Paoli to return from the precipice towards which he had been advancing. He assured the General that if he would come to Bastia and work with the Commissioners all might still be well. Paoli, he says, argued that, when he was well again, he would come and co-operate in the defence of the island, but this was impracticable for him at the moment. Saliceti suggested that, in that case, Paoli might choose to retire from government until he was well and then go to Paris to receive the thanks of the Convention for the work that he had done. He might then return to a well-earned rest in Rostino. This, according to Saliceti, set off a tirade, which certainly sounds like Paoli: 'French enthusiasm,' said Paoli, 'is a vapour. If someone writes an article, if someone speaks in a club, if a few hot heads present an address to the Convention, then down goes the altar set up to today's idol and the string is ripped from the garlands to form a noose for his neck. The *lanterne* is not far from the Pantheon. If Franklin with his buckleless shoes and leather-striped breeches arrived in France today, his sober dress would not save him from being hanged as an aristocrat. He would be a diversion, not to the elegant ladies of Versailles, but to the murderous shrews at the foot of the guillotine.'

They had several more conversations at a rather lower temperature during Saliceti's three days at Corte, but they got nowhere. Saliceti rode back to Bastia with nothing decided. Paoli had been, except for his outburst, polite; he had seemed willing to make concessions, but Saliceti could obtain no firm commitments. However, he did not despair. On his arrival at Bastia he and the other Commissioners drafted a letter to Paoli, thanking the General for his hospitality and hoping that he might, in the near future, be able to come to Bastia and renew their discussions.

The day after the letter was sent, however, the stalemate was rudely shattered. A boat brought the news of the decree of 2nd April to the Commissioners.

21

THE BREAK WITH FRANCE

Saliceti was furious. He despatched an agonised letter to Andrei, saying that the decree ruined all his careful planning to bring about a compromise. The news, somewhat embroidered, reached Paoli quickly too. Indeed, little of moment happened in that island that was not immediately reported to the General. Paoli, learning of the part played in his condemnation by Lucien, was highly indignant. He recalled how he had tried to further the career of the young Buonaparte and said bitterly that he was nothing but a little serpent.

Both Paoli and Saliceti knew that the next few days would be critical and both immediately set their forces in motion. Saliceti declared that Bastia was now the capital of the island and the seat of the government for the time being. He appointed Raffaello Casabianca as the interim commander of the Twenty-Third Division, and he sent an order to the Municipality of Corte for the arrest of Pozzo and Paoli. This was ignored and the *gendarme* who had carried the message reported that he had only escaped hanging by the enraged citizens through the intervention of Paoli's guards. Saliceti immediately sent troops to reinforce the garrison he had steadily been building up in San Fiorenzo. But there was heavy fighting before they crossed the mountain passes behind the town and a similar attempt to reinforce Cervione was repulsed.

On the other side, Panattieri, leading Paolist troops, gathered together the men of the Balagna and easily overran Isola Rossa where the Arena house went up in flames. He then tried to occupy Calvi but the regular troops there rapidly retreated into the citadel, and from that rocky eminence easily repulsed the first ill-organised attack. But besides Calvi, only Bastia and San Fiorenzo and the hill villages of Patrimonio and Barbaggio held out. The chief ports and the interior, every town, every village of it, declared unequivocably for Paoli. The nights after the decree of 2nd April was published in the island were brightened, up and down Corsica, by the burning of effigies of the Commissioners. Trees of liberty as the symbol of the French were hacked down. Resolutions declaring absolute loyalty to the *Babbo* – or Father, Paoli's affectionate nickname – were drawn up in every part of the island. But many men were divided in their minds at this parting of the ways. Napoleon at Ajaccio, for instance, tried to reconcile the two parties. For his own patriotic club he drew up a defence of Paoli and attempted to unite the club with the Friends of Liberty and Equality, where his old enemy Peraldi was the driving force. But Joseph, seeing the way things were going, and believing no reconciliation possible, made his way to Bastia where Napoleon, after some indecision, decided to join him; he reached the seaport with difficulty after a series of hair-breadth escapes. In Calvi itself, there was sudden rising and for a day it seemed as if the town might fall to the Paolists, but the garrison commander, Maudet, showed a great deal of resolution, and, at the critical moment, he received the help of the crews of the *Perle* and *Proselyte*, which were in the harbour, and so saved the day for the French. Within a week, the split was clear. It was a very familiar one. Paoli controlled all the island except the three sea-ports of Bastia, San Fiorenzo and Calvi, where the French garrisons dominated the town.

A pause followed the first clashes. The more judicious of the French, particularly the military who had some experience of Corsica, were deeply dismayed by what had occurred. General Brunet for one, sent a deeply-felt, closely-reasoned letter from Provence to Pache, pointing out that most of the trouble had been caused by the old spirit of vendetta, so plainly shown by Saliceti and Arena. He lamented the folly of arousing the opposition of the islanders by the appointment of such partial Commissioners, and he recalled the fate of the French armies in 1769, saying that if Corsica were to be held it could not be ruled by force, unless the French were prepared to assemble as huge an army as that of the Comte de Vaux.

St Martin, Casabianca's successor, as the commander of the Twenty-First Division, said much the same thing and pointed out how ridiculous it was to undertake a war against men who had openly declared their wish to remain French at all costs.

Paoli himself hastily dispatched two representatives, Marsily and Bertola, to go to the Convention and put his point of view. The news became known to Saliceti, who immediately sent a courier after them. The courier alerted the authorities at Nice, Marsily and Bartola were pursued and arrested and then sent to the prisons of Toulon.

But Constantini, that busy promoter of schemes, the former advocate of the attack on Sardinia and Lieutenant-Colonel Ferrandi, a Corsican officer who had distinguished himself in the Army of the North, both being already on the spot in Paris, were of more help. Instructed by Paoli to put the case of the islanders as strongly as they could, they joined forces with Bozio and Andrei, and managed by their unceasing efforts to produce a marked change in feeling towards the island and its General. They had an unexpected recruit. Chiappe, brutal and anti-clerical as he was, had been tormented for some time by Saliceti's policy towards Paoli. He had seen Saliceti as the opponent, but not as the destroyer, of Paoli on the island and after the condemnation of 2nd April, realising that Paoli's very existence was in danger, he changed sides abruptly and added his sullen force to that of the Paolists. The five were indefatigable. Speaking at the Bar of the Convention, petitioning the Committee of Public Safety, intriguing in the Clubs of the Cordeliers and the Jacobins, attacking Barère, wheedling Marat and even braving Robespierre himself, they hammered away at the twin themes of Paoli's innocence and Saliceti's folly, emphasising over and over again the island's loyalty to the French.

Paoli, meanwhile, proposed a National Assembly which he hoped would take place on 27th April at Corte. In his letters to the local administrators and leaders making the proposal, he wrote that since the Commissioners now refused to see, or indeed even to correspond with, the Directory it was necessary to take some joint action to demonstrate to the Convention the feelings of the islanders. He was out to demonstrate that he and the Directory were the *de facto* rulers of Corsica and to establish a government independent of the Commissioners, whose authority he was determined to ignore. But before the Assembly met he wrote a letter to the Convention, explaining his policy and setting out his actions. It was a tactful and moderate letter. He cited his old age and infirmities again. It was these, he said, which prevented him from crossing the sea and answering his calumniators at the Bar of the Assembly itself. But he asserted once more that his love for France was as strong as ever. He desired the approbation and the goodwill of that good hearted nation, he wrote. He would always keep faith with his undertaking to the cause of liberty. If he himself were the stumbling block, he would be willing to go into exile for the second time, willing for the sake of his country and of the Revolution, secure in a good conscience and proud of the love the Corsicans bore for him.

On 16th May, the letter was read to the Convention. It caused a reaction in his favour, for the panic caused by Dumouriez's treason had now died down. Moreover, it had become widely known that, on 27th March, five days before Paoli's condemnation, the Minister of the Interior had put on record that it was understood that the indiscipline of the Marseillais was responsible for many of the disturbances which had occurred in Corsica during the Sardinian invasion and that he looked to Paoli to show new proofs of the selflessness that had hitherto always been so evident. But perhaps working even more strongly in the General's favour than these new revelations was the realisation in Paris that the island was solidly behind Paoli, and that if he were really determined to assert his power, it was evident that the French could not hope to prevail against him, without a prolonged and expensive struggle.

On the 23rd May, Barère, preparing for a *volte-face,* declared that the Convention was not the Court of Versailles and that free men would ever listen to the voice of reason and reconsider their actions. Two Commissioners, he said, would be dispatched to Corsica to join the three already there and bring a detached view to what was rapidly becoming a partisan struggle. On 30th May, Antiboul and Bo were named as the new Commissioners and on 5th June, the decree against Paoli and Pozzo was suspended until the two had reported back. But Fate again took a hand. The suspension of the decree occurred three days after the expulsion of the Girondin Deputies, and by June throughout the south of France rebellion had broken out against the rule of the Jacobins. Antiboul and Bo got as far as Marseilles, only to be there thrown into prison. They were released some weeks later and made their way to Corsica, but, by this time, the effect of their mission had been destroyed.

For news of the uprisings against the Convention which were taking place throughout France led many Corsicans to believe that the island struggle was related to a provincial revolt against misgovernment and this belief made them defiant of compromise.

The day after Paoli's letter had been written the Convention opened at Corte in the convent of San Francesco. It was the largest Convention that had been held in the island. Over 1,000 Deputies were present and feeling ran very high. Pozzo and Paoli (who was dressed in the uniform of a French General) made their way to the Convention through streets of wildly cheering people. Volleys of musketry marked their path, and in the background the thunder of cannon rolled up and down the encircling mountains. Paoli was determined to damp down the feeling as far as possible and he began by reading his letter to the Convention. He followed this by an oration, in which he repeated his unshakeable adherence to the French Republic. The Assembly then settled to a debate. There was little of it. Saliceti's supporters were not represented, as Saliceti had let it be known that the Assembly should be regarded as an illegal Assembly. The first resolutions condemned the calumnious lies that had been directed against General Paoli. They were the work of the wicked and mendacious, it was said, who sought to overthrow Corsica. All the lies and actions of the General's critics had only disgusted the people of Corsica, it was said, and had in no way affected their esteem for their illustrious and intrepid General. In General Paoli the people recognised the founder of the nation, the prop of freedom and the incarnation of liberty. Pasquale Paoli, they declared, was 'the father of his country, the soul of his people, the upholder of law'. The decree of 2nd April was a monument of lies and deception and the present Congress would transmit the facts to the National Convention so that truth and justice might prevail.

This was followed by a more restrained, but nevertheless glowing, tribute to Pozzo di Borgo. The Congress declared that, as he had shown many proofs of his virtue and his talent, he should retain his post as Procurator General Syndic.

The first session had gone very quietly, but on the second day Galeazzi, the President of the General Council, made a savage attack on the Commissioners. They had betrayed the people, he said, and attempted to destroy all legality. They had branded true patriots as subversive and they had called the seditious and ambitious virtuous. They had attempted to corrupt the general will and to divide the public. Then he launched into a scarcely veiled attack on France, where such things were possible. He called on the Corsicans, by their disciplined behaviour, to establish a unity which would spare them the awful perils of civil war. He ended with a call for vengeance on those hypocrites who had usurped the fair name of patriot and sought in public office only their own selfish ends. His oratory was much more to the taste of the Assembly than Paoli's diplomatic caution. It was greeted with wild enthusiasm and, while the mood he aroused was still prevalent, seven resolutions were passed.

The Commissioners were not to be recognised on the island, the authorities which had been in existence before their arrival were to continue in their posts; the four battalions of light infantry that the Commissioners intended to set up were declared to be illegal; the authorities of Bastia were to be informed that they should cease to obey any orders that the Commissioners might give to them; any alterations made by the Commissioners in the magistracy, the administration, the *gendarmerie* or the National Guard were cancelled; the General Paoli was requested to redouble his zeal and vigilance to maintain liberty and peace and Saliceti, Multedo and Casabianca, the Deputies to the Convention, were declared to be deprived of their mandate.

All these regulations were to be printed and circulated to be in force until the National Convention ordered otherwise. On the last day of the Consulta, the Arena and the Buonapartes were condemned 'to perpetual execration and infamy'.

Before the Conference broke up a subscription was set on foot for the needs of all true patriots.

As soon as the Commissioners heard of the resolutions which had been passed in the Assembly, they immediately declared them illegal, but while the Conference was meeting they were engaged on other business. For the young Napoleon had persuaded them to an attack on Ajaccio, while the leaders of their enemies were engaged in legislating. Almost as soon as he had arrived in San Fiorenzo, Napoleon had begun to bombard the Commissioners with advice about the fortifications of the port. He saw it as one of the great harbours of Corsica which could easily contain a fleet, but which was terribly open to attack. His letters and the presence of a respected elder brother in Joseph, together with the possibility of action against Paoli, appealed to Saliceti. Napoleon, asked to prepare a plan for action, succeeded in convincing the other Commissioners that Ajaccio only needed the slightest assistance from the French for the people to rise against Paoli and his minions. He then drew up a plan. Detachments of the *Salis Grison* Regiment, stationed at Sartene, Vico and Corte were to be instructed to make their way to Ajaccio under the pretence of embarkation for France. But once in the town, they would join their force to that of the Fifty-Second Regiment, which would sail in by sea.

On the night of 23rd May, Lacombe St Michel, Saliceti, Joseph and Napoleon set sail from San Fiorenzo at the head of 400 men in the greatest secrecy; Napoleon was in command of the artillery. But the plan went badly awry. During the night a storm blew up and continued for some days. It was not until the 31st that the fleet entered the harbour at Ajaccio. They remarked with satisfaction that the tricolour still floated above the citadel, but their high hopes were shattered as, when they approached the harbour, the guns of the fortress thundered against them. No damage was done, but they sailed out of gun-shot and held a shipboard council of war.

It was decided to make a landing near the Capoletto fort on the opposite side of the Bay of Ajaccio and to send a letter summoning the garrison to surrender. The landing was easily made and the letter sent, but the answer was not encouraging. The commander, Vincetto Colonna-Lecca, replied that he was loyal to the French Republic, but that they would not allow the French Commissioners to enter the town. He requested them to retire, lest their efforts should seem to be the result of their personal vindictiveness. All Corsicans, he said, were French Republicans who would always obey the French Republic, but they would not obey the commands of Saliceti. Reports reached the Commissioners that from all the neighbouring glens men were pouring to the help of Ajaccio. Napoleon himself, reconnoitring in force near the walls, was jeered at by some countrymen as a traitor to the nation. He sent a cannon shot among them by way of retaliation. But the position was hopeless. Saliceti had not enough troops to risk an attack and the garrison was being reinforced at every moment. The fleet sailed back to San Fiorenzo with nothing achieved.

Now the Paolists retaliated and Leonetti, Paoli's nephew, launched a fresh attack on Calvi. He soon overran the surrounding countryside, but the black, whale-backed hump of the citadel, surrounded on three sides by the sea, survived all his attempts. One incident pointed to something new in the conflict:

the French reported that some of the attackers were heard to be swearing vengeance for the death of the King.

Paoli's own actions had, at first, cloaked the divisions which existed in the ranks of his followers. He had never ceased to be a republican, however much he disapproved of the actual execution of the King. His position was summed up after 10th August 1792 by his letter to the Legislative Assembly: 'Law exists always,' he wrote, 'France has been without Kings before without suffering any discomfort. The supreme good of the Constitution is that the presence or absence of an individual does nothing to alter the life of the nation.' But the faith in natural man that promoted this remark, and that dominated all his actions, had never really found an echo in many of his countrymen; the non-juring priests, who rejoiced in his protection, as well as many of his most fervent supporters, saw in the death of Louis another instance of French godlessness. Moreover, the reaction which had followed the rule of Saliceti had let out of prison many who looked beyond Paoli and the short years left to him to the Bourbons and *émigrés*. They could not make the distinctions that Paoli made.

He, for his part, was sure that Republican France was sound at heart and that the actions of a faction, the Jacobins, lay at the root of the present trouble: 'The insurrection in France is general,' he wrote on 26th June. 'The armies at the front are defeated. But in spite of all this, the French people are sound and will fight on. It is the Convention which ruins everything. Paris has risen and 26 Deputies, the best men in the Assembly, have been cut down. The Jacobins rage; they may have the advantage in Paris, but they have thrown all the Departments into a turmoil.' But he simplified. The rebellion which was sweeping the west and south of France was as mixed in its motives as some of his own followers – and as capable of misrepresentation.

Saliceti sailed for France on 21st June, despairing of being able to do anything to contain the triumphant progress of the Paolists. On 17th July, the Convention, acting on the report of Delcher and Barère with whom Saliceti had closely cooperated, decreed Paoli a traitor to the French Republic and an outlaw. With him were included Pozzo, Peraldi and twenty-five other Corsican leaders. Andrei protested vainly against Saliceti's vendetta. He was soon imprisoned. Chiappe unexpectedly rose to the occasion. In a defiant oration he pointed out how one-sided the order was and tried to move an amendment which would have allowed the proscribed to go into temporary exile, while the French restored order in Corsica. But he had few supporters. Not many in the Convention were willing to make distinctions. Everywhere the forces of the government were fighting for their lives. Corsica seemed but one part of a great struggle against a common enemy. Moreover, it was the Jacobins who now dominated the Convention completely, and Saliceti was, and always had been, one of the most admired and extreme of them. His conflict with Paoli had come at last to open war.

Paoli's attempt at steering his way clear of the reefs had failed. After the news of his outlawry had reached the island, a parting of the ways took place between the General and many of his former supporters. Many families felt that he had gone too far in his defiance, and that if they had to choose they chose France as the legal authority, however doubtful in its present shape that authority might appear. Many families either settled in the French-held ports or sailed for the mainland. In all, members of more than seventy clans chose to break with Paoli and crowd into the seaboard towns. Among these were the Abbatucci, the Ceccaldi, the Mattei and the Bozio, all clans whose members almost without exception had been among his most loyal supporters during the Corsican struggles for liberty against the Genoese. Among these departures, some caused Paoli a good deal of private grief. Zampaglino had been one of his most loyal supporters throughout all the years of his exile, but the old partisan's sons, the Bonelli brothers, chose France. Abbatucci, Paoli's old lieutenant in the *Oltremonti,* and the martyr of Marbeuf's injustice, likewise threw in his lot with France. So did Gentili, whose defection was perhaps to Paoli's mind the saddest one of all. The companion of his exile, one of the most loyal and able of Paoli's followers, a tower of strength in the dubious Directories of Arena and Saliceti, he had slipped out of politics after 1792. But now, faced with the decision, his loyalty to France and the Convention proved greater than his loyalty to the person of Paoli.

But it was not only friends but families that were split. In one way, it might be argued that Paoli's long struggle to make the Corsicans true to principle rather than to person had been successful. But, if he thought of it, it was an ironic consolation.

At the end of June another threat manifested itself. Paoli received news from Leghorn that the combined Anglo-Spanish fleet was cruising in Italian waters.

He was aware that this would encourage those among his supporters whose support for him was support for what they imagined to be the lesser evil, or those who still longed in their hearts for the authority of the *ancien régime*. But he also knew that the presence of the Allies provided him with an opportunity. For by an alliance with the English he could spike the guns of his opponents in the island, and at the same time obtain for himself a powerful backing against any expedition that the French might mount.

However, he moved towards such an alliance slowly. There is no suggestion of any English connection in his letters during July. In the middle of that month, indeed, he seems to have seen the English almost in the light of opponents: 'The nation is at peace although there is a threat from the *émigrés,* who believe that they will have at their disposition the Anglo-Spanish fleet which is in these waters. They think that by its means they will overcome our resolution and our desire to preserve our liberty. But we hate subjection and oppression in whatever guise they may appear.' But by the end of that month the English fleet was visible from the island to remind Paoli of the importance of English sea-power in the Mediterranean and of the decisive effect it might have for the future of the island, even if only as a counter-weight to Saliceti.

In some ways, it was 1768 all over again. But France was now a different France and England a different England. There had been an odd reversal in their roles, for it was England, which in 1768 had been the unique model for government by sensible men, which now seemed the conservative power. Paoli's position was by no means simple. Although he had broken with the Jacobins, only chance and Saliceti had brought about the break. He had grown up on French principles, his fundamental beliefs had been drawn from texts of the French '*Philosophes*'. And behind the English stood the *émigrés*.

Moreover, although he admired England, and numbered many Englishmen amongst his dearest friends, he was under no illusions about English politicians. He was, after all, a politician himself. Napoleon on St Helena has, for a historian, a dangerous memory, but if his recollection of Paoli's assessment of the English seems unnaturally cold and unqualified for Paoli, it states accurately what Paoli thought of English politicians. (It provides, incidentally, with 'shopkeepers' substituted for 'merchants' one of the most famous of all Napoleonic quotations) :

I recollect that Paoli, who was a great friend to your nation – in fact who was almost an Englishman – said, on hearing the English extolled as the most generous, the most liberal, and the most unprejudiced nation on earth, 'Softly, you go too far; they are not so generous, nor so unprejudiced as you imagine; they are very self-interested; they are a nation of merchants, and generally have gain in view. Whenever they do anything, they always calculate what profit they shall derive from it. They are the most calculating people in existence.'

If Paoli had, then, a great deal of thinking to do on the advantages of making overtures to the English, he had not long in which to make up his mind. For in the Midi, the Royalists had seen in the rebellion against the Convention an opportunity to enlist the Allies on their side, and in Marseilles, as later at Toulon, an appeal had gone out to Lord Hood, the commander of the English fleet, to take over the port. Paoli had been informed that in Ajaccio the Royalist element was strong. They had been forced into support for him in order to save themselves from Saliceti. They were in a minority, but if the English had resolved to possess themselves of the town and its useful harbour the Royalists might easily have been the means by which the English would have conquered, and indeed their nominal excuse for intervention. If this event had come about, then Paoli and all who thought like him would have become merely *interim* rulers in Corsica, rebels to both sides.

Certainly, Paoli was in a good position to bargain with the English. He knew that his reputation stood very high in England in many quarters. He might hope to preserve not only his country's liberty but also its Constitution by alliance with England and it was only by such an alliance that he could hope for untroubled power in Corsica, come what may on the French Mediterranean coast. Moreover, he had a strong hand in the harbours of Corsica, those he possessed and those he could hope to take with the assistance from the fleet of a strong naval power like England. For he knew, and the English knew, that he who held Corsica could threaten the French Mediterranean supply lines and dominate the north Italian coast.

By the end of August Paoli had made up his mind. The necessity to decide was emphasised by the news that the British had established an agent, Francis Drake, in Genoa, one of whose duties was to sound out the extent and the views of the various parties in the island. Drake was to endeavour to open a correspondence with General Paoli or other persons of influence in Corsica and, almost at the same time as he heard this, Paoli was informed that Buttofuoco and Gaffori were in Leghorn preparing to launch a Royalist invasion. If he delayed long he realised that he might be forestalled by Royalist overtures to the English.

His doubts put aside, Paoli sent off two letters: one to Hood on 25th August and one to Grenville, the English Foreign Minister, on 1st September. Although the letters went into some detail about Paoli's position, *vis-à-vis* the French, they were vague about the connection with England that Paoli proposed. They were evidently meant to sound out the English; the most important passage requested 'England's protection for Corsica's political existence'. This, however, was good enough for Hood and Grenville. Paoli might be only offering what in form was a pact for joint operations against a common enemy, but both sides knew that, once in being, such a pact was the first step on the path to a much closer and more important alliance.

22

THE KING OF CORSICA

His decision taken, Paoli had only to wait. On 13th September 1793, the English fleet appeared off Calvi; on the 15th, two officers, carrying a white flag of truce, were rowed to the rocks beneath the massive citadel and called for the Governor, Lacombe St Michel, who had decided that Calvi was the most likely point of attack and had settled in there. He conducted a dialogue with them. He was a brave man; he was also sanguine and vainglorious and given to declarations. To a request for surrender, the officers received a long sermon which concluded ringingly: 'Go back and say to your masters, Englishmen, that although philosophy accounts the English friends of humanity the black treason of these actions dishonours your race.' The English, however, although unrepentant, had decided that Calvi was far too hard a nut to crack and, as Napoleon had perciffiently prophesied, they estimated that San Fiorenzo was the weakest link in the French defence. The fleet, therefore, sailed first to attack the Mortella fort, which commanded the entry to the magnificent bay, at the end of which lay the port. After a heavy bombardment, they landed and easily overcame the fort's resistance. Nevertheless, the English were so impressed with the fort's construction that they took it (and the name with two vowels transposed) as the pattern for the Martello forts which were later built along the English and Irish coasts against the threat of French invasion.

Then the fleet sailed to bombard the Formali fort which lay deep in the bay just opposite the town of San Fiorenzo itself. The same pattern followed: a heavy bombardment, followed by a landing. But this time, they found the French garrison under Paoli's old comrade, Gentili, well-positioned in the fortifications that Napoleon had repaired and, after a few hours of useless fighting, they re-embarked.

The English were now collaborating with Paoli closely. They

provided him with small arms, light cannon and ammunition and thus enabled his nephew, Leonetti, to second the attack on San Fiorenzo with an attack on the high villages of Patrimonio and Barbaggio (which the French had occupied) the keys to the route which went through the mountain passes between San Fiorenzo and Bastia. The fighting at the villages was severe; some of it took place in the streets, but at the end of the day the French were still in possession and Leonetti, defeated and discouraged, retreated into the interior. Paoli now put the country on a war footing and moved forward his headquarters to Murato to be ready for the campaign.

It was not until October that the English fleet was again off the French fort. This time they concerted their attack with Paoli's forces; while Paoli attacked from the landward side the English fleet bombarded the port from the sea. The loss amongst the defenders was high, but they held on grimly and at nightfall the English fleet sailed out of the harbour with the fort unconquered, not without having suffered some scars, while Paoli had in the attack lost one of the greatest of his captains in Masseria.

The English did not return until January, a few days after Toulon had fallen to the troops of the Revolutionary Army.

By this time the nature of Corsica's probable future connection with the English was clearer. Drake quickly realised that Paoli would accept 'any conditions provided that the inhabitants are left at liberty to govern themselves by their own laws and magistracies. This independency,' Drake wrote, 'with respect to their internal government appears to be a leading consideration with them and is the only point on which difficulties can possibly occur.'

Paoli soon categorically confirmed this surmise. That the Corsicans should govern themselves was, he insisted, the *sine qua non* of any agreement. He himself, he wrote (and was to repeat, no doubt to the delight of the Spirits Ironic), favoured a government based on the Irish model. George III would be King of Corsica even as he was King of Ireland; and as, theoretically at least, was the position in Ireland, the island would in all that concerned its internal affairs be independent. If this were politically impossible he suggested a treaty of subsidy and protection, with the English given the right to a permanent garrison in a Corsican port and the Corsicans furnishing a guarantee that they would, in future, align their foreign policy with that of Great Britain.

But the form of the agreement was immaterial to him, so long as he secured his one essential demand: that Corsica should, in all that concerned her internal affairs, be self-governing. In return he outlined the future advantages England would gain from such an alliance: when 'by the beneficial effect of an Enlightened government and of a wise administration' Corsica prospered, England, he declared, would find that she had gained a rich ally indeed.

The English government was willing enough to fall in with Paoli's predilection for an Anglo-Corsican kingdom, but in the last month of 1793 the main preoccupation of its diplomacy, and of its fleet in the Mediterranean, was the retention of Toulon, which had surrendered to Admiral Lord Hood in August. Hood's subsequent inability to furnish Paoli with the assistance he needed, even though he had now thrown in his lot with England, meant an anxious winter for the General. Throughout these months, Paoli time and time again bombarded the English with appeals for help and support. He wrote repeatedly to Drake, the English representative at Genoa, and to his friends at Leghorn, requesting them to obtain assistance: 'We lack money and munitions,' he wrote desperately. 'We have not the means to lay siege to the ports and indeed we cannot even afford to keep a regular force of soldiers in being.'

At the beginning of November, he was pointing out how easily French ships were now able to revictual in Bastia and provide the garrison with munitions of war. At the end of the same month, he complained that the French squadrons operating from San Fiorenzo were now raiding along the entire coast of Corsica. His complaints were fruitless, however; for the English already had their hands full and had no time to spare for Corsica. The *status quo* in the island was threatened from another direction. While he complained, Saliceti was busy organising an expedition against the island in Provence; by the end of January, he was writing confidently that the island would soon be again in French hands.

The fall of Toulon, which made Corsica far more important to the English, upset all Saliceti's calculations; it also meant the end of Paoli's prolonged period of waiting and ended his most pressing anxieties. Yet between October and the middle of

January, when the English sailed again to his assistance, he had
not been altogether unhappy in the island despite his misgivings
about its vulnerability. It was, in a fashion, almost a return to
those halcyon days between 1755 and 1760 when, in spite of
Genoese power in the ports, he had ruled in the island, secure
in the goodwill of the people and confident of bringing them
peace and a measure of progress. But there were differences,
too; some very great, although not immediately obvious. Some
of his most enthusiastic supporters, some of the most enthusiastic patriots in the island and some of those who had been
closest to his way of thinking had chosen to join the French;
and he no longer possessed the energy and health of his first
period of rule which had enabled him to move around freely
and assess the feelings of his countrymen. More and more, he
had to leave the daily management of affairs to his lieutenants,
particularly Pozzo di Borgo, who had become, indeed, a sort
of heir to his ideas and who boasted proudly at this time that:
'Paoli is the head: I am the hand.'

Immediately after the fall of Toulon, the English sent a delegation to the island to assure themselves of the extent of Paoli's
power and of his ability to guarantee that the islanders would
accept a connection with the English crown. The delegation
consisted of Sir Gilbert Elliot, Lieutenant-Colonel Moore and
Major Kochler. Through Sir Gilbert, Paoli learnt of Lord
Hood's proposal that the General should summon a Consulta
to agree to the proposed annexation of Corsica to the English
crown; Sir Gilbert further informed him that he, Sir Gilbert,
was the principal political representative and was to report on
the political situation in the island, even as the officers were to
report on the military situation. All went well. Sir Gilbert, who
was highly impressionable, was enchanted with the Corsicans
and with Paoli. Everywhere, he wrote, he was warmly greeted
with volleys of musketry and cries of: *'Viva Paoli et la nazione
inglese!'*; everywhere he heard Paoli praised extravagantly. And
Paoli himself charmed Sir Gilbert in the same way that he had
charmed Boswell so many years before. Sir Gilbert insisted that
the time he spent in Corsica was the most interesting and entertaining that he had ever spent and he remarked how differently
Paoli appeared in Corsica from the remembrance he had of him
at the 'Tabby Assemblies' in London. At the same time, he
remarked that the General's health seemed to be failing fast.

284

There was certainly no doubt that Paoli had not exaggerated the plight of the Corsicans. The General's stock of arms, powder and lead was nearly exhausted; his funds also were very depleted. He immediately requested from the English a loan of £4,000, together with ammunition and provisions. At the same time, he pointed out that any General Consulta to determine the future Constitution of the island would be difficult to convoke until the French were finally defeated. He thought that the best solution would be a *de facto* administration until the French were driven out, and then he would hold the Assembly which would determine Corsica's future links with England. The delegation agreed to take his proposal back to Lord Hood. Lord Hood, in due course, approved Paoli's counter-proposals and, as a result, on 21st June the English fleet was again in Corsican waters. On 7th July, it launched an all-out attack on the Formali fort. The French fought bravely. Attacked by the Paolists from the west, and by the English who had landed to the north, they also underwent repeated bombardments from the English ships in the bay. They held out for eleven days, then they evacuated the crumbling fort and retreated into San Fiorenzo. They had come off not without honour, but their determination to resist had dissipated itself. On the heights inland they knew Paoli's forces were besieging Patrimonio and Barbaggio which, if taken, would trap them against the side of the mountains; Lacombe's exhortations alone rallied them and saved them from a complete rout, but they abandoned the town and retreated wearily through the mountains to Bastia and a temporary safety.

The Bastians were not discouraged. Exhorted by Lacombe, and encouraged by news from the mainland that the French were preparing to come to their assistance, they made ready to withstand a long siege. But two weeks later, as the English fleet sailed into sight, with their white sails seeming to cover the whole of the sea, their hopes fell. To discourage them still further, almost at the same time as the English bombardment from the sea began, a column of English troops crossed the passes of the mountain to occupy the heights to the east of Bastia, while Paolist troops moved in force into all the hill villages of the eastern plain. Lacombe reported that his troops were in good spirits in spite of all this amassing of enemy forces. 'Their enthusiasm is such,' he wrote in his usual grandiloquent fashion, 'that even the wounded are eager to leave hospital to join in the battle.'

He was optimistic about the outcome of any siege. He had more reason for his optimism than he knew, for the first of a series of quarrels had broken out between Lord Hood and General Dundas who commanded the English troops. The General held that the wisest course to take was to try to starve out Bastia. Hood was for trying to take the place by storm. Dundas and Hood had never been on a friendly footing; now they openly quarrelled, and Hood demanded that Dundas retire since they were unable to agree on a plan of action. Accordingly, on 14th March, Dundas sailed from San Fiorenzo. But his successor, Colonel Stuart, was no more willing than Dundas to launch an all-out attack on the heavily-fortified port and, like Dundas, advised a siege. Hood, in a fury, declared that he would take the town with his sailors alone and, shortly afterwards, he began a heavy bombardment of the town from the sea. There were fierce exchanges as ships and forts cannonaded each other furiously. But the Bastians held on grimly, and manfully drove off all the attacks which were made on them.

Sir Gilbert was concerned about the dissension between the naval and the military commanders, and he had good reason to be, for it was the presage of a conflict between the two Services that was to continue as long as the English held Corsica. However, for him better things were on the way. While the attacks were going on, he heard that he had been entrusted with new powers, no less than the general supervision of political affairs in the Mediterranean. By the middle of April he was again in Italy, visiting Piedmont and Tuscany and talking with the agents of the Pope and the King of Naples. His observations concerning the Italian States' ability to resist a French invasion were pessimistic and reinforced the impression that he had already gained that the possession of Corsica was going to be essential to the English in the near future.

He was followed to the Continent, to the amazement and distress of the Bastians, by Lacombe St Michel. Lacombe's departure marked the effective end of the resistance. He himself explained his defection by the necessity to stop Saliceti launching a fruitless expedition for the relief of the island. If that were indeed his intention, he was only just in time, for on 8th May, Saliceti was given carte-blanche by the Committee of Public Safety to set the fleet, which had been assembling at Toulon, in motion. But Lacombe brought the news that eighteen Spanish ships were now in Leghorn, ready to sail to the island and reinforce the English and he also brought an excited account of just how near the Bastians were to surrender. Saliceti reported these facts to Paris and the expedition was countermanded. The loss of their leader spelt the end of French rule in Bastia. When he heard the news of Lacombe's flight, Paoli convoked the Consulta at Corte for 10th June, for he knew that the surrender of the garrison was very close, and he was eager to arrange for the islanders to have full diplomatic recognition as soon as possible. Before it met, Bastia had been taken on 21st May; on the 27th, the English fleet was off Calvi; when the Consulta met, the English had already begun the bombardment of the last French stronghold on the island.

Sir Gilbert hastened back to Corsica as soon as he received news of the end of Bastia's resistance. He was delighted once again, as he wended his way to Corte, by the enthusiasm of his reception: 'We had hospitality wherever we went, in every form, and whenever we slept illuminations, bonfires and muskets fired in our faces.' Paoli sent him a 'handsome, prancing horse' for his entry into Corte. Sir Gilbert's account of that event was, in its Shakespearian imagery, oddly prophetic: 'At our arrival our prancing was prettily heightened by the discharge of cannon in our ears and I entered bare-headed, bowing and prancing like Bolingbroke. I met and embraced Old Richard at his door. However, the likeness does not hold, for although I am a sort of successor he would have far more "God bless him's" than I and could send Bolingbroke into the kennel without the help of Roan Barbary.'

At the first session of the Assembly, Paoli waited outside, while the Deputies deliberated on the choice of President. This was a purely symbolic gesture for they did not deliberate long. As soon as the election was open, there was a great shout for Paoli. The old man appeared to frantic cheering and was nearly lifted into the Presidential chair by the enthusiastic Deputies. He at once chose Pozzo di Borgo and Muselli for his secretaries and thanked them for their past services. He then launched into a justification of his conduct. He did not overelaborate much on his break with the French; his argument was that, in placing the island under English protection, he had avoided a lengthy and bloody civil war.

When his speech was over, a Commission was elected to outline the new Constitution for the island. The Commission included most of the eminent lawyers in Corsica, but Paoli also sought Sir Gilbert's advice very frequently. Sir Gilbert's hand was very evident indeed in some of the legislation – in the property qualification for electors, for instance. But, in essence, the Constitution was very like that of Paoli's old Constitution of the 1770s; the great difference, of course, was that it was a monarchial constitution and the monarch was now George III of Great Britain. Under the Constitution the powers of the King were carefully balanced by the rights of the nation. The only source of law was to be the Parliament but the King was to have the right of veto. The King's representative in the island was to be a Viceroy, who would have a Council of State and nominate a Secretary of State; but the Parliament was to have the right of requesting the recall of any Viceroy. The King had the right to dissolve Parliament but he must convene another within forty days. The military affairs of the island and its foreign policy were to be in the hands of the King, but this was to be without prejudice to Corsica and its dependencies. The King was to nominate all the magistracies, while the nation would elect its Municipalities. Symbolically, the national flag was to have the head of a Moor united to the Royal arms.

As for the Parliament itself, it was to be composed of men of over twenty-five years in age and possessing a property of not less than 6,000 francs. Its normal term was two years.

The old ideals of the Enlightenment, and of course the influence of the English Constitution, were everywhere visible: a *habeas corpus* Act was instituted; the press was to be free; the national religion was to be the Roman Catholic religion but all other cults were to be tolerated; Parliament was to fix the number of parishes, priests and bishops; the efficient function of the episcopate was to be ensured by an agreement with the Holy See; all civil and criminal cases of importance were to be judged by a jury (and in the first instance in Corsica). For the crime of treason a special tribunal was to be set up, with a judge nominated by the King but this, too, was to have a jury.

The Constitution did not take long to agree and, on 19th

June, Sir Gilbert Elliot went formally to the Assembly to receive the Constitutional Act. He took it on behalf of the King of England, and made a graceful speech after having received it. He then declared in the name of King George III, his sovereign, that he accepted the Constitution and took an oath to maintain it. Four Commissioners were then appointed to carry the document to King George.

There was still a great deal of work to be done in drafting all the legislation that the Constitution demanded, and Sir Gilbert accordingly settled down at Corte to undertake this task in conjunction with Paoli's legal advisers, confident in the expectation that his own appointment as Viceroy would not be long delayed.

Sir Gilbert was to be the most important figure during the last years of Paoli's life on the island. As the English representative, he seemed a good choice. Indeed, he might have been chosen by a board of professional interviewers for his post. He was a Scot, and might have been expected to have a natural sympathy for the Corsican temperament and social system. Like so many other observers, he was very well aware of the similarities of Corsica and Scotland, for in 1802, he sent a copy of Sir Walter Scott's *Introduction to the Border Minstrelsy* to Pozzo di Borgo, remarking to him that he would find many things there that were familiar to him. He came from a Presbyterian family which had been devoted adherents to the Parliamentary cause in Scotland; a family which, as a result, had risen rapidly in rank, land and wealth after the Glorious Revolution. He was very fond of Italy and Italians and he had more than a little knowledge of Italian culture and literature. He was familiar with French affairs, too, for he had passed part of his schooldays in France and had been educated with Mirabeau, whom he had afterwards entertained in England. He was happily married, an affectionate and considerate husband and father; and he was reckoned, both in London and on his Roxburghshire estate, to be a good master.

Yet, with all these advantages and virtues, his character and his temperament were to render his period in Corsica, in the last resort, disastrous. In spite of his being a Scot, or perhaps because of it, he believed that the English system of government was the most perfect that mankind had yet devised and that the misfortunes of other countries arose from the degree

K

to which they differed from it. Particularly, he believed that the rich and the poor were divinely ordained and that all forms of democracy led to anarchy and misery; he believed that events in France provided a terrible vindication of such a belief. It was a simple belief and indeed Sir Gilbert had a large streak of simplicity in his character, for, although he was prepared to be as devious as any politician, he accepted men easily at their own valuation if they shared his outlook and attitudes. In a country of born diplomats and natural pleasers, such as Corsica, this attitude was to be very dangerous. He was also emotional and thin-skinned. He took affronts, or suspected affronts, very hard and he reacted equally exaggeratedly in the opposite direction, laying too much stress on a compliment or a gift, with both of which, of course, the Corsicans could always make great play. Paoli's reserve was, of course, partly natural, but it was also partly a mechanism by which he preserved himself from some of the more dubious traits of his countrymen. Sir Gilbert had *hauteur,* but among those he considered his equals or his collaborators he was inclined to be both too open and too unwary. It was to cost him dear.

23

THE ANGLO-CORSICAN
KINGDOM

Only the news from England and his own legal powerlessness
marred the summer for Sir Gilbert. Otherwise he found Corsica
perfectly delightful. He spent the summer of 1794 at Corte and
Orezza, helping to draft the legislation which stemmed from
the June Consulta.

His letters to his wife in England were enthusiastic, indeed
almost lyrical: 'Orezza,' he wrote, 'is the name of the district
where the mineral waters of that name are. The Convent at
which I am to lodge with Paoli and other grandees and statesmen of this country is about a couple of miles from the spring.
It is the centre of the sweet chestnut woods and in the beautiful
mountainous country. The elevation is such as to promise a
degree of freshness and there is abundance of shade, of water
and of ferns.' Of Corte he wrote: 'It is like Scotland with a
fine climate. The rivers are rapid, craggy and crystal. There
never was water so perfectly pure and of such a beautiful white
transparency as the Restonica which flows by Corte. It falls
into another river almost as beautiful, close to this my capital.
The brightness and splendour of the Restonica make it what
one might call precious water, as one talks of the precious
stones. I have heard of the water of a diamond before, now I
see it, for it is really diamonds in solution. This is no exaggera-
tion as you will see when you come.' Already he anticipated the
arrival of his family. 'I could build you a palace of precious
stones,' he wrote gaily, 'but for the sake of cheapness it shall
be merely of marble.'

The charm of his surroundings was enhanced by the com-
panionship of his collaborators. Paoli continued to be charming and considerate. Pozzo di Borgo showed himself brilliant
and witty as well as being extremely talented. Pietri, the former
Deputy to the Legislative Assembly, and now one of the four
Commissioners appointed to carry a loyal address to King

George, was his constant companion during his rides and walks through the countryside. Sir Gilbert found him 'a scholar and a remarkably good sort of man' with whom he could discuss philosophy and literature and who, as their friendship ripened, helped him greatly with his readings in Dante. The other Commissioners were equally charming and received due mention in Sir Gilbert's letters home. Colonna, a 'man with a fine military' bearing was of course that Colonna Cesari who had led the ill-fated expedition to La Maddalena. Savelli and Galliazzi were members of Paoli's provisional government. They all went out of their way to be helpful to Sir Gilbert. Sir Gilbert's idyll was further enhanced by his labours, his political labours, on the Constitution. Burke had chaffed him years before about his enthusiasm for building new worlds, gently reminding him that politics was mainly a matter of cobbling. But Sir Gilbert felt he had now left cobbling behind and had, all for himself, a new world to bring into being. He found the opportunity of turning this island Eden into what he intended it to be, a more perfect England, vastly exhilarating. It was all the more exhilarating when contrasted with the news from home, for in England the political skies continued to darken. The *de facto* alliance with the *émigrés*, into which Admiral Hood had entered at Toulon, contributed, together with the flow of refugees into England from France, to harden the lines of conviction and party. Burke was now deeply estranged from Fox and Sheridan and provided, with his *Reflections on the Revolution in France*, an intellectual justification for an upsurge of patriotism which the steady improvement in the French military position, as well as the increasing flow of revolutionary propaganda from France, had heightened. In July, the Portland Whigs, who had had for some time growing misgivings about Fox's stand and viewed the evidence of unrest in England apprehensively, at last entered Pitt's administration in defence of throne, country and property. Portland himself, a good friend of Sir Gilbert, took the Home Office. If anything, they became more zealous for the cause of King and Country than Pitt himself. Wyndham indeed, who in the new Coalition had become Secretary for War, was to become known for his enthusiastic espousal of the refugees' cause as the Minister for the *émigrés*.

There was, in governing circles, a condition something akin

to panic because of the lack of reliable information about the intentions and actions of the working class. With no police force and no c.i.d. to provide reliable information, informers were the only source from which the government could obtain news, and in this situation informers tended to run riot. For the proliferation of branches of the Constitutional Society in 1793, in Manchester, Stockport, Norwich and Sheffield, the addresses that were sent from the working men of England to the French Convention, and the delighted enthusiasm with which the news of French victories was received in some of the English industrial towns, could all be represented as evidences of a huge plot to implant Jacobinism into England. The local magistrates readily accepted all these events as evidence of just such a plot and used all their considerable influence and connections to hunt down those whom they, rightly or wrongly, believed to be their mortal enemies. The suspension of *habeas corpus* in England in 1794 seemed to Sir Gilbert a logical conclusion to the way in which things in England were moving.

Not only the news from home distressed Sir Gilbert: every wind that blew brought to that rumour-ridden island stories of the unparalleled wickedness of the French Jacobins; and Pozzo di Borgo was always on hand to confirm Sir Gilbert's fears and apprehensions by the addition of horribly realistic details about the wickedness of the French leaders, many of whom, of course, he had known at first hand.

To turn his attention again to Corsica after these glances abroad was always a relief for Sir Gilbert. He could always console himself, when events looked black elsewhere, by the reflection that in Corsica at least things were handled very differently. There were, even so, a few serpents in his Corsican Eden. One was the way in which Paoli treated the islanders. The General, indeed, acted as he had always done; easy of access, infinitely patient, he was always ready to listen for hours to the complaints of his fellow countrymen and equally ready to harangue them on any matter on which he thought they should be informed. It all smacked, Sir Gilbert was to say later, of the demagogue. He appreciated the virtues of Paoli but he thought that he was lacking in the qualities to build up reverence for the majesty of the new régime. However, he kept his criticisms to himself, for he was after all only the representative of the sovereign by courtesy. Until his commission arrived from

England, legal authority lay in the hands of Paoli's provisional government, and if Paoli wished the title of address to be 'citizen' as he certainly did, Sir Gilbert, unhappily conscious that the term was evidence of a fundamental difference in their political attitudes, could only observe and silently demur. He was uneasily aware, too, that he had no monopoly of unspoken criticism. All Paoli's courtesy and the attentions of his followers to Sir Gilbert could not conceal the fact that many Corsicans, perhaps at times Paoli himself, harboured a certain suspicion of the English government and feared that the delay in according Sir Gilbert his credentials might conceal some intricate plot which would involve the handing over of power on the island to the hated monarchists. While the island waited then, Paoli governed and, a fact which added somewhat more to Sir Gilbert's irritation, the commanders of the English regiments collaborated with him very willingly, obeying his commands and abiding by his advice, often without any reference to Sir Gilbert.

From May, when he first asked for authority, until October, and in spite of repeated remonstrances, no communication arrived from England which might authorise Sir Gilbert to take over the control of the island. The continuing irritation of being potentially so powerful and practically so powerless, led to his writing, on 7th August 1794, an irritated and exasperated letter to Dundas, an old friend and now the Secretary for War and Colonies, in which all his fears and suspicions welled to the surface when he wrote that he feared Paoli really intended to govern the island solely in his own interest, using English troops and protected by the English fleet. However, when he reflected on Paoli's charm, his constant attentions and his willingness to be useful in every way, Sir Gilbert became ashamed of his letter and left it unsent.

Pozzo di Borgo was a great solace to Sir Gilbert during this stay in limbo; the future diplomat had his own worries: he was above all things ambitious and it was painfully clear to him that, in supporting Paoli, he ran the risk of finding his career as uncertain as it might be inglorious, for while he remained in Corsica the most he could hope to be was an important man in a tiny state. He had already tasted much greater power and he had far greater ambitions. The friendship of Sir Gilbert offered him grander, if vaguer, glories than those of the Procurator General Syndicship. Pozzo used all his diplomatic arts. A story which Sir Gilbert delightedly reported to Lady Elliot is typical of Pozzo's attitude at this time:

> It is a current anecdote and I think honourable to the sagacity and large views, as well as to the spirit and courage of the man that on 20th June 1792, Pozzo di Borgo, one of the Corsican Deputies to the Legislative Assembly, said to Pietri, one of his colleagues, that it was now becoming impossible to continue any further connection with France and that he was sure it must end in the union of Corsica with England.

This statement was a tribute to Pozzo's versatility as well as to his perspicacity, for on 16th July in the same year, acting as one of the four Commissioners for foreign affairs, he had thundered against Kings and declared:

> our enemies doubtless hope that passing dissensions which now trouble us augur the dissolution of our government. But it is not so. We will not fulfil their evil expectations. We realise that a change in our political constitution must lead inevitably to the overthrow of law, the suppression of authority, the destruction of our country, the growth of licence and the end of all liberty.

Pozzo grew on Sir Gilbert, day by day. He had many things to recommend him. He was certainly an attractive figure: good-looking, well-mannered, charming and energetic; he also commanded brilliant executive ability which he placed entirely at Sir Gilbert's disposal. He had, moreover, been a protégé of Mirabeau, even as Sir Gilbert, in his time, had been Mirabeau's friend. Sir Gilbert found him, too, easier to be familiar with than Paoli. To begin with, they were more of an age and then Pozzo was quite willing to accept patronage, while Paoli was far too grand and remote ever to be patronised. In temperament, too, they had much in common; both were fond of cutting a figure in the world; both distrusted general ideas and preferred the hurly-burly and compromises of normal, political life; both, too, had come to value order in society very highly and thought, always with the Jacobin Convention at the back of their minds, that the pursuit of democracy and constitutions was erosive of that order. In this, of course, Paoli was very different from his younger colleagues; nearer, indeed, in some ways, to the idealists of the Convention which had condemned him, for his whole life long he never stopped dreaming of the democratic republic that he had first admired in his youth.

Pozzo and Sir Gilbert were by no means reactionary; they, too, shared many of Paoli's hopes; what Pozzo, and Sir Gilbert in his more insular way, represented was one of the mutations of the Enlightenment; they were to be typical of those liberals who were, for a generation, hamstrung by the memory of Revolutionary France. They were men of a new kind, and to them Paoli seemed at times painfully impractical and out of touch with the politics of the day.

At the end of the summer, Sir Gilbert heard with delight the news that his wife would soon be arriving in Corsica. His happiness was complete when, on 1st October 1794, he heard that he had been at long last invested with the Vice-Regality. The news of Sir Gilbert's appointment was followed after a few days by a handsome acknowledgement to the Corsicans in general, and their leader in particular, of the honour they had done the King of England in adding the island to his possessions. For Paoli himself, there was a portrait of the King encrusted in diamonds, which would be sent to him in the very near future. Paoli was quick to acknowledge these marks of favour as evidence of the trust placed by the King in the Corsican people, rather than as personal gifts.

The drafting of the legislation had now been completed and Sir Gilbert was happy to visit Bastia more frequently to prepare a suitable home for his wife. Naturally, he took Pozzo di Borgo with him to help. Paoli, for his part, was happy to return to Rostino. His health was not good and he could now hope that Sir Gilbert, aided by Pozzo, whose intimacy with the Viceroy he strongly approved, would now take over the day to day business of government. He hoped that Pozzo would fulfil his own role and be the link between Sir Gilbert and the islanders. But events were to disappoint him.

In Bastia, Sir Gilbert found another sort of society to the one he had been concerned with at Corte and in the mountains. Instead of voluble delegations and rough mountaineers he found that the French *émigrés,* who had sought sanctuary in the town, had created a similacrum of the *ancien régime.* Into this tiny courtly world the naval officers of the fleet, whose ships had brought the *émigrés* to Bastia from France and Italy and whose influence protected them, fitted easily to provide a reassuring and sizeable British element. Unfortunately, in the little court there had grown up a distaste for the provinciality of the Corsicans. The exiles, with the ever-optimistic faith of political exiles, believed that a restoration was just around the corner and that Corsica was a brief, rather distressing, interlude to be passed as pleasantly as conditions allowed. This being so, they made no effort to trim their conduct to the habits of their hosts or to pay much respect to their leader, who was, in any case, tainted with the suspicion of Jacobinism. There was in Bastian society, too, an element which had a great dislike for Paoli. It was composed of those Corsican *émigrés* who had fled the island on Paoli's accession of power and who had now returned from Italy, confident of English protection. As for Pozzo, suspect at first, he was adaptable and he could easily make a scapegoat of the French revolutionaries to account for his revolutionary past. He quickly adopted the manners and the tone of his surroundings. Unfortunately for the peace of the Viceroy's government, he also began to adopt their outlook. As Sir Gilbert's relations with the Society of Bastia developed, his relations with the English regiments steadily deteriorated. They had been growing strained for some time. The English officers would not acknowledge Sir Gilbert until he was invested with full powers. Even when this was done, they questioned the extent of those powers. Sir Gilbert, irritated beyond measure by repeated disagreements, petitioned for the recall of Stuart, whom he found unmanageable and placed his reliance more and more on the battalions of the *émigrés* that he was engaged in recruiting to support the English troops in the island, now sadly depleted by disease and withdrawal.

The arrival of Lady Elliot, in the middle of December, confirmed Sir Gilbert in the course he was pursuing. His wife was enchanted with her surroundings and enraptured by the natural scenery of the island. Unfortunately, she was less enthusiastic about the people – 'All that Nature had done for the island is lovely and all that man has added filthy.' However, there were compensations in the presence of the officers of the fleet and the society of Bastia, to the intricacies of which she was introduced by the ever-ready help of 'Pozzo di Borgo, the

President of the Council and Sir Gilbert's prime favourite,' whom she thought 'a most uncommonly sensible and agreeable man'. Her parties were a great joy to her:

> The almond and cherry blossoms have been long over, but the apricots and the apples are charming. All the fruit trees are in leaf excepting figs and vines and they are peeping. Our garden is a little cape, the sea serving as a fence half around it. It is elevated about fifty feet and has a beautiful view of the coast; it is full of orange and lemon trees, rose and myrtle hedges. In such a spot my banishment does not sit as heavily on my heart as it did on Seneca's. In this garden the bands of the regiment play when I have my assemblies and the company walk and dance on a terrace above it, washed by the sea; last night the scene was quite like a fairy tale the moon rising out of the sea exactly opposite the great glass folding doors which lead from the rooms to the terrace. It was one of the most charming things I ever saw.

'If,' she sighed, 'the country were in a state of cultivation and the people in a state of civilisation it would be Elysium.'

By the beginning of the year 1795, Sir Gilbert had recovered his composure completely. The news that Paoli had determined to retire finally from politics aroused his enthusiasm. He congratulated the General warmly on his assumption of the position of an elder statesman. It was a sad misjudgement. It was true that Paoli had little taste, at the end of 1794, for politics. He was ill himself and his mind was deeply distressed at the illness of his brother, Clemente, whose increasing weakness, he rightly surmised, marked his last days. But while he lived, Paoli, because of his unique position, could not be, whatever his own feelings, other than a political figure. Faced by the English, from whom they differed temperamentally and politically, the Corsicans looked to Paoli for explanations. Pozzo di Borgo might, if he had acted discreetly, have taken Paoli's place, but he had not acted discreetly; he had become too closely associated with the Bastians and the English.

With the example of Saliceti before him, Sir Gilbert would have been wise to be cautious. He was not. He believed that he was now in complete control of the island. It was at this point of euphoria that he made a fatal mistake. He decided that it would be wiser to transfer the capital of the island from

Corte to Bastia. No sooner had the idea come to him, than he issued a decree to that effect. From his point of view it was a perfectly logical step. Bastia was now his home, and a place in which most of the business of the island was done. The society there he found charming, and the respect with which he and his family were treated flattering. There were advantages, too, from the administrative point of view, for with Bastia as the capital of the island he would have quicker and readier access to the fleet and thus to the government in England. But in Corsican terms, Sir Gilbert's decision was a disastrous one; it immediately recalled to the Corsicans the days of the French occupation and the brutal repression the island had suffered under the Royal government. Ever on the alert as the islanders were for signs of party, it seemed to place the government firmly in the hands of two bodies of foreigners – the *émigrés* and the English – and Sir Gilbert's close association with the *émigrés* increased the fears that the removal of the capital aroused. It seemed to suggest, too, that Paoli was no longer a guarantee against the exploitation of foreigners. Paoli, for his part, realised the danger at once. Offered the Presidency of the Parliament, when it was convoked on 15th January, he immediately refused it, for he had no desire to become the head of a faction. He saw, only too clearly, what would happen in Bastia. Indeed, at the first sessions of the Parliament it had already begun to happen, for already opposition to Pozzo was forming. Sir Gilbert's attitude to government magnified his error. For Sir Gilbert did not mean to concern himself with this day to day business of running the country. He deliberately left these matters to Pozzo. His aim was to create in Corsica a copy of England and, since in this state he was the Viceroy, he had cast Pozzo for the post of a loyal Prime Minister. But Pozzo had no party; only the favour of Sir Gilbert. Nor, considering his new connections, was he in a position to create one. His character, and the fact that he had learnt the arts of government in Revolutionary France, hindered his efforts; he was far less easy of access than Paoli had been, far more peremptory, and he had all the impatience of his brilliance and of his youth. He conducted business very briskly and with very little respect for persons. He was sure that he knew the way the country ought to be governed and he set about governing it; he had little time for formality or ceremony. In that formal and ceremonious society he quickly offended the *amour propre* of the Corsicans. To them, his new broom seemed ominously like the old ones they remembered and he was soon accused of being proud and overbearing.

However, the first sessions of the new Parliament which met at Bastia on 9th February 1795, went reasonably well. Sir Gilbert had a few anxious days while he awaited the result of the Assembly's invitation to Paoli to become the President of the Assembly. He was much relieved when he heard that the General had refused. Deprived of the General's presence, the Assembly voted for the installation of his bust as the next best thing. At the session of 20th February, the bust was solemnly installed in the Great Hall of the Parliament with the inscription: 'The Nation and its General Assembly of the year 1795 decrees this statue to Pasquale Paoli, the founder and restorer of the liberty of his country and the tutelary genius of Corsica.' The ceremony that attended its unveiling might have been a warning to Sir Gilbert. As the President, Giafferi, unveiled the bust and the artillery fired, a great cheer spread from the Hall into the streets outside, and was taken up throughout the town by a crowd, which was massed in ranks, waiting for the signal; at the same time, every bell in the town began to ring.

After this demonstration, the Parliament got down to business. The legislation it enacted was, on the whole, unexceptionable. The jury system was instituted, laws were passed that were meant to suppress the vendetta in any form it might appear. Torture was abolished. Civil and political crimes were invested with the appropriate penalties and laws were provided for the punishment of political crimes. Laws were passed against prostitution, against the exposure of children, against theft and so forth.

All this legislation was meant to perform the very necessary task of establishing a criminal code of law in Corsica, where, the laws, after the rule and the varying requirements of the monarchy, the Revolutionary government and Paoli's Provisional government, were in a confused state. Apart from the criminal legislation, the chief work the Parliament did was to legislate for the establishment of a new university at Corte, a project always dear to Paoli's heart. Before the session finished, a darker turn was given to legislation when the Parliament passed a Bill of Penalties against all *émigrés* from the island.

Since this Statute decreed the banishment, under pain of death, of all those who had emigrated from the island and who had not returned by a given date, and for the confiscation of their goods, it was strongly opposed by many of the Deputies. Although in theory it applied to both Royalists and Republicans, it was evident to many that, considering the influence the Royalists already possessed at Bastia, its application would be unilateral and that only the French Republicans would suffer under the law. However, in spite of the unrest which marked the last sessions of the Parliament, on the whole Sir Gilbert had no reason to feel dissatisfied with the conduct of the Assembly.

While things were going reasonably well for him in the Assembly, he was suddenly reminded of the existence of the outside world. On the 13th and 14th March 1795, there was a running fight off Leghorn between a French squadron, which had emerged from Toulon, and several ships of the British fleet. In the fight, the French frigates the *Ça Ira* and the *Censeur* were captured and brought into San Fiorenzo where the prisoners were disembarked and sent to Bastia. Their appearance reinforced the Elliots' horror of all things connected with the Revolution. Lady Elliot wrote:

> The common men will be packed into large churches and the officers sent to Corte and are to be on their parole; though certainly not one of them had any idea of what that means; but if they try to escape the Corsicans will make no scruple of shooting them. The officers came here from St Fiorenzo on their way the day before yesterday; and only conceive, Sir Gilbert had six of them to dine with us. To describe their appearance is impossible; but my idea of them was a gaol-delivery. We had the two captains of the *Ça Ira*; the first was a decent-looking man, the second conveyed to me the notion of Blue Beard; their filth was shocking. I was so filled with horror and astonishment that I was perfectly silent for two hours!

The capture of the frigates had certainly proved the superiority of the British navy. But it was an unpleasant reminder to Sir Gilbert that the French Republicans still coveted the island, and a confirmation of the rumours which came to him every day, concerning the preparations that were being made on the coast of France for an invasion. Moreover, there were persistent stories, some of them certainly true, of the landing of French agents at points on the Corsican coast. Joined to this was the under-current of opposition to Pozzo's government. The opposition was at first very minor: insults offered to Pozzo's officials and a refusal of certain individuals to pay taxes. Pozzo reacted vigorously to this opposition, making an example whenever he thought it necessary, but the examples, in their turn, produced fresh outbreaks. Gradually the position began to worsen. Minor outbreaks grew and become major ones. There were some lethal brushes between Pozzo's soldiers and disaffected Corsicans. Lieutenant-Colonel (later, and immortally, Sir John) Moore, who had been in the island since January, was already celebrated as being among the most efficient (and incidentally the most handsome) of the English command. He also had the more particular distinction of having made himself the best informed of all the English about the customs and affairs of the islanders. Moore, writing in his journal at this time, saw clearly the cause of all the disquiet. It was, he correctly surmised, all due to distrust of Pozzo and the destruction of confidence in the Viceroy caused by the removal of the capital of the island to Bastia. As trouble continued and grew in the mountain villages, so stories arrived in Bastia which Paoli's enemies sedulously circulated: Paoli had spoken against the Viceroy and the government; Paoli was still in communication with Saliceti; Paoli was encouraging French Republican elements on the east coast; he was plotting rebellion; he was plotting the setting up of a new General Consulta to replace the one in Bastia. These rumours were without a shred of truth, but Sir Gilbert, whose nerve was badly shaken by the disorders in the interior of the island, and yet who still trusted Pozzo di Borgo implicitly, believed many of them and dutifully reported them back to England.

Paoli was very badly equipped to deal with a situation of this kind. Sir Gilbert had created a Court. Paoli was debarred by his past, his health and, above all, by his temperament from being a successful courtier. Yet, the arts of a courtier alone could have averted the situation which was steadily being created. Far from plotting rebellion, Paoli did his best to damp down the disturbances wherever they occurred. Colonel Moore, who now had far more dealings with the Corsicans of the interior than the Viceroy, realized the truth of the situation very quickly. He had had his suspicions of both Paoli and Sir Gilbert in the past. In the unfortunate affair of the siege of Bastia he had been openly critical of both. Paoli, he had said then, was a politician rather than a soldier – which was shrewd enough. Sir Gilbert, he thought merely artful. He soon changed his opinion about Paoli, if not about Sir Gilbert. Along with the conviction that Paoli's influence was by far the strongest in the island, and that it was being used to preserve peace and contain the rising anger of the glens, came the conviction that if the General ever turned against the English a bloody insurrection must ensue, whose result would be the penning of the English into the sea-ports. Moore was too good a soldier, and had too much knowledge of the battles of 1769, to doubt that, if a revolt broke out, the English would be as unable as the French had been to control the island. He was also uneasily aware that on the continent the French armies were going from strength to strength, as the First Coalition broke apart under the hammer blows of the Revolutionary armies.

Throughout April, the situation steadily worsened as more and more incidents were reported of opposition to Sir Gilbert and Pozzo. Early in May, Paoli tried to quiet the growing unrest by paying a visit to Bastia to discuss the situation with Sir Gilbert; ostensibly, he was making a visit to Lady Elliot. The General reached the capital by way of San Fiorenzo and, as he came down from the hills into the plain of the Nebbio, it was observed that something like an army followed him. To the relief of Sir Gilbert, who was horrified at the implication of the first reports, closer acquaintance proved that the army was composed of a handful of Paoli's close associates and a great crowd of admirers and well-wishers, who had decided to follow the General as a mark of their respect and admiration. Sir Gilbert was none too happy at the prospect of this procession arriving at Bastia for, in spite of the innocence of its assembly, it had begun to assume the proportions of a popular demonstration. He, therefore, sent a courier to San Fiorenzo with an offer to Paoli of a guard of troops on the last stretch of the journey from San Fiorenzo to Bastia, so that the procession might have at least a quasi-official appearance. Paoli politely declined the offer, saying that he had not come as an official, but as a simple citizen. The simple citizen, accompanied by his huge retinue of followers, entered the capital next day, rather like a king entering into his kingdom. If the society of Bastia did not flock to welcome him the Viceroy observed that the lower orders poured out of every crack and cranny to hail their beloved chief. Paoli lodged in the house of a friend. Sir Gilbert immediately sent two sentinels to stand before his door, ostensibly as a mark of respect. Paoli politely sent the sentinels back to Sir Gilbert with the comment that an honest man did not need to be protected by soldiers; he was quite satisfied with the protection that the Constitution afforded. After he had paid his respects to Lady Elliot, Paoli had two long conversations with Sir Gilbert, at both of which Pozzo di Borgo was present. Sir Gilbert faced Paoli bluntly, so he wrote to Portland, with the demand to know why the General was provoking opposition to the government of the Viceroy in every quarter of the island. Paoli's reaction, reported Sir Gilbert, was an angry one. He demanded proof of the accusations, whereupon, wrote Sir Gilbert, he laid before Paoli many proofs of visits that had been made to Paoli by the leaders of various villages and glens, some of which had afterwards been involved in disturbances. Paoli retorted that Sir Gilbert confused the desire of the islanders to seek information from their old chief with disloyal conspiracies. He delivered this part of his speech, said Sir Gilbert, in the manner of an old actor, ranting about liberty and equality, as though he believed there was an audience in the next room. Some of Paoli's words must have touched Sir Gilbert to the quick though, for he then set out to explain that stories Paoli might have heard of his opposition to the proposal to elect the General to the President of the Assembly were indeed true. Sir Gilbert explained that his opposition to Paoli's candidature was not, however, based on any distrust of Paoli, but on Sir Gilbert's belief that the time had come to end the form of Paoli's government, which had been a personal government, and to establish a new order of things in the island. Charges of loyalty and disloyalty were then bandied about for some time and Paoli, according to Sir Gilbert, lost his usual sangfroid and became extremely angry, although he later subsided into comparative calm and ended by declaring that when the military situation permitted he would retire from the island. He came forward, said Sir Gilbert, with only one positive proposal which Sir Gilbert cited as an example of his mischief-making. This was that Deputies should be paid four shillings a day for their attendance at the Parliament. In this way, said Sir Gilbert, he wished to facilitate the entry of the lower orders into the Assembly. Sir Gilbert left Paoli in no doubt of his opposition to this measure. But his failure to understand the reasons for Paoli's proposal unintentionally illustrated his lack of comprehension of the nature of the islanders' society. There was, of course, a very good practical reason for the proposal and this was that, in a predominantly agrarian society, attendance at the Parliament meant, very often, financial hardship for the Deputies. The landowners of Corsica were a very different class from the landowners of England, and of this Sir Gilbert still only had a shaky grasp. However, Sir Gilbert congratulated himself, in spite of the inconclusive nature of the interview, he had expressed his opinions and suspicions to Paoli very forcibly; he believed that the General was disconcerted to have all his plans discovered and that, in the future, the country would be far more quiet than it had been in the past.

In reality, the meeting did much more harm than good. General Moore noted this in his journal on 16th May, recording that Paoli, who until now had always been most circumspect, was beginning to criticise the Viceroy openly. Paoli told him that he resented the Viceroy's conduct so much that he had written to England to complain of it. Moore, for his part, was, he said, convinced that Sir Gilbert has 'written often enough misrepresenting Paoli', which was a shrewd enough surmise.

The situation deteriorated from day to day. Sir Gilbert and Pozzo di Borgo were soon committed to an open struggle against what they regarded as the forces of disorder and disruption. When, at the end of June, Sir Gilbert took the opportunity of his wife's absence in Italy to go on a progress through the island, he had to be escorted by a large body of troops, and his visit was accompanied by very evident expressions of dislike, directed not so much against him as against Pozzo, who was burnt in effigy in village after village as the column wound its way through the valleys of the island. Significantly, it was only in the Greek colony of Cargese and in the villages of the west coast, where Pozzo's clan held sway, that Sir Gilbert had an enthusiastic welcome. On the way, Sir Gilbert stopped at Morosaglia and spent the afternoon of 26th June with Paoli, but although he was received courteously and hospitably entertained, the gap between the two was now too wide to close by a visit. Before Sir Gilbert's progress through the island had ended, a scandal broke out which was to lead inevitably to the exile of Paoli and the destruction of the English power on the island.

The occasion of the scandal was a ball at Ajaccio, given at the end of July to celebrate the visit of the Viceroy. It was held in the hall of the Municipality where, as was the case in many official buildings on the island, there stood a bust of the General Paoli. Captain Colonna, the aide-de-camp of the Viceroy, was in the hall with a party of officers, making the final arrangements for the ball which was to take place that evening, when Colonna, either through drink or in a fit of bravado, suddenly cried out, 'What business has that old charlatan here?' and knocked the bust of Paoli from its pedestal. Some of the other officers then stuck their daggers into the bust and damaged it beyond repair. It was then thrown into a closet. The ball duly took place that evening; nothing untoward was noticed and the next day Sir Gilbert and Pozzo di Borgo set off for Bonifacio. When they reached the town they learnt that the countryside behind them was in an uproar. One of the officers, who had been present when Colonna had damaged the bust, had set down his impressions in a *procès verbal,* which was printed the next day and before long was circulating through the island. The Viceroy returned hurriedly to Ajaccio and found the bust in the self-same place with, as he reported to Dundas, only a slight sliver removed from the nose. The Paolists maintained this was a substituted bust. Colonna protested that it was the original, which had been put away in a place of safety before the ball. The Viceroy, incredible as it seems, given the circumstances and the character of the Corsicans, made no further enquiry but took the word of Colonna as the truth.

From every part of the island petitions now poured in, demanding the dismissal of Pozzo and Colonna. Deputations set out from village after village, making for Rostino to assure Paoli of the loyalty of the Corsicans and of the sympathy they felt for the insult he had suffered. Sir Gilbert returned hurriedly to Bastia through a country on the edge of civil war. Pozzo wrote at once to Paoli, assuring him of the falseness of the story which was circulating. So did Colonna. Paoli answered that he laughed at the whole incident, but that, since the agitation had deeper springs, Pozzo must satisfy the people of Corsica for the actions of his government. The people of Corsica, in the meantime, became more and more insistent that the government must be reconstructed. Signs of unrest were everywhere. In Bastia the Corsican battalion was thought to be on the verge of rebellion and was ordered at once to Corte. Moore noted that it went quietly and in very good order. On 11th August, the Council formally requested the dismissal of Pozzo di Borgo. Sir Gilbert was panic-stricken. He said that he would rather die than give up Pozzo. It began to look as though he might do both. The English troops in the island were hopelessly outnumbered. General Trigge, who had replaced Stuart, owed his position to Sir Gilbert's correct assumption that he would be loyal and unquestioning; unfortunately he was also indecisive. He did nothing. But Moore, who was an independent-minded and able officer, feared greatly for the safety of his troops and, on his own authority, set out immediately for Rostino to see Paoli and possibly pacify him. With him went Lord Huntley, Colonel Oakes and Colonel Grampella. On the way to Paoli they noticed that every village through which they passed in the Casinca was seething with fury and that, in some, the villages had already taken up arms. However, when they arrived at Morosaglia everything was calm. Paoli greeted them with his usual charm and was his usual courteous self. Moore noted that he spoke with great moderation, although he had very little that was good to say of Pozzo and he was more sharply critical of the Viceroy than he had ever been before. Of the Viceroy he said that he regretted his lack of judgement as a misfortune to his country. In spite of Paoli's harsh words about the Viceroy and his companions, Moore returned to Bastia convinced that Paoli had no thought of fermenting an insurrection and would do all he could to preserve peace. All Moore's criticism was of the Viceroy, who was said to be confused and agitated byond measure by the situation. Moore had little sympathy with the Viceroy's distress. He thought that he had brought it on his own head:

Had the Viceroy in the first instant dismissed his aide-de-camp, Captain Colonna, for a very foolish, mean action he would have prevented all this uproar. By a series of rash, absurd actions he committed the troops as far as depended on him. Had the Corsicans been equally intemperate, and one shot been fired, we must have been driven out of the country. The fact is that the people in general have great goodwill towards us individually. Paoli's party, the one that Sir Gilbert has quarrelled with, wish to be united with us as a nation and dread the misconduct of Sir Gilbert as most likely to bring about a rupture.

Paoli, for his part, was doing everything he could to preserve peace. He wrote letters to all the villages where disturbances had occurred, counselling moderation and patience. One of these letters was instrumental in preventing a serious clash between the Corsicans and the English near Ajaccio. But Sir Gilbert's actions tended to exacerbate the situation. He had already dispensed with his Council. Now he announced that the Parliament, which was due to begin its new session on September 1st, would be prorogued indefinitely. As a result, there were risings in the Mezzana, in Borgo and in the valley of the Fiumale. Sir Gilbert's actions exasperated Paoli: 'The very stones are crying tyranny,' he wrote to a friend. He pinned his hopes for a happy resolution of the unhappy situation on the English government. It was an article of his belief that in England the opinion of responsible men prevailed in the long run, and that once the news of the disturbances and the almost unanimous opposition to the Viceroy in the island reached the English, together with his own account of events, and that when this had been reinforced by the representations of the Commissioners in London, whom he had provided with a full account of the troubles, a halt would be called to the Viceroy's headlong career. He also hoped that the arrival of Lord North, who was due to take up the duties of the Secretary of State, might help to ameliorate things. He had had some acquaintance with North in England and he hoped that if the new Secretary of State could be persuaded to visit the interior 'he would be able to see the loyalty of the population and the falseness of these unreliable counsellors.'
But he deceived himself. While he tried to preserve the peace and hoped for better times, the Viceroy had already written to England requesting that not only Paoli but Colonel Moore

should be recalled. Certainly, he was in a panic. He believed that he had evidence that Moore and Paoli had been plotting to overthrow him, with Paoli as the new Viceroy and Moore as commander of the troops in the island. On 3rd August, he had written to Dundas: 'General Paoli threatens the tranquillity of the island and the stability of the government. His conduct is dishonourable, absurd and ignoble. It is necessary to act without delay.'

Portland, for his part, whatever he might have thought of the stream of complaints that issued continually from Sir Gilbert, had no intention of playing a judge in the case. The year had been full of disasters for the First Coalition; in April, the Prussians had been glad to make peace with the French; in May, Holland had followed suit; in June, the ill-fated expedition to the Vendée came to its bitter end; in July, the French had forced Spain out of the Coalition; everywhere England stood on the defensive. Portland knew Elliot, liked him and trusted him. He had no intention of weakening the King's government in Corsica at a time when the island's strategic position in Europe was becoming more and more valuable. On 13th September, he assured Elliot that Moore would be recalled and that he was already engaged in putting the question of Paoli's departure from the island before the King. Some days later, Sir Gilbert received the news for which he had been feverishly waiting: that Paoli was to be requested to retire from the island.

On 2nd October, Sir Gilbert informed General Trigge that Moore had been formally recalled to England. On 5th October, Lord North reported from Pontenuovo that he had had an interview with Paoli in which he had communicated to him the King's desire that he should retire from the island. Moore had no choice but to go, but Paoli demanded a little time to think the question over. North reported apprehensively that he did not seem eager to go. Sir Gilbert took this as a call to arms and made ready for a civil war.

But, as was unfortunately usual throughout the crisis, he had misjudged the situation. After a few days of silence, Paoli announced that he was preparing to go to England and that he would depart on 14th October. He had really little choice. He could easily have roused the island and driven the English into the ports. But this would have been, at the best, to return to the position of 1793. He was not sufficiently in love with power to subject his countrymen to the ensuing privation and misery. Besides, he could hope that in England, where he had powerful friends, he might be able to influence the action of the English government and ameliorate, if he could not remove, the government of Sir Gilbert. On 14th October 1795, therefore, he set sail from San Fiorenzo.

Sir Gilbert did all he could to make the departure seem a voluntary one. He sent an expensive carriage to Rostino to convey the General along the roads to San Fiorenzo; he gave instructions that the General was to be accorded full military honours; he himself came to San Fiorenzo to bid Paoli farewell. Paoli, however, was shocked and contemptuous at the Viceroy's hypocrisy, and the leave-taking was decidedly cold. Sir Gilbert had hoped Paoli's departure would be a comparatively simple affair. He was disappointed. The news spread quickly. From every village in the Nebbio, men came to say farewell to the General. As the frigate, the *Dauphin,* which was to carry Paoli from the island, sailed out of the harbour thousands of people were left weeping unashamedly on the shore. They stood there, a great army, staring out to sea as the frigate passed the far point of the Mortella Fort and sank slowly over the horizon.

PART IV

The Babbo

24

THE DESTRUCTION OF
THE KINGDOM

So the second exile of Pasquale Paoli began. He was never to
see Corsica again. A month later, on 18th November 1795, he
met Moore at Cuxhaven to await the English boat and they
had two long conversations before they sailed. Moore revealed
that he had had a most distressing last interview with the
Viceroy. Angrily repudiating the Viceroy's charges, his 'feelings
were so strong and my indignation such that, at times, to bring
tears to my eyes and for moments to stop my speech'. Paoli, for
his part, with justifiable but uncharacteristic bitterness, called
Sir Gilbert the meanest of mankind; he believed, he said, that
the Viceroy was actuated chiefly by self-interest and vanity.
But he had little hope of obtaining redress from Pitt or Dundas,
the latter of whom indeed he represented, on the strength of
information he had received from the Corsican Commissioners,
as a man without morals. Above all, he was tormented with
the idea that Pitt would, in the future, give up Corsica to the
French. Moore, during these conversations, strongly urged
Paoli to justify himself; he had already written an open letter
to that effect to the General before he left Corsica. For Moore
and his future it was absolutely essential that Paoli did so.
Paoli at 68, could, at the best, even if the political climate
should change completely, have but few years of active politics
left to him. Moore, on the other hand, was a comparatively
young man and had all his military career before him; he was
horrified at the thought that it might now, by Sir Gilbert's
brutal action, be terminated before it had really begun.

Paoli's arrival in England with Moore was of a far different
kind from the triumphal landing of 1769. By the advice of the
Viceroy his disembarkation was unmarked by any ceremony,
welcome or acknowledgement, for the government meant to
emphasise that he returned as a private citizen to lead a private
life. Paoli returned to London to live a comparatively secluded

existence for the rest of his days. Any hope that he might have had of influencing the English government soon vanished. Dundas, indeed, gave him an interview, but only after informing him that the King no longer wished to see him, but that he, Dundas, was willing to hear him state his case. It was a very heated interview. Paoli began by outlining his case against the Viceroy, but before he had got very far, Dundas interrupted him and warned him against the effect of jealousy. Naturally, this provoked Paoli to some bitter retorts. He already had little respect for the character of Dundas and, before it finished, the interview developed into an unseemly wrangle and ended bitterly with Dundas stiffly requesting Paoli to communicate all that he had said on the subject of the government of Corsica to paper, in order that he, Dundas, might communicate it to the King. He told Paoli that a reply would be sent to him, either through the English Secretary of State or through the Viceroy of Corsica.

Moore fared a good deal better in his campaign of justification. He saw Pitt, whom he found stiff and cold; he saw Portland, whom he found embarrassed, but who assured him that his military career would not suffer as a result of the Corsican imbroglio and he saw Dundas, who listened to him very carefully, asking him many questions and committed himself to the remark that 'Sir Gilbert upon several occasions had displayed a degree of jealousy he had not thought him capable of.' Moore found that 'Sir Gilbert's character is not altogether unknown in this country'. Sir Gilbert's quarrel with General Stuart was remembered and Stuart himself joined with Moore's friends in a campaign to reinstate the reputation of the maligned Colonel. All this activity soon had the desired effect. A few days after Moore's interview with Dundas, he was promoted to brigadier-general and attached to a brigade of foreign troops, assembling in the Isle of Wight for an expedition to the West Indies. So recommenced a career which was to end gloriously and immortally in 1809 on the heights of Corunna.

But for Paoli there was to be no beginning again. True, he, too, had powerful friends; Fox and Sheridan, in particular, placed all their brilliant talents at his disposal, flayed the folly of Sir Gilbert and poured scorn on Pitt's policy. But they were no longer in accordance with the mood of the country. Pitt took the simple attitude that Sir Gilbert was an English representative in a difficult position and in a foreign country. His countrymen, as a whole, had little inclination to argue the justice of Paoli's case. Patriotism for 'Old England' was the creed of the hour. The approved attitude was that of a bluff John Bull, contemptuous alike of ideas and foreigners. In this light, Paoli was merely another exile among many exiles and one, moreover, who was suspect because of his close association with the revolutionary governments. The picture of Corsica had changed for Englishmen. It was no longer a romantic, misty island, fighting valiantly for its liberty, but merely another part of the European battlefield, where Englishmen sought everywhere to defeat their mortal enemies, the French. When J. H. Mortimer, almost a quarter of a century before, had painted his series on the 'Hero's Life', which hangs now in the Tate Gallery, he had depicted the 'Hero's' family as vaguely rustic in its trappings, but noble and gentle in its attitude and statuesquely classical in its pose; it took its place, naturally enough, among Mortimer's numerous scenes of life among the *banditti*. Gilray's savage cartoon on the same subject, painted some time after Paoli's return to England and aimed of course at Napoleon, depicted a household of lusty, squalling brats, eyes bulging and mouths greedily watering as they gazed up at the hunting trophies which their brigand father displayed at the door of their squalid hut. Public sympathy for Corsica was dead.

Paoli's years after his return were sad. Many of the oldest and dearest friends of his first exile were dead: Johnson was dead, Reynolds had died in 1792, Lord Pembroke in January 1794, Boswell in the July before his return. His good friend, Count Burzynski, the former Polish Ambassador, with whom he had once visited Edinburgh, was now in exile far from London. There was at first, too, a coolness towards Paoli in some quarters as a supposedly false friend of Britain. But it would be wrong to paint the picture too darkly and to depict Paoli as isolated or in any sense a social outcast; and as the Viceroy's misjudgement about Corsican affairs became evident, Paoli's acceptance by English society became general once more. From the first, he found good friends among that branch of the Whigs which deplored the war against France and in addition to these he soon renewed his acquaintanceship with many who had always esteemed him as the valued friend and companion of former years, rather than as the public man he had since become. One of these was the Chevalier Ruspini who was instrumental in Paoli's subsequently joining the highly exclusive Prince of Wales Lodge of Freemasons, a preserve of the Prince and his friends, which numbered among its members the Dukes of York and Clarence and many distinguished in military and court circles. But his political position, outlawed by the Convention and exiled by an unrelenting English government, had no meaning in contemporary political terms; he was thus rendered powerless to do anything at all for the cause which always lay closest to his heart, the welfare of his beloved homeland. George Dance's pencil drawing of him, made in July 1797, is a melancholy one. The old broad, self-confident head is no longer there. The lines of the face have become rigid. He stares blankly in front of him. It is the head of an old, sad and disappointed man. By this time, of course, his fears had been fulfilled: the English government in the island had come to an end and the French were again in full possession.

The Viceroy's government in the island had lasted just one year. At first, it seemed as if its duration would be very short indeed. Hardly had the excitement, caused by Paoli's departure, died away when the news came that a village in the Bozio had refused to pay its taxes. The symbolic significance of this was very evident. It was in the Bozio, in 1729, that a refusal to pay taxes had begun the Corsican rebellion against the Genoese. A body of three hundred soldiers, drawn from the Third Battalion of the Corsican Regiment was sent immediately by the Viceroy to the Bozio to enforce payment. To Sir Gilbert's anger, not only did this produce no result, but the magistrates who accompanied the troops fraternised with the rebels and returned with the soldiers to Corte, saying that it was quite impossible to enforce the payment of the taxes. Sir Gilbert had been expecting something of this sort and he immediately ordered Major Pringle to lead a small army of six hundred men to the Bozio in order to enforce obedience. Pringle acted with dash and vigour, and the troops were in possession of the key points of the hill villages before any resistance could be organised. Sullenly, the inhabitants gave way and paid their taxes. This action left Sir Gilbert cock-a-hoop. 'That affair,' he wrote gleefully, 'cost us very little blood and less than twenty pounds.'

Having shown his power and his resolution, the Viceroy proceeded to convoke Parliament, on 25th November, at Corte. Corte was chosen, partly as a concession to Corsican pride, partly to demonstrate to the islanders that there, in the very heart of Paoli's State, a new power which intended to govern, and to govern firmly, was in command. Sir Gilbert and Pozzo planned the business of the Parliament carefully. After the Bishop had opened and preached submission to the civil power, Sir Gilbert took the rostrum and delivered a long harangue on the duties of the Corsicans, on the necessity to preserve peace and order, and on the determination of his Majesty's government to ensure that peace and order were preserved. There was little opposition. What opposition there was came from Leonetti, Paoli's nephew, and, ironically enough, from Captain Colonna, the Viceroy's former aide-de-camp, whose conduct had been responsible for the occasion of Paoli's exile. He was now an object of hatred throughout Corsica, had resigned his post and hoped by his opposition to the English to restore his sullied reputation in the eyes of his fellow countrymen.

The Viceroy, however, was contemptuous of all opposition. The measures that he and Pozzo concerted showed his determination to stamp out any possible opposition on the island. The effect of the Parliament was to legalise a state of emergency. In the first instance, the jury system was abolished. Then, any assembly of more than twenty men was forbidden without special authorisation from the Viceroy. A court-martial of three judges was set up to try any offence against the security of the State and at the same time, legislation was passed which authorised the government to search the premises of any suspected enemy of the State. This done, the Viceroy prorogued the Parliament until 5th April.

Sir Gilbert now proceeded to organise his troops. He had never had any confidence in the Corsican battalions. He suspected them of still being loyal to Paoli, and the incident in the Bozio had done nothing to calm his suspicions. He, therefore, resolved to reduce the battalions from four to two and to dismiss all the Corsican officers and all those non-commissioned officers whose loyalty was suspect, replacing them all by Englishmen. In order to make up for the reduction this inevitably caused in soldiers, he increased the *gendarmerie* by 400 men, relying on relatively high rates of pay to ensure himself of their loyalty. While he was thus engaged on this re-organisation of the army, the English government sent twelve warships to reinforce the naval strength of the island. Dundas was now convinced, as he said in a letter to Elliot, that the island was secure from all ill.

Sir Gilbert thought the same. With great pleasure, he re-counted the events of 24th January, when the birthday of King George had been celebrated: *feux de joie,* salvos of cannon and all the ships in the harbour dressed overall. No disturbances. Not the slightest show of opposition. The Viceroy luxuriated in his new-found security. Sure of himself in the island, he now sought fresh fields to conquer. Sardinia had revolted against the government of King Victor Amadeus and Sir Gilbert bruited an expedition, either to conquer it for Great Britain or to restore it to its Sardinian overlord. Timely con-cessions by the Sardinian King, however, removed this possi-bility. Then, at the end of March 1796, the world, Sir Gilbert's world, began to tumble about his ears.

The avalanche began with a single stone. Major Pringle, now promoted colonel, had been sent to Corte to reorganise the Corsican battalion. From Corte he set out for Ajaccio to per-form the same office there. He carried instructions with him which prescribed the leaving of two Commissioners at Bocog-nano, who, supported by two companies of *gendarmes,* would collect the taxes for the district. The Commissioners passed freely through the district, but the *gendarmes* met with a great deal of hostility. Colonel Pringle pointed out to the Munici-pality the folly of any resistance, and, since the Municipality seemed to acquiesce in his reasoning, he took the road to Ajaccio, confident that all was well. No sooner had he and his two Commissioners departed, than the inhabitants of Bocog-nano rose and made their way to the house where the *gen-darmes* were quartered, demanding that the *gendarmes* should lay down their arms and leave the village. The *gendarmes* refused, whereupon the inhabitants immediately surrounded the house and opened fire on the occupants. A state of siege then began. When he heard of this, the Viceroy immediately ordered a two-pronged attack to relieve the besieged. General Trigge was to lead out a battalion from Bastia and Colonel Pringle was to attack from Ajaccio.

The Viceroy was in no doubt about the importance of the operation. The village of Bocognano was an important one, lying across the direct route from Corte to Ajaccio. He who held it could cut the island in half. To the Viceroy's amazement, General Trigge refused to lead his troops, saying that if the Corsicans intended to hold Bocognano it was almost impossible to storm it, being, as it was, so easy to fortify and so difficult to assail. Angrily ignoring Trigge, Elliot ordered Major Logas to march on Bocognano, storm it and restore it to order without delay. Logas set off at the head of three hundred of the Viceroy's most trusted troops. But he never reached Bocognano. Already, the country between Corte and the coast was in a ferment. The Corsicans had already fortified the approaches to the pass over the mountains at Vizzavona by entrenching themselves in the strategic village of Vivario, and heavy falls of snow made any attack by the English forces quite impossible. Knowing that the Corsicans were assembling in the country behind them, ready to cut their lines of communication to Bastia, and fearful of being trapped in a valley, the English retreated. Colonel Pringle was more unlucky. He had launched a full-scale attack from the side of Ajaccio. The attack was a disastrous failure, as man after man was picked off by the Corsican sharpshooters when the English column attempted to storm through the mountain passes. Colonel Pringle's forces were halted and then, counter-attacked from all sides, they broke and ran, leaving all their baggage and equipment in the hands of the Corsicans. Force having failed, diplomacy was tried. A Commissioner, Belgodère, who had been sent by Elliot to accompany the troops for the purposes of proclaiming martial law in the recaptured village, obtained a safe conduct from the Corsicans to go to Bocognano and negotiate the surrender of the *gendarmes*; this he did without much difficulty, by giving an undertaking that the *gendarmes* would lay down their arms and leave the village peacefully. But old hatreds were stirring anew. Bocognano had always been one of the centres of Corsican resistance against the French, and consequently it had suffered brutal retaliation after the failure of the revolt of 1774. For years after the revolt had been put down those of its inhabitants who had taken to the hills were hunted as bandits. One of the most celebrated of these was Zampaglino, father of the two Bonelli brothers,

319

two of the most enthusiastic partisans of the French cause, who were now with Napoleon's armies in Provence, awaiting an opportunity to invade their native country. Among the most zealous of the former persecutors of the Paolist rebels were the officers of the Provincial Corsican Regiment, which had been set up under the Monarchy, many of whose officers had re-emerged with the exile of Paoli. Two of these, one from the Vittini and one from the Casabianca clans, were now officers in the *gendarmerie*. After Belgodère had negotiated the surrender, the *gendarmes* filed out of the house and began to lay down their arms, but no sooner had Vittini and Casabianca laid down theirs, than they were brutally assassinated by a gang made up of the relatives of their former victims.

When he heard the news, the Viceroy condemned the Corsican vice of the vendetta in the strongest terms he could command as a most barbarous threat to peace and good order. But the words rang hollow. He himself had been responsible for removing the one sure brake on its savage operation; he himself had been responsible for creating the conditions in which it could operate once more; and he himself bore the responsibility for the dismissal of Colonel Moore, the one English soldier whose military and political knowledge of the island might have, in some measure, enabled him to deal with it.

It was at this critical period that Sir Gilbert received an unexpected windfall, for two long-awaited regiments of reinforcements now arrived in Bastia. The same ship that brought them to Bastia brought also Colonel Villettes, and the Viceroy immediately replaced Trigge by the colonel and gave him orders to advance with the Viceroy's troops and one of the new regiments to Bocognano. He had the other regiment re-embarked and sent to Ajaccio. It was indeed necessary to act very quickly. The whole of the eastern part of the island, inspired by the example of Bocognano, had risen in rebellion, and Colonel Pringle was penned within the town of Ajaccio itself. Elsewhere in the island there were constant reports of disturbances, with bands of armed men everywhere roaming the countryside. The Viceroy knew that the critical moment of his rule had come. Very conscious of the decisive nature of the campaign which had now begun, he took the resolution to accompany the army of Villettes to Bocognano.

At first, all seemed to go well. The two thousand men of

the Expeditionary Force marched rapidly along the road to Corte and then, descending into the valley of the Vecchio, they stormed the Corsican entrenchments at Vivario. Elated by their victory, the regiments of Villettes swept through the pass of Vizzavona and appeared before Bocognano before the Corsicans had organised their defences fully. After the briefest of pauses, Villettes threw his troops into an attack on the town; but the attack was bloodily repulsed. To try to storm the village directly meant heavy and bloody losses. As Villette's men took up their dispositions for the grim battle of attrition, which they knew they must fight to gain the village, disquieting news came to them. At Bistuglio, two miles distant from Corte, the Corsicans of the surrounding districts were rallying. Villettes realised what this meant: in a few days his army would be trapped between two forces. The Viceroy and Villettes had hasty consultations, and, as a result of them, they decided to grant full pardon to all the Bocognanans if they would lay down their arms. The question of the taxes was not entered into; nor was the question of the murder of the former regimental officers of the Provincial Corsican Regiment.

The army of the Viceroy then hurriedly took the road for Bistuglio. When they arrived there, they found that the Corsicans were gathering in force. Already they numbered eight hundred or so men and the news was that detachments were still hurrying from the glens to join them. Couriers brought reports to Elliot that other Corsican insurgents had already attacked the strategic bridges of Ponteleccia and Francardo, over which the road from Corte to Bastia passed. The detachments of English troops at the bridges had beaten off the attackers but the Corsicans were already regrouping and awaiting the arrival of yet more supporters from the surrounding glens. Elliot received the news, too, that the road from Bastia along the east coast was threatened, and there were even stories that an army of Corsicans was preparing to descend from the hills to attack the capital itself. What Elliot feared on the departure of Paoli had now come about: the country was in a state of civil war.

Villettes was eager that the Viceroy should launch an attack on the Corsicans' stronghold at Bistuglio. But Elliot was discouraged and depressed. He had seen the failure of his policy of the firm hand. He had no faith in the judge-

L

ment of his fire-eating commander, newly-arrived as he was, and ignorant of Corsican ways and of the background of the struggle. Moreover, it was reported that the leaders at Bistuglio included some of the most educated men and powerful chiefs of the district. Gambini, Santini, Franzini and three well-respected doctors, della Croce, Ponticaccia and della Campana were among them. Sir Gilbert resolved on negotiations and arranged a meeting with the leaders of the Corsicans. He found that he was dealing with a revolutionary committee, which claimed that it could speak for most of the island. After some preliminary discussion, the revolutionary committee suddenly provided him with something like an ultimatum, in the shape of a long list of the members of the Council to whom they most objected, saying that it was impossible for him to govern by means of them, since they were detested by the majority of Corsicans. At the same time, they repeated over and over again that they had no quarrel with the Viceroy himself, who, they said, had been misled. It was a very familiar formula for rebellion, but the Viceroy judged that he had no alternative but to accept it and, with a great deal of private repining, he agreed that he would revise his Council and dismiss all the proscribed Councillors. He further agreed to a full pardon for all the insurgents and to the revision of the land and salt taxes.

With the agreement signed, peace was restored. But it was a peace that marked the complete bankruptcy of the Viceroy's government: in a financial as well as a moral sense. For, as Elliot wrote bitterly to Portland, they had thrown away the right to claim a penny piece in the interior of the island for the sake of peace. Only the English money which circulated there and the administration of justice which, as the French sympathisers sardonically said, the Corsicans did not object to unless it affected them personally, were left as evidences of English rule. The list of Elliot's former advisers, whom he had been forced to dispense with, was very long. At the head of them, of course, was Pozzo di Borgo, who was forced to retire to his dwelling in Bastia, divested of all public authority and reduced to the rank of simple citizen: which part he played extremely well, being affable and friendly with all men in the streets of Bastia and bearing his disgrace with great insouciance.

Elliot had not Pozzo's resilience and was terribly depressed. Even his new Councillors, he reflected, would do little to ease the troubled situation in the island. For, with their appointment, a whole new class of opponents to his government had arisen – all those who had not obtained employment in the Viceroy's new administration. Neither the Viceroy, nor anyone around him, had anything like Paoli's authority or ability to reconcile factions for the good of the country as a whole. The vendetta in its milder and most lethal forms became endemic. There was universal dislike and distrust of the *émigrés,* and, to an increasing extent, of the English themselves. Differences of religion, differences of interest made their mark. Horse play by some English soldiers on the quay at Ajaccio involved some Corsican fishermen and developed into a near riot. An English sergeant at Bastia, rather than reveal the name of a thief, went to the scaffold, declaring that he would rather be hanged a thousand times than betray a fellow countryman to a Papist. There were continual complaints from the island's clergy that the English treated neither their religion nor their churches with due respect. Elliot believed that behind all this turmoil were Paoli's followers, provoking discontent, organising opposition, plotting and planning for the return of the General to the island. His letters to England became full of his suspicions, almost to the point of obsession.

But the really menacing plots against his rule were being organised not in London but on the south coast of France. For there, Napoleon was methodically arranging for the dispatch of agents to the island in order to stir up trouble and to exploit grievances wherever they occurred: 'You will go to Corsica with eighteen men of your own choice. Citizen Sapey is instructed to arrange your journey and to provide you with all the necessary powder and arms. Twenty-four thousand *livres* in silver will be given to you in order that you may encourage the patriots with it': thus wrote Napoleon on 21st May 1796. And again on 20th July, to Bonelli: 'I have received your letter from Bocognano dated 23rd June. I congratulate you on your arrival in Corsica. I have ordered all the refugees to make ready to lead the brave Corsican patriots, in order that they may break the English yoke and to reconquer liberty, the perpetual aim of all our compatriots.' To counteract all this activity by the French, Sir Gilbert offered a reward of 5,000 francs for every French agent captured, but there were very few rewards claimed.

Realising much too late in the day the ineffectiveness of regular troops to deal with the situation that was being created, Elliot decided to form bodies of paid Corsican Volunteers in each village. The operation, however, proved a farce. After his agents had enrolled a certain number of Volunteers in a village they all too frequently, on arriving at the next village, found themselves preceded by their recruits, who, if they were able to escape detection, had themselves inscribed a second time. Although the deception was not invariably successful, nevertheless the English found that in any emergency there were always a great many more troops on paper than there were in actuality. These 'paper' troops increased substantially the expenses of the English government in the island, expenses which were already considerable. For Elliot was already resorting to bribery on a large scale to secure representatives, whom he hoped would be favourable to his own government. All this was additional to the expense the administration had to bear from the loss of taxes, which the agreement at Bistuglio had brought about. Elliot reckoned that the agreement alone had lost him ten thousand pounds a year in revenue.

Yet he was not entirely despondent. Although he realised that there was nothing to be proud of in the actual government of Corsica, yet he still maintained that he had at least preserved Corsica as a haven for British ships: a bastion in a Europe dominated by the power of the Directory. He saw it as a springboard from which the English might leap to safeguard their interests along the Mediterranean littoral and harrass the enclosing semicircle of the French. He had other plans, too. He had always had better relations with the navy than with the army, and he was very conscious of the power the English fleet possessed. He, therefore, resolved to offset the blow to English prestige in Corsica itself by occupying the Italian islands in the Mediterranean. Accordingly, on 17th July, he was able to send a detailed report to Dundas, describing his unopposed occupation of the island of Elba. On the day after he sent it the English fleet likewise obtained the surrender of the island of Capraja without any spilling of blood. Sir Gilbert, who was inclined to shoot from the depths of despair to the heights of exultation, determined that he would next send an expedition to Leghorn to safeguard English interests there, and he appointed a rendezvous for the fleet on 17th August at Bastia. But before he could embark his troops for the expedition, a letter came from Portland, instructing him to evacuate the Hundredth Division from the island. This withdrawal of the most trusted of his troops presaged an even greater withdrawal. Elliot was full of foreboding, and justly so, for some days later another letter from Portland instructed him to make all preparations for the withdrawal of all the English troops on the island. The English government had decided that the cost of holding Corsica was too great, and that it was necessary, since the French were uniformly victorious on the shores of the Mediterranean, to withdraw all the English outposts to Gibraltar. Elliot obeyed his instructions with a heavy heart, drawing some consolation from the fact that the English plans for withdrawal were still only precautionary and might now never be implemented. Indeed, at the end of September he was still setting out details of the measures he had believed necessary for the retention of Corsica as an English base. In this he was, incidentally, warmly supported by Nelson who was always conscious of the advantage given to the fleet by the possession of the Corsican harbours.

But there was to be no respite for Sir Gilbert, for his letter on this subject crossed with one of Portland's, ordering him to quit Corsica as soon as possible. Elliot performed his last duties in the island conscientiously. He was particularly determined that the situation that had existed at Toulon should not occur in Corsica, and he was therefore very concerned that all the *émigrés* and the Corsicans who had revolted against the French and had loyally supported him against Paoli, should he embarked with the garrison of the island. He also arranged for pensions to be paid to all the exiles. Nothing indeed became him in the island so much as the manner of his going. In all, 7,000 French *émigrés* and a little over 5,000 Corsican refugees embarked with the English fleet. As they sailed out of the island, the French armies, under the command of General Gentili and with Saliceti as the Commissioner, sailed in. There was a brush between English and French troops, but, on the whole, very little fighting. The French merely took over as the English moved out. Saliceti, as the French representative, was quickly succeeded by André François Miot, whose post was that of

General Commissioner for the island. It was a wise move on the part of the Directory, for Saliceti, in the brief span of his government, showed a regrettable tendency to pursue the old Corsican custom of vendetta, while Miot was, from the first, determined to govern judiciously and fairly and to try and moderate the partisan spirit which raged. He began by declaring an amnesty for all who had fought against the French. This specific measure was immediately countermanded by Napoleon, who produced a detailed list (at the head of which was Pozzo di Borgo) of all those who were to be hunted down. This list numbered about thirty individuals and to it Napoleon added a general instruction that any *émigrés* found in the island were to be immediately arrested and an exhortation to punish with the whole vigour of the law anyone found pursuing a vendetta. But, in spite of this setback to a conciliatory policy, with Miot as its Commissioner and Gentili as its General, the island found for a certain time a certain measure of peace.

25

PAOLI'S LAST YEARS

Sir Gilbert and Pozzo di Borgo returned to England by way of Rome and Naples; they arrived in England early in March 1797. The failure of the Viceroy's government did not mean a vindication of Paoli, for the government showed great solicitude for Sir Gilbert and, in October of that year, conferred a peerage on him; as the General sardonically said : 'It is the custom of ministers to protect their creatures.' The government's concern was, however, solely for Sir Gilbert. If Pozzo had retained any hope of success for his plan to play once again the part of a minister of a great power it was soon destroyed. His part in bringing about the English débâcle was known to the English Ministers, even if only imperfectly, and no matter how brilliant his talents, and he was certainly very gifted, there was no place for him in the closed little worlds of the Court and the Government other than as the dependant of Sir Gilbert. He had served the English purpose and, in the last resort, he had served it badly; his use was over. His credit and his career became entirely dependent on the goodwill Sir Gilbert bore him; when, in 1799, Sir Gilbert left England on a mission to Vienna, Pozzo accompanied him as a mere member of his household.

Paoli had, by the time of their arrival, ceased to have any hope that he might return to Corsica. At the most, he thought that he might be able to make his way to Italy and there spend the remainder of his days in comfort, close to his homeland and his countrymen. Italy, too, would have relieved the strain on his pension, for England in wartime was an expensive place in which to live and Paoli, surrounded by dependants who had followed him into exile, had many outlays. There were other reasons for his wishing to find an Italian home, for in Italy he might be of more use to his relatives, particularly his sister and her children who might, he feared, be the victims of the reprisals of the victorious French. He advised her that, if danger threatened, she should make her way with her children to Italy and there await his arrival. If his way to Italy should be barred by the French army he hoped, he wrote, to find asylum for her and himself in one of the smaller German states. His nephews seemed to have taken his advice, for three years later he was playfully referring in his letters to his Livornese and Pisan nephews. But he himself was never to leave England again while he lived. Why this was so, it is not possible to establish with certainty. Perhaps he found that the English government had taken Sir Gilbert's advice which had followed Paoli from the island: that is, not to allow Paoli to leave England again; or perhaps he found that the long arm of the French State reached wherever he might wish to set up a new home; or perhaps it was the simple fact that his health was now very bad: a fact to which he makes constant reference in his letters of this period. In 1800, he had a momentary flash of hope, for, with Napoleon as the First Consul, many of the French *émigrés* began returning to France and he hoped, for a brief space, that those who had suffered from the violence of Saliceti might be considered by Buonaparte to be in the same category as those who had fled the Revolution. Those hopes were shattered in the August of that same year when he heard that Buonaparte had sent Saliceti himself to subdue a rebellion which had broken out in Corsica.

His information was inaccurate, for Saliceti had not been sent to repress a rebellion: he had caused it and was now desperately striving to restore the *status quo*. The occasion of the rising was the forced recruitment of Corsicans by Saliceti for yet another invasion of the island of Sardinia. It was a very serious rebellion. At its height, it threatened the total destruction of French power in the island and the French were all the more concerned about it, since it came hard on the heels of the so-called Rebellion of the Cross which had taken place two years before, in 1798. The Rebellion of the Cross had been a religious and a Royalist rebellion but Paoli's name had, ironically enough, been invoked in it by the partisans of the old order and, so confused was the situation in Corsica, not unsuccessfully.

The rebellion of 1800 was, fantastic though it seems, organised in the name of Paul I, the Emperor of All the Russias and, however much truth there was in the statement that Russia was behind the rebellion, it is a fact that the rebels were plentifully supplied from some source with money and arms. Amongst their leaders, as a final bizarre touch, was Paoli's old enemy, Buttafuoco, leading men who had been raised out of the ground, or rather out of the chestnut groves, by the magic of Paoli's name. But, in fact, Paoli was neither consulted nor wished to have any part in these rebellions. He defined his position to rebellion, both at that time and in subsequent letters, clearly enough. In the Europe of that time, he wrote, divided as it was into great states, each of which relentlessly pursued its own ends, it was hopeless for a small island, such as Corsica, to dream of independence. The English experiment, he believed, had failed for good and all, and the best that could be hoped from England was that her influence might be used to place Corsica under the aegis of one of the smaller European Powers. In this, Paoli saw no advantage. What good would it profit Corsica, he wrote, to be nominally ruled by a Power which had no real interest in it and could not protect it? He recalled his youthful rejection of the idea that Corsica might come under the patronage of the Pope. This was still his position. The status of a dependency, he held, was of no advantage to Corsica, then or now.

Since English goodwill, even if it were regained, promised the Corsicans nothing, then there was no sense in the Corsicans expending their energy to create a useless diversion. This could bring misery in its wake and he held that, with all their misfortunes, the Corsicans had, in their present state one consolation, a consolation that, he wrote, he often repeated to himself – that in all the turmoil of Europe it was, at least, spared the fate of some greater states on the continental mainland, continually exposed as they were to the chances of war with their people suffering all the hardships that trampling armies passing to and fro through their territory could bring upon them.

Moreover, he thought that the islanders had some good cards to play. Corsica, small and so near to France, must always be an object of great military concern to the French, and, in an island so easily invaded, he thought that the Corsicans might draw some advantage from this. The vulnerability of the island to invasion from the sea would make the French eager to purchase Corsican support by a *de facto* alliance, and the French as allies, he believed, had a good deal to offer Corsica, apart from an opportunity to recuperate after its long struggle. The French flag could protect the Corsican fishers; French expertise and assistance might advance the state of Corsican agriculture; above all, France, in its new guise, might open a career for the talents.

It was in this respect that he thought Corsican collaboration with France might produce the most fruitful results for the Corsicans. The career open to the talents is a theme that sounds again and again in his last letters. It was as an example of a Corsican who had seized the opportunity open to him that Paoli regarded Napoleon. In this light, although in this light only, he considered that Napoleon would be a shining example to future generations of Corsicans. For the rest, he considered Napoleon merely a rebel against the legitimately-constituted government of his native land – and an ungrateful rebel at that. But it was on this shaky foundation that future generations of Buonapartist historians had to build their posthumous reconciliation between Buonaparte and Paoli.

Even while he was formulating this doctrine of collaboration in his letters, events in the island were making nonsense of it. Paoli had some knowledge of this, for, in September 1800, he wrote a measured condemnation of Saliceti's character: 'Saliceti will not succeed in any military undertaking because he is unthinking; and he will never do anything good in civil life because he is too passionate and violent in his actions.' Saliceti's repression of the rebellion in the island was indeed violent. Villages were burnt and men, women and children were massacred, churches were looted and the sacraments insulted. In fairness to Saliceti, this was rather the result of the Republican troops getting out of hand than result of any cold-blooded policy of repression. But the outcome was the same. When Saliceti, at the end of the year, left the island he left the Corsicans subdued, indeed, but thirsting for vengeance. He left in his place once again Miot, whose pacific policy had once before proved successful, immediately after the retreat of the English. Miot came as Administrator-General, a post really equivalent to Dictator, for he had complete control of the administration of the island where, since the island was really in a state of emergency, all the normal laws had been suspended. Miot ruled a Corsica cast in a new mould, for Saliceti before his departure had acted on instructions from France where Napoleon had resolved on root and branch reorganisation. The old democratic *Podestas* and the Fathers of the Commune, for so long the basis of government in Corsica, were by his edict, replaced by Municipal Councils, on which sat a high proportion of French officials.

Miot's rule was short-lived. He was soon deposed by a conspiracy organised by the military and the administrators in the island, and in his place came the grim General Morand, who for ten years was to rule Corsica with an iron hand. The price General Morand had to pay for Miot's going was a return to constitutional government, but so threatening was the Corsican attitude to the French that he soon managed to have himself invested with plenary powers, and for the next decade he used these ruthlessly whenever, and wherever, there was a threat to the French control of the island.

Paoli kept himself fairly closely informed of all these events, for his informants and friends, drawn from all parts of the island, came in course of time to number those who had made their peace with the French as well as those who continued intransigent. In return, he provided them with information about the Corsican exiles, about whom his knowledge was very comprehensive:

Giacomo Pietro has passed to a better life, leaving a daughter and a great many debts. His son, who is only nine years old, is very dear to me. Giacomo, Orso and Graziani are well enough and I have taken them into my service. Balestrini no longer thinks of going to Italy: his daughter has married a young painter; and she is happy. Marti del Borgo on the eve of being promoted to a company has left Martinique; in India Massei di Bastia is in the same position. The son of Signor Bartolani is in the island of Ceylon. Lord North who is the Governor there likes him, esteems him and has promoted him.

To the Corsicans in England he was the *Babbo,* 'Father', to a greater extent than he had ever been before, even in Corsica; he guided them in their relations with the English; he kept them informed, as far as he was able, of the doings of their countrymen; above all, he devoted the greater part of his income to providing them with help and relief.

His uncertain health now troubled him greatly. Because of his arthritis and failing sight he was no longer able to read or write easily; he suffered a great deal from catarrh and from the stone. In 1802, his health was very bad indeed and his letters took a valedictory tone. He had gone to Bristol to escape the suffocating heat of a London summer and in a letter, written from the port in September, he bequeathed all his writings and the sword which had been given to him by Frederick of Prussia to the confraternity of Morosaglia. He gave his regards to the parish priest of his native village and to the remaining religious of the convent which he had known so well. And to the men and women of his native village he sent what looks as if it were intended to be a last message:

> Say to them that I loved them above all others. Their story will always be remembered in the history of our glens. It will tell how, for the liberty of their country, they shed more blood than any, and the memory of this will put courage in those who will come after and make them eager to preserve the reputation which their ancestors have acquired.

Just before Christmas, in the year 1802, he was at a low ebb. He wrote that he suffered a great deal from the stone, that he suffered great effusions of blood and that every little thing threatened to end his life. To add to the agonies of the body, he heard of the death of one of his nephews. He was deeply affected: 'I never had any reason to be anything but pleased with him. I valued his worth and I loved him greatly.'

He sought to cheer himself with the illusion that his country had won her freedom – which it had not. He wrote that he forgave all his enemies and anyone who had spoken ill of him, and he included Saliceti and Arena specifically among these. If Paoli's life had ended here on a dying fall, in the winter of 1802, or in 1803, in the English spring, which he always believed might be fatal to him, his life would have conformed to a familiar human pattern. In his last days he would have turned to look backwards with forgiveness and charity into the past, even as in his passionate youth he had looked eagerly and intemperately forward into the future. It is a pattern not without beauty, but it was not to be that of Paoli's life. His last days were to be more typical of the theme that ran through his life – the Enlightenment. His letters are naturally few in the last few years of his life when he suffered from very bad health, but there rings out again and again the old notes which had sustained his youth and inspired his manhood. In July 1803, in a letter to the Abbé Paoletti at Morosaglia, he laments that the increased cost of living in England had forced him to discontinue some of his benefactions to the children of the refugees. He doubted that, in the circumstances, he would leave very much behind him, but he wrote: 'If on my death any property remains, let my glen and my country know that what was dearest to my heart was to promote the education of our youth, for I have always believed that our young men are both able and willing to profit from the advances in the sciences, which on every side now open such great roads to advancement.' His will, after bequests to family and friends, was devoted to that end.

His last days were taken up by using every channel of influence that he commanded to ensure the establishment of the new university he dreamed of and for which his will provided. In 1805, writing to Pietri, one of Napoleon's prefects in Corsica, he outlined in great detail what each of the chairs was to teach. In his emphasis on the syllabus for each Corsican instructor, the old Enlightened administrator was revealed for the last time. For the last time he prepared a programme inspired by those Enlightened principles from which his spirit had never departed. The programme was the same as ever: to produce a responsible and educated electorate, politicians devoted only to the well-being of their country, and an educated and responsible clergy.

Each professor was to give a two-year course. The first chair was to teach the fundamental principles of natural theology and revealed religion, with an emphasis on the use of reason and a bias against the uncritical acceptance of texts. The second was to teach politics and philosophy so that the students might learn to govern well and with probity.

The third chair was to give courses in logic, metaphysics and mathematics. Logic and metaphysics were to 'direct and assist man's natural faculty of reason and understanding in the consideration of general ideas' and mathematics was to provide the foundation for a future study of the natural sciences, as well as enabling the future administrator to manage the nation's finances wisely. Paoli hoped that, after all this had been arranged, there might still be enough money to set up a school in his native glen of Rostino, where the children of the glen might learn reading, writing and arithmetic. If this proved impossible, he wished the money to go to provide five scholarships, by means of which five Corsican students could go to the mainland and study at some university. So he hoped he might leave his native country 'in possession of something that may be of use to it'.

So, still dreaming of the Enlightened future of his beloved country, he passed his last years in exile. His powerful constitution, which had been subject to so many stresses and strains, fought a last hard battle against the pain and penalties of old age. But he was very tired. On 4th March 1806, he wrote: 'I have lived long enough and I would not wish to begin again. Unless, that is, I might be permitted to remember my former life and so correct its errors and avoid its follies.' The sentiment might be common to many men but, with its implicit restatement of Paoli's ineradicable belief, that reason was supreme and, properly applied, could overcome all man's weaknesses and failings, it was no unworthy farewell.

Just a little under a year later, on 2nd February 1807, he became very ill. He lingered until the 5th and then, at midnight, he died in the arms of his fellow exile, Giacomorsi. He was eighty-two years of age.

He was buried in the cemetery of St Pancras, the burial ground at that time of all Catholics in London, in a lead coffin carrying the inscription in Latin:

PASCAL DE PAOLI
ONCE THE SUPREME LEADER AND LEGISLATOR OF CORSICA
BORN 5TH APRIL A.D. 1725
DIED LONDON A.D. 1807

His death stirred many memories, but England was at war and every day brought fresh news of the mortal struggle against his fellow-countrymen and one-time follower, Napoleon Buonaparte; although the pattern of Paoli's life was complex, he had never ceased to profess principles which were now looked at askance by most of the embattled English; he did not fit the simple pattern of the English hero of the day and his passing did not arouse a great deal of notice. Nevertheless, he had many friends in London, and by their united efforts a memorial to him was placed in Westminster Abbey with a bust by Flaxman and a lengthy epitaph which reads (deprived of its concluding laudatory lines to George III):

D.O.M.

TO THE MEMORY OF

PASQUALE DE PAOLI

ONE OF THE MOST EMINENT AND MOST ILLUSTRIOUS CHARACTERS
OF THE AGE IN WHICH HE LIVED.

HE WAS BORN IN CORSICA, APRIL 5TH 1725.

WAS UNANIMOUSLY CHOSEN, AT THE AGE OF THIRTY SUPREME
HEAD OF THAT COUNTRY

AND DIED IN THIS METROPOLIS FEBY THE 5TH 1807

AGED 82 YEARS

THE EARLY AND BETTER PART OF HIS LIFE HE DEVOTED TO
THE CAUSE OF LIBERTY;

NOBLY MAINTAINING IT AGAINST THE USURPATION
OF GENOESE AND FRENCH TYRANNY;

BY HIS MANY SPLENDID ACHIEVEMENTS,

HIS USEFUL AND BENEVOLENT INSTITUTIONS,

HIS PATRIOTIC AND PUBLIC ZEAL MANIFESTED UPON EVERY
OCCASION HE, AMONGST THE FEW WHO HAVE MERITED
SO GLORIOUS A TITLE,

MOST JUSTLY DESERVED TO BE HAILED

THE FATHER OF HIS COUNTRY

BEING OBLIGED BY THE SUPERIOR FORCE OF HIS ENEMIES
TO RETIRE FROM CORSICA,

HE SOUGHT REFUGE IN THIS LAND OF LIBERTY;

AND WAS HERE MOST GRACIOUSLY RECEIVED

(AMIDST THE GENERAL APPLAUSE OF A MAGNANIMOUS NATION)

INTO THE PROTECTION OF HIS MAJESTY KING GEORGE THE THIRD.

That epitaph has, even more than most epitaphs, evasions and ambiguities tangled in it, but its bland phrases are only too true of the way in which Paoli's memory has been preserved in England. Except for a curious few, his life ends on the day he disappears from the papers of Boswell's *Life of Johnson*.

In France, this was not possible. Since the greatest of the French heroes had admired Paoli in his boyhood and served him in his youth and since Paoli's memory continued to be in

Corsica so honoured and venerated, a posthumous reconciliation had to be effected by French historians. Napoleon, ever considerate of his future hagiographers, provided very useful material. On St Helena he told what was essentially the same story to Las Cases and to O'Meara : 'I passed a short time with Paoli ... who was very partial to me, and to whom I was then most attached. Paoli espoused the cause of the English faction and I that of the French and consequently most of my family were driven away from Corsica. Paoli often patted me on the head saying, "You are one of Plutarch's men." He divined that I should be something extraordinary.' When he had heard of Paoli's death, Napoleon said he was filled with chagrin. It would have been a great happiness for him, and, he believed, much to his credit if he had recalled Paoli: 'But taken up as I was with affairs of State I rarely had the opportunity of indulging my personal desires.' To balance this, apocryphal anecdotes were created to show that Paoli had, in his last years, been won over by the exploits of Napoleon. Even Chuquet, who is remarkably clearsighted about the young Napoleon, repeats the story that Paoli, when he heard, in 1796, that Napoleon had abolished the Republic of Genoa, cried out: 'It is by the hand of a Corsican that Genoa has received the *coup de grâce*!' Even Tomaso's collection of Paoli's letters (which contains ample evidence to call the story into question) repeats the tale that Paoli, when he heard in 1800 that Buonaparte had been elected the First Consul, illuminated all the windows of his house in Oxford Street to show his joy. To account for the split between Paoli and Napoleon, the picture of an old and enfeebled General, totally subverted by a repellent Pozzo di Borgo, was created. Thus Paoli passed into the French popular memory in a guise pretty accurately portrayed in Abel Gance's famous, heroic film, *Napoleon*. The later career of Pozzo di Borgo, ironically enough, clinched the legend. As the agent of Alexander I of Russia, Pozzo became, in his day, famous throughout Europe as the arch-enemy of Napoleon and one of the prime architects of his destruction. Later, as the Ambassador of Russia in Paris, from 1815 to 1835, he became to the Liberals of a new generation the symbol of reaction and the archetypal opponent of everything that Liberalism, which increasingly hailed Buonaparte as one of its Founding Fathers, stood for. His name echoes and re-echoes among the memorialists and diarists of the period who were, indeed, excessively numerous and many of whom, of course, knew him. But, remarkably, his break with Paoli is hardly mentioned at all, either by him or by others; it confused a simple picture. Pozzo and Paoli, indissolubly united, suited the memories both of Pozzo and the Buonapartes, and in the last years, talking about his early life with Capefigue, the break disappeared completely from Pozzo's memory and he recalled that the happiest days in his life had been spent with Paoli in Corsica, struggling for Corsican liberty. So, quite unconsciously, he helped to perpetrate the legend of his being Paoli's evil genius during his last years.

But Paoli's death did not mean that Corsica had done with him. In 1848, Louis-Philippe, hoping to associate his régime with one of the most glorious epochs of French history, had the body of Napoleon brought from St Helena to its final resting place in Les Invalides. Just under half a century later, the Third Republic, fortified by the fact that Corsica had now been for almost a century united to France, and seeing no harm, and perhaps some good, coming from a similar gesture, permitted Franceschini Pietri, who had been the Secretary of Napoleon III, to organise a subscription throughout the island with the object of bringing back the Father of his country to his own beloved soil. Paoli's memory always was, and always will be, green in Corsica; there was not a Commune in the island that did not contribute to the cost of the reinterment. Accordingly, on 2nd September 1889, Paoli's remains were exhumed from the old St Pancras cemetery, placed on an English frigate and taken back to their native land. There, in a mausoleum constructed in his own house at the head of the glen in Morosaglia, Paoli was finally buried. Here he lies today: his remains secure amongst his fellow-countrymen. His fame, securer still, will rest forever in their hearts.

BIBLIOGRAPHY

PART I

UNPUBLISHED PRIMARY SOURCES

PUBLIC RECORD OFFICE

Foreign Office Records : Corsica F.O. 20 1–22
France F.O. 27 33A–35
Genoa F.O. 28 6–13

ARCHIVES NATIONALES

There is a great deal of material in the Archives which concerns
Corsica during the period of Paoli's life. The Archives are particularly rich in documents which relate to French rule from 1769 to
1789 and during the Revolution. I have found the following to be
most useful :

Série AA   AA 15 : 479, 739–40, 751–752, 757–758
            AA 56
Série D   D III^{51}
Série F   F^{60} 6
Série K   K 1225$^{1-14}$
            K 1226$^{4-6}$ (contains reports on Corsica made by de
            Vaux, Buttafuoco and Marbeuf and written shortly after
            the conquest of Corsica by France in 1769.)
            K 1226$^{9-40}$
            K 1227^{10}
            K 1227$^{12-13}$
            K 1227$^{18-21}$
            K 1227^{31}
Série M   M 663^{10}

PART II

PUBLISHED PRIMARY SOURCES

1. 'Lettere di Pasquale de' Paoli', *Archivio Storico Italiano*
(Florence 1846)

Bibliography

2. 'Lettres de Pasquale Paoli à Giuseppe Ottavio Nobili-Savelli', Ed. A. Costa, *Bulletin de la Société des Sciences Historiques et Naturelles de la Corse* (Bastia, 1930, 1931)
3. 'Lettres divers à Paoli', Ed. Francois di Morati-Gentili, *Bulletin de la Société des Sciences Historiques et Naturelles de la Corse* (Bastia 1901)
4. 'Lettres', Ed. by M. le docteur Perelli, *Bulletin de la Société des Sciences Historiques et Naturelles de la Corse* (Bastia 1881–99)
5. *Lettere inedite di Pasquale Paoli*, Ed. P. di C. (Ajaccio 1933)
6. 'Lettere inedite di Pasquale de' Paoli', Ed. by G. Livi, *Archivio Storico Italiano* (Florence 1889–1890)
7. 'Lettere inedite di Pasquale de' Paoli', *Miscellanea di Storia Italiana* (Turin 1880)

PART III

PUBLISHED SECONDARY SOURCES

Acton, H., *The Bourbons of Naples (1734–1825)* (London 1956)
Anon., *A Review of the conduct of P. Paoli addressed to the Rt. Hon. W. Beckford* (London 1770)
Annual Register, 1768, 1769
Arblay, d', *The Diary and Letters of Madame d'Arblay*, Ed. A. Dobson (London 1904)
Arrighi, A., *Histoire de Pascal Paoli* (Paris 1843)
Bartoli, *Histoire de Pascal Paoli* (Bastia 1889)
Benson, R., *Sketches of Corsica* (London 1825)
Bordin, P., *Le Retour triumphant de Paoli, le vengeur de la liberté* (1790)
Boswell, J., *An Account of Corsica, the Journal of a Tour in that Island and Memoirs of Pascal Paoli* (London 1768)
Boswell, J., Ed. *Essays in Favour of the Brave Corsicans* (London 1768)
Boswell, J., *Life of Johnson*, Ed. G. B. Hill (London 1950)
Buonarroti, F. M., *La Conjuration de Corse* (Paris 1794)
Burnaby, A., *Journal of a Tour to Corsica in the year 1766* (London 1804)
Caird, L. H., *History of Corsica* (London 1899)
Chiari, J., *The Scented Isle* (Glasgow 1948)
Chuquet, A., *La Jeunesse de Napoléon* (Paris 1899)
Colonna de Cesari Rocca, *Histoire de la Corse* (Paris 1907)
Colonna de Cesari Rocca, *La Vendetta dans l'Histoire* (Paris 1908)
Colonna de Cesari Rocca and L. Villat, *Histoire des Corses* (Paris 1916)
Collucci, Southwell E., 'Un canzone alla Corsica attributa a P. Paoli', *Archivio Storico di Corsica* (Leghorn 1930)

Bibliography

Cristiani, L., *Pascal Paoli* (Ajaccio 1954)

Colvill, *The Cyrnean Hero* (1772)

Duperrier Dumouriez, C. F., *Mémoires* (Paris 1843)

Eisenstein, Elizabeth L., *The First Professional Revolutionary, Filippo Michèle Buonarotti (1761–1837)* (Cambridge, Massachusetts 1954)

Fairchild, H. M., *The Noble Savage* (New York 1928)

Fenn, T., *Prince of Wales Lodge No. 259* (London 1910)

Feiling, K., *The Second Tory Party* (London 1938)

Fitzmaurice, Lord, *Life of William, Earl of Shelburne* (London 1912)

Flaubert, G., *Voyages* (Paris 1948)

Fontana, M., *Le Constitution du Généralat de Pascal Paoli en Corse* (Paris 1907)

Forester, L., *Rambles in the islands of Corsica and Sardinia* (London 1868)

Forster, J., *Life and adventures of Oliver Goldsmith* (London 1848)

Gai, Dom J-B., *La tragique histoire des Corses* (Paris 1951)

Galletti, J-A. (l'Abbé), *Histoire illustrée de la Corse* (Paris 1863)

Giamarchi, F. M., *Vita Politica di Pasquale Paoli* (Bastia 1858)

Gregorovius, F., *Wanderings in Corsica*, trans. A. Muir (Edinburgh 1860)

Guerruzi, F. D., *Pasquale Paoli* (1864)

Gay, P., *The Enlightenment* (London 1967)

Gay, P., *The Party of Humanity* (London 1964)

Hobsbawm, E. J., *The Age of Revolution* (London 1962)

Jacobi, J. M., *Histoire Générale de la Corse* (Paris 1835)

Jollivet, M., *La 'Révolution Française' en Corse* (Paris 1892)

Jollivet, M., *Les Anglais dans la Méditerranée (1794–1797)* (Paris 1896)

Las Cases, M. J. E. D., Comte de, *Mémorial de Ste-Hélène* (Brussels 1828)

Lecky, W. E. H., *History of England in the 18th Century* (London 1878)

Lencisa, F., *Pasquale Paoli e le guerre d'Indepependenza della Corsica* (Milan 1790)

Macknight, T., *History of the Life and Times of Edmund Burke* (London 1858)

Maggiolo, A., *Pozzo di Borgo* (Paris 1890)

Mérimée, P., *Colomba* (Paris 1850)

Mérimée, P., *Notes d'un Voyage en Corse* (Paris 1840)

Michel, E., 'Giudizi Francesi su Pasquale Paoli all 'inizio del suo Generalat', *Archivio Istorico di Corsica* (Leghorn 1928)

Michel, E., 'Pasquale Paoli e il Bey di Tunisia', *Archivio Istorico di Corsica* (Leghorn 1937)

Bibliography

Michel, E., 'Pasquale Paoli ufficiale dell 'escrito Napoletano 1741–1745', *Archivio Istorico di Corsica* (Leghorn 1928)

Michel, E., 'Pasquale Paoli a Livorno', *Archivio Istorico di Corsica* (Leghorn 1936)

Minto, First Earl of, *Life and Letters of Sir Gilbert Elliot, First Earl of Minto,* Ed. by the Countess of Minto (London 1814)

Montesquieu, Charles de Secondat, Baron de, *Oeuvres* (Paris 1820)

Moore, Sir John, *Diary,* Ed. by Major-General Sir J. F. Maurice (London 1904)

Morandi, C., 'La Conquista Franchese della Corsica nel pensiva di Pietro e Alessandro Verril', *Archivio Istorico di Corsica* (Leghorn 1938)

Neuhoff, F. de', *The Description of Corsica* (London 1795)

Ordioni, P., *Pozzo di Borgo* (Paris 1935)

Oria, J. d', *Pasquale de' Paoli* (Genoa 1869)

O'Meara, B. E., *Napoleon at St Helena* (London 1888)

Past Master, *An Account of the Lodge of the Nine Muses No. 235, 1777–1939* (London 1940)

Paoli, P., *Discours prononcés a l'Assemblée Nationale par le Général Paoli* (Paris 1790)

Paoli, P., *Il Generale Paoli ai suoi compatrioti* (Corte 1774)

Pompei (Marshal Sebastiani), *Etat actuel de la Corse* (Paris 1821)

Potolicchio, A., 'Pasquale Paoli e Antonio Genovese', *Archivio Storico di Corsica* (Leghorn 1932)

Ravenna, L., *Pasquale Paoli etc.* (Florence 1928)

Rota, E., *Pasquale Paoli* (Turin 1941)

Sandri, L., 'Gian Giacomo Rousseau e il suo Progeti di Constituzione per la Corsica', *Archivio Storico di Corsica* (Leghorn 1936)

Segre, C., 'Rousseau e l'Indipendenza Corsa', *Archivio Storico di Corsica* (Leghorn 1930)

Sorel, A., *L'Europe et la Révolution Française* (Paris 1885)

Smith, Preserved, *The Enlightenment* (New York 1954)

Rava, L., 'Pasquale Paoli, Vittorio Alfieri e il Segretario Polidori', *Archivio Storico di Corsica* (Leghorn 1931)

Renucci, F. O., *Storia di Corsica* (Bastia 1833)

Rousseau, J-J., *Oeuvres* (Paris 1823)

Valery (pseud.) Pasquin, A. C., *Voyages en Corse à l'isle d'Elbe et en Sardaigne* (Paris 1837)

Vallance, A., *The Summer King* (London 1956)

Vicens, E., *Histoire de la République de Gènes* (Paris 1842)

Villet, A., *Le Corse de 1768 à 1789* (Besançon 1924)

Voltaire, F-M. A., *Oeuvres* (Paris 1801)

INDEX

Abbatucci clan, 277
Abbatucci, Giacomo Pietro, 87–8, 101–102, 139–40, 146, 182, 277
Account of Corsica, An, 98–9, 100, 123, 133
Agostini, Ferdinando, 59, 131, 146, 147
Ajaccio, importance of, 25, under Genoa, 32, 60, 86, 90–1, 101; French occupation of, 61, 115, 139–40, 142, 146–7, 153, 186, 187; Paolist occupation of, 111–12; and evacuation from, 113; unrest in, under French, 192,194, 195, 197; and return of Paoli, 209, 211; disturbances in, 225, 240–3; under the Directory, 235, 237, 240–3, 244; and the Sardinian expedition, 249–51, 253; Napoleon's association with, 270, 274–5; attack on, 274–5; under Elliot, 318–9, 320, 323
Aleria, 13, 25, 50, 53, 74, 76, 80, 87, 88, 89, 180, 226, 232
Alexander I, Czar of Russia, 43, 336
Alfieri, 97
Algajola, 25, 30, 60, 138, 139, 142
Andrei, 247, 262, 263, 264, 266, 269, 271, 276
Angelis, Crescentio *see* Segni, bishop of
Anselme, 249–50, 251
Antiboul, 272
Antisanti, 81
Arcambal, General, 127, 128–9
Arena, Bartolomeo, relationship of, with Paoli, 199, 262, 266, 332; anti-French attitude of, 201; as head of administration, 217, 220–1, 234; expelled from Corsica, 222; escape and return of, 223–4; in elections, 228, 229; and the Sardinian Expedition, 249, 250; censured, 264; with Saliceti, 266
Arena clan, 211, 234, 252, 274
Arena, Filippo, 199, 233–4

Arena, Guiseppe, 199, 234
Arrighi, Tomasi, 204, 243
Astolfi, 135
Austria, 38, 43, 249, 266

Bach, Johan Christian, 172
Bailly, 196, 204–205
Balagna, 15, 30, 66, 84, 117, 137, 151, 153, 234, 269
Baldassari, Giacomo, 81
Balestrini, 331
Banconi, Filippo, 138
Barbaggio, 119, 120, 142, 145, 282, 285, 285,
Barbaroux, 259
Barbibi, 106
Barère, 271, 272, 276
Barrin, Vicomte de, 183, 190, 191–2, 194–5, 197–8, 199, 201, 208
Barry, Madame du, 161, 167
Bartolozzi, 172
Bastelica, 209
Bastelica, Sampiero da, 24
Bastia, Genoese in, 16, 35, 54, 60, 61, 72, 73, 75, 76, 88, 91; importance of, 25; Matra in, 80, 88; Paolists in, 90; French in, 116, 117, 118, 119, 130, 131, 142, 180, 183, 186, 192, 195; rebellion in, 197–8; and Paoli's return, 201, 202, 208, 209, 210, 217; rebellion against the Directory in, 220–4; Marseillais in, 253, 255; Saliceti in, 266, 267, 269; attacked by English and Paolists, 285–6, 287; Elliot in, 296–7, 298–9, 302, 307, 320, 322–4; unrest in, 307, 322–3
Bath, 166
Bartolani, 331
Belgodère, 319, 320
Bertola, 270–1
Biron, Duc de, 204, 207, 229, 235, 259, 261–2
Bistuglio, 321, 322, 324

343

Index

Index

with Paoli, 107; attitude of, to Genoa, 110; and England, 111; and the siege of Ajaccio, 111–12; signing of 1768 treaty by, 113; Corsican attitude to, 115–16; attack on Corsicans by, 117–18, 119–22; England's attitude to, 122–4, 133, 134–5; campaigns of, in Corsica, 126–32, 138–40, 143–7, 149–53; intimidation of Corsicans by, 153; pacification of Corsica, 154; dismissal of Choiseul in, 167; Paoli in, 204–207; in Corsica after Paoli's return, 209–11; attack on Tuileries in, 245; and the invasion of Sardinia, 249–57; suspicions of Paoli in, 259–60; 1793 war with England, Paoli recalled to, 261–2; growing criticism of Paoli in, 262–4, 265–6; order issued to seize Paoli by, 266; Commissioners sent to Corsica by, 269–71, 274; rising under the National Convention, 271–2, 272–6; declares Paoli traitor, 276–7; fights England in Corsica, 281–2, 285; defeated in naval battle, 301; success of, against First Coalition, 309; agents of, in Corsica, 323–4; and Rebellion of the Cross in Corsica, 328–9; repression of Corsicans by, 330–1 *see also* Corsica; Barrin; Marbeuf; Paoli, Pasquale

Franceschi, Angelo di, 135–6
Franzini, 322
Frasseto, 193
Frederick the Great, King of Prussia, 43, 98, 124, 332
French Royal Africa Company, 185
Furiani, 61, 62, 89, 126–7

Gaeta, 38
Gaffori, Maréchal de Camp, lands with French troops, 194–5; attitude of Corsicans to, 195, 197, 201–202; and Paoli, 197; activities of, in Corsica, 197, 199, 201–202, 210; character of, 201; deportation of, 210; prepares for invasion of Corsica, 280
Gaffori, Captain, 151
Gaffori, General, 24, 34–5, 48, 50, 58
Galeazziani, 200
Galeria, 182
Gallipoli, 38
Gambini, 322
Gance, Abel, 336
Garrick, David, 163

Gascoigne, Charles, 168
Geneva, 135
Giacomorsi, 334
Gibraltar, 92, 110, 325
Genoa, rule of, in Corsica, 13; and Paoli, 13; support of first Matra invasion by, 13; use of vendetta, 24, 32, 35; garrisons of, 25–6, 60; exploitation of Corsica by, 30–2; and 1729 Corsican revolt, 32–4, 36; and France, 34–5, 60–1; campaigns of, in Corsica, 34, 61–2, 71–3; and Isola Rossa, 66–7; and the Corsican navy, 67, 86, 91–2; and the Churches, 69–71; and the Grand Deputation, 73; encourages disaffection in Corsica 73–4; and second Matra invasion, 74–7; and third Matra invasion, 80–1; and fourth Matra invasion, 86–7, 88–9; and the Ajaccio rebellion, 90–1; trade and, 91, 92; and the blockade of San Fiorenzo, 91–2; negotiations of, with French for aid, 92–3; and the Treaty of Compiègne, 93–5; requests to French for further aid, 102–103; Corsican capture of Capraja from, 104–109; French attitude to, 110–11; and the siege of Ajaccio, 111–12; and the 1768 treaty, 113
Genovesi, 40, 65
Gentili, Antonio, 196–7, 216, 217, 218, 265, 277, 281, 325
Gentili, Count Aubanis, 152, 158, 168
George III, King of England, 99, 159, 165, 282, 288, 289, 291–2, 296, 314
Germany, Germans, 32, 124, 182
Geufucci, Abbé, 58, 158
Ghisoni, 219
Gilray, 315
Giornale Pattrioto, 218
Goldsmith, Oliver, 164, 169
Golo, bay of, 53, 208
Goupilleau, 259
Goya, 214
Goyetche, Captain, 256–7
Grafton, Lord, 123, 134, 135, 157, 162–3, 167, 172
Grampella, Colonel, 307
Grand-Maison, General, 121–2, 129, 131, 143–4, 145, 146, 150
Greeks, 183, 193, 199
Grenville, Lord, 280
Grimaldi, Giocante, 131, 151, 152
Grimaldi, Marchése, 62
Grimm, Frédéric-Melchior, 97, 98

Index

Grothous, 158
Guagno, 146
Guasco, 138
Guasco, Abbé, 221, 223
Guasco, Captain, 200

Hague, the, 158
Harwich, 158
Holland, 158, 309
Holland, Lord, 133, 134
Hood, Lord, 279, 280, 283, 284–5, 286, 292
Huntley, Lord, 307
Ingratestone, 158
Intoduction to the Border Minstrelsy, 289
Ireland, 25, 28, 133, 282
Isola Rossa, construction of, 66–7; Paoli's reputation in, 117; French attack on, 138–9; Corsican retreat to, 153; rebellion in, 199; withdrawal of French from, 201; Arena in, 201, 211, 233–4; disturbances in, 225, 233–4; Paolists in, 269
d'Istria, Ottavio Colonna, 174
d'Istria, Vincentello, 24
Italy, 28, 32, 81, 87, 97, 98, 157–8, 259, 287

Jacobi, Gian Battista, 75
Jacobi, Giuseppina, 75–6
Johnson, Dr Samuel, 159–61, 163, 164, 168, 169–70, 173, 315
Joseph II, Emperor of Austria, 43, 97–8, 158
Journal of a Voyage to Corsica, 163, 181

Kochler, Major, 284

Lafayette, General, 196, 197, 205, 206
Lagobenetto, 130
La Harpe, 43
La Maddalena, 252, 256, 292
Lameth, 196
La Platta, 209
Las Cases, 336
Leghorn, Corsican exiles in, 48, 136, 154, 173; Paoli in, 53; English trade with, 61, 82, 98, 122; enthusiasm for Paoli in, 157; naval battle off, 301; mentioned, 187, 278, 283
Lento, 151
Leonetti, Felice Antonio, 228, 229, 275–6, 282
Leoni, Giovanni Battista, 317
Letourmer, 261

Life of Johnson, 335
Logas, Major, 319
Lomellino, Agostino, Doge of Genoa, 71, 72–4
Longone, 48, 56, 59
Loreto, 130
Louis, XIV, King of France, 40, 43, 44, 92
Louis XVI, King of France, 143, 204, 207, 226, 258–9, 276
Louis-Philippe, 337
Luca, 61
Luciana, 131
Ludre, Colonel de, 130, 131, 132
Lugo, 75
Luri, Domenici de, 174, 180
Lusinghi, Carlo, 38, 46–7, 62
Lyttleton, Lord, 163

Macaulay, Mrs., 163, 166
Macinaggio, 60, 72, 75, 91, 105
Maillard, Colonel, 240, 241, 242
Maillebois, 147
Malta, Maltese, 49, 138
Mann, Sir Horace, 122, 158
Mansfield, Lord Chief Justice, 124
Mantua, 158
Marat, 271
Marbeuf, Comte de, character of, 94, 174, 181–2; in charge of garrison troops, 94, 111; relationship of, with Paoli, 112; duplicity of, 113, 117–8, 119; campaigns of, 119–20, 122, 143, 149–50; commander-in-chief in Corsica, 174, 176, 181–3; return of, to Paris, 181; attempts of, at colonisation, 182–3, 193; death of, 183; mentioned, 185, 187
Mariani, 49
Maroti, 239
Marsily, 270
Martello fort, 281
Martinetti, Giacomo, 74
Massesi, Grand Chancellor, 140–1
Massesi, Matteo, 140
Massiani, Sergeant, 89
Matra, Alerio Francesco, 50, 80–1, 88
Matra, Angelo, 147
Matra, Antonuccio, 74–5, 77, 78, 107, 108
Matra clan, 211
Matra, Emanuele, 13, 14–15, 16–19, 50, 55
Mattei clan, 277
Maudet, 270

348

Index

Reale Albergo dei Poveri, 39
Reflections on the Revolution in France, 202
Reynolds, Sir Joshua, 164, 169, 171
Ristori, Gian Battista, 105, 126, 127, 134
Rivarola, Count Domenico, 34
Robespierre, Maximilien, 206, 231, 232, 247, 258, 271
Rocca, 91, 92
Rocco, Father, 39
Rocco-Serra, 241
Rochfort, 124
Rogliano, 26, 60, 72, 105, 120
Rome, 327
Rossi, Comte de, 193, 194
Rossi, Antonio, 235, 240, 245, 266
Rostini, Abbé, 58, 136
Rostino, 34, 36, 65, 151, 267, 296, 307, 310, 334
Round tower, 66, 106, 120, 281
Rousseau, Jean-Jacques, 29, 96-7, 99, 107
Royal Society, 172
Royeur, 261
Ruins, 262
Rully, Colonel, 195, 198, 199, 202
Ruspini, Chevalier, 172, 316
Russia, 97, 166

St Helena, 336, 337
St Martin, 270
St Michel, Lacombe, 260, 267, 281, 285-7
St Petersburg, 166
Saliceti, Abbé, 144-5
Saliceti, Cristoforo, as deputy to Estates General, 190, 194, 197, 224; and Corsican assimilation with France, 200; Paoli and, 205, 206, 231-2, 233, 234-5, 244, 259, 332; appearance and character of, 206, 232-3, 300; in the Directory, 219-20, 240, 244-5; as Procurator General Syndic, 217, 230, 234-5, 240; and Napoleon, 240, 258, 260; Jacobinism of, 231-2, 258-9; suppression of convents by, 237; during National Convention elections, 245-7; in Paris, 247, 248, 258-9; urges Sardinian expedition, 249; growing importance of, 258-9; opposition to Paoli of, 259-61; as Commissioner, 260-1, 266-9; criticism of, 263, 264, 271; deprived of mandate, 274, 275; return of, to France, 276; organises expedition against Corsica,

283, 328; return of, to Corsica, 325-6, 328; Paoli on, 330
Saliceti, Gian Carlo, opposition of, to Genoese, 80; and Matra, 80-1; in command at Cervione, 88; at Furiani, 126; campaigns of, 80-1, 88, 126, 131, 149, 151
Saliceti, Giulio, 144
Sampiero da Corso, 24, 147
San Antonio della Casabianca, 54, 128, 148
San Fiorenzo, size and importance of, 25, 30; Genoese in, 60, 71; French in, 60; Corsican navy in, 67, 102; siege of, 72, 91-2, 94; Paolists in, 86, 91; French occupation of, 117-8, 119, 120, 121, 186, 191; Paolist attacks on, 143, 145-6; on return of Paoli, 209; Marseillais in, 253; Saliceti in, 269, 270; Napoleon in, 274-7, 281; English-Corsican attack on, 251-2; Paoli's departure from, 310
San Pietro, 75, 76
San Pietro di Tenda, 149
San Rocca, 26
San Stephano, 256, 257
Sansonetti clan, 211
Santa Raparata, 138
Santucci, Tomaso, 59
Sapey, Citizen, 323
Sardinia, 92, 249, 250, 253-7, 318, 328
Sartene, 25, 193, 201, 275
Savelli, 292
Savelli clan, 233-4
Sawbridge, Alderman, 166
Scotland, 25, 26, 133, 164, 168, 289
Scott, Sir Walter, 289
Segni, bishop of, 70, 71
Sentini, 322
Serpentini, Giulio, 81, 129, 131, 149, 153
Serpentini, Rosanna, 131
Seven Years' War, 60, 110
Shelburne, Lord, 123-4, 134-5
She Stoops to Conquer, 169
Sheridan, Richard, 172, 292, 314
Sicily, 46-7, 62
Sieyes, Abbé, 205
Sinipitio, 106
Sionville, Brigadier, 180-1
Smith, Admiral, 149, 154, 157
Sorba, 92, 93, 102-103, 107, 111, 112, 113
Spain, 111, 167, 287, 308

351

Index